THE VISIBLE PAST

BY THE SAME AUTHOR

The World of Rome

Myths of the Greeks and Romans

The Civilizations of Europe

The Ancient Mediterranean

Herod the Great

Ancient History Atlas

Cleopatra

The Jews and the Roman World

The Army of the Caesars

The Twelve Caesars

The Ancient Historians

Saint Paul

Jesus

The History of Rome

The Etruscans

The Dawn of the Middle Ages

The History of Ancient Israel

The Roman Emperors

The Rise of the Greeks

The Classical Greeks

From Alexander to Cleopatra

The Fall of the Roman Empire

THE VISIBLE PAST

Greek and Roman History from Archaeology
1960–1990

Michael Grant

CHARLES SCRIBNER'S SONS
NEW YORK

Maxwell Macmillan International
New York Oxford Singapore Sydney

Charles Scribner's Sons
Macmillan Publishing Company
866 Third Avenue, New York, NY 10022

Collier Macmillan Canada, Inc.
1200 Eglinton Avenue East, Suite 200
Don Mills, Ontario M3C 3N1

Library of Congress Cataloging-in-Publication Data

Grant, Michael, 1914–
The visible past : Greek and Roman history from archaeology / Michael Grant.
p. cm.
Includes bibliographical references and index.

1. Greece—History—To 146 B.C. 2. Rome—History. 3. Classical antiquities. I. Title.
DE86.G734 1990 90-42241 CIP
938—dc20

PRINTED IN THE UNITED STATES OF AMERICA

None of us knows enough
P. Throckmorton, *Shipwrecks and Archaeology: The Unharvested Sea*, 1969, p. xii

Archaeology can play a key role . . . in providing a new understanding of the world in which we live.
G. F. Bass, *Archaeology*, January/February 1989, p. 105

CONTENTS

PART II: ITALY AND THE ROMAN EMPIRE

ILLUSTRATIONS

MAPS

Maps appear between pages 164 and 171

INTRODUCTION

In classical archaeology – the study of the material remains of the Greeks and Etruscans and Romans – the last few decades have in many countries produced new discoveries of many kinds, and of many ancient epochs, telling us a great deal about the things that happened, and why they happened as they did.

These discoveries have enlarged, and indeed transformed, our knowledge of classical history. However, the precise, theoretical relationship between history and archaeology has come in for much discussion and argument. The classical historian has an absolute need of the archaeologist; archaeology is visible history. True, history and archaeology are independent disciplines, each based upon its own set of methods; yet although archaeology has tended, of late, to gravitate increasingly towards scientific fields and methods – of which something will be said in Appendix 1 – it continues to interact with historical studies to an inextricable extent. It is that necessary interaction which, by focusing upon recent discoveries, this volume will seek to point out and confirm.

Am I, as a classicist and ancient historian, attempting to launch an old-fashioned manifesto designed to deprecate archaeology's links with the sciences? No, not at all, because such links are, surely, to be welcomed. It is difficult to feel otherwise (although some try), because these scientific associations have revivified archaeology. Nevertheless, there does exist a danger that the increasedly scientific character of the subject may well cause its imperative connections with history to be edged aside, or regarded as secondary. It is partly in the hope of helping to prevent this that I have written the present book, though my main purpose is to be useful to historians.

What I shall be doing, then, is to list some fifty archaeological sites or projects, dating from the past thirty years, which appear to me to have made particularly valuable new contributions to our knowledge of the Greek and Roman worlds and their history. 'Rescue' (salvage) archaeology, to preserve sites, is mentioned only when it happens to have made such contributions. I have also included a few artistic, epigraphic and numismatic items, which form part, I feel, of the archaeological picture.

The admission of certain of these sites and projects to my list is defensible, and indeed inevitable; that of others is, perhaps, less so, while no doubt some people might have preferred to include quite different examples instead of, or in addition to, those I have chosen. It is a rash undertaking to select so few sites or projects out of the tens of thousands that have provided archaeological evidence during the past three decades. But that is what, nevertheless, I have attempted to do. So this is a very personal book – incorporating my own choice of what should appear, a choice which must to some extent be based on my own historical interests. I offer apologies, therefore, to any individuals or groups who may feel that I have not given them or their activities a fair deal.

And there is something more to be added. It may well be that if I had been writing in five years' time my list would have been substantially different. Appendix II says something about that possibility, but gives only a few examples out of many: for there are, in fact, immense and varied contributions to our still very defective knowledge of ancient history that classical archaeology has yet to make. Indeed, it is busy doing so at this very moment – stimulated by enlarged public interest – on an even more breathtaking scale than the past three decades have witnessed.

Having made my fifty-odd selections, I decided not to group them according to themes or archaeological techniques, since more than one of these themes or techniques are often simultaneously illuminated by any single enterprise and, besides, what I am writing about is the contribution of these enterprises to *history*. This being so, I have preferred to follow a historical, approximately chronological, approach divided between the Greek and Roman worlds. It seemed to me that this arrangement would throw most light on what, as I have said, I had in mind – namely, the extent to which these archaeological discoveries have benefited historical studies.

Yet while the choices I have made are my own, it is obvious that the information that I have collected was largely obtained from other people. Out of the many who have written about these diverse subjects, I shall list a selection in the bibliography at the end of the work. This will, I hope – like the Notes – enable those who are interested to pursue the various topics further. I have also felt impelled to quote, word for word, much of what these writers say: partly in order to record my indebtedness and partly because such quotations, from persons directly concerned with what I am writing about, often provide the vividness and immediacy which this exciting theme requires. So I am grateful to the following for quotations from their writings: R. Agache, M. Andronikos, J. Barron, G.F. Bass, P. Bernard, L.R. Binford, S. Bisel, M. Bound, D.J. Breeze, O.H. Bullitt, A. Bullock, A.R. Burn, J.M. Camp, H.W. Catling, D.

Clarke, P.E. Cleator, J.F. Coates, J. N. Coldstream, T.J. Cornell, J.J. Coulton, M. Crawford, R. W. Davies, E. M. De Juliis, D. De Solla Price, J.J. Deiss, W.G. East, K. Erim, A. Farkas, G. Foti, R.J. Fowler, M.W. Frederiksen, K. Greene, N.G.L. Hammond, F.M. Heichelheim, J.G.F. Hind, K.G. Holum (and R.L. Hohlfelder, R.J. Bull, A. Raban), S.C. Humphreys, M.H. Jameson, A. W. Johnston (and M .A. R. Colledge), V. Karageorghis, J.P.C. Kent, A.G. King, C. Kraay, J.G. Landels, W. Leppmann, C.M. Lerici, P. Levi, J. McIntosh, A.G. McKay, P. MacKendrick, F.G.A. Miller, I. Morris, J.S. Morrison, O. Murray, W. Murray (and P. Petsas), S.T. Parker, *Past Worlds* (authors of), S. Piggott, J.J. Pollitt, M.K. Popham (and E. Toulupa and L.H. Sackett), T.W. Potter, M.J. Price (and B.L. Trell), P. Rahtz, F. Rainey, C. Renfrew, D. Ridgway, T.L. Shear jr., A. Sherratt, S.M. Sherwin-White, G. Shipley, H. Sigurdsson, A.M. Snodgrass, R.J.A. Talbert, T. Tatton-Brown, P. Throckmorton, E.G. Turner, C. Valenziano, G. Webster, K.D. White, D.R. Wilson, A.G. Woodhead and Y. Yadin.

I want to add, too, a special word of thanks, appreciation and admiration to all those upon whose work I have drawn not only by direct quotation but for much other information as well. Archaeologists, in particular, do not have an easy life. The obstacles that they have to overcome are formidable indeed: harsh working conditions, looting, governmental and military obstructions and convulsions, and the inevitable diversion of limited funds to the rescue and conservation of sites threatened by industry, agriculture, nature or war (see above). I have not said much about these difficulties in this book, but it is impossible not to be aware of them.

In addition, a number of people have helped me directly, and to these I want to offer a special acknowledgement: Mr Robert Anderson, Mr C.H. Annis, M. Jean-Louis Astier, Mr Robin Birley, Professor Baldassare Conticello, Mr Mensun Bound, Professor Keith De Vries, Herr Helmut Feller, Mr David Gibbins, Mr Thomas C. Gillmer, Professor C. Holliger, Dr Henry Hurst, Professor Michael H. Jameson, Signor Carlo Knight, Dr Antje Krug, Dr Silvana Luppino, Professor Giovanna Menci, Diplom Forstwirt Mechthild Neyses, Professor S. Thomas Parker, Mrs Veronica M. Palmer, Signora Luciana Valentini, Dr Gerd Rupprecht, Mrs Patricia Vanags and Dr Graham Webster. I also owe much gratitude to Mrs Anne Marriott, Mr Marcus Harpur, Mr Malcolm Gerratt and Miss Jocelyn Burton of Messrs Weidenfeld & Nicolson for skilfully seeing the book through the press, to Miss Maria Ellis for typing the manuscript and making useful suggestions, to Mr Tom Graves and Miss Emma Harman for securing the illustrations, and to Mr Ken Wass for making the maps.

Michael Grant
1990

THE VISIBLE PAST

PART I

THE GREEKS

CHAPTER 1

THE 'DARK AGE'

Towards the end of the second millennium BC the Mycenaean Bronze Age civilization, which had extended over most of Greece and much of the eastern Mediterranean region, collapsed, undermined from both within and without. The external pressure perhaps came from the Dorian invasion which arrived from the north and enveloped most of the Peloponnese, although the transformation may have been a more complex and longlasting affair than a straightforward invasion, involving successive groups of immigrants. These movements heralded or accompanied the beginning of the Iron Age, in which iron gradually succeeded bronze as the principal metal and instrument of weaponry. But this earliest Iron Age has also been customarily described as a 'Dark Age', for two reasons: first because at the time of the Mycenaean collapse living standards appear to have fallen sharply, and secondly because we ourselves (like the ancient Greek historians before us) know so little about what was happening at that time.

The men of Athens always maintained that they themselves had successfully resisted the Dorian invaders and had consequently escaped occupation and destruction at their hands. Instead, they received flocks of refugees who then joined many Athenians in departing to colonize Ionia in western Asia Minor. But any suggestion that Athens was the only Greek state to continue to flourish during this 'Dark Age' is misguided, for there were also other pockets of survival and prosperity (at least at the top of the social scale). One of these places, as excavations have now shown, was Lefkandi on the island of Euboea just to the north of Attica and Boeotia, while another was Salamis in Cyprus. Spectacular prosperity of the governing classes at these two centres, despite the lowering of life at most other eastern Mediterranean localities, is what the archaeologists have revealed to us.

1 *Lefkandi: The Not So Dark Age*

The finds made at Lefkandi from the 1960s onwards have, as has just been said, thrown entirely new light on what was hitherto regarded as the 'Dark Age' of Greece, between the collapse of the Mycenaean civilization and the emergence of the subsequent Greece that we know.

The Lelantine Plain in the western part of Euboea, the island's most fertile region, faces the Euripus strait (between the island and the mainland), which ships coasting in Aegean waters used so as to avoid the rocks and currents of the eastern Euboean coast, facing the open sea. The plain took its name from the Lelanton stream or torrent. During the Mycenaean epoch, this flat land had been dominated by mainland Boeotia. Its importance, however, dates from the period that followed. Containing mines producing both copper and iron, it extended between Chalcis and Eretria – two cities which led Greek recovery and development during the early Iron Age and which competed for the ownership of the territory that lay between them.

Before this struggle came to a head, however, one place on the coast between Chalcis and Eretria, beside the Euripus strait and with the Lelantine Plain as its hinterland, assumed conspicuous importance, as is made clear by archaeological discoveries. This was where the village of Lefkandi is situated now, its name perhaps indicating that the ancient habitation centre on the site was called Lelanton or Lelantion. It was already a centre in the late Mycenaean age (mid-twelfth century BC), but in the subsequent post-Mycenaean 'Dark Age' – the time of the Dorian invasions of Greece – the settlement became unexpectedly prosperous, although its population remained small.

What has come to light at Lefkandi – although only a minute proportion of the site has so far been unearthed – is a group of very early Greek (Iron Age) tombs, and the study of tombs constitutes an essential branch of archaeology (cf. section 2, and Chapter 3, section 4). 'The burial customs of Lefkandi', writes J. N. Coldstream, 'represent a curious compromise, unparalleled elsewhere. With few exceptions, cremation was the prevailing rite [there], from Sub-Mycenaean times until the final burials in the later ninth century. The corpse was burnt on a pyre, onto which some vessels, jewellery and dress ornaments were thrown. Afterwards the cremated remains were not placed in an urn, as in Athens; instead, only a token amount of burnt bones was placed in the open grave, together with the unburnt pots and personal belongings, which were sometimes placed as though round an inhumed body.'[1]

It is these collections of objects, lodged in the graves of Lefkandi, which show it to have been one of the first localities in post-Mycenaean Greece to have imported luxury objects from the near east, especially from northern Syria and Phoenicia and, perhaps indirectly, Egypt. Thus the earliest finds at Toumba – a hill rising up from the Lelantine Plain to the north, and overlooking the sea to the west – include a faience (bluish glass) necklace of near-eastern origin, in addition to glass and blue frit (a component of glass) beads, an Egyptian ring, vases, a human-headed scaraboid, and an arrangement of bronze wheels that may have originated in Cyprus.

'At Lefkandi', continues Coldstream, 'it is the finery rather than the weapons which first attracts our attention. To account for this wealth, a ready explanation is at hand: the bronze foundry which had been in operation on the settlement around or just before 900 BC, when there is also some slight evidence of trade between Euboea and Cyprus: one of the obvious motives would have been the supply of Cypriot copper for the foundry.'[2] Athenian imports, too, have appeared at Lefkandi, including Protogeometric pots of *c.*950–900 BC (along with Euboean counterparts), and a contemporary, surprisingly early, figurine of a centaur, fourteen inches high – while, conversely, an iron spear and sword of local manufacture discovered in the graves recall that Athens, and other cities, may have learnt their ironworking from Euboea.

'Apart from Athens and Lefkandi,' observes Coldstream, 'no other Greek city displays any comparable symptoms of prosperity as early as this. In view of the Levantine imports, and the Levantine skills which were copied by local craftsmen, one assumes that this prosperity was founded to some extent on commercial exchange with the eastern Mediterranean; and it was probably from that direction that the materials of gold and ivory were obtained.' He goes on to discuss the likelihood that Phoenicians acted as intermediaries in the procurement of these materials.

Excavations at Lefkandi in 1981 also revealed the remains of an apsidal building, made of mud-brick with a stone foundation, which apparently dates from the tenth century BC and is the largest 'Dark Age' building yet known. Indeed, the substantial dimensions of this edifice – it was 30 feet wide, and at least 135 feet long – are unexpected, as are various features of its design and construction. For example, the exterior was flanked by porticos or verandas colonnaded with rectangular wooden posts. 'This discovery', writes J. J. Coulton, 'pushes back the origin of the surrounding portico by at least a century. Furthermore, the building can scarcely have been conceived at this early date as an imitation temple to honour a dead hero [*heroon*]; pits for storage jars in the rear room indicate rather that it was envisaged as a glorified house, so suggesting that the veranda arose in a secular, not a sacred context.'[3]

The structure turned out to have been erected some 7½ feet above a rich burial place containing two splendidly furnished tombs. One of these contained the remains of a warrior, now known as the 'Hero of Lefkandi'. To judge from the grandeur of his interment, he must have belonged to the local royal house. Beside his remains lay the iron spear and sword to which reference was made above. His bones and ashes, placed in a bronze amphora decorated with reliefs, were wrapped in strips of cloth, portions of which have, uniquely, survived. Their patterns and textures can still be seen, giving life to the woven garments that we find depicted on painted pottery, and increasing our defective knowledge of early textiles. As M. R. Popham, E. Touloupa and L. H. Sackett report, 'The cloth, which had been folded and packed around the inside of the amphora, is astonishingly well preserved owing to the unusually favourable conditions of humidity and association with bronze. Considerably damaged by the collapse of the amphora, it appears to be a robe of ankle length, made of two sheets of linen sewn up the sides. The borders and bottom half are plain, but the upper part is of shaggy weave, resembling on a much smaller scale the modern Greek "flokata".'[4]

The second of the two graves contained the cremated remains of a woman. Her jewellery is of interest because little is otherwise known of the dress or adornment of the period. She was buried wearing a decorated gold neckpiece, a brassière of gold discs, gilded hair-rollers, and ear-rings, and her garment was fastened by pins of bronze and gilt iron. The presence of a knife may indicate that she died as a sacrificial victim. In an associated grave-shaft the remains of four sacrificed horses have been found, as in tombs at Salamis in Cyprus (see section 2).

The building constructed on top of these two graves evolved from a substantial tumulus which was erected to house the burials shortly after they had taken place; outside the entrance to the building a cemetery sprang up. These circumstances have prompted conjectures that, despite what Coulton said, we have here a cult of persons who had recently died, a hero-cult, the earliest yet known. 'Greek hero-cult', writes Anthony Snodgrass, 'could include not only the worship of the remote and anonymous Bronze Age dead but also the heroization of the recently deceased. The discovery in 1981 of a pair of exceptionally rich burials of the tenth century BC at Lefkandi, over which a large building, apparently a heroon (centre of hero-cult) had been almost at once constructed, posed insuperable problems for those who believed in the influence of Ionian epic on such practices: for who could believe that the great burial scenes in Homer, or even their earlier prototypes, were known to the people of the island of Euboea as early as about 950 BC? We can now see this phenomenon for what it probably is: an unusually early manifestation of a strand of hero worship that we know well from classical times – the elevation of prominent persons to the ranks of the heroes immediately after their death.'[5] This interpretation of the Lefkandi tombs, it has also been pointed out, is confirmed by the identification of another tenth-century hero's grave on the island of Naxos.

At Lefkandi, an adjacent foundry, dating from *c.*900, shows that by that time the importation of near-eastern metal objects was no longer considered sufficient for local needs, so that their techniques were imitated on the spot. Nevertheless, imports did not stop; indeed, they continued on an increased scale. In *c.*865, however, cremation burials at Lefkandi abruptly ceased. Was the place attacked by Chalcis? We cannot be sure. But at all events, although life at Lefkandi still continued for more than a century and a half, it was on a minor scale: the great age of the place was over.

In revealing that climax, however, these excavations have revealed how wrong we were to regard this age following the Mycenaean collapse as wholly 'Dark'. Euboea, evidently, had avoided the general decline of standards associated with the Dorian invasion or immigrations. Athens, likewise, as we have seen, claimed to have held out against the Dorians. In parts of Cyprus there was no apparent recession, as the next section will suggest. Crete, perhaps, should be added to the list as well.

2 *Salamis in Cyprus: Homeric Analogies?*

Cyprus lies fifty miles south of Cilicia Tracheia or Aspera (Rough Cilicia) in south-eastern Asia Minor, and was thus excellently placed to act as a point of communication between that peninsula and other near eastern and Aegean regions. Upon the island, between ranges of mountains, the thickly wooded central plain of Mesaoria provided timber for shipbuilding and for the smelting of copper ores from Cypriot mines. During the Late Bronze Age, as the second millennium BC was drawing to a close, groups of migrants from the Greek (Mycenaean) mainland came and settled in Cyprus. Thereafter, it was the object of first Syrian and then Phoenician penetration in *c.*1000 BC and *c.*800 BC respectively.

The leading city of the island was Salamis, situated beside its east coast, five miles to the north of the modern Famagusta. An acropolis, rising above a plateau, overlooked a sandy bay providing a natural harbour (now silted up) at the mouth of the River Pediaeus or Pedias (Pidias). Salamis, founded in about 1075 BC, is now known to have been the successor of a Bronze Age (Mycenaean) settlement at Enkomi, a mile and a half inland. According to the mythology of the Greeks, the creator of Salamis, after the Trojan War, was Teucer, son of Telamon, king of the island of the same name off the coast of Attica, and the first colonists of Cypriot Salamis may indeed have been refugees from Mycenaean Greece.

But then, after Mycenae, came a new phase. As has been mentioned, one of the island's principal claims to importance lies in the fact that, along with the communities of Euboea (see section 1 above), its cities give the lie to the tradition that the 'Dark Age' was uniformly dark. In the earliest phase of the post-Mycenaean towns of Cyprus, marking their transition to the Iron Age, political life centred round the local kings and their aristocratic followers. At this time, continuing relations with the near east are demonstrated by the contents of tombs. Connections with the Aegean coastlands and islands, too, and especially with Euboea, are attested by various finds and influences. During what was, evidently, a period of wealth and prosperity, Aegean links included an export trade in copper and iron, as a number of discoveries confirm. Metallurgy, which had already been prominent in earlier times, flourished more than ever before, and it may even have been by way of Cyprus (rather than by way of Euboea, as was suggested above) that the Greek knowledge of ironwork originated.

Salamis illustrates these island developments well, while at the same time reinforcing the evidence from Lefkandi (section 1 above) of the historical information that tombs can provide about the early Greeks; for the richness of some of the Salaminian burial places, whose antique Bronze Age echoes hint at the persistence of old ideas along with new, suggests that, already by the middle of the eleventh century BC, the post-Mycenaean city was established on a stable basis and comprised a prosperous community. In addition to Greek (notably Athenian) material, graves contained objects exported from, and reflecting the influence of, the near east, thus recalling the tradition that it was with the assistance of Belus, king of Sidon, that Teucer had gained possession of Salamis.

These 'royal' Salaminian tombs, excavated from 1956 onwards, date from the eighth and seventh centuries BC. 'Their splendour', remarks Vassos Karageorghis, 'is an almost unique phenomenon in Cyprus'[6] – and is at least equal to anything discovered elsewhere. A feature of their contents, which has already been encountered at Lefkandi, was the sacrifice of pairs of yoked horses (with or without their chariots) in honour of the dead – recalling Homer's funeral of Patroclus.[7] The horses were sacrificed within the broad anterooms (*dromoi*), in front of the main tomb-chambers in which the body of the dead person was buried, along with his or her personal belongings. The varied origins of these latter mirror the widespread commercial and cultural contacts which the ruling classes of the place enjoyed at this time.

Thus 'Tomb 1' reveals Egyptianizing architectural features, and has yielded different types of imported Greek pottery as well as Cypriot pots. The female body which they accompany was cremated in the Greek fashion – an unusual feature at Salamis, where inhumation was customary – and her necklace of gold and rock-crystal beads was discovered in a bronze cauldron, together with her incinerated skeleton. Perhaps she was a Greek princess, married to a member of the Salaminian royal house, who, when she died, had her dowry interred with her body.

The most magnificent of the graves, 'Tomb 79', was a rectangular structure built of two very large blocks of stone, with a gabled roof and monumental entrance. Within it were three thrones and a bed, made of wood and decorated with ivory plaques, one of which was coated with thin sheets of silver fastened by decorative silver nails with gilded heads. A stool, adorned in similar fashion, resembles the 'silver-studded' throne described by Homer.[8] One of the thrones, too, displays an elaborate decorative technique reminiscent of Penelope's bed in the *Odyssey*.[9] In the case of a bedstead of Egyptianizing Phoenician style, Homeric descriptions seem once again analogous.

'Tomb 79' was employed twice, at the end of the eighth century and then again shortly afterwards. On both occasions four-horse chariots, with their horses, were sacrificed, as a symbol of the lofty rank of the dead persons. These chariots have now been reconstructed, together with the hearses that they contained. The wheels of one of them were fastened by lynch pins nearly two feet long, with the bronze head of a sphinx at one end and, at the other, the hollow bronze figure of a warrior wearing a crested helmet, a scaled cuirass inlaid with blue glass, and a long sword hanging from a baldric. The horses' bronze and iron trappings have also partially survived, including breastplates, blinkers, front bands and pendant side-ornaments bearing *repoussé* reliefs which combine an eclectic variety of near-eastern and Egyptian motifs and styles.

'Tomb 79' also contained a large bronze cauldron with griffins' heads and sirens (or sphinxes) round its rim, a sort of object that is found abundantly throughout the Mediterranean world, but which is believed to have originated in Syria. Also to be seen was a pair of iron fire-dogs and a bundle of a dozen spits (both possibly of Cypriot construction), which remind one of Homer's descriptions of the roasting of meat as food for a hero. In addition, the tomb furniture included ivory plaques and three ivory chairs, one of which was still in fairly good condition.

'Tomb 3', of the seventh century BC, was apparently the work of architects from Asia Minor (or imitators of their work), such mainland affinities being suggested by the tumulus of earth that covered the grave. Here, once again, a chariot and two horses were offered for sacrifice to the dead. In addition to the horses' equipment the grave contained a spear, shield and quiver, as well as an iron sword whose silver-plated nails, attaching the pommel, once again recall passages in Homer. So does the mention of olive-oil displayed by a Greek inscription, in the Cypriot syllabary, found upon an amphora inside the grave. The same, too, can be said of a human skeleton, discovered in 'Tomb 2', with its hands bound in front of the body; for, according to the *Iliad*, Achilles placed on Patroclus's pyre the bodies of twelve Trojans whom he had slain as human sacrifices. (There is also evidence elsewhere on the Salamis site of the sacrifice of a slave to serve his dead master.)

Anthony Snodgrass sees these tombs as reflecting a practice of the time, which he had already noted at Lefkandi, 'that of giving an actual "heroic burial" to the newly deceased members of a ruling class. [At Salamis] a whole series of burials, beginning about 750 BC, emulate the great funeral rituals of the *Iliad*: slaughter of animals (including the chariot-horses), offering of jars of oil, human sacrifice, cremation of the dead (a new practice for Cyprus), quenching of the pyre with wine, placing of the ashes in an urn wrapped in cloth, and final heaping up of a tumulus.'[10]

At Lefkandi, as we have seen, such practices were pre-Homeric. But at Salamis, as Coldstream observes, 'it is the combination of so many features in the tombs which should incline us to take the Homeric comparisons seriously . . . Let us suppose, then, that the princely burials of Salamis were influenced in large measure by the circulation of epic poetry, and especially of the *Iliad*'[11] – which was being composed in the course of the eighth century. Alternatively, we might consider the possibility that the poet who composed the *Iliad*, whom we know as Homer, was aware of, and chose to perpetuate, an *earlier*, continuing way of life which we have seen at Lefkandi, and about which we now learn more from the Salaminian graves – a way of life which may well also have survived in parts of western Asia Minor, though little or no material record has come down to us. (Whether early Italian tombs can likewise be described as 'Homeric' is discussed elsewhere [Chapter 5, section 4].) That is to say, the tombs at Salamis, like those at Lefkandi, although offering Homeric comparisons, need not necessarily have been influenced by Homer at all; he, on the contrary, may have been reproducing, independently of the tombs, the tradition that they, too, perpetuated.

But some will not accept these Homeric analogies in the case of Salamis at all – whether its graves are regarded as influenced by Homer or preserving a tradition by which he himself was independently influenced – preferring to believe that the burial-worships at Salamis (as, perhaps, also at Lefkandi) may not have been based on the Trojan War ideology in any substantial way, but upon alternative, possibly earlier, sagas – perhaps those of a Silver Race who, as the poet Hesiod recorded, had lived on the earth before the heroes.[12] This cannot be regarded as proven but, whether it is correct or not, I. Morris, who indicates the possibility, comments perceptively on the atmosphere and background of these Salaminian rituals, and of the tomb-cults in general, which increased enormously – not only in Salamis – during the course of the eighth century. 'The cults show the conflict of ideologies... fitting into the very centre of the struggles between the old, Dark Age, aristocratic structures and the emergent polis. The distant past was probably never far from people's minds as they moved among the ruins of other ages, and when the social system came under pressure in the eighth century they turned instinctively for help to the men who had peopled these other worlds... The cults seem ambiguous, meaning different things to different people... Some tombs were visited only once, some countless times, and some locations had shrines built at them.'[13]

This group of architectural graves at Salamis, concentrated within a single zone of the city's territory, was apparently reserved for the Salaminian royal family and its aristocratic followers. In another part of the necropolis ordinary citizens were buried in plain rock-cut tombs. Several infant burials, in imported jars, were discovered. Remains of the contemporary town itself, however, have so far scarcely come to light. A place bearing the name of Sillua or Sillume, mentioned among tributaries of the Assyrian King Esarhaddon (*c.*672), appears to be identifiable with Salamis. Later, a king of the place, Euelthon (*c.*560–525), claimed to be the independent ruler of the entire island. But in 545 the Persians gained control of Cyprus, which thenceforward oscillated between Persian-influenced and independent régimes until it came into the hands of Alexander the Great. From that final period, under a tumulus, was a large cenotaph ('Tomb 77'), which was probably erected in honour of the city's last monarch, Nicocreon, who committed suicide, with the members of his family, in 311 BC, and was buried amid the ruins of his palace.

CHAPTER 2

THE ARCHAIC GREEKS

After the so-called 'Dark Age' many more Greeks re-emerged, establishing their city-states and embarking on that explosive programme of expansion which involved massive commerce and the colonization of regions as far afield and apart as south Italy, Sicily, the Black Sea coasts and north Africa – events of which the traditional chronologies can be partly controlled by recent archaeological explorations. The first Greek trading stations and colonies in the west, established by the Euboeans at Pithecusae (Ischia) and Cumae, are now illuminated by excavations which have also thrown light on the relations of these places with Etruscan city-states (Chapter 5, sections 1–4). Modern scientific devices have located a leading Greek commercial city – Sybaris – in south-eastern Sicily.

Further information, too, concerning early Greek commerce on the Italian coasts has been derived from a vessel wrecked off the island of Igilium (Giglio), a prime specimen of the flourishing and developing techniques for examining shipwrecks. Ancient sites that are now underwater are the concern of another branch of maritime archaeology – Halieis in the Peloponnese will be quoted as an example.

As for Greek colonies and settlements farther east, investigations of Olbia have opened up the vast and (outside the Soviet Union) too little-known field of Black Sea studies, while evidence collected at Naucratis and other Egyptian sites raises practical queries, and questions of principle, relating to possible contradictions between archaeological and literary evidence.

1 Pithecusae (Ischia) and Cumae: The West

Campania, in south-western Italy, extends between the Apennine Mountains and the Tyrrhenian Sea, and between the boundaries of Latium to the north-west and Lucania to the south-east. The volcanic Campanian soil was productive, but it was for commercial rather than agricultural purposes that the earliest of many markets – subsequently developed into cities – were established by Greek traders. The first of these visitors, in the eighth century BC, were men from Euboea, who based themselves first upon the island of Pithecusae (Ischia), off the north-western extremity of the Gulf of Cumae (Bay of Naples), and subsequently at Cumae (Cuma) on the mainland.

Pithecusae, or Inarime or Arime (the Roman Aenaria, now Ischia), is a fertile island seven miles from the north-western extremity of the Gulf of Cumae. Mycenaean habitation upon the lofty promontory of Monte Vico at the north-western end of the island was followed by an early Iron Age village – unearthed at Castiglione, 2½ miles to the east. A Greek commercial post (*emporion*) was also established below Monte Vico itself, where artefacts from Greece found in its cemetery go back at least to the second quarter of the eighth century BC. In this region of the Valle di San Montano an initial series of campaigns (1952–61) produced almost 730 tombs; twenty years later, after excavation work had been resumed, the total had risen to 1,300.

The occupants of the post came from the Euboean cities of Chalcis and Eretria, these being centres which, following the example of Lefkandi (Chapter 1, section 1), were leaders of the new outburst of Greek colonization. The traders were accompanied by a party from another Euboean town, Cyme (not to be confused with the famous city of that name in western Asia Minor). The majority of the visitors (though not all) seem to have been unpretentious: 'Further study of the San Montano cemetery', wrote M. W. Frederiksen, 'confirms that most of the tombs are of relatively modest or lower class, though there are signs too of family plots in which the better-off were cremated and the poor simply buried.'[1]

An early vase found at Pithecusae depicts a nautical scene (a shipwreck). It is an indication, perhaps, of how the Greek trading post on the island was very largely concerned to develop maritime contacts with Etruria, (farther to the north, beyond the River Tiber), a country possessing metal resources – and especially iron and copper – which were sought after by the Greeks. Thus a piece of haematite (iron in its natural state) which has come to light in the earliest Greek strata of Pithecusae turns out to have originated from the Etruscan island of Aethalia (Ilva, Elba), and at Pithecusae itself the remains of iron-workings have been discovered.

In return for iron and copper, the rulers of the Etruscan city-states wanted gold – which we see in such abundance in the cemeteries of their homeland. The Euboeans at Pithecusae were able to give it to them because they had obtained it from Greek trading-posts such as Al Mina, Posidium (Ras El-Bassit) and Paltus (Tell Sukas) in northern Syria, which included a strong, and at first predominant, Euboean element and which enjoyed access to a number of different Asian sources of gold ore. This Levantine link is corroborated by the appearance of a variety of near-eastern finds at Pithecusae, including objects from Phoenicia in north-western Syria. Such a link is not surprising, since at the time Pithecusae was the only permanent Greek establishment in the west, and therefore a natural magnet for foreign commercial exchanges.

In the third quarter of the eighth century, however, the Euboeans on the island moved over to the Campanian mainland. Here they established a second market, which became the city of Cumae. The supersession of Pithecusae, which this development inaugurated, was accelerated, at about the end of the sixth century, by an eruption of the island's Mount Montagnone, a secondary crater of Mount Epomaeus (Epomeo), an active volcano in ancient times.

Cumae, formerly Cyme (Cuma), lay just beyond the northern extremity of the gulf that bore its name (which was also known as the Crater and is now the Bay of Naples). The Cumaean acropolis overlooked beaches providing anchorage for ships, as well as a protected harbour at the outlet (no longer existent) of Lake Lucrinus (Fusaro). The acropolis was inhabited by a native population (Opici) from the early tenth century BC. In *c.*750–725, as we saw, the place became a Greek trading post, manned by merchants from Pithecusae. Most of the new settlers at Cumae, under the leadership of Megasthenes, had originated from the Euboean city of Chalcis, but some (like those at Pithecusae) were from the smaller town of Cyme on the same island, and it was they who gave the new Campanian trading post its name (just as they named Cyme of Aeolis in Western Asia Minor).

In *c.*730–725 Cumae attained the status of a Greek colony, and asserted its independence. From the immediately ensuing period dates the Artiaco Tomb, the earliest south Italian burial of what is known as the 'princely' type (further described elsewhere, Chapter 5, section 4), containing the ashes of men and women of the noble warrior class, who were buried with the silver ornaments, bronze vessels and iron weapons which had been their pride. The Artiaco Tomb was discovered at the beginning of the present century, but recent re-examination has demonstrated that – despite the Etruscan character of many of its contents, which once caused this grave to be interpreted as Etruscan – the tomb, like the burials at Salamis in Cyprus (Chapter 1, section 2), reflects Greek forms of ritual. Early architectural ornaments at Cumae, which contributed to what was known as a 'Campanian style', have also now been shown to be Greek.

Cumaeans and Etruscans soon colonized Zancle on the strategic Sicilian Strait (Strait of Messina); later, Cumae asserted control over a wide area of its own Campanian coast as well, founding Dicaearchia (Puteoli; see

Appendix II (iii)) in *c.*621 BC and Neapolis (Naples) in *c.*600, and exporting its pottery over an extensive region. Moreover, the Cumaeans also looked north. For although the Artiaco Tomb reflects Greek burial practices, the Etruscan character of some of its contents confirms the dominant role that the city fulfilled in the rapidly developing relationship between its Greek colonists and the city-states of Etruria, a relationship based (as we have seen at Pithecusae) upon the exchange of Etruscan iron and copper for eastern gold brought to Campania by the Euboeans. Moreover, the art of writing came to Etruria from the Campanian Greeks, and especially, it would seem, from the Cumaeans. Nevertheless, as Cumae became a major political power in its region, relations with the Etruscans (whose local capital Capua was not far away) began to deteriorate, erupting during the later years of the sixth century BC into open warfare, in which the Cumaean ruler Aristodemus twice repelled Etruscan threats.

Cumae also owed a great deal to its religious fame as the home of one of the Sibyls – prophetic mouthpieces of Apollo – whose vaulted chambers and galleries can still be seen within the depths of the acropolis. These have long been known. But much other archaeological material is new, for our knowledge of the early history of this area, wrote Martin Frederiksen (1979), 'has changed dramatically within the last few years, and is still changing with a speed that defies any ambition to offer definitive statements.'[2]

2 *Sybaris: The Magnetometer*

Since the Second World War there has been extensive employment of electrical, electronic and magnetic methods designed to tell the archaeologist where his digging is likely to prove most fruitful. Two kinds of device, in particular, can be distinguished: potentiometers, measuring the electrical resistivity of the earth, and magnetometers. The work of the potentiometer will be illustrated later by an Etruscan site, Tarquinii (Chapter 5, section 1) while an example of the effectiveness of the magnetometer is provided by Sybaris.

Sybaris was a Greek city in Bruttii (the modern Calabria), situated upon the Ionian Sea, in the Gulf of Taras (Tarentum, Taranto), the 'instep' of Italy. The town had been founded in *c.*720 BC by immigrants from Achaea in the northern Peloponnese, joined by colonists from Troezen in the Argolid, the north-eastern part of the same peninsula. Sybaris occupied a large site between the river of the same name (now the Coscile) and another river, the Crathis (Crati), where the two streams debouched into the Gulf of Taras, within an area still known as the plain of Sibari.

Sybaris became powerful – and notoriously luxurious – by expanding its territory throughout this fertile, cattle-rich, alluvial plain, a process assisted by a pact with the local native tribe of the Serdaioi. The Sybarites also founded colonies of their own, including Posidonia (Paestum), upon the western coast of Italy, bordering upon the Tyrrhenian Sea, which enabled their merchants to trade with the city-states of Etruria. In 510, however, internal strife at Sybaris gave Croton (Crotone), a longstanding rival, an opportunity to capture the city and obliterate it completely – or so the historians recorded,[3] but on this see further below – diverting the Crathis to flow over the site: and it is true enough that from about that time onwards Sybaris remained buried, so that even its location was no longer identifiable. All that was known until $2\frac{1}{2}$ millennia later was that the city must have been somewhere on the plain created by the two rivers' deltas.

But the plain extends over forty square miles, and the search for Sybaris proved difficult. In the early 1960s, nearly a century after the quest began, the first survey by a team from the University of Pennsylvania Museum (in conjunction with the Lerici Foundation, Chapter 5, section 1) revealed that one of the many earthquakes to which the region has been subject lowered the ground level by fifteen feet, so that the sea rushed in and created a lagoon. Subsequently the lagoon silted up. Then it was recreated by floods, and later silted up once more. Sybaris, or whatever was left of the town, might have lain anywhere in the area, between twelve and twenty feet beneath the earth.

At this point, the magnetometer was introduced into the operation. This is an electrical resistance apparatus, designed to measure, at any point, the strength and intensity of the earth's magnetic field. This science of archaeomagnetism, the measurement of the earth's magnetic field, had been in embryonic existence for some time, but its practical application, on a substantial scale, dates only from recent decades. Its instrument, the magnetometer, is able to locate certain archaeological objects and features.

Use was first made of a proton magnetometer. This, observes P. E. Cleator, is 'a development of the ordinary magnetometer, in which use is made of the magnetic properties of the proton (hydrogen nucleus) content of a bottle of water or alcohol. When an electric current is passed through an enveloping coil of wire, the hydrogen atoms of the liquid align themselves to the magnetic field thus created. If the current is then suddenly switched off, the protons readjust to the prevailing terrestrial magnetism, and in so doing induce in the coil a weak response proportional to the field strength producing it, which voltage is amplified and recorded on a dial. By operating the device at regular intervals along a straight line, any local anomalies caused by soil disturbance, or the presence of iron-containing substances (for example, baked clay), are duly revealed. Such features, moreover, can be rapidly located and their position charted for possible investigation in the future.'[4]

David Wilson recalls that 'the first suggestion that such a machine might be made to help archaeologists came ... in 1956. This was only two years after the discovery of ... nuclear physics, on which all the subsequent machines are based, had first been applied to geophysical work. The basic discovery was that the nucleus of a hydrogen atom – a proton – seems to spin around ... The proton at the centre of a hydrogen atom [gyrates] in the earth's magnetic field. The stronger the magnetic field, the faster a proton in it will gyrate ... The basic sensing device of a proton magnetometer is simple – it is nothing more than a bottle of water, which contains a great many hydrogen atoms ... A proton magnetometer has a very light, portable and easily manoeuvrable sensor head, from which a light-electric cable can lead back to the electronics and meters as much as a hundred yards away. It is extremely sensitive to the variations in the magnetic field caused by disturbances of the earth from former ditches or pits or the foundations of long-buried buildings.'[5]

Just how these variations and disturbances are revealed was explained in 1962 by F. Rainey, with special reference to Sybaris where he brought the instrument into use. 'The proton magnetometer is a sensitive detector of magnetic intensity because of a fortuitous fundamental principle – namely, the fact that the speed of gyration of protons is dependent upon the strength of the magnetic field in which they are located ... When the current is passed through the coil, the protons are upset and want to realign themselves with magnetic north because of their built-in dipoles (minute equivalents to bar magnets). They then gyrate in a manner similar to a top, and their speed of gyration, as measured by the instrument, is determined by the magnetic intensity of the earth beneath the detector-bottle ... At Sybaris the proton magnetometer is by far the most successful survey instrument. Operating on the principle of measuring slight variations in magnetic intensity in the ground, it is particularly successful on the Sybaris plain because there is here a substratum of clay or high magnetic intensity lying normally between ten and eighteen feet in depth. Thus a low magnetic reading on the proton magnetometer at any given point usually indicates an archaeological feature (an anomaly) which at that point displaces the magnetic clay.'[6] Power-driven drills of various types were then brought in to explore the locations where the magnetometer had shown that such anomalies existed.

What the proton magnetometer achieved, however, was to find not Sybaris itself, but its much later successor, the remains of the Roman city of Copia (193 BC) that was built later on the same, or an adjacent, site.

The proton magnetometer could not penetrate deep enough to find the Greek town (besides causing confusion where there were pockets of soil which produced 'false anomalies', i.e. material that was not archaeological after all), so that the original Sybaris still remained to be discovered.

Experimentation with a rubidium magnetometer came next. This was more sensitive and probed deeper, but could not be operated by hand, and was not designed for this type of fieldwork. Then, however, in 1967, a caesium (cesium) magnetometer was brought onto the scene, its active material, caesium, being a rare but widely distributed metallic element of the alkali group, and the most reactive of all metals.

'At either end of an aluminium tube,' writes O. H. Bullitt, 'about one inch in diameter, is fastened a can... One man walks across the field, carrying this odd-looking contraption. An electric wire runs from this back to a second man who is following some fifty feet to the rear. On this second man's chest is hung a viewfinder containing discs which have numbers around them like the odometer [instrument for measuring mileage] on an automobile speedometer. On his back are the batteries, and a wire runs from him to another piece of equipment set in the ground. The instrument in the hand of the first man is the sensor of the magnetometer. In one can is caesium, and when an electric current from the batteries is passed through it, it heats and becomes a gas. Simple so far, but now the electrons begin jumping between energy levels of the atoms... The speed at which the electrons jump will be governed by the intensity of the magnetic field on the ground. In other words, if the magnetometer is carried over ground that has a stone structure beneath it, even if this is twenty feet down, the speed of the electrons will be slowed down, as the stone has less magnetism, and conversely, if it is over a magnificent Greek vase, they will go faster. The later magnetometers were so sensitive that in one spot they showed a large piece of iron lying on a stone floor.'[7]

The employment of the caesium magnetometer made it possible to survey as much as ten acres of land in a single day. At points where it had detected magnetic disturbances, test borings brought up fragments of ancient pottery and tiles. They were found under water, but trenches dug where they had been discovered confirmed that the locations in question contained the foundations of buildings. Sybaris, finally, had been rediscovered.

Further applications of the caesium magnetometer indicated that old river-beds lay both to the north and south of these Greek remains, confirming ancient assertions that Sybaris lay between the two rivers, the Sybaris and the Crathis. Within this area, it has subsequently been determined that the archaic Greek settlement was built on a row of dunes parallel to the shore, and more than a mile inland from the present coastline.

An account of the campaigns conducted in the 1960s described six soundings which made it clear that the destruction of the city in the sixth century BC was almost total. But whether this annihilation was, in fact, wholly or primarily caused by a deliberate inundation undertaken by the hostile Crotoniates, as had been reported, remains doubtful. It would have been hard to obliterate a town constructed on a line of sand-dunes in this way. What may well have happened was that an earthquake caused the shoreland to subside, perhaps by as much as nine feet, creating an inland rush of seawater which made part of the plain into a lagoon; while subsequently, no doubt, the Crotoniates inflicted on the weakened Sybaris whatever further and fatal damage they could. From that time onwards soil has continued to be brought down by the rivers from the uplands, enlarging the flood plain under which the remains of Sybaris continued to sink deeper and deeper.

In 1969 the threatened construction of a petrochemical and thermoelectric complex almost on top of the site was warded off, and investigations were resumed with the assistance of infra-red aerial film and scanning equipment (Chapter 6, section 3). Thanks, also, to the 'well-point' system – which pumped off water so as to allow dry excavation down to a depth of at least eighteen feet – substantial portions of the theatre of Sybaris were cleared, together with parts of an adjoining building. The ancient town-plan has been reconstructed, the Greek harbour tentatively retraced and a residential quarter of the sixth century BC has been identified.

Yet only a small fraction of the ancient city's buildings has so far been found, and the obstacles involved make it uncertain whether much more of Sybaris can ever be disinterred. Meanwhile, problems of preserving what has so far been discovered, involving continued, expensive pumping, remain acute. Despite these difficulties at Sybaris itself, however, examinations of the whole territory adjoining the city have also been undertaken, confirming, in particular, an ancient tradition regarding the extensive network of subject towns which the city controlled.

3 Igilium (Giglio): Shipwrecks

Underwater archaeology has developed into a huge and invaluable continuation and supplementation of terrestrial archaeology, producing enlightenment not merely about technical matters, but also on all manner of social, economic, nautical, political and religious aspects of ancient history and life.

This branch of archaeology can be divided into two distinct parts: underwater sites and shipwrecked vessels. Halieis will be quoted as an example of a partly underwater site (section 4), with more being said on the subject in connection with Herod's Caesarea (Chapter 6, section 3) and the submerged shore of Puteoli (Appendix II (iii)). The present section will concern itself with the investigation of ancient shipwrecks – 'the recovery of a lost dimension of history: man's encounter with the sea and the part which this encounter had played in the development of human civilization.'[8]

For at least four thousand years, a large proportion of the world's goods has travelled by sea, and it is believed that until less than two centuries ago as much as five per cent of all this material was lost, every year, by shipwreck. Extrapolation from the eighteenth- and nineteenth-century figures which exist for British coasts has suggested plausible statistics relating to earlier losses in other seas. During the first millennium BC, for example, it has been estimated that as many as 15,000 merchant ships and 5,000 warships went down in the Mediterranean Sea alone – the richest museum of underwater antiquities in the world. Not all of these ships have been completely lost to us, however, for – despite the obvious and frequently discussed technical difficulties involved – an ever-increasing number of such vessels has been located, both in shallow and in deep water, every one of which is a 'time capsule' adding to our comprehension of ancient shipbuilding, trade routes and maritime traffic in general.

The breakthrough was the discovery of the aqualung, an automatic compressed-air diving lung, pioneered by Jacques-Yves Cousteau (1942). 'Before Cousteau,' wrote Peter Throckmorton, 'men explored the undersea world like timid savages living at the edge of a hostile jungle which they visited with trepidation and explored at risk of their lives. Cousteau changed all that ... He got Émile Gagnan to adapt to underwater use an air-regulating device originally built to meter gas in wartime wood-burning automobile engines ... The invention of the aqualung has indeed revolutionized not only diving, but our understanding of the sea itself, enabling non-specialist divers to explore the shallow edge of continental shelves to a depth of 200–300 feet ... Now, for the first time, it became possible to conceive of a new kind of *treasure* from the sea – treasure that would add significantly to the sum of human knowledge ... However, for archaeology the immediate impact of the marvellous invention was negative. The aqualung became available to the general public in 1947. *And in the next decade every known ancient wreck off the south of France and the Ligurian coast of Italy was destroyed.*'[9]

This book, and our present discussion, are concerned not with this tragic series of events but with the happier period that followed. Yet it has been happier only to a limited degree: in the words of George F. Bass, who has dominated this branch of archaeology, 'some [ancient wrecks] have been surveyed or photographed, a few salvaged, and very few excavated.'[10] And while all this has been laboriously done, people have gone on asking just how such investigations ought to be carried out, what should be done with the objects and remains that are discovered (bearing in mind the advantages of leaving them where they are), and how – if they *are* left where they are – it could be possible to prevent them from being plundered.

'Since it is rarely feasible', comment the authors of *Past Worlds* (The Times Atlas of Archaeology), 'to lift an entire vessel to the surface or transport it to land... much of the archaeological work has to be done underwater. This can often be hazardous and difficult... like any archaeological site, each wreck poses new problems. The condition of vessels can range from almost totally destroyed to virtually intact, from free-standing to completely buried. Much depends on how and why they sank, the type of bed they lie on, the depth of water and the existence of currents. Strong sites and currents can cause rapid burial by sand, which helps to preserve the remains... The position of the cargo on the sea bed results from the way in which the ship went down, its impact on the bottom and the angle of tilt... It is slowly becoming possible to chart the history of maritime technology.'[11]

One such historic discovery was the archaic Greek ship found in the waters beside the island of Giglio, the ancient Igilium, off the coast of Tuscany. The vessel lay at a depth of 150 feet, so that its examination, and the recovery of its contents, posed intractable problems.

The man who had, in 1961, first paid attention to the wreck was Reg Vallintine, while the excavations of 1982–6 were led by Mensun Bound. The renewed search that was necessary, in order to find the ship Vallintine had sighted, was described by Bound as follows. 'In the search for the wreck I based my hopes on three things. First: the various accounts of underwater divers who spoke of a cave in the rocks which it had been necessary to pass right through in order to reach the place. This once found, and two other underwater clues, we should be on the right road to find the wreck. Secondly: Reg Vallintine had spoken of "large shields" of bronze which could be seen on the site. These, I thought, were probably copper ingots, and if that was so they would powerfully stimulate our metal detector. All those which had been visible at the original stage, in

1961, had been taken, but surely at least one or two ought to have remained beneath the sand. Third: Reg said that he would be at Giglio for three or four days at the beginning of the campaign. Although twenty years had gone by since then, and memory of the underwater landscape had naturally become fainter, he was sure he would be able to guide us at least into the vicinity in order to enable us to begin our search.

'Once at Giglio, we easily found the cave, and it was from there that a pair of divers got started with the search. For three days nothing was seen, but the last time Reg went down we found, at a depth of a hundred and fifty feet, three or four small fragments of amphora. Clearly we were in the right zone, but as we expected nothing could be seen on the sea-floor to show the exact position of the wreck... The search continued with metal detectors and a magnetometer [section 2 above]. Two divers, about two days later, came back speaking excitedly of a strong reaction on the metal detector showing a substantial presence of metals under the sand. One of the two, Dr David Corps, and I, went down to verify. Moving away the layers of sand, we came upon a large mass of iron.'[12] The object turned out to be the handle of an Etruscan amphora, and after making further finds the investigators concluded that they had found the wrecked ship.

It proved to have sunk in about 600 BC, during the archaic period of Greek history. Our information about this period is only patchy. but the Igilium ship has done something to rectify this, for although many objects from the vessel suffered dispersal, what remained has given us a more intimate understanding of the epoch, as well as of the trading ships and operations which played so large a part in its life. Take, for example, pottery, which is of such importance to archaeology, because of its ubiquity, the permanence of the materials of which it is composed and the approximate datability of its painted designs. The pottery on board the Igilium ship came from six or seven separate geographical locations. Pots of Corinthian origin predominated, but others originated from Sparta, eastern Greece, a Carthaginian centre, and Etruria. Many of these vases were amphoras – commonly used for the transportation of ancient commodities – but other forms of pottery discovered in the wreck included *oinochoai* (jugs), *crateres* (wine-mixing bowls), and *lekythoi*, receptacles for oil which, like the wine, was preserved by the inclusion of pitch.

The wreck also contained many ingots of copper and lead, metals found in neighbouring Etruria, to which, in consequence, scholars have tentatively ascribed the ship's origin, calling attention also to the presence of pots from that region, as well as to the discovery of musicians' pipes, reminders of the Etruscan predilection for wind music. A superb helmet, however, made from a single sheet of bronze, comes not from Etruria, but from the Greek city of Corinth. This helmet, now in a private German collection, is a prestige object indicating the rank of the personage to whom it belonged.

The cargo on the Igilium vessel, and its other contents, was mixed. The finds included lamps, amber, fishing weights, fragments of ornate inlaid furniture, an elaborately carved lid, coins, arrowheads, a wooden plate, a writing plaque, and wooden shipbuilding tools, including a pair of calipers (instruments for measuring distances between two points, especially on a curved surface). The only calipers to have come down to us from antiquity, they remained sealed up in the wreck, so that worm parasites could not destroy them.

The ship, with these impressive and diversified contents, cannot have been just a tramp calling in at various harbours in search of business. Its captain, or the merchant who gave him orders, must have been well acquainted with the maritime markets and what they wanted. Evidently Greco-Etruscan commercial patterns and networks were a good deal more intricate and highly developed than there was previously any reason to believe.

An earlier example of shipwreck excavation is provided by a vessel made at Rhodes, which met its fate off Anticythera (Chapter 4, section 4). In 1967, the discovery of another ancient wreck, of much later date, off Ceryneia (Cyrenia) in northern Cyprus provided us with new insight into the nature and design of such merchant vessels and set a new and higher standard for the investigation of wrecked vessels by modern archaeologists: a standard which those who examined the Igilium ship were later able to emulate. And now, the mid-sixth century BC Plemmyrium ('Plemmirio C') shipwreck – discovered in 1987 – has proved to be the oldest wreck so far known off eastern Sicily. Although much looted, this merchantman was still found to contain a composite cargo, including amphoras from both Corinth and Massalia. Another sixth-century Sicilian wreck has now been located in the Fosso di Camarina.

4 Halieis: Underwater Site

In discussing the Igilium (Giglio) shipwreck (last section), it was recalled that underwater archaeology comprises the examination not only of wrecked vessels but also of submerged sites.

This second form of underwater investigation is illustrated by the study of Halieis. Lying near the southern extremity of the Argolid peninsula – the north-eastern region of the Peloponnese – in low rolling country, Halieis was situated beside an excellent natural harbour, on the north side of which stands the modern village of Porto Cheli. The ancient town has experienced one of those major changes of coastline which have so greatly affected ancient shores, for at some places the sea has receded (Chapter 5, section 3), while at others it has encroached. At Haleis, as elsewhere, (next section, and Chapter 6, section 3), it has encroached, and large tracts of what was once the inhabited area now lie under the sea. Inundation has occurred for as much as 150 feet inland. In particular, the southern and eastern sides of the harbour have undergone such a substantial rise in sea-level that parts of the ancient town are now more than six feet under water.

The excavation of Halieis was begun in 1962, and the submerged remains were tackled in 1965. With such a useful harbour at its disposal, Halieis had been a habitation centre from the early years of the first millennium BC; the name means 'salty places', with reference to the principal local product. After a period when the Spartans maintained a garrison in the place (*c.*640–590 BC), it received Athenian refugees in 480 (Chapter 4, section 2). Some ten years later a fresh draft of refugees arrived – this time from Tiryns, overrun by its neighbour Argos, so that henceforward the local silver coinage of Halieis bore the name of the Tirynthians. For the next century and a half the port served as a naval base in struggles between the leading Greek city-states. Before 300 BC, however, Halieis was gradually abandoned, though it was partly reoccupied in late Roman times.

It was perhaps in that late Roman epoch that a substantial part of the ancient town's remains went beneath the sea – radiocarbon examination of a wooden post suggests a date of about AD 400. The excavation of this inundated area provided an opportunity to apply techniques of shallow-water archaeology. First, swimmers using masks and snorkels located most of the visible remains and measured them by triangulation. 'Divers in pairs', indicated the leader of the operation Michael Jameson, 'used air-hoses supplied by a portable compressor on board a thirty-foot kaïk or on a flat-bottomed, fibre-glass boat equipped with an outboard motor... In 1967 an adjustable nozzle was used on the end of a fire-hose supplied by a pump mounted on the kaïk... In 1968 we used two kinds of portable dredge powered by portable pumps in the boats or set in a crate in shallow water... Besides removing accumulation the dredge could be used effectively for digging test trenches into the harbour bottom and, by keeping the water in the trench relatively clear, permit the observation, to some degree, of stratigraphy and the removal of samples of mud and potsherds from different levels....'[13]

But the discharge of what was brought out proved too close to the working area, and visibility under water was often defective. In 1970, therefore, a new system of metal irrigation pipes was used. These carried the discharge far enough away to avoid serious interference. Moreover, a gap of nearly 500 feet in the middle of the submerged sector was reconstructed by probing systematically beneath the mud. This was done with the help of metal-tipped surveyors' poles, along lines fixed at measured intervals.

At the same time, as Jameson reported, his colleagues 'were trying out their balloon-borne camera for shallow-water photography . . . A tethered balloon of three metres (nearly 10 feet) diameter, filled with hydrogen, suspended a camera. Shutter release and film advance (after 1967) were activated by radio controls . . .[14] Photographic coverage taken with a camera suspended from a balloon not only served for planimetric measurements [measurements of plane surfaces], supplementing and checking those secured by conventional surveying methods, but in a number of notable cases identified remains which had escaped detection in previous seasons . . . On early, windless mornings, as long as possible after excavating has ceased disturbing the water . . . forms often meaningless at close range may, by careful interpretation of the film, lead to identification of significant archaeological remains. The washing of silt or the growth of seaweed in meaningful geometric patterns, however vague, are recorded by the aerial camera though not recognizable by the diver right over them . . .[15] The great advantage of balloon-borne photography is that it permits a perspective of remains in shallow water, both before and after excavation, which is not available to the swimmer or diver. Unknown remains have been detected and much more accurate and detailed surveying and recording have been done. But for good results the water must be calm and clear . . . Wind conditions are often a problem.'

These various means have made it possible to locate the submerged city-walls of Halieis (probably of early fourth-century date like the fortifications of the acropolis) as well as a water-gate and three circular defence towers (bringing the total for the city to fifteen). One underwater sector within the walls, however, of roughly 330 × 165 feet, although trenched extensively, provided no evidence of construction of any date. The excavators interpret this empty area as a marine corridor which formed the entrance, in ancient times, to an enclosed harbour.

Next, in 1974, at the east end of the bay, some five hundred yards from the town itself, a shrine was discovered. It has been interpreted as the city's chief temple, dedicated to Apollo, who appears on local coinage.[17] In its earliest form, the building dated back to *c*.675 BC. A second temple nearby has been attributed to *c*.600. Like the first, this second shrine may have been dedicated to Apollo, but the Laconian tiles that form its roof suggest that it was built by the Spartans, at a time when they had a garrison at Halieis (*c*.640–590 BC). A stadium more than 600 feet long was found in the vicinity of the temples.

Progress has also been made in reconstructing successive phases of the town plan, including residential units and a structure in which coin blanks were found, leading to its identification as the city's mint.

As regards underwater excavation in general, *Past Worlds* has recently (1988) listed some of the devices that are nowadays employed: '1: Cables lowered by crane serve to lift heavy items. 2: Lifting balloon: air bubbles from its vent equalise pressure and regulate the speed of ascent. 3: Narghile or hooker hose: uses air pumped from the surface to allow longer but less mobile dives. 4: Air lift: with float, catch bag and basket serves to suck up debris [this is principally but not exclusively applicable to shipwrecks, see below, and so is 5: the step-frame]. 6: Plane table: to measure relative elevations. 7: Photography tower: made of light metal and standing 4 metres [12 feet] high. 8: Air-filled telephone booth: provides contact with the dive barge.'[18]

5 *Olbia: The Greek North-East*

The Greek north-east, and in particular the northern shorelands of the Black (Euxine) Sea, the coastland of Scythia, tends to be neglected in books about the Greeks. This is partly because surviving ancient authors (with a few exceptions) said little about the history of the area, except at moments when it happened to impinge on mainland Greece; partly because modern chauvinisms, too, tend to equate the Greeks with mainland Greece itself; and partly, also, because most of the modern excavation reports are in Russian, a language of which the west is still largely ignorant. But the reports exist and the tale they tell shows how the archaeology of the northern Black Sea region has transformed what we had hitherto known about the area's history.

The 'Scythians' of the hinterland were central Asian tribes of Indo-European origin and speech, comprising a mixed collection of peoples, including a substantial Thracian element. As Ann Farkas pointed out, 'by the time that Herodotus wrote, in the middle of the fifth century BC, the Scythians of the Black Sea area were grouped into a large confederation of separate tribes. In its most precise form the term "Scythians" refers to some tribes who lived on the northern shores of the Black Sea, but the "Scythian culture" was shared by various tribes spread over a large territory, with similar ways of life and close interrelations, promoted by nomadic cattle-breeding. The horse made direct communication possible between people living at great distances from each other, and it is no mere coincidence that horse equipment, specifically, is similar over the whole territory inhabited by tribes of the so-called Scythian culture.'[19]

W. Gordon East likewise draws upon Herodotus. 'The country of the Scythians,' he writes, 'which was many times greater than the area of classical Greece, appeared to the Greeks an alien world, remarkable both for its many large and useful rivers . . . (which yielded, near their estuaries, both sturgeon and salt) . . . and for the great extent of its "level and deep-soiled plains". It fronted the Black Sea and the Sea of Azov [Lake Maeotis], from the delta of the Danube to the mouth of the Don [River Tanais]; inland, it stretched a distance comparable with that of its coastline – a journey of some twenty days . . . The Scythians remained staunch to the nomadism which they had brought with them from central Asia. They drove cattle and horses over the rich pastures of the steppe, and sustained themselves mainly by the milk of mares and by making cheese and butter. In the most southerly parts of Scythia which bordered the sea the people sowed and lived on wheat, millet, lentils, onions and garlic. Others too, nearby, grew wheat, "not for food, but for sale". The reasons for this defection from nomadism were doubtless the penetration of Greek cultural influences and the chance and ease of trade in grain by means of the seaways . . . Scythia, contrasting as it did both geographically and economically with the city-states of classical Greece, afforded the latter an accessible and fruitful field of trade. Greek cities, which were founded near the mouths of the Danube and the south Russian rivers, served as means of contact and centres of exchange.'[20]

The major element in this phenomenon was the Greek city of Olbia (Olvia, near Parutino). Situated upon the coast of what is now the Soviet Republic of the Ukraine, Olbia stood at the north-western extremity of the Black Sea, beside the west (right) bank of the Hypanis (Bug), not far from the entrance of the extensive *liman* (estuary gulf) of that river – into which another river, the Ingul, also debouched – and facing the *liman* of the Borysthenes (Dnieper), which in ancient times did not follow the course that it follows today. It was the River Borysthenes which at first gave its name to the new colony, until the town subsequently assumed the name of Olbia or Olbiopolis, after *olbos*, happiness.

The settlement was established during the first half of the sixth century BC by a group of migrants including, especially, those most enterprising of ancient explorers, the men of Miletus in Ionia (western Asia Minor); and Olbia continued to cherish the Milesian connection. The site the new arrivals chose for themselves comprised a lower town fronting the *liman* of the Hypanis, beneath an upper town extending across a plateau 120 feet above sea-level. The lower town is now partially under water, owing to encroachment of the sea (such as also took place at Halieis; see last section). But it has recently proved possible first to map out a number of these underwater zones by air photography, and then to excavate them.

The results of this suggest that the occupants of the town originally numbered about 6,000 and soon increased to approximately 10,000. In the upper town, the public buildings appear to date from the years 550–500 BC. One area comprises the Agora (see Chapter 3, section 2), flanked by a colonnade, a court-house (*dikasterion*) and sacred precincts containing shrines of Zeus and Delphic Apollo.

North of the Agora, private houses have also been excavated. Some of these, containing storage facilities, display considerable size and wealth, and evidently belonged to prosperous merchants. At the other end of the economic scale, about forty more or less diminutive huts of mid-sixth-century date have also been brought to light. Another early residential district has been identified at the western end of the city, overlooking the gorge known as the Zayach'ya Balka (Hare's Ravine). Inscriptions found in this area indicate the existence of a temple of Zeus Eleutherios, the divine protector of the city's freedom, and record a committee of seven citizens responsible for the construction and repair of walls.

The territory of Olbia was nearly forty miles wide and thirty deep, and examinations of this area have revealed a network of no less than seventy settlements, linked by a communications system that almost entitles the area to be regarded as an entire second Greece. Excavations at Berezan, twenty-three miles west-south-west of Olbia, have proved particularly useful. Located on an island which in ancient times was a promontory or peninsula, Berezan stands at the entrance of the sea-channel leading into the estuaries of the Hypanis and Borysthenes (after which the place is named). It is possible that the Greek *emporion* (market) and harbour at Berezan were established earlier than Olbia. 'In my view,' writes J. G. F. Hind, 'the settlement at Berezan was undoubtedly the first in the Dnieper [Borysthenes] estuary and the whole north Black Sea area, and was an embryo *polis* from the start, gradually (by the early 6th century?) becoming a significant *emporion* for substantial traders.'[21] The houses of Berezan prove to have been single-roomed, thatched-roofed dwellings which were set low in the ground, for protection from the winter cold, and possessed fireplaces. Light has been thrown on local economic conditions by the discovery, within the crack of a wall, of a private letter of *c.*500, written on lead, in the Ionic dialect, and rolled into a scroll.[22] This document, the earliest business letter that has come down to us, confirms the major contribution that epigraphy makes to our knowledge of Greek history (cf. Chapter 4, section 2). In particular, it demonstrates the existence of a class of professional merchants at these Black Sea centres and illuminates their way of life.

Olbia and its dependent zone lived on commerce. The city was geographically well placed to dominate movements upon and beside the massive rivers which flowed and debouched nearby, and to control the region's natural resources of timber and minerals – iron, copper, gold and quartzite sand (for glass). The literary authorities, although they describe Black Sea trade at later epochs, are silent about what had happened before the fifth century. But archaeological evidence has now allowed a partial reconstruction of developments in the earlier period, at least from the years after 600. As far as land communications were concerned, Olbia's principal trade-route northwards to the forest steppe ran up through the valley of the Ingul. But the city also did business up the Hypanis, for at least two hundred miles, as indicated by the discovery of east Greek pottery of the later seventh century at that distance. With regard to sea-routes, stones found on inland sites of the southern Ukraine had evidently come from Greek lands as ballast; such links were encouraged when Miletus founded a further colony, Tyras (Belgorod Dniestrovsky) on the *liman* of the river of the same name (now the Dniester). Tyras stood halfway between Olbia and yet another Milesian colony, Istrus (now Histria in Rumania), which in turn established its own *emporion* at Istrian Harbour, near Olbia.

Herodotus enlarges on the rich pastures and products of the lower plain of the Borysthenes.[23] Not only did fish swarm in the river-mouths, but there was salt, too, to preserve them. The principal source, however, of Olbia's wealth was grain imported from its hinterland. Greek and Roman writers dwell on the enormous quantities of grain brought from the 'Black Earth' lands of the Ukraine, and the part that the Olbians played in this traffic is illustrated by discoveries a mile south of their city. Here a dozen storage pits have been unearthed, as well as an oven, which may have been used for drying the grain.

Other inland products, too, were brought down to Olbia for re-exportation. Polybius refers to cattle, wax and honey. The forests of the interior supplied timber, furs and hides. Metals came by land and river from Transylvania. And many slaves were transported from the interior to Olbia and other Black Sea ports, whence they were sent on to other Greek lands, mostly on Milesian ships. In exchange, Greek vessels calling at Black Sea harbours brought wine and olive oil, not only for their compatriots in the region, but also for Scythians and other non-Greek populations over a vast hinterland area, for Olbia maintained a close relationship with its Scythian neighbours – an association epitomized by an anecdote of Herodotus, who visited the city in the mid-fifth century.

He tells of a Scythian king, Scyles, who, having acquired pro-Greek tastes from his Greek mother, indulged them by frequent periods of residence at Olbia, where he owned a house and kept a Greek wife – until, that is, his Scythian compatriots found out about these visits, and put an end to them by killing him.[25] The story may be untrue, or untypical, but archaeological discoveries confirm a kind of Greco-Scythian symbiosis contrasting with the hostility which, for example, some Greeks living in more western countries displayed towards their indigenous neighbours. 'It is likely enough', writes Sally Humphreys, 'that Greek colonies had to develop sufficient flexibility of institutions to serve as intermediaries between the professional traders and markets of Greece and a quite different economic pattern among their barbarian neighbours, and that in consequence their social and economic development was different from that of the old Greek cities. The Russian excavations at Olbia, for instance, have revealed an Agora flanked by large fifth-century stoas which seem to have been used for trade ... Commercial public building on this scale is not a common feature in the Agoras of old Greece as early as the fifth century, as far as we know (we know very little).'[26] It is possible, too, the state may have exercised a greater control over trade in fifth-century Olbia than it did in Greece.

Mention should also be made of the superb goldwork produced by Milesian goldsmiths for whom Olbia provided temporary or permanent accommodation – a craft and art founded on the spectacular, exaggerated, accentuated depiction of animals, the 'animal style', which remained a Black Sea speciality. Such local motifs were employed because these gold objects, although made by Milesians, were largely intended for the Scythian peoples of the interior. Intermarriage occurred between Greeks and Scythians, and at least one nomadic people, the Callipidae, became sedentary 'Helleno-Scythians' under Olbian influence. The Gute Maritzyn Warriors' Tomb of *c.*490 at Olbia displays a thoroughgoing cultural fusion: its numerous objects of Greek manufacture were interred within a grave of Scythian design. Moreover, the grave contained 377 bronze arrowheads of a socketed form introduced to the Scythians by the Greeks.

In the light of this relationship between the two peoples, it has even been conjectured that Olbia (which was not easily defensible) owed its very existence, from its earliest years, to the protection of its Scythian neighbours. This may well have been so, although the further suggestion that Scythians actually formed a significant section of the Olbian ruling class remains unproven.

But the position of the city continued to be precarious. The Scythian expedition of the Persian king Darius I in *c.*513–512 BC must have caused anxiety to the merchants of Olbia, not least because it severed their access to one of their commercial outlets, the mining country of Transylvania. Not long afterwards, too, Olbia's role as the principal Black Sea centre was gradually taken over by Panticapaeum (Kerch) on the Cimmerian Bosphorus, where first the Archaeanactid dynasty (480s) and then the

Spartocids (438) ruled over a kingdom that proved highly durable. Archaeological explorations have pointed to a series of sharp political and economic ups and downs for the territory of Olbia throughout the Archaeanactid and Spartocid periods. Settlements were abandoned in the fifth century BC, reinstated in the fourth, and evacuated again in the early third, before recovering their prosperity during the first centuries of the Christian era.

6 *Naucratis: Archaeology Against History?*

Sometimes the archaeological record seems, at least at first sight, to conflict with what the literary authorities have told us.

Greek (Ionian) soldiers, together with non-Greek Carians, came to Egypt's Nile delta in about 660 BC. They may have been mercenaries employed by King Gyges of Lydia in Asia Minor, or free-lances with piratical intentions. When they arrived, they found employment under the Egyptian king Psammetichus (Psamtik) I (*c.*664/3–610/609), who subsequently posted or settled a number of them in garrison towns. Herodotus names these places as the Stratopeda or 'camps' in the eastern Nile delta, on its Pelusiac branch, a short distance from the sea.[27] And then too, as Strabo reports, Psammetichus settled men from Miletus at the 'Fort of the Milesians' beside a westerly (the Bolbinitic) mouth of the river. Later, after they had helped him put down a pretender, Inarus, he allowed them to establish a commercial post (*emporion*) at Naucratis (now Kom Gieif) upon the Canopic (most westerly) mouth of the Nile.[28] A subsequent monarch, Aphries or Hophra (589–570), employed a force of Ionian and Carian mercenaries against a rival Amasis (Ahmose), but without success, since Amasis was finally victorious and succeeded Aphries as pharaoh (570–526). It was Amasis, we are told, who singled out Naucratis for favours and privileges, thus setting it on its way to becoming a great Greek trading city (beside an Egyptian quarter), including merchants from many parts of the Greek world, engaged in a famous cooperative enterprise.

That is, approximately, what the literary authority, Herodotus, tells us. However, at first sight the excavations look as though they contradict him, so that a conflict seems to arise between the literary and archaeological evidence. What Herodotus wrote was this: 'Amasis liked the Greeks and granted them a number of privileges, of which the chief was the gift of Naucratis as a commercial headquarters for any who wished to settle in the country.'[29] And, he added, Greek trade was now concentrated at Naucratis to the exclusion of other ports. The clash between these statements and what the archaeologists have discovered is, in its first stages, an old story, going back for more than a hundred years. For excavations of Naucratis from 1884 onwards already indicated that Greeks had been settled there, permanently, a good deal before the reign of Amasis ever began. Moreover, Greek pottery belonging to the time of Amasis was discovered at Egyptian centres *outside* Naucratis, thus apparently refuting Herodotus's second statement also – about the exclusive concentration of Greek settlers at Naucratis – or at least making it hard to ascribe any such initiative to Amasis.

The most recent developments seem only to reinforce this second contradiction. Investigations in 1978 revealed a dozen further Greek sites in the north-eastern Nile delta, containing material from most of the sixth century BC, including its last years, after Amasis' death. It must therefore be concluded, with more force than ever, not only that Greeks were settled at Naucratis before 600 BC, and thus well before the reign of Amasis, but that his reign, moreover, neither exercised any detectable effect on the condition of Naucratis, nor brought about the withdrawal of the mercenaries from the frontier posts to that city.

But it is not quite as simple as that, as Anthony Snodgrass points out, in terms that sum up the delicate, and sometimes tantalizingly inconclusive, interrelationship between archaeologist and ancient or modern historian. 'Has the evidence of excavation therefore destroyed the credit of Herodotus's account? Not really, I would argue ... It is perfectly possible that ... the Greek pottery at places outside Naucratis was traded by non-Greek middlemen, and (although this is the hardest obstacle to overcome) that Herodotus's phrase about 'giving the Greeks Naucratis' was intended to cover some purely institutional change of the kind that leaves no material trace. But it also seems to me that ... the claim that Herodotus's account has been falsified by archaeology ... assumes that archaeology and history are operating in essentially the same order of historical reality; that archaeological observations are made, so to speak, in the same language as historical statements. In fact the overlap between the two is small and occurs, in the main, only in those cases where the activities of a significant part of the community are directly influenced by contemporary historical events ... Much of life goes on unchanged ... The archaeological evidence ... has revealed Herodotus's account as being a very inadequate summary of the history of the Greek presence in Egypt in these years. But it has not destroyed the entire credibility of Herodotus's account, because it is not in the nature of the archaeological evidence to do so. What it has rather done is to cast doubt on the chosen *emphasis* of the historian's version.'[30] That is to say, both Herodotus and the archaeologists have given us versions of the truth – but they are widely divergent versions because they approach the matter, inevitably, from different angles.

More recently, Snodgrass has enlarged further on this same problem, quoting a passage from Thucydides[31] that again does not seem to fit in with the archaeological evidence. Once more he concludes that we ought 'perhaps even to entertain the notion that the two classes of evidence may, quite simply, not bear closely on each other at all'.[32] It is the 'positivist fallacy', he suggests, to require the evidence of excavation, which is so often incomplete and ambiguous, to express itself in the language of historical narrative. 'Archaeological data', as David Clarke remarked, 'are not historical data and consequently archaeology is not history.'[33] Yet archaeology can and should be 'visible history' (see Introduction) – and these observations suggest what the modern classical historian ought, and ought not, to expect from the archaeologists. He has to grasp what they have to offer, and turn it, if he can, into the sort of history he wants. Opinions on this subject are referred to in Appendix I.

CHAPTER 3

THE CLASSICAL GREEKS

We have seen, in recent years, the reconstruction of the trireme, which, although probably invented in earlier times by the Corinthians, became famous as the war-vessel used by their successors to supreme sea-power, the men of Athens – both to win their empire after the Persian Wars (490, 480–479), and to wage the Peloponnesian War against the Spartans (431–404). Recent excavations have also provided a clearer picture of the topography of Athens itself during this peak century, revealing, for instance, the Painted Portico (Stoa Poikile) in the Agora, the central area in which so much of the city's public life was conducted. It was this period, too, which produced the supreme masterpieces of Greek classical art, exemplified by the two bronze statues found in the sea off Riace in south-eastern Italy.

During the following century Thebes succeeded Sparta as the principal mainland leader, while Athens temporarily recovered its empire only to succumb, with other cities, to Philip II of Macedonia at Chaeronea (338). Much more is now known about Philip's régime and kingdom, thanks to discoveries at Vergina and Pella. In Sicily, throughout this period, Syracuse was the greatest power, and a variety of archaeological evidence shows that the praises heaped by ancient writers on Timoleon (*c.*351–336), as the agent of the island's new prosperity, were by no means overstated, as had sometimes been supposed.

1 *Corinth and Athens: The Trireme*

Elsewhere in this volume reference is made to the ships wrecked off the island of Igilium (Giglio) and off Ceryneia (Cyrenia) in Cyprus, which have thrown light on Greek life and trade in *c.*600 and *c.*300 BC (Chapter 2, section 3). In the earlier of those periods Corinth had established commercial supremacy in Greece, but between the dates of the two shipwrecks it was overtaken by the Athenian empire.

The sea was essential to the creation and maintenance of any such dominant role. In consequence, shipbuilding became the largest and most complex commercial activity of the Greeks; and – since war was even more important than commerce – the war-galley formed one of the most vital instruments of city-state power. Thus the decisive weapon both in the rise of Corinth, and in the creation and maintenance of the Athenian empire that followed, was the oared trireme (*trieres*): one of the most significant warships in history, and the bulwark of any ancient political authority that was able to create a sufficient number of them.

At least one, and very possibly all three, of the principal successive forms of Greek warships, the penteconter, bireme and trireme, was invented by Corinthian naval designers. It remains disputed as to what extent these innovations belonged to the age of the Corinthian 'tyrants' or dictators, Cypselus (*c*.658/7 to *c*.628) and his son Periander (*c*.628–586), or to the preceding or subsequent periods in the history of the same city-state. It is unquestionable, however, that with the assistance of Syrian and Phoenician expertise, as well as with the aid of earlier Greek experience (which we knew about from paintings on pottery), these developments must have helped substantially to build up the Corinthian dictators' power. Versions of the penteconter appeared on vases before 700 BC, and this form of vessel then became predominant. Strengthened at the prow by a bronze-sheathed ram, it accommodated twenty-four rowers, in two rows, with two steering oars at the stern.

Since however these penteconters, though capable of rapid movement, were perilously long and slender, and by no means easy to manoeuvre, the development of another warship, the bireme, followed shortly afterwards. Biremes, probably influenced by Phoenician models, sat their twenty-four oarsmen in two rows of benches, one above the other, twelve along the gunwale and twelve along the lower thwarts (with their oars protruding through port-holes), so that length was diminished while speed was increased.

From ships of this kind, perhaps in the late sixth century (though its invention may have come somewhat earlier), developed the trireme – apparently once again at Corinth, as Thucydides indicates.[1] A trireme provided room for twenty-seven rowers at each of two levels, with the superimposition of a third row of thirty-one oarsmen on either side, each man plying his own single oar (rather than two or three to an oar), the topmost row working their oars through a laterally projecting outrigger (*parexeeirsia*).

It has taken a long time for the assumption that this was the character of a trireme to receive general acceptance (with some, but only some, help from the ancient Greek writers, for the ship was too familiar to them to need very detailed description), in opposition to the view, propounded from the sixteenth century onwards, that these vessels were propelled by three men to an oar. Within the last few years, however, this supposition has become a virtual certainty – enabling a ship actually to be built incorporating the features of the ancient trireme. The construction of this vessel was begun at the Piraeus in 1985, and it underwent sea-trials off Poros in 1987, after which its launching took place successfully in the following year.

'The reconstruction', wrote John Morrison, who directed the whole process, 'is a serious and thoroughly researched example of experimental archaeology, which reflects the partnership of naval architecture with classical scholarship. As an experiment to test the design practically and to provide data of performance it is unique because it is based on no actual surviving remains. The experiment is important for many reasons: the ship and her trials will help historians to fill a notorious deficiency in the accounts of naval engagements and the movement of fleets ... But perhaps the most important achievement of all will be for the student of ancient literature, enabling him or her to recreate accurately the maritime events described ... We have known the ancient Athenians as poets and dramatists, historians and philosophers. Now, in this recreated ship, we see them in a new and rather unexpected role as the builders and exploiters of a technologically advanced naval vessel'[2] – though elsewhere Morrison and J. F. Coates, partners in the reconstruction, agree (rightly, as suggested above) to give more of the credit to the Corinthians.

Morrison also refers to the effect that the reconstruction has exercised upon our general concepts of the nature and limitations of sea-power in antiquity. The recreated vessel shows how the trireme, sacrificing weight to mobility, was able to improve on all its forerunners in speed, ramming force (its bronze-covered ram terminated in three prongs instead of one) and manoeuvrable buoyancy within the sheltered waters that were habitually chosen for sea-battles.

The trireme could operate either under oar or under sail, but it was unusual for both methods to be adopted simultaneously. Mainsails, it appears, were not employed in battles, and when a battle was anticipated they were left ashore. Triremes could accommodate five officers and twenty-five petty officers, and were furnished with a light deck for the stationing of eighteen marines, fourteen infantrymen armed with spears and four archers. They proved ideal for amphibious operations because they were light and could easily be beached. Battle was not their only function, however, for they could also be utilized as troop or horse transports, or protectors of convoys.

These researches have confirmed what an effective ship the trireme was. As Coates observed, 'The Athenians were very good indeed. They pushed the outer limits of the designs, materials and men'[3] (and, incidentally, the collaborative functioning of the men aboard, in cramped quarters, proved an acid test of democracy in action). Nevertheless, the trireme did suffer from certain disadvantages. For one thing, it needed expert skill and training, which city-states less rich than Corinth and Athens found hard to afford and achieve. Also, owing to their lack of space, these craft could not carry more than a few days' rations on board – indeed, they were drawn up on shore every night, so that their crews could eat and sleep. Furthermore, their low gunwales were vulnerable to the open sea and bad weather. Nonetheless, it was the development of the trireme, corrected and refined throughout several centuries, that created the decisive element in naval warfare for a long time to come.

2 Athens: The Painted Portico

The Agora was the heart of an ancient Greek city and city-state: people questioned whether a place could be considered a true city if it did not have one. An Agora was a large open square, in which citizens could meet together for various functions and activities. It was a place, for example, in which trading was undertaken, and, indeed, 'Agora' is usually translated as 'market-place'. But the term is misleading, since so much else happened within its boundaries as well. Thus it was the centre of a city's civil government and the centre, too, of its political and legislative deliberations. It provided a stage for religious worship and ceremonial at its altars and shrines, as well as for many processions and athletic contests and dramatic performances. And people congregated there for purely social purposes, too, in order to talk about politics or philosophy or business or anything else.

The Agora of Athens, west of the Acropolis, incorporated all these aspects of Greek life, and symbolized the unique achievements of its city. Within this square, observed John M. Camp, who is joint-director of the Agora excavations today, 'monuments were set up to commemorate her triumphs, along its edges were the civic buildings for the administration of her democracy, while beyond its borders crowded the houses and workshops of those who made Athens the foremost city of Greece. The archaeological exploration of the Agora of Athens has thus led to a greater understanding not just of a single site but of all aspects of classical Greek civilization. Conversely, the extensive literary tradition we have for Athens, and Athens alone, sheds unique light on the Agora and its buildings... Nowhere else in Greece do the sources so enliven our understanding of the remains.'[4]

'We always felt we were privileged', wrote Homer Thompson to whom the rediscovery of this Athenian Agora was due, 'to be allowed to work in the most distinguished Greek city-state, and in the very heart of it – the cradle of western civic life and judicial procedure. We were unearthing the remains, coming to a better understanding of the civic and political life by knowing more of the physical setting. If you follow Socrates [469–399 BC] around the Agora, he meets tradesmen, shoemakers, philosophers, politicians. I still believe that it is of some general importance and consequence to know something about the physical setting of ancient life in one of the greatest city-states – that is, the circumstances under which a leader like Pericles [*c*.495–429 BC] or Demosthenes [384–322 BC] lived.'[5]

The layout of the Athenian Agora has been revealed by these excavations: the five hundred members of the city's Boule (Council) met every day in the Bouleuterion along the west side of the space; lawcourts were situated at its south-west and north-west corners; numerous shrines bore witness to its religious activities; in the Metroon the central archives were stored, and long stoas or porticos lined the square – open colonnades which provided meeting-places affording some protection from heat and from cold.

The South Portico (South Stoa I) was brought to light in the 1930s. It lay along the south side of the square, and proved to be a structure of partly preserved mud-brick. Pottery suggests that the remains that have survived should be dated to the 420s BC. While we do not know the ancient name of this portico, the large number of bronze coins found on the site suggest that the various uses which it served included employment for some public commercial purpose, perhaps associated with banking. In addition, an inscription of the *metronomoi* (inspectors of weights and measures) found in one of the rooms seems to indicate that it may have been the place where the small commission concerned with such matters, together with others that helped to run the city's daily administration, held their meetings.

The Royal Portico took its name (Basileios) from the King Archon, whose antique office gradually became largely formal. This structure was identified in 1970 (between the Portico of Zeus Eleutherios, protector of the city's freedom, and the road named the Panathenaic Way) and three more of the column drums which formed part of its colonnade were unearthed in 1980. Once again, inscriptional evidence contributed towards its identification. In front of it stands a large unworked block of hard limestone, apparently the stone on which incoming magistrates swore allegiance before taking office. It was here that Socrates had to answer the indictment which led to his trial and death in 399 BC.

In historical terms, one of the most important of recent archaeological finds has been the discovery and convincing recognition, in 1981, of another such edifice – the Painted Portico (Stoa Poikile), lying along the north side of the Agora and looking up the Panathenaic Way to the Acropolis. As T. L. Shear Jr, who shared the direction of the excavation with Camp, reported: 'Exploration of the area on the east side of the street [13 Hadrian St.] brought to light the west end of a colonnaded building of the fifth century BC, which, from its massive scale, its superb construction, and its orientation, must have been one of the most important early classical buildings in the Agora... All of the evidence points to the identification of the new building with the Stoa Poikile.'[6]

This portico, gradually disentangled from modern houses, was about forty feet wide and over a hundred feet long. Combining an exterior Doric with an interior Ionic order, it was built mainly of limestone, though the Ionic capitals were of marble. The pottery found on the site indicates construction in 470–460 BC, ten to twenty years after the Persian Wars. The Painted Portico first bore the name Peisianaktios, after its architect Peisianax, probably the brother-in-law of the conservative politician Cimon, who lavishly endowed the city with new buildings. Soon after its erection, however, the structure assumed the popular (and later official) designation of the Painted Portico, for it was adorned with a series of important paintings, now entirely lost (as are all of the Greek wall- and panel-paintings before the later fourth century BC, Chapter 3, section 4). Executed on large wooden panels by outstanding Athenian artists – Polygnotus, Micon and Panaenus – these pictures represented various mythological and historical Athenian military exploits. The most famous, attributed to Panaenus (or sometimes to one of the other two artists who worked on the portico), depicted the victory over the Persians at Marathon in 490 BC. The paintings were described by the travel-writer Pausanias in the second century AD, but had vanished by the time of the bishop Synesius, who wrote *c.*AD 398. 'All that is left to us', he said, 'is to walk around and wonder at the Academy and the Lyceum, and, by Zeus, the Painted Portico... no longer many-coloured: a proconsul took away the panels.'[7] Modern excavators of the site have found, inserted in the limestone, iron pins that may have fastened the grid of beams on which the paintings hung.

Moreover, in addition to these pictures, the Painted Portico contained yet further mementos of the Athenians' past military triumphs, such as shields (smeared with pitch for protection) taken from the Spartan force whose capture in 425 BC on the island of Sphacteria (Pylos) was Athens' greatest success in the Peloponnesian War.

A particularly wide range of activities took place in the Painted Portico. As far as official functions were concerned, it was the scene, every year, of a proclamation summoning those who were entitled to attend the Eleusinian Mysteries. There is evidence, too, of legal proceedings there. But, in addition, it was thronged by a crowd of people engaged in almost every other sort of activity, from fishmongers to jugglers, sword-swallowers to beggars. Above all, the portico was famous for the philosophers who held their meetings and attracted audiences within its colonnade. Cynics and many others gathered there, but the Painted Portico was best known as the meeting-place of the Stoics, who took their name from its Greek designation, Stoa Poikile. When Synesius deplored the removal of the paintings, he duly noted that this was 'the portico after which the philosophy of Chrysippus was named'[8] – Chrysippus having been the third head of the Stoic school from 232 BC until his death in 207. But in fact the portico had already been used by Zeno, the founder of the same school (*c.*300 BC), for his lectures and discussions. The Stoics, meeting here, were presided over by a continuous series of official directors until at least AD 260, and probably later, though by the time the Byzantine Christian emperor Justinian I closed down the last philosophical schools at Athens in AD 529, theirs had already ceased to exist.

Indeed, in that and the previous century the whole area gradually fell into disuse and disrepair. 'Damaged by the attacks of the Heruli, Alaric and the Slavs,' remarked Camp, 'the Agora ceased to be of significance only when Athens herself finally sank into obscurity at the end of antiquity. Finally abandoned in the seventh century AD, [its] area seems to have been totally deserted throughout the eighth and ninth centuries, if we may judge from the archaeological evidence. Only in the tenth century do we find signs of occupation once again, this time in the form of small private houses. By the end of the century there was apparently a large enough population to justify the construction of the little church of the Holy Apostles, which dates to the years around AD 1000. From this time on, the area was a populous residential district until the start of excavations, despite extensive damage in 1205 and again in 1826. Since 1931 the dozens of ancient buildings and thousands of inscriptions which tell the story of Athens and her Agora have gradually come to light . . .' leading, fifty years on, to the discovery of this portico, one of the Agora's most notable buildings.

3 Riace: Peak of Classical Sculpture

Art history should not be excluded from classical archaeology, for it is an important part of the historical evidence that classical archaeology can provide. 'Research and teaching connected with the history of Greek and

Roman art', observes Anthony Snodgrass, 'have accounted for a very large proportion of the activities, over the past two hundred years, of those called classical archaeologists. Even now, more than half of the sum of their work must be of this kind... The capacity [of classical archaeology] to integrate ancient art history into the study of the total material culture of the classical civilizations opens the way to a kind of art-historical approach that is often impossible in the case of other epochs... True classical art-history is now alive and well, practised indeed by several dissident schools simultaneously.'[9]

This same discipline has relatively recently had an amazing stroke of luck, for two exceptional bronze statues, of the classical Greek period, have been found. In August 1972 these two figures, known as the Riace Bronzes (Statues A and B), were located by a deep-sea diver about three hundred yards off Porto Forticcio (Riace, Calabria), at a depth of about twenty-four feet. Underwater archaeology (Chapter 2, sections 3 and 4) had thus, fortuitously, registered one of its outstanding discoveries. First, an arm of Statue B emerged from the sand, and four days later, despite problems caused by an alarmingly turbulent sea, the whole statue was gradually brought to the surface, with the aid of an oxygen-filled balloon. On the following day, Statue A was raised out of the water. An accidental deflation of the balloon plunged it back again, but it was brought up once more, and set down safely on land.

Next, after the removal of the small stones and sand and chalk which adhered to their surfaces, the process of cleaning the two bronzes was begun. This task was undertaken at Reggio di Calabria (the ancient Rhegium) until 1975. They were then transferred to the Restoration Centre at Florence, where the task continued. 'The cleansing of the statues in Florence', wrote Giuseppe Foti, who had directed the operation at Reggio, 'was exclusively mechanical, relying on scalpels, small hammers powered by compressed air, ultrasonic sound and punches in tempered steel, made especially for the job. In this way it was possible to use percussion to lift much of the encrustation, which contained only limited quantities of corrosive substances and which was thus only loosely attached to the surface. The only instances in which the encrustations were more compact and more strongly attached to the surface were where this took certain specific forms. Thus we used an ultrasonic probe to bring to light the eyes, the eye-lids, the lips and, in Statue A, the teeth, which are covered in a thick plate of metal. The same probe was used to clean the area around the groin, the beard and the hair.'[10] Protective treatment, too, was provided, so as to repel destructive elements in the atmosphere. In 1980 the work had been completed, and in order to determine to what extent the metal was liable to deterioration, tests were applied, involving storage in rooms in which humidity was maintained at ninety-eight per cent. Finally, after special exhibitions at Florence and Rome, the statues were transferred to their location in the National Museum at Reggio, in which gauges have been installed to control humidity, temperature and carbon dioxide.

The two figures are about six feet in height. Their faces are bearded, and each figure shows the remains of a shield-strap on its left arm. Each may also have held a short sword in its right hand. It would appear, therefore, that they do represent not athletes but warriors.

Statue A, the more youthful of the two, stands with his weight on his right leg; his left leg is extended forward. His hair is long and abundant, curling about his ears. Round his head was a band, which seems originally to have been coated with a gold or silver layer, perhaps in the form of a garland. His nipples and parted lips are made of cast copper. The corneas of his eyes are of vitreous paste, but the eye-balls are missing. His teeth, of which a glimpse can be seen, display an inlay of silver. He is a powerful figure, with wide shoulders, impressive chest and strong muscles. His confident turn of head, with a far-off but resolute gaze, is more theatrical than any known counterpart in the sculpture of this epoch.

The lips and nipples of Statue B are once again of copper, and one of his eye-balls survives, made of a mixture of ivory and a calcareous substance. This man is older, with a fuller beard, and makes a less assertive impact than his counterpart. Examination by gamma rays (Chapter 4, section 4) reveals a curious fact: his right arm, and the lower portion of his left arm, are composed of different metals from the rest of the figure, onto which, at some subsequent ancient period, they were soldered. That is to say, they are antique replacements of the original arms, which must have become detached. The helmet which the figure originally wore (of which little is now to be seen) confirms the suggestion, offered above, that these men are warriors.

The two statues are of such outstanding quality that, for the most part, the marble statues made by the Greeks, even when they are available in originals, look lifeless beside them. Although arguments have been put forward to the contrary, technical considerations suggest that both masterpieces were executed in one and the same workshop, and perhaps in the same fairly short duration of time. It also seems likely, though again there are opposing views, that they are the work of a single man. In terms of the labels utilized to define successive stages of fifth-century sculpture, they represent a moment of transition from Early Classical (Severe) to High Classical style. That is to say, the stances of the figures recall previous Severe art, while the easier pose and greater anatomical accuracy that have now been achieved – even though complete realism is still ruled out by

2.1 The island of Pithecusae (Ischia) off the north coast of the Gulf of Cumae (Bay of Naples). The Mycenaeans had occupied the promontory of Monte Vico, and the Greeks (Euboeans) established their earliest western commercial post, now excavated, in the Valle di San Montano below.

2.2a The magnetometer employed to locate the buried remains of Sybaris.

2.2b Silver stater of Sybaris, 6th century BC, showing a bull.

2.5 Silver coin of the Milesian colony of Olbia, on the north coast of the Black Sea, 3rd century BC. Head of Demeter; sea eagle carrying dolphin.

3.2b Silver tetradrachm of Athens, 5th century BC, showing head of Athena and her owl.

3.5a Silver stater of Syracuse under Timoleon of Corinth (345–337 BC), showing the Corinthian types of head of Athena and Pegasus.

3.5b Silver stater of Corinth. These coins of Corinth and its colonies appeared abundantly in Sicily under the domination of Timoleon of Syracuse (345–337 BC).

3.1 The Athenian trireme. This version painted by Bill Gilkerson differs in detail from the reconstruction of J. S. Morrison and J. F. Coates.

2.3 Imaginary picture of underwater archaeology as practised today.

W.B.D., JR. - 1981

3.2a Reconstruction of the Painted Portico (Stoa Poikile) in the Agora at Athens.

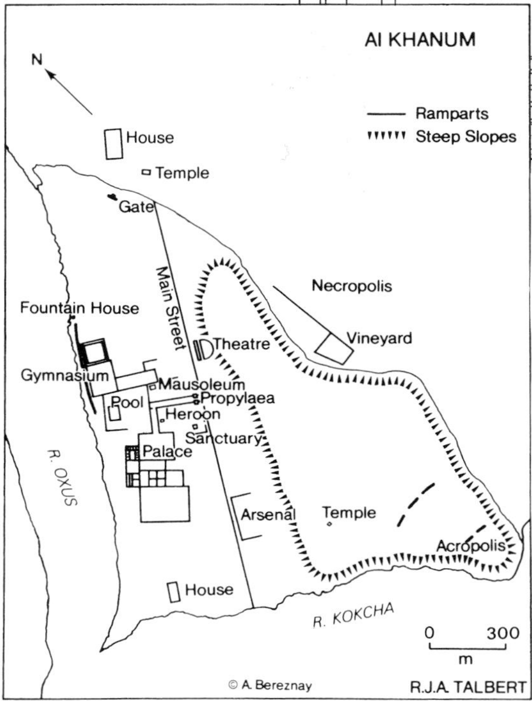

AI KHANUM
N
Ramparts
Steep Slopes
House
Temple
Gate
Main Street
Necropolis
Fountain House
Theatre
Vineyard
Gymnasium
Mausoleum
Pool
Propylaea
Heroon
Sanctuary
Palace
R. OXUS
Arsenal
Temple
Acropolis
House
R. KOKCHA
0 300
m
© A. Bereznay
R.J.A. TALBERT

4.1 Aï Khanum, one of the remotest of all Greek settlements, in Afghanistan; the ancient Alexandria or Seleucia Oxiana.

3.4 Pebble Floor Mosaic at Pella, Macedonia, showing two men fighting a lion, late 4th century BC.

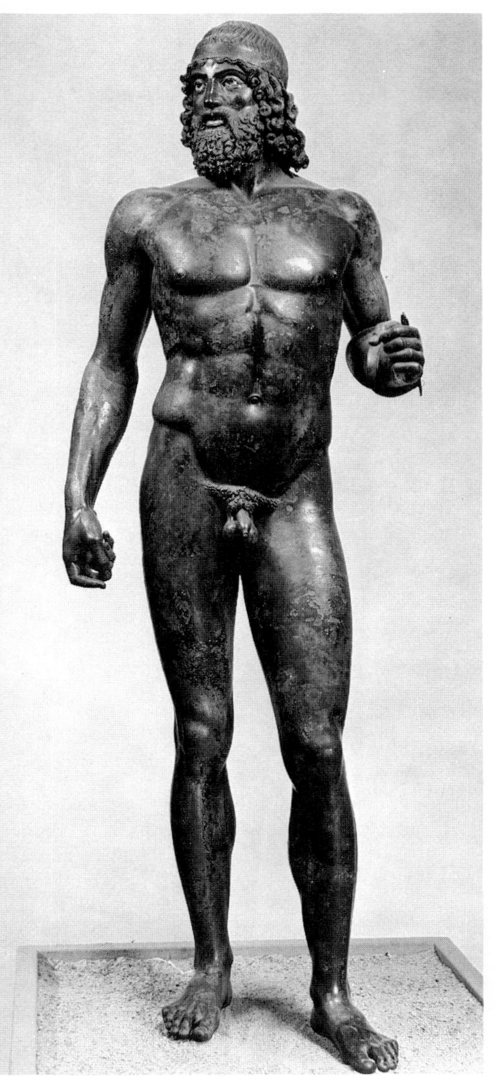

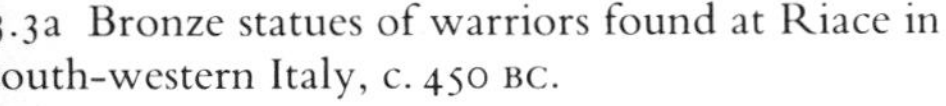

3.3a Bronze statues of warriors found at Riace in south-western Italy, c. 450 BC.

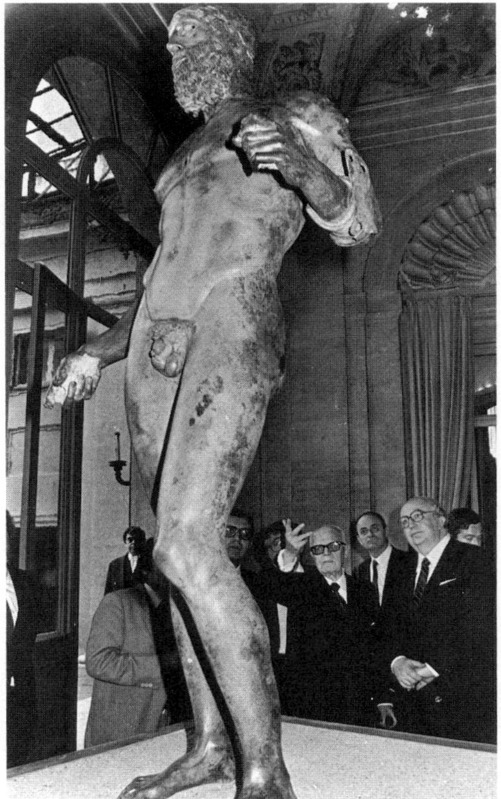

3.3b One of the Riace Bronzes inspected by the late former President of the Italian Republic, Sandro Pertini, and the President of the Senate, Giovanni Spadolini.

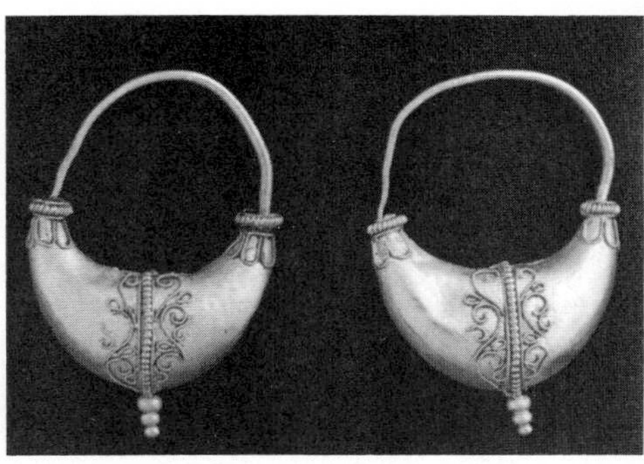

4.3 A specimen of the gold jewellery which was a speciality of the south Italian city of Taras (Tarentum, Taranto).

4.2 *left* Inscription found at Troezen purporting to reproduce Themistocles' decree of 481 BC, but probably altering it, perhaps in c. 323.

4.4a The mechanism found on a wrecked ship off Anticythera, and apparently made at Rhodes in the early 1st century BC. A calendrical instrument of extraordinary ingenuity.

4.4b Silver drachm of Rhodes, showing head of Helios (the Sun) and rose, c. 80 BC.

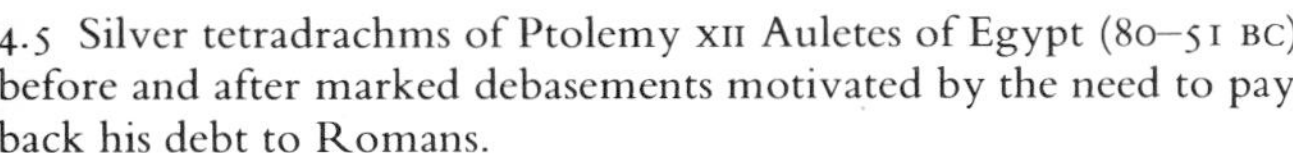

4.5 Silver tetradrachms of Ptolemy XII Auletes of Egypt (80–51 BC) before and after marked debasements motivated by the need to pay back his debt to Romans.

5.1 The four electrodes employed at Tarquinii and elsewhere to measure the electrical resistivity of the soil and detect empty spaces.

5.2 Etruscan inscription, one of two found with a Punic paraphrase, on sheets of gold foil at Pyrgi, a port of Caere (Cerveteri) in Etruria, end of 6th century BC.

idealistic considerations – mark the beginnings of the High Classical epoch. Both figures can therefore be ascribed to the years around 450 BC.

Who, then, are the two personages, that is to say the two warriors, intended to be? In about 465 the Athenian sculptor Phidias is known to have composed a group of statuary for the Athenian Treasury at Delphi, commemorating the battle of Marathon (490) and including representations of the two principal Athenian heroes of the Persian Wars, Miltiades and Themistocles. However, there is no particular reason to suppose that the Riace statues had ever formed part of that group, or indeed, that Phidias (or any of his students) was responsible for the creation of either or both of them. They have also been conjecturally supposed to have formed part of another bronze ensemble, designed by Onatas of Aegina to depict the Greek heroes of the legendary Trojan War. Argos, Sicyon, Corinth and Thebes have all been likewise proposed as possible places of origin. So has nearby Rhegium (Reggio di Calabria), which possessed, at the time, an eminent sculptor, Pythagoras – described by Diogenes Laertius as the 'earliest to aim at rhythm and proportion', and by Pliny the elder as the 'earliest to reproduce anatomical details such as sinews and veins and hair'.[11] No positive cause, however, for regarding Pythagoras as the sculptor of the two bronzes has been put forward. Instead, it is best to agree with John Barron that 'there is every likelihood that this is mainland work'.[12] The treatment of the beard of Statue B, as he points out, is reminiscent of a statue of the Athenian statesman Pericles (of which copies exist) by Cresilas, from Cydonia in Crete, who worked mainly at Athens during the second half of the fifth century BC. We are thus back to a tentative Athenian attribution, which conjectural references to Phidias had, earlier, failed to recommend.

As to how these statues came to be in the sea at that particular place, we have no idea. Maybe a Roman art collector or looter, in some much later century, was transporting them from one place to another – but there is no way of knowing. All that can be said is that the underwater archaeology that has yielded them up, and the restorers to whom we owe their present condition, have made a major contribution to our knowledge of Greek fifth-century art.

4 *Aegae (Vergina) and Pella: Macedonia Revealed*

Macedonia is the central part of the Balkan peninsula. From all its bordering territories, Thrace, southern Illyricum and the regions south of the Danube, thoroughfares converged upon the fertile Macedonian plain, formed by the rivers Haliacmon, Lydias and Axius (Vardar) at the head of the Thermaic Gulf of the Aegean Sea. This plain, which was enclosed by rings of hills and mountains – inhabited by fierce independent peoples – remained the nucleus of the country. The Bronze Age culture of Macedonia, which was more or less impervious to Mycenaean civilization, was overtaken during the twelfth century BC by a northern people, followed by Dorian invaders or immigrants whose descendants, mingled with other races, came to constitute the Macedonian upper class of subsequent ages. They spoke a language related to Greek, and the later Argead royal dynasty of Macedonia claimed to have originated from Argos (though the Greekness, or otherwise, of these kings of the controversial Macedonian region remained a political issue among their southern neighbours).

In about 640 BC one of these monarchs, Perdiccas I, expanded his domination eastward from the Haliacmon area to occupy those parts of the Macedonian plain that he had not controlled before, and moved his capital from Lebaea to Aegae. Amyntas I and Alexander I (*c.*495–450) collaborated with Darius I and Xerxes I of Persia when the two Persian monarchs invaded the Balkans and Greece (512, 490; 480), though Alexander hedged his bets and organized a national infantry and cavalry army of his own. His son Perdiccas II (*c.*450–413) played off the Spartans against the Athenians in the Peloponnesian War and was the father of Archelaus (413–399), whose modernization plans included the transfer of his capital from Aegae to the more convenient site of Pella. Philip II (359–336) hugely strengthened, enlarged and enriched the Macedonian kingdom, gaining control of the city-states of Greece itself by defeating them at Chaeronea in Boeotia (338). After Philip's son Alexander III the Great (336–323) had overthrown the Persian empire and carried his conquests to the Nile and the Indus, the Succession Wars gave control of Macedonia to Cassander (316), whose death in 298/7 was followed by the stabilization of the country under the Antigonid monarchy, which survived until it was crushed by Rome (168).

Of the three successive Macedonian capitals Lebaea remains unidentified, but excavations of Aegae and Pella, which in turn took its place, have multiplied our knowledge not only of the country itself but of Greek art and architecture and military equipment at more than one period. As these finds have established, the ancient Aegae was the modern Vergina – in the region of Pieria, south of the Haliacmon. There, in addition to a necropolis of three hundred tumuli on the edge of the plain beside the river, one of the most recent discoveries (1988) is that of a tomb containing Corinthian pottery which enables the burial to be dated to *c.*500 BC. Although the skeleton has decayed, except for its set of teeth, its fine array of gold jewellery – some of it engraved with mythological scenes – reveals that it belonged to a woman. She wore a gold diadem, a necklace of gold beads, a pair of large gilded pins, a robe edged with strips of gold, and sandals with soles of silver. 'In the absence of written history,' writes Manolis Andronikos to whom these discoveries are owed, 'it has taken archaeology to reveal how rich the lives of the Macedonians were, even as early as the fifth century BC.'[13]

The discovery of this tomb is the most recent among a long series of finds on the site. Excavations in 1861 and 1937, and then again under Andronikos in 1952 and 1957–63, had not amounted to a great deal. But during the past dozen years, under his leadership, no less than eleven mainly rectangular, barrel-vaulted graves have come to light, their architectural façades resembling those of religious or civic buildings. The first stages of these operations were concerned with the Great Mound, which was piled over a series of three smaller mounds and crowned by an arched roof, providing an early example of vaults that later became characteristic of Roman times. 'Andronikos', wrote A. W. Johnston and M. A. R. Colledge, 'returned to the Great Mound, particularly to its southern edge, late in the 1977 season... In early October, he found stone blocks. Soon a handsomely-built chamber of a type already known in the area was revealed. The door, as was to be expected, had been broken in and the contents were looted. But Andronikos was more than adequately compensated by finding painted friezes on the upper walls of the chamber. These were not only rare, but were also of high quality. The dig continued and another tomb was located farther into the mound. The excited archaeologists found that its door was still in position and there was no visible sign of forced entry. Andronikos entered the tomb on 8 November and found himself amid the decayed remnants of what was obviously an important and intact burial'[14] – the Great Tomb, containing a cremation burial inside a gold casket.

The paintings mentioned in that account are notable for their colouring, shading, dramatic strength, and almost impressionistic technique. They thus provide exceptional evidence for the ancient Greek art of wall-painting, which is otherwise – in contrast to the less ambitious paintings on pottery – wholly lost to us as far as the classical period is concerned (with the exception of paintings in tombs of Etruria [Chapter 5, section 1], which are in many ways more Etruscan than Greek). In the paintings at Aegae (Vergina), on the other hand, the character and quality of this major branch of the visual arts of Greece at last becomes apparent. One of these pictures (from the Small Chamber Tomb found under the Great Mound) depicts the abduction of Persephone (Kore) by Pluto (Hades) at Henna in Sicily, employing a subtle range of pink, brown and mauve. 'The ease and sureness of touch,' wrote Andronikos, 'the inspired draughtsmanship, the delicate colour-scheme, the expressive power, and the profound knowledge of perspective prove this to be the work of a very great artist indeed.'[15] 'Here,' adds J. J. Pollitt, 'rapid, impressionistic brushwork contributes to the sense of agitation in the dramatic subject and creates effects that anticipate and call to mind frescos of later European baroque painting. The second tomb at Vergina, containing an unplundered royal burial... has a hunt scene painted on its façade that belongs in the mainstream of the development of Hellenistic royal iconography. It shows an interest in elements of landscape (the hunters are shown in a grove of trees) that continued to grow throughout the Hellenistic period.'[16] Nor is this the only painting that has been discovered on this site, for a tomb discovered in 1978 contained a painting of a chariot-race in its antechamber, and a grave known as the Macedonian Tomb displayed a vigorous picture of a lion-hunt.

The quality of these works makes it hard to imagine that the graves which contained them could have housed the ashes of anyone but members of the Macedonian royal family; and this conclusion is confirmed by an inscription on one of three statue bases that have now come to light in a small adjoining temple, which reads 'dedicated by Eurydice, [daughter] of Sirra, to Eucleia'.[17] For whereas Eucleia was a goddess, the name 'Eurydice' played a leading part in the nomenclature of the Macedonian royal house. Moreover, the supposition that these are royal burials is further corroborated by weaponry, horse harness and traces of a mud-brick altar found on top of the Great Mound, which echo heroic, Homeric customs.

Such considerations suggest association with Philip II, whose portrait (along with the earliest known representation of his son, Alexander the Great) has been tentatively recognized in the Lion-Hunt painting. Furthermore, the Great Tomb contained within a golden casket (displaying the Macedonian symbol of a sun-burst on its lid) bones and ashes which are believed – despite suggestions to the contrary – to be the remains of Philip II himself. The wounds he sustained during his campaigns included not only a broken shoulder and arm but the loss of an eye (from an arrow in 354) and a crippled leg: it is therefore significant that a skull unearthed from the Vergina tomb shows damage indicating a missile wound from above that would have blinded one eye, and that a small ivory bust too, some three centimetres in height – one of a set of what would seem to be royal portraits – appears to show a mutilated eye. Another discovery bearing upon this point is that of a pair of golden greaves of different lengths and shapes, one of which could well have been made to fit Philip's injured leg.

Further finds included a helmet and corselet of iron – the latter ornamented with gold studs fashioned as lions' heads on the front – and a ceremonial parade shield. This was found disintegrated behind a large bronze cover but has now been painstakingly reconstructed. Set in a leather frame, it was composed of bands of ivory, glass and gold, with a carved ivory centrepiece, and is the most grandiose piece of parade-armour that has come to light from the Greco-Roman world. Of equally skilful workmanship was a wreath of interlacing golden oak leaves and acorns.

A second unrobbed grave, located in the antechamber of the Great Tomb and cleared in 1979, housed a single, female, cremation burial. 'There were also', wrote Paul MacKendrick, 'two silver-plated bronze containers, silver vessels, gilt bronze greaves, a silver-plated iron lampstand, a gilt bronze strigil, another with gold appliqué and a gilt spearpoint, and fragments of ceremonial dress in leather and cloth, with gold décor.'[18] Here, as in the other tomb, a gold wreath or crown was discovered, surmounting another (smaller) golden casket. In this casket were found the bones of the dead woman, wrapped in a shroud of purple and gold, finely decorated with floral designs. The shroud, within its airtight container, was excellently preserved, yet even so, once it had been removed, the treatment of the cloth required great expertise. This applied, too, to fragments of leather, including the remains of a case for bow and quiver. Covered by an embossed and chased gilt silver casing, this is the sort of piece that has previously been found in Greco-Scythian south Russia (Chapter 2, section 5), whence, indeed this case itself may have originated.

The ancient town of Aegae extended between Vergina and another village, Palatitsa, about a mile and a half to the west. On a small plateau between Aegae's acropolis and a cemetery stands the remains of a royal palace of the third century BC, containing peristyle courts, double-storeyed colonnades and circular halls. To the east of the Agora were found pottery workshops which contained terracotta figures, together with moulds of good quality for making them, as well as moulds for making pots. Many additional terracotta objects were discovered in a circular sanctuary of Demeter and her daughter Persephone (Kore), datable to the second century BC.

The acropolis of Aegae proves to have been much larger than was supposed, comprising no less than six large building units, now in the process of being excavated. Investigations of the town itself indicate that it was designed according to the symmetrical plan known as Hippodamian, after Hippodamus of Miletus (born *c.*500 BC). The theatre in which Philip II was murdered was located in 1982.

King Archelaus, as we saw, made Pella, instead of Aegae, the capital of

Macedonia towards the end of the fifth century BC. Pella lay to the north-east of Aegae, on the other side of Haliacmon, upon a slope beside a lake formed by the River Lydias, which was navigable from this point down to its estuary in the Thermaic Gulf.

The men of distinction whom Archelaus invited to his new capital included Euripides – who wrote his *Archelaus* while at the Macedonian court and, indeed, died in the country – as well as another eminent poet, Timotheus of Miletus, and the painter Zeuxis of Heraclea in Lucania. Alexander III the Great was born at Pella in 356, and the city reached its zenith under Antigonus II Gonatas (274–239). Superseded under Roman rule as the Macedonian capital by Thessalonica, it became a Roman citizen colony.

Since 1958, numerous remains of Pella have been discovered between the modern villages of Palea (Old) Pella and Nea (New) Pella and Phakos, three miles to the south (where the royal treasury proves to have been located). Air photographs give a good impression of this widespread ancient site, while investigations on the most westerly of the two hills that formed its acropolis have disclosed a palace comprising two architectural complexes erected side by side. They date back originally to Philip II (whose enlargement of Pella is recorded by Strabo[19]), but underwent alterations more than a century later. A hall and colonnaded court have been revealed, and excavations have also cleared two further courtyards on the main axis of the palace, separating the royal quarters from the town's administrative centre.

A sanctuary has been found, too, which should perhaps be identified with the shrine of Athena Alcidemus referred to by Livy.[20] In the central area of the ancient town is a colonnaded Agora (with shops, and a storm-water drainage system), on whose northern side a porticoed temple of Aphrodite and the earth-goddess Cybele can be seen. Terracotta statuettes of Aphrodite and her son Eros have also been excavated. Additional finds include half-a-dozen blocks of Hellenistic houses, sometimes two storeys high, dating from both before and after 300 BC. They were sometimes furnished with colonnaded courtyards, and showed black and white pebble mosaic pavements (forerunners of tessellated mosaics) which displayed qualities of refinement that had not hitherto been suspected of this art, and which must have approximated, in their general effect, to the achievements of contemporary painters. These mosaics, now in the local museum, depict a battle with Amazons, the rape of Helen by Theseus, a griffin slaying a stag, and the nude Dionysus riding a panther. There are hunting scenes as well, showing two men with swords and spears engaged in combat with a lion; a mosaic picture of a stag hunt is inscribed with the words 'made by Gnosis'. At Kanali, three hundred yards south of the main site, another mosaic depicts a young centaur in a rocky setting amid trees and caves; the border of the design shows lilies and poppies. In one house human skeletons were found – possibly victims of an earthquake. Work has also been carried out on the water and drainage systems of ancient Pella.

Examination of an area seven hundred yards to the east of the archaeological zone reveals burial places belonging to what is described as the 'Eastern Cemetery', including large rock-cut graves for burials, and smaller graves for cremations. Three of the larger tombs, which had until then remained undisturbed, were found to contain a varied array of artefacts mostly of Hellenistic date. An exhibition illustrating thirty years of excavation at Pella was organized at Salonica at the end of 1987, but many more important discoveries are still expected from the site.

5 Syracuse: Archaeology and Economics

There are a hundred, or a thousand, different ways in which the archaeologist contributes, or can contribute, to the work of an economic historian of Greece and Rome – and many chapters in the present book bear witness to the various interrelationships of the two disciplines (*cf.* also Appendix 1). There are also, however, more comprehensive situations in which a host of separate archaeological elements can be pieced together to provide a new economic picture of an entire country.

'Any study of the economic history of the ancient world', wrote Sally Humphreys, 'must begin with the relative importance of country and town, autarkic (subsistence and manorial) farming and production for the market, the agricultural basis and the superstructure supported by it... The fourth century is the most obvious period for research on Greek trade at present.'[21] Humphreys argues that progress can be achieved by increasing those forms of excavation that add to our knowledge of farmers rather than philosophers, that tell us about villages rather than cities. The cogency of this suggestion will be underlined when we come to Italian villa-farms such as Francolise and Settefinestre (Chapter 5, section 5). Another, more general, line of approach lies in examining how a complete, geographically defined, *group of cities*, together with their territories, fared economically within a specific period.

Here a field of enquiry is provided by Sicily under the direction of Timoleon of Syracuse, in the third quarter of the fourth century BC. That city's powerful autocrat ('tyrant') Dionysius I had kept the Greek cities of the island united, in a certain sense, by dint of knocking people's heads together, transplanting them from place to place and enlisting them –

with the support of mercenaries – against the supposed common enemy Carthage (along with its fellow-Semitic communities in western Sicily). After his death in 367, however, the whole island, reaping this unhappy heritage, sank back into its customary state of warfare between one Greek city and another, and of savage faction within each city's walls. The result was devastation, underpopulation and ruin. In the middle of this internecine strife, however, a group of Syracusans appealed to their mother city of Corinth to send a liberation force. The request was granted, and a Corinthian in his mid-sixties named Timoleon was dispatched to command the contingent.

Hitherto, Timoleon had been known for little but the murder of his brother. But now, although he had only nine or ten ships and not more than a thousand mercenaries, he eluded a Carthaginian fleet, landed in Sicily, overthrew those who resisted him, and became master of Syracuse (345). There, helped by reinforcements from Corinth, he introduced a new form of government, ostensibly led not by himself, but by the priest of Olympian Zeus, the divinity to whom a famous shrine outside the city was dedicated. Next, he campaigned successfully both against the dictators of other Sicilian cities, and also against two further Carthaginian invading forces (*c*.343, *c*.341), of which the first withdrew, and the second was heavily defeated beside the River Crimisus (Helice Sinistro). The subsequent peace, re-establishing the frontier between the Greek and Carthaginian spheres of Sicilian influence on the River Halycus (Platani), enabled Timoleon to execute those of the island's Greek autocrats who had hitherto remained alive, and to embark on the much needed social and economic reconstruction which earned him such fulsome praise in ancient times.

At one stage or another, he imported into Sicily, from the south Italian mainland and from Greece, settlers who were said to have totalled as many as 60,000. Moreover, writes R. J. A. Talbert, 'excavations carried out in the Greek zone of Sicily since the Second World War have enabled us to view the Timoleontic period in a completely new light. The old idea that the Timoleontic revival was a brief and insignificant episode shamelessly over-praised by biased sources has now been superseded; and the wealth of evidence for the island's revival seems to present us with a strange case where the ancient authors' generous praise is perhaps not sufficiently lavish... The contrast between the desolation of southern Sicily in the first half of the fourth century and its rapid recovery of prosperity in the second half is certainly striking.'[22]

The evidence for these assertions is archaeological, based on urban excavations. They have proved, for example, that the initial impetus for the revival of the city of Megara Hyblaea dates back to the time of

Timoleon. Similar investigation also points to the reconstruction of Camarina, Scornavacche, Castiglione and Helorus in this period. As for Morgantina, the town flourished most conspicuously later on, but it was evidently under Timoleon that its ambitious expansion had been planned. It was Gela, however, as archaeologists have shown, that most completely exemplified the rebirth of a Sicilian city under Timoleon; we can see why he was considered its second founder. Aerial photography seems to justify a comparable assertion regarding Acragas (Agrigento); the same is perhaps true of Tyndaris (Tindari) and Heraclea Minoa.

Certainly, this emphasis on the Timoleontic period should not lead to the exclusion of later epochs, since the reign of Hiero II (270–215 BC) was also an important watershed, to which, for example, further progress at Acragas may be ascribed. But the fact is surely that both periods witnessed advances, and that the attributions to Timoleon remain largely valid. In accordance, too, with Sally Humphreys' observations, the rural hinterlands of Acragas and Gela and Camarina (on whose territory particularly careful explorations have taken place) are now shown by archaeologists to have joined fully in the general recovery. Nor was the indigenous population excluded, as studies of Greek-native interaction confirm.

Pottery, that all-important aid to dating (Chapter 2, section 3), appears to add to the story. After a decline in the first half of the fourth century, the Sicilian production of red-figure vases seems to have flourished after *c.*350 BC, and the eminent 'Manfria' painter came to the island from Campania after *c.*340. Coinage, too, to whose historical importance allusion is made elsewhere (Chapter 4, section 5 and Chapter 9, section 1), enlarges our knowledge of this revival of Sicilian prosperity as inaugurated by Timoleon. For it must be that which lies behind the predominance of Corinthian coins on the island during the period in question. This predominance is revealed by the coin-hoards which, as so often, fulfil a huge and ever-increasing role in the numismatic contribution to history. 'Of thirty substantial hoards buried in Sicily between 340 and 290,' wrote Colin Kraay, 'in only two does the proportion of Corinthian coinage fall below seventy per cent.'[23] Talbert adds: 'It seems certain that this appearance of Pegasi [Corinthian coins, showing the winged horse Pegasus] is connected with Timoleon's successful expedition to the island... It is probably reasonable to place the first significant appearance of Pegasi in the years after the battle of the River Crimisus... The flow of Pegasi into Sicily must be the result of enormously increased exports from the island to mainland Greece and elsewhere. Agricultural produce will presumably have formed the bulk of these exports. Certainly Diodorus Siculus believed that it was the revival of agriculture which quickly restored Sicilian prosperity, and we have no reason to doubt his testimony on this point.'[24]

Evidently, too, the mintage of further Pegasi by no less than fifteen of Corinth's western dependencies (on the main sailing route between Sicily and Greece) was designed to take advantage of the island's new economic efflorescence, and of the consequent trade between Corinth and the Sicilian cities.

Thus Timoleon, although his eulogists unduly glossed over the violent methods he sometimes felt obliged to apply, provided Sicily, for all too short a period, with the most effective and beneficial régime it had ever enjoyed. After his retirement (337) and death, therefore, one can see why his fellow-citizens voted him conspicuous honours. Once he was dead, it is true, the island split apart once more, but, as the archaeologists show, the economic revival inaugurated by Timoleon did not come to an end – even after a subsequent autocrat, Agathocles, had put a stop to these convulsions by installing a rule of force at Syracuse (317). Moreover, the good times during the following century, under Hiero II, owed a very great deal to the achievements of Timoleon.

CHAPTER 4

THE HELLENISTIC GREEKS

When Alexander III the Great of Macedonia (336–323 BC) expanded Greek horizons to such a spectacular extent, one of the most distant of the settlements that he created (unless it was founded by one of his principal successors, Seleucus I Nicator) was a city on the River Oxus (Amu Darya) in what is now northern Afghanistan. This city, Alexandria or Seleucia Oxiana, has been discovered and excavated.

After the death of Alexander, the Athenians tried, in vain, to revolt against Macedonian rule; at this juncture, it would seem, Athens' ally Troezen set up an inscription apparently altering an Athenian decree of 481 (during the glorious period of the Persian Wars) in the light of the current political crisis.

Meanwhile the Greek west was dominated by Taras (Taranto), whose goldwork and jewellery, knowledge of which is much augmented by recent studies, occupied a leading role among the artistic products of the epoch. These western Greeks, unless they chose to invite mainland generals over to help them in local disputes, remained relatively unaffected by the activities of Alexander and the Successor Kingdoms. In the eastern Mediterranean area, too, there were still city-states which retained their independence. Conspicuous among them was Rhodes, which produced complex technological instruments, notably a calendar-calculator found in a shipwreck off Anticythera. Egypt, ruled by the Ptolemies, was the scene of the Successor Kingdom that lasted longest, but the precariousness of that state's later survival, under the shadow of the Romans, is illustrated by the coinage of Ptolemy XII Auletes – the abrupt metallic debasement of these issues, confirmed by scientific methods that are now utilized for numismatic analysis, can be convincingly ascribed to his indebtedness to Roman creditors.

1 *Alexandria (or Seleucia) Oxiana (Aï Khanum): The Farthest Greek East*

After Alexander the Great had conquered the Persian empire and founded a number of Alexandrias as far as Soviet Central Asia and the approaches to the Indus, the Seleucid monarchs who, a few years after his death, established themselves in the eastern parts of his territories, continued and extended his colonization process, spreading some seventy colonies throughout their dominions. They thus exceeded even the earlier, archaic age of Greek colonization in the amount of the territory they covered.

Many of these settlements were in Asia Minor, Syria and Mesopotamia. But there was also a far-flung, if less longlasting, semi-circle of foundations around the distant fringes of the Iranian plateau – as well as in lands even farther to the east, namely Bactria and adjacent regions. Settlements in this area have now come to light, telling us more of this Greco-Bactrian civilization. One such colony was Alexandria in Arachosia (southern Afghanistan). Another, which will be discussed here, was at Aï Khanum, in north-eastern Bactria, now beside Afghanistan's frontier with the Soviet Union. The discovery of this foundation has thrown unexpected light upon Greek expansion into this remote territory.

The town, of which the plan has now been largely reconstructed, is on the bank of the upper River Oxus (Amu Darya) at its confluence with the Kokcha, which descends from a mountainous region containing mines of lapis lazuli, the extraction of which was no doubt taxed or controlled by the city. Aï Khanum possessed natural defences, for it stood on the only section of the Oxus for miles around where the river was too deep to ford. Moreover, it was not only conveniently situated for the development of its own fertile, well-cultivated plain (containing canals which had existed from an early date) but could also monitor the approaches to Bactria from the north and east, as well as dominate the silk route from China, and control the annual migration routes of nomadic shepherds.

In 1961 King Zahir of Afghanistan was hunting in the region when he came upon a Corinthian column and a stone pillar, which proved, on investigation, to be the remains of Aï Khanum's Greek city, lying only inches beneath the soil. An acropolis, reinforced by ramparts (this was the 'Hill of the Lady', Aï Khanum), rose to a height of 180 feet, and from its foot ran the town's straight main street. On the flat land between this and the left bank of the Oxus was housed a series of public buildings, including a palace, a courtyard originally surrounded by 116 columns, and a treasury which was found to contain a mass of metal ingots.

The same area has yielded remains of three temples. One of these, a walled shrine with Corinthian capitals known as the 'Temple with Indented Niches', is flanked by two sacristies. The discoveries made on this site display mixtures of Greek and oriental artistic styles. One object brought to light in the temple is a repoussé silver plaque bearing a relief of the goddess Cybele. 'Two discreetly dancing lions', remarks Peter Levi, 'are pulling a chariot across a mountainous landscape towards a purely Persian altar of seven steps, which faces her. A priest in a long robe and conical hat sacrifices. Behind the chariot comes a Persian priest holding an umbrella over the head of a Greek goddess... She rides in a chariot, which is driven by a Greek girl. A star, a crescent moon, and the head of a young Greek sun god with thirteen rays sprouting from him survey the mysterious scene. We know that Cybele was originally a regional mother goddess adopted by the Greeks in Asia Minor. She was worshipped in Greece itself only by guilds of foreigners, never publicly until the Roman empire, but she was the Asian goddess the Greeks knew best in the third century BC.

'The temple was rebuilt. At first its outer walls had a series of recessed square niches, each one receding in a series of three diminishing frames, one inside the other... At the rebuilding the walls were smothered over in massive clay-brick, with some use of stucco and white paint. A carbonized wooden Ionic capital has been recovered almost complete.'[1] A cult statue found on the site was of enormous dimensions. The marble foot that survives wears a sandal adorned with a thunderbolt, suggesting that the figure represented Zeus.

Elsewhere the small shrine of a hero has an entrance framed by a pair of columns; the building was reconstructed on several occasions. Inside the shrine were two brick graves containing sarcophagi, one of which may have been the tomb of Cineas, who had been the founder of the Greek colony. Another temple nearby contained an inscription in Greek verse, whose lettering can be dated to before 250 BC. It describes how a certain Clearchus – probably Aristotle's pupil Clearchus of Soli in Cilicia – made a journey to Delphi in order to copy out the moral precepts of famous men of ancient times, relating to the virtues proper to the different ages of human life; and he brought back these precepts to Aï Khanum, where a section of his list has survived.[2] Another sign, too, of Aristotle's doctrine seems to be provided by the reverse traces of a papyrus, on decomposed mud-brick, containing what looks like a dialogue by a member of his school.[3]

Further testimony to the extension of Greek culture to this faraway corner of the Hellenistic world is supplied by a gymnasium or wrestling school (*palaestra*) and a theatre. There was a rectangular arsenal as well –

comprising a series of long store-rooms – from which portions of the armour of a cataphract (heavy cavalryman) have been recovered. Residential quarters, too, are to be seen, equipped with two- or three-unit baths adorned with stucco and mosaic. Some of these buildings lie outside the city walls, where irrigation channels and a mausoleum (in a necropolis area) have also been noted.

The history of Aï Khanum, if it was ever written down, has not survived. But some of its principal features can, nevertheless, be reconstructed. Earlier on, as the pre-Greek cultivation of the area has suggested, a town must have existed under the rule of the Persians, whose governors' palace has been tentatively identified (on the strength of the discovery of at least one Persian column base); hydraulic remains, too, reveal Persian settlement. Then Alexander the Great crossed the Oxus not far away (328), and it is not unlikely that, while establishing a network of garrison cities in elevated positions along the river, he visited Aï Khanum and marked it out for future development. The place could even for a time have been named, like other cities, Alexandria – Alexandria Oxiana – though it does not resemble any of those Alexandrias for which records exist. The surviving remains of the place date mostly from *c.*300 BC, and its principal foundation could have been the work of the first Seleucid ruler Seleucus I Nicator (312–281), who is thought to have established no less than thirty colonies. If so, Aï Khanum no doubt became known as Seleucia (Oxiana).

Subsequently, it must have passed from Seleucid control into the non-Greek Parthian empire, from which, however, it was recovered by the Greek (or Indo-Greek) rulers who later established themselves in Bactria. A fire which, as excavations have shown, destroyed a large part of the city can be attributed to *c.*145 BC or a generation or two later, when the Sacae (Scythians) overran the area. During their incursion, the forest of columns was felled with axes, and Aï Khanum never saw human occupation again – although, many centuries later, it served as a polo ground.

The Greek population lived exclusively in a quarter of its own, parasitic upon the rural inhabitants who were compelled to support this superimposed enclave. Inscriptions show names of Greek, Macedonian and Asian origin. 'The material from Aï Khanum and other new Hellenistic sites in the Middle East', writes Susan Sherwin-White, 'is providing the stimulus for a new appraisal of the character of Hellenism in the ancient east during this period . . . Older ideas of a 'fusion' (or synthesis) of Greek and 'Oriental' culture, with the overtone of an easy 'Instant Whip', are generally – and it seems rightly – now regarded as too crude to be of much use in analysing the complicated processes of culture change. Hellenistic historians have also learnt from the modern experience of decolonisation that different cultures do not communicate as easily as older approaches once assumed... Current orthodoxy tends to see the general pattern of contact between Greeks and non-Greeks as the juxtaposition or co-existence of Greek and non-Greek cultures with little interchange except in the case of local non-Greek élites.'[4] Indeed, the wall at Aï Khanum, which appears to divide the city in two, has been interpreted as a means of separating the Greeks from the natives, as at Massalia (Marseille). For Hellenistic cities were not particularly accommodating to local populations – not as cooperative as Olbia, for example, had been in the past (Chapter 2, section 5) – although a more open approach was favoured by some rulers and their envoys.

2 Troezen: Inscriptions and History

Some of the complex relationships between epigraphy and history are illustrated by an inscription found at Troezen in the Argolid (north-east Peloponnese). It relates to the Persian Wars of the early fifth century BC, but appears to have been made much later, during the months following the death of Alexander the Great in 323.

After the Athenians had repulsed the forces of Darius at Marathon (490), it was clear that his successor, Xerxes I, would seek his revenge. Accordingly, faced by the imminent threat of another Persian invasion, Sparta, the leading land-power in Greece, summoned the earliest of what were subsequently called 'Panhellenic' Congresses at the Isthmus of Corinth (autumn 481). The thirty-one states which sent delegates included thirteen in the Peloponnese; but another that took part was Athens. Unusually, the Athenians had conferred the supreme command of their forces upon a single man, Themistocles, although the overall inter-allied command, both on land and sea, remained in Spartan hands.

Victory did not come at once to the Greek defenders. Their original intention had been to hold the narrow valley of Tempe between Macedonia and Thessaly. Since, however, this line could be penetrated elsewhere (and since, also, the Thessalians were unreliable), this project was rapidly abandoned. The Greeks decided, therefore, to concentrate their forces instead on the eastern shore, stationing their army of 6,000 heavy infantry (hoplites), commanded by the Spartan king Leonidas I, on the narrow coastal pass at Thermopylae, and their fleet of 271 triremes off Artemisium in northern Euboea, under the command of another Spartan, Eurybiades – advised by Themistocles, whose Athenian flotilla was by far the largest. Leonidas and his Spartans fell, gallantly, before overwhelming enemy force. Their resistance had been brief, but it was enough to save the Greek ships at Artemisium – after three days of fighting, costly to both sides – from inevitable destruction at the hands of the Persian navy (damaged by storms though it was). However, after the annihilation of Leonidas the Greek fleet's position at Artemisium was no longer tenable, and it had to retreat, hastily and after dark, through the Euripus strait between Boeotia and Euboea.

Bowing to necessity, most of the Athenians followed the proposal of Themistocles and evacuated their city, which Xerxes took and burnt. The fugitive Athenian wives and children left for Troezen, Aegina and Salamis, whither the government of the city also moved. Somehow, Themistocles persuaded the Peloponnesians not to retreat to the Isthmus of Corinth as they had wished to do – arguing that as long as the Persian fleet remained undefeated any isthmus fortification could be turned – but instead to fight well ahead of the Isthmus, in the narrow strait of Salamis. And there a naval victory, one of the most famous of all time, was won. Xerxes withdrew to Asia Minor to prepare for the next year's war, which culminated at Plataea, while for many generations to come the relative parts played in the strategies and successes of 480 by the Spartans, Athenians and others were widely discussed and disputed.

After the first Panhellenic Congress in autumn 481 – that is to say, before the evacuation of Tempe, and before the campaigns of Thermopylae, Artemisium and Salamis – the Athenian government had passed a decree, which Herodotus reports in the following terms. 'The Athenians decided formally, taking counsel after the oracle, to meet the barbarian invading Greece with their ships and all their forces, in obedience to the gods, together with those of the Greeks who were willing.'[5] According to this version, then, the Athenians were from the outset determined to go all out to save Greece as a whole. To do so meant resisting in the north at Artemisium, with the implication that the Isthmus and Salamis, at this early stage, were still only secondary considerations to the Athenians. This looks very much like the true version of how the Athenians' minds must have worked, since 'saving Greece as a whole', by fighting in the north, meant saving Athens as well.

But now we come to the 'Troezen decree', which tells a rather disconcertingly different tale. That was the place where, in 1959, an inscription bearing on these events was discovered by Michael Jameson. Before discussing this particular inscription, however, a word or two should be said about the whole question of epigraphy. It provides one of archaeology's most essential and extensive contributions to ancient historical enquiries. 'There have been few major civilizations', writes Fergus Millar, 'in which the incision of words on stone or metal for permanent display or record has played no part at all. But if the making and display of inscriptions is attested in many cultures, it was so distinctive a feature of Graeco-Roman civilization that it deserves consideration as a major cultural phenomenon in its own right. As a consequence of this, the sheer volume of inscriptions from the ancient world, primarily but not only in Greek and Latin, gives epigraphy a central importance in the study of its history and culture in a way which is not characteristic of historical approaches to most other periods or areas... It is the reading of inscriptions... which will provide the essential direct acquaintance, the 'feel' for ancient society, without which the formulation of precise historical questions or hypotheses is an empty exercise, indeed cannot properly proceed at all.'[6]

Thus, A. G. Woodhead remarked, 'one of the principal features about the study of Greek inscriptions is the closeness of contact which they give us with the ancient world'. The lead letter from Berezan (Chapter 2, section 5), and the gold leaves from Pyrgi (Chapter 5, section 2), are conspicuous examples. Yet, although duly respecting epigraphy as a frequent supplement and corrective to the historical record, the same writer adds a warning: 'It is sometimes claimed for inscriptions that they provide not only a vivid but also an objective witness of the events with which they are related, that whereas a literary author writes with his own ideas and interpretation as a basis, an inscription is an official record, whose objectivity can do much to redress the balance of the ancient historian's subjective account. But... a record which is committed to stone does not on that account derive some additional and indisputable veracity. Few people who read the eulogies on gravestones of a century ago would be prepared to believe all the superlatives they see there... As with a modern communiqué, there is sometimes more reading between the lines than on them, and the art of propaganda, although brought to its finest pitch by modern techniques, was not absent from the armoury of the politician of antiquity.'[7]

The inscription discovered at Troezen has brought this whole question of authenticity to the forefront. It purports to reproduce Themistocles's Athenian decree of 481, the year preceding the second Persian invasion of Greece, under Xerxes I. Herodotus had told us that this related solely, and in general terms, to fighting in order to save Greece, that is to say, going up north to fight. But the Troezen version tells a divergent story, indicating that the decree of 481 had already proposed that the major part of the Greek fleet should take up its position further south, in the Salamis strait, while Athens itself was to be evacuated. Orders were already given, at this stage, according to the Troezen text, for the evacuation of non-combatants (except temple treasurers and priestesses) from Attica to Troezen and Salamis. Apart from the ships due to go to Salamis, a flotilla was to guard the Attic coast, while a hundred further vessels would proceed to Artemisium.

The text of the Troezen inscription, in translation and with gaps filled in as far as possible, reads as follows: 'This decree was passed by the Council and the Assembly: Themistocles, the son of Neocles, of Phrearrhioi, proposed it: the city is to be entrusted to Athena, the guardian of Athens, and to all the other gods, for protection and defence against the barbarian [Persian] on behalf of the land. As for the Athenians themselves and the aliens dwelling in Athens, children and women are to be taken to Troezen and the protection of Pittheus, founder of the place. Old men and movable property (*ktemata*, slaves) are to be taken to Salamis. Treasures and priestesses are to remain on the Acropolis guarding the possessions of the gods. All other Athenians and resident aliens of military age are to embark on the two hundred ships, which have been made ready, and ward off the barbarian for the sake of freedom, both their own and that of the other Greeks, with the help of Spartans, Corinthians, Aeginetans and others who wish to share in the danger. The generals, beginning tomorrow, are to appoint two hundred ship-commanders (trierarchs), one for each ship, from among those who possess land and a home at Athens and have legitimate children and who are not over fifty years of age, and to these men they are to assign the ships by lot... when the ships have been manned, with a hundred of them they are to render service at Artemisium in Euboea and with the other hundred they are to be in wait around Salamis and the rest of Attica and guard the land.'[8] Then follow directions regarding the possibility of amnesties for Athenian exiles.

This inscription raises two distinct though interrelated questions. The first is whether it dates from the actual time when the decree (worded differently, as we have seen, by Herodotus) came into being (481). The second question is whether it reproduces the decree authentically (which, in that case, Herodotus does not). As to the first question, the answer is certain. The inscription cannot belong to as early a time as 481, for it contains several features characteristic not of that date, but of a later epoch: notably, the specifications of the patronymic and deme of the mover, which do not, in other texts, appear earlier than the mid-fourth century BC. Moreover, the Troezen inscription's smoothly fluent style differs from the abrupt, bare and economical phrasing of decrees of genuinely Themistoclean date. Such an argument, it is true, is not entirely conclusive as a refutation of the inscription's essential genuineness, because the Greeks did not expect copies to maintain word-for-word fidelity; but there is more to it than that. For one thing, the detailed arrangements for the manning of the two hundred ships sound, for technical reasons, far more appropriate to the fourth century than to the fifth. Other features, too, seem anachronistic.

In any case it would be hard to suppose that even an approximate copy of Themistocles' decree could actually have survived. In the desperate emergency of 481–480, such a copy would not have been inscribed on stone, and it can hardly be supposed that any Athenian would have thought of taking it down on papyrus, for eventual transfer to stone, whenever that might become possible. For such reasons, then, it is necessary not only to ascribe the inscription to a date well after the fifth century BC, but also to doubt whether (in substance as well as in detailed style) it accurately mirrors the original of 481 BC at all. 'Its language', concludes Oswyn Murray, 'recalls an occasion like that in 323 BC, when the Athenians decided to revolt from Macedonian rule on the news of the death of Alexander the Great. The language [of their decree passed on that occasion and recorded by Diodorus Siculus][9] echoes that of the Themistocles decree: and it was most probably on this occasion (or another similar to it) that the Troezen inscription was carved by the people of Troezen, as a sign that they accepted the new alliance' (and as a reminder of the unity and courage that, once before, the Greeks had shown in the face of a foreign invader, planning well in advance the retreat as far as Salamis, proposed by the self-sacrificing Athenians). The Themistocles decree had in fact been serving such propaganda purposes since at least 348, when the orator Aeschines quoted it[10] (our earliest reference to the Decree; perhaps he quoted the same text as is preserved by the inscription) during a tour of the Peloponnese designed to whip up support against another aggressor, Philip II of Macedonia.[11]

All this being so, the next question – hotly debated – that arises concerning the Troezen inscription is this: was it, then, a *forgery* made in the interests of one of these fourth-century calls to political unity and patriotism? A number of other Persian War documents, after all, are known or thought to have been forged for precisely those purposes. On the one hand, certain details in the inscription do not look like inventions of a later forger, and were probably derived from a genuine document. On the other hand, 'form and language owe a great deal to the fourth century, and this debt is not just the consequence of a superficial reworking of an earlier document. The whole structure of the decree is literary; its coherence and organization are unparalleled in any genuine inscription of the period; it is a synthetic attempt to cover all aspects of the great event.' Moreover, as we have seen, the strategy reflected in its text, which implies that Salamis and Attica were seen to fulfil a prominent role from the start, seems to contradict the decree quoted by Herodotus, which had made the Athenians throw their entire initial weight behind the Artemisium effort, without thinking, as yet, of Salamis at all. So perhaps, suggests Murray, this Troezen inscription *was* the work of a forger, who 'had special reasons for giving an unorthodox account of the strategy of the Athenians. For instance, he may have wanted to include in his document references to both the great naval battles of the war: an unnatural striving after completeness is a common fault of forgers . . . Or [he] may have intended his document to endorse a particular strategy appropriate to his own day. Here we might compare the strategy of split forces put forward in 323, a strategy which is there associated with the Persian War, and which may well go back to the 340s and the first production of this document.'[12]

True, Murray concludes that 'on the issue of authenticity no agreement has been or ever will be reached'. All the same, he has pointed to some disquieting possibilities – or likelihoods. Nicholas Hammond, however, is not impressed by them (1982), and will not believe that the inscription is a fourth-century forgery. At the same time, however, he does not regard it as faithfully reproducing the original decree, interpreting it, rather, as a literary, but basically reliable, version of that decree. 'We can see', he indicates, 'what happened to the Decree of Themistocles over two centuries. Herodotus placed it where it belonged, just after Athens had consulted the Oracle of Delphi in late summer 481 . . . Other authors moved the decree and its concomitants down to the eve of Salamis . . . This move occurred already in the fourth century. Any forger in that century would have followed suit in order to impose his version on his contemporaries. The Decree of Themistocles which has been found at Troezen was so worded that it could not be placed on the eve of Salamis. We conclude, therefore, that this Decree is a copy made in the third century, not of a fourth-century forgery, but of a literary version of the original decree of September 481.'[13] But A. R. Burn, while conceding that this 'attractively explains at least some problems', does not abandon his own, on the whole, more sceptical view – concluding that the topic still remains controversial[14]: justifiably so, since the possible motives of the forger postulated by Murray cannot be discounted and seem indeed, to provide the best interpretation.

Moreover, if we see the inscription as a forgery, the forger could well have been prompted by a second, interrelated purpose as well, which would enhance his attempted adaptation of the historical record to his own fourth-century requirements. For he was able to make the Athenians' planning of 481–480 look calmer, more rational and more the product of inter-allied agreement (as well as more deliberately self-sacrificing) than the panic-stricken scramble and improvisation that had actually been forced on them by successive emergencies. In this way, too, the personal ingenuity and brilliance of Themistocles in creating these successive emergency plans, which Herodotus had emphasized but which later Athenians were more unwilling to acknowledge, would receive much less of the limelight.

In Chapter 2, section 6, archaeology at first sight seemed to be correcting Herodotus although, in fact, closer examination proved that it was rather a case of two sources operating along different lines. Here is another clash – this time between Herodotus and epigraphy – in which, factually speaking, the historian would appear to come off better than the inscription.

3 Taras (Taranto): Jewellery

Taras, on the gulf of the same name (now the Gulf of Taranto) on the 'instep' of south-eastern Italy, was one of the most important Greek cities, justifying the description of the southern part of the Italian peninsula as 'Great Greece' or Magna Graecia. Among numerous finds on and around the site is magnificent Hellenistic jewellery, the finest from the whole of the ancient world. Perhaps the theme ought not, strictly speaking, to be introduced here, since many of these objects were known long before the period of the past thirty years covered by this book. Tarantine jewellery deserves a mention all the same, because our knowledge of the subject has been considerably increased by recent discoveries which, together with older finds, have now been collected together in an exhibition at Milan – containing 300 pieces of jewellery, and the contents of 20 tombs found at Taranto, and in its province and in three adjoining provinces.[15]

After a prolonged Neolithic and Bronze Age history, Taras had been refounded, according to tradition, by men from Sparta in 706 BC. Standing on a promontory or peninsula – virtually an island in ancient times – the site, with its acropolis, extended between its inner harbour (an inland tidal lagoon) and a larger outer harbour, which was the safest and most spacious in Italy. Left by the decline of Croton (Crotone) in the mid-fifth century as the leading Greek city in the area (Chapter 2, section 2), Taras founded a colony (Heraclea in Lucania [Policoro]) that became the headquarters of a League of Italiot Greeks. In this League the Tarantines played a leading role.

During the years after 400, under the rule of the Pythagorean philosopher Archytas, Taras reached new heights of power and prosperity. Later in the century, as Strabo records,[16] it began to call in a series of mercenary leaders from elsewhere in the Greek world in order to repel adjacent tribes. The last of these leaders was Pyrrhus of Epirus, to whom the Tarantines appealed to save them from Rome. When he withdrew, Taras had to surrender to the Romans, remaining thereafter (except for a traumatic four years of Carthaginian occupation during the second Punic War) under their control. In 133 BC the Romans established a citizen colony there.

The site of early Taras is gradually becoming better known. A Doric temple of Poseidon of *c.*575 BC, on the acropolis, is now disinterred and restored, and a precinct of Persephone and Dionysus has been identified. An altar which has likewise come to light appears to have belonged to a sanctuary of Aphrodite. Two theatres are recorded, but neither has been located, nor have the defences of the acropolis. However, remains of the fortifications that encircled the city itself can be seen below the present waterline.

Like the Spartans who had been their ancestors, the Tarantines buried their dead within the walls, and excavations have uncovered thousands of graves, ranging in date from before 600 BC onwards. In 1979 a further 120 tombs, of the fifth and fourth centuries, were disinterred, regularly disposed in separate blocks. Then in 1980 another twenty-nine burials, dating from *c.*400 to 250, were discovered in another section. Near the centre of the Greek city, also, two burial pits seem to have been in uninterrupted use, from the sixth century onwards, for nearly three hundred years.

The territory of Taras produced pears, figs, grapes, chestnuts and famous horses – depicted on its renowned coinage. The city also derived abundant wool from flocks in the fertile hinterland, and this wool was dyed with the purple of *murex* mussels, found in the neighbouring waters, so as to make a fashionable woman's robe, the *tarantinon* or *tarantinidion*. Taras was notable also for various other products and exports. It was the centre, for example, of a school of Apulian pottery from *c.*420 BC. In the later fourth century, too, the sculptor Lysippus of Sicyon arrived in the city, and made colossal statues of Zeus and Heracles to symbolize the Tarantines' leadership of the Italiot League. Local artists not only designed architectural sculptures in limestone, displaying human figures, but also made graceful terracotta figurines, evolved from an earlier craft and foreshadowing the statuettes of Athens and Tanagra. Thirty thousand of these miniature figures have been discovered in the precinct of Persephone and Dionysus, in addition to others, near the shore, offered as dedications by arriving and departing voyagers.

It had been at a fairly early date, too, that Taras began making the jewellery which became its most important product. A goldsmiths' industry had already been operating in the city at least as early as the fifth century BC, although at that time neither its techniques nor its iconography had yet become distinguishable from those of other Greek lands. Later, when the conquests of Alexander the Great (d.323 BC) exploded the confines of the Greek world, a greatly increased amount of gold became available, so that jewellery became much more abundant. This development prompted the introduction of new types of ornament and new motifs, which brought about, as time went on, a radical overhaul and diversification of the somewhat austere fashions displayed by the jewellery of the earlier, classical epoch. The most important centres of this production in the Hellenistic world seem to have been Alexandria, Antioch and Taras.

It was above all in the third century BC, when the wealth of Taras was still famous, that the jewellery of the city not only multiplied in quantity but assumed characteristics of its own, including a taste for certain stylistic and iconographical motifs. During this climactic phase, which continued after 200, the jewels of Taras obtained a wide distribution not only in neighbouring Apulia, but also in Lucania (where the Tarantine colony Heraclea was naturally receptive), and as far afield as Campania and Etruria.

The metal wreath is one of the most frequently found objects at Taras. It was never a type of jewellery designed for female adornment – not being solid enough, indeed, for the most part, to have been worn by living persons – but was intended as an offering for the dead, making its appearance both in men's and women's tombs (cf. Pella, Chapter 3, section 4). The first wreaths known to have been made at Taras (*c.*500 BC) had been made of silver gilt, reproducing myrtle leaves and berries. In about the middle of the fourth century this silver gilt was replaced by gilded bronze, which continued to be employed for a long time thereafter. Gold, too, was used for wreaths, but in very thin leaves. These metal garlands exhibit a gradual transition from naturalistic styles to more schematic types of design.

In contrast to wreaths, diadems of varying lavishness were made at Taras for female adornment. Many have been discovered on the site and some of the most resplendent examples found elsewhere, notably a diadem of late third-century date, with a design of flowers, from the Tomba degli Ori at Canusium (Canosa) in Apulia, were probably of Tarantine manufacture. So too were diadems found at another Apulian centre, Ginos (the ancient Genusia), with a 'Heracles knot', a reef-knot credited with magical powers.

The tombs at Taras also contained numerous women's ear-rings. One widespread type, displaying small models of a ship, is represented by a Tarantine example of exceptional size. More frequent in the city's graves, however (and more and more popular as time went on), are ear-rings comprising a hoop of coiled wire tapering to a point at one end and displaying a miniature head at the other, the heads at Taras often being of lions. Spiral designs also occur from the middle of the fourth until the beginning of the third century BC. Other types of ear-ring make increasing use of semiprecious stones, which appear in *c.*300 and become predominant in Roman times.

Most abundant of all Tarantine jewellery, however, were finger-rings, from the fourth to the first century BC. Ettore De Juliis, analysing the Milan exhibition, has divided the finger-rings of the region into four principal categories, of which the relative popularity varied from one period to another: 1: scarab seal-rings, with revolving faces, in hard stone; 2: rings entirely of metal, with their faces smooth, incised or in relief; 3: rings with precious stones inserted in their faces; 4: rings of thread-like design.[17] The working of stones in categories (1) and (3) took place at Taras itself. With regard to (1), which ended in the mid-third century BC, such signet rings often occurred in female burials, bearing witness to the authority that women possessed in the private sphere.

4 Rhodes: Calendar-Calculator from Anticythera

The piece of machinery that will be discussed in this section was not found at Rhodes, where it seems – as a result of recent research – to have been constructed, but made its appearance under the sea beside Anticythera (Aegilia), a small island between southern Greece and Crete. Off that island, in AD 1900, a sponge-diver discovered, upon the sea-bed 180 feet below the surface, the remains of an ancient ship loaded with bronze and marble statues, amphoras and other objects. The ship, made of elmwood, was wrecked early in the first century BC, for reasons we do not know. The recovery of its cargo was one of the first major achievements of shipwreck archaeology (Chapter 2, section 3).

Among the objects recovered was something that turned out to be a bronze scientific instrument, the 'Anticythera mechanism'. Corroded and encrusted with calcareous deposits, it was at first ignored. But then investigators noticed that one calcified lump of corroded bronze, which had split open as it dried out, contained fragments of what looked like clockwork. Examination proved that four major pieces of the instrument, and several smaller ones, had survived; and that the inner sides of the fragments possessed attachments consisting of bronze dials, geared cog-wheels and inscriptions, of which parts were dimly legible. The original mechanism, to which all these pieces belonged, was apparently covered by a wood casing with hinged doors. This casing, which seems to have stood just over a foot high, had burst into fragments, but must originally have looked rather like an eighteenth-century clock.

In 1959, after eight years' careful study and various mistaken attempts at interpretation, it was decided that the instrument's purpose had been to enable its dials and wheels to show the past, present and future phases of the moon. Then, in 1971, new techniques of gamma-radiography were applied. Gamma rays are high frequency electromagnetic radiations emitted by radioactive bodies; photographs are produced on film by their passage through an object. The application of this process to the Anticythera mechanism helped Derek de Solla Price, after working through all the layers of encrustation and corrosion, to determine how its components were related to known astronomical and calendrical data of various kinds (not relating only to the moon).

Activated by hand, the mechanism was a sort of calculator, or computer, equipped with three outside dials, one in front and two on the back. The frontal dial had two scales: one fixed, showing the signs of the zodiac, the other on an adjustable slip ring, indicating months of the year. Both scales were marked off in degrees. A handle at one side could set this frontal dial to any required point in the calendar or zodiac circle. The dials at the back, by their rotations, indicated the positions of the sun and the moon.

The mechanism was also found to possess at least twenty interlocking brass gear wheels, each possessing teeth which enabled it to rotate at a prescribed rate within the gear train. Their operation, it could be seen, involved the *differential* principle, enabling the two shafts, which the instrument contained, to rotate at different speeds. Thus one shaft, for example, could revolve at an increased pace while the other was checked – like the system that makes it possible for a modern car to turn on the curve of a road. De Solla Price describes it as one of the greatest of all basic inventions. This differential device took the form of a turntable at the back which the moon-dial drive sent in one direction, and the sun-dial drive in the opposite direction – in obedience to the fact that, as the moon orbits the earth, the sun moves at a slower speed.

Thus it proved possible, in the end, to decipher the mathematical basis which lay behind this mechanism. Each of the twenty or more gears, it turned out, represented a particular calendrical or astronomical cycle. Set in motion by an axle (which was turned either by hand or by some automatic device like a water-clock), the gear wheels worked a system of pointers on graduate dials (some with a smaller subsidiary dial like the seconds dial on a watch), from which, when the axle was turned and the pointers moved, it was possible to read off the astronomical cycles known to the Greeks – not only the motions of the moon and sun, but also the risings and settings of constellations and planets (Mercury, Venus, Mars, Jupiter, Saturn and possibly other planets as well).

For whose information and enlightenment was this mass of complex calendrical data intended? Any idea that, because it was found on a ship, the instrument had merely been planned for the assistance of navigation appears to be misplaced – it was there only because someone on board had it with him. Could the instrument have been designed to serve an educational, instructional purpose? Or could its machinery, planned to work backwards and forwards from present time, have possessed some arcane significance for astrologers? Their bogus art was widely studied and favoured, and not clearly distinguished from astronomy.

The most probable, as well as the most obvious, solution is that the object was intended to assist the compilation of an astronomical calendar or almanac. For the arithmetic that lay behind the mechanism's creation, writes J. G. Landels, 'was based on the nineteen-year cycle discovered by Meton in Athens (*c*.432 BC), by which the sidereal orbit of the moon around the signs of the zodiac, which takes about 27½ days, and the lunar month, which is about two days longer, could be brought into relationship with the solar year. Meton held, in fact, that the period of 19 solar years was exactly equal to 235 lunar months and 254 orbits of the moon round the zodiac.' Despite slight errors, Landels adds, the accuracy of his system was creditable, considering that it was founded on observations by the naked eye, assisted by only the most elementary sighting instruments.[19]

However, the Anticythera mechanism was made nearly 350 years after the time of Meton, and was apparently constructed, not at Athens, but at Rhodes. This emerges from a study of the inscriptions incised on the instrument's surface, explaining how it should be used. The best preserved of these inscriptions reproduces part of an astronomical calendar written by Geminus, a mathematician of the early first century BC who belonged to the philosophical school of the Stoic Posidonius. This was situated on Rhodes, an island which had been no stranger to advanced technology, since it was also the place of origin, for example, of the most complex catapult of which knowledge has survived. What Rhodian however – if it was a Rhodian – made the Anticythera mechanism we cannot tell, any more than we can trace the stages of the earlier evolutionary process that made its creation possible. However, De Solla Price did succeed in deducing, from the slip-ring indicating the position of the stars, the instrument's date: it was made in about 87 BC, and subsequently repaired on two occasions, the second being in 80 BC, when it was set for the last time shortly before the ship carrying it was wrecked.

With the exception of a few striking inventions, such as the Rhodian catapult that has just been mentioned, and the Corinthian and Athenian trireme (Chapter 3, section 1), Greek and Roman technology sometimes strikes us as sporadic and disappointing. Yet this mechanism challenges any assumption of technological backwardness. True, it is only a miniature affair, and there is no evidence of any intention to scale up its various potentially useful elements so that they could serve any practical purposes, yet it is a device of exceptionally sophisticated design. Nothing like it has ever been seen again: though it should not be thought that astronomical and calendrical interests were declining, then or later. They were illustrated once more by the Tower of Winds at Athens, of about the same period, which is evidently a kind of planetarium of the ancient world. A number of Greco-Roman sundials, of various dates, made of marble and bronze, have also been found, and another, quite different, mechanism for the measurement of time was devised at Rome later in the same first century BC, during the reign of the emperor Augustus (Chapter 6, section 4).

5 *Alexandria in Egypt: Debasing the Coinage*

The significance of the finds and types and styles of ancient coins is discussed elsewhere (Chapter 3, section 5; Chapter 9, section 1). Here, however, mention will be made of another aspect of historical numismatics which has gained increasing impetus in recent years: namely, the application of scientific techniques (so widely applied to archaeology in general) to the peculiar problems inherent in the study of coins.

In 1946 I published some results of spectrographic analyses of monetary issues of Augustus, with a view to determining certain of his political and economic policies.[20] But since then, and particularly since the Royal Numismatic Society's 1970 symposium on the study of coins by scientific techniques, this form of investigation has rapidly advanced and diversified. Just how varied and numerous those new methods have become is suggested by the articles under the heading of 'Scientific Techniques in Numismatics' published by the International Numismatic Commission in 1986. The titles of these articles were: Physical Methods of Analysis; X-Ray Fluorescence and Lead Isotope Analysis; Activation Analysis; Chemical, Spectroscopic and Statistical Methods of Analysis; and The Application of Computers.[21]

One of the subjects upon which these techniques throw light is the debasement of ancient coinage, and its economic or political causes and implications. A debasement introduced in the Ptolemaic kingdom of Egypt, in the first century BC, provides an example. In 80 BC Cleopatra VII's father Ptolemy XII Auletes (the Piper) had been placed, precariously, upon the throne of Egypt by the Romans. Actual annexation by the Romans remained a threat, however. In the 60s, Auletes succeeded in averting it by giving lavish assistance to Pompey (Cnaeus Pompeius

Magnus), who was now in the east, although this did not endear him to his own subjects. In 59 Pompey and Caesar (now members, along with Crassus, of the 'First Triumvirate' that ruled Rome) agreed to back Auletes against his rebellious subjects, confirming his kingship as 'friend and ally of the Roman people', provided only that the monarch handed over to Pompey and Caesar six thousand talents – estimated as the equivalent of the entire revenue of the Egyptian state for between six months and a year.

Since Pompey and Caesar wanted the money immediately, Auletes borrowed it from a Roman financier, Gaius Rabirius Postumus, and handed it over to them. Then, of course, he had to consider how he was ever going to repay Rabirius, plus interest: and in order to do this he had to mulct his subjects. In the hope of softening their hostile reactions, he began by declaring an amnesty, cancelling all impending prosecutions. But then he was obliged to increase taxes. This infuriated the Alexandrians, as did his failure to prevent Rome's seizure of Ptolemaic Cyprus from his brother (likewise called Ptolemy). The people revolted, and Auletes fled for his life. He went to Italy, where Rabirius Postumus, who had not received his loan back, was urging Pompey and Caesar to reinstate the monarch on his throne, since otherwise no money would be forthcoming at all. Auletes distributed bribes at Rome, and finally a henchman of Pompey, Aulus Gabinius, undertook to re-establish him in Egypt, in return for the sum of ten thousand talents (from which Pompey and Caesar would again take their cut). And so, despite opposition and chaos in Egypt, Auletes returned there. Rabirius insisted on accompanying him in order to make sure his debt was repaid, and, in pursuit of this aim, set himself up as the country's economic overlord. In 51 Auletes died.

It has often been wondered how Auletes, faced with the national recalcitrance to higher taxation, set about repaying the enormous debts he had incurred from the Romans in order to keep, and resume, his throne. Now, with the help of scientific techniques, one of his principal methods has come to light – he undertook the debasement of his royal silver coinage, the first serious move in this direction during the nearly three centuries of Ptolemaic rule. Chemical analysis shows what happened: at the beginning of his reign in 80 BC, his coins contained 84.85% of silver, while in 53/52 the proportion had fallen to 64%; the weight of the pieces, too, had sunk to the lowest level of the reign.[22] As Michael Crawford points out, this was one way in which Auletes tried to save on costs, so as to repay his debts to the Romans.[23] The debasement of the coinage helped to make this possible, and the whole episode illustrates the kind of contribution numismatics can make to historical studies.

PART II

ITALY AND THE ROMAN EMPIRE

CHAPTER 5

ETRUSCAN AND REPUBLICAN ITALY

Those parts of Italy which were not Greek possessed a long history of their own which can be elucidated with the aid of archaeologists. North-west of the Tiber lay Etruria, where the absence of literary historical sources is glaring. Excavators, however, have done much to fill the gap. The cemeteries of Tarquinii, for instance, have yielded a wealth of informative painted tombs, revealed in many cases by novel techniques of investigation.

Furthermore, light is shed on the history of Etruscan cities by the inscriptions which have been found. An example is provided by the wafers of gold found at Pyrgi, one of the ports of Caere (Cerveteri), which bear two inscriptions in Etruscan together with a paraphrase in Punic (Carthaginian). Other places along the Etruscan shore have found their way into history through the recognition, and archaeological investigation, of substantial ancient changes of coastline. Thus the sea-lagoon off Orbetello (formerly an Etruscan city) is now closed by two sandbars, but in Etruscan times the lagoon contained openings to the Tyrrhenian Sea, giving Orbetello a valuable harbour. Vetulonia and Rusellae also possessed harbours, or rather they possessed more than a single port each, since the plainland above which they now stand was formerly the sea-lagoon Lake Prilius.

These are a few of many reminders that the Etruscan city-states engaged in maritime activity. Moreover, similar enterprises prompted extension of their power beyond Etruria itself: in addition to their territorial and economic expansions in northern Italy, recent archaeology has demonstrated the character and prosperity of the settlements that they founded in the south, as far away as Picentia (Pontecagnano) near the farthest extremity of Campania.

As to the Romans who gradually took over all these Etruscan posts and dependencies, recent excavation has brought to light their villa-farms dating from the first century BC at Settefinestre in Etruria and Francolise in northern Campania. On the Campanian coast, too, the discovery of a large villa at Oplontis, of similar date, has added this to the centres subsequently destroyed by the eruption of Vesuvius; the paintings on its walls have added much to our knowledge of this art from the first century BC onwards.

1 Tarquinii: Potentiometer, Periscope

Situated in south-western Etruria (now Lazio), five miles from the Tyrrhenian Sea, Tarquinii (Tarquinia) was reputedly the earliest Etruscan centre to achieve metallic wealth and political power, so that the tenth and ninth centuries BC have been described as a period of 'Tarquinian Civilization' – an estimate which excavations have confirmed. In the later eighth century the villages on the site, enriched by the copper of Mount Tolfa, amalgamated into the nucleus of a city and city-state. From *c.*675 local chamber-tombs bear witness to a new epoch of prosperity, and the years after *c.*550 produced an efflorescence of wall-painting (such as is not to be seen in Greek lands until very much later, Chapter 3, section 4) combining both Greek and Etruscan characteristics. As elsewhere in Etruria, our evidence nearly all comes from graves and not from the residential areas of the city which have, for the most part, vanished, though their systematic excavation has now begun.

Investigations of the tombs, however, were started a long time ago, during the first half of the nineteenth century. G. M. Dennis wrote of his visit to one of them (1842), with a romanticism which, as we shall see, modern science has rendered somewhat out of date. 'Among the half-destroyed tumuli of the Monterozzi is a pit, six or eight feet deep, overgrown by lentiscus; and at the bottom is a hole, barely large enough for a man to squeeze himself through, and which no one would care to enter unless aware of something within to repay him for the trouble, and the filth unavoidably contracted. Having wormed myself through this aperture, I found myself in a dark, damp chamber, half-choked with the débris of the walls and ceiling. Yet the walls have not wholly fallen in, for when my eyes were somewhat accustomed to the gloom, I perceived them to be painted, and the taper's light disclosed on the inner wall a banquet in the open air.'[1] Since then, a hundred tombs have become visible at Tarquinii, including a score which extend over a period of three centuries and which are reasonably well preserved.

However, it is during the past thirty years that our knowledge of these graves has been particularly increased by scientific methods. It has been a period when, at various centres, electrical, electronic and magnetic devices have been employed for 'seeing through' the ground and noting disturbances, so that likely areas for digging can be identified. These devices include magnetometers and potentiometers, for the former of which, see Sybaris (Chapter 2, section 2).

Potentiometers, employed at Tarquinii, are based on the principle that variations in what lies underground offer differing resistance to the passage of an electric current.

'The electric resistivity method of the geologist', writes P. E. Cleator, 'was first applied to the making of an archaeological survey by R. J. C. Atkinson in 1946. It operates on the principle of the varying resistance to the passage of an electric current between steel rods inserted in the ground, a variation which is governed by the amount of moisture present. A damp area (in the guise, say, of a filled-in pit) will offer less, and a comparatively dry formation (such as a stone wall) will provide more, resistance than the surrounding soil, and these differing measurements are recorded in graph form. Where the presence of buried structure such as a wall or roadway is known or suspected, its assumed position is traversed at right-angles so as to provide a single straight line of readings from four electrodes, spaced at predetermined intervals. Otherwise, a more extensive survey is undertaken, in which the results of a series of parallel traverses are combined to give an indication of anything unusual within a chosen area. But this resistivity procedure, too, has its limitations, in that its effective range extends only a few feet below the surface, and it makes no clear distinction between such features as a man-made tunnel and a natural hollow. Nevertheless, it has been used with outstanding success by the Italian engineer Carlo M. Lerici in his search for Etruscan tombs.'[2]

Lerici found that electrical-resistivity surveying with this potentiometer, sensitive to the difference between solid earth and empty subterranean space, made it possible to locate the hollow spaces of Etruscan graves. When possible, he began his operations by undertaking or arranging aerial photography of a site that he had in mind. But he found that between 75% and 80% of the tombs at Tarquinii (and 50% of those at Caere [Cerveteri] were not close enough to the surface for archaeological details to become apparent to air photography, which showed them only if they were less than about six feet below the surface. It was for this reason that he instead made use of a potentiometer. 'If two metal rods (electrodes)', he explains, 'are pushed into the ground and a current passed between them, we can measure the electrical resistance between them ... As we move the electrodes farther apart, the resistance will increase, but if the earth is uniform, the resistivity will remain constant. The farther apart the electrodes are placed, the more the current will travel to deeper layers as it passes from one electrode to the other. Thus if there is a lower layer of earth through which the current passes more easily (i.e. a lower resistivity), this will eventually start to contribute to the result, and the overall resistivity will fall. If the electrodes are over an empty tomb, the reverse may happen, since air has a very high resistivity, and the resistivity will rise, as the electrodes are moved apart.'[3]

As Cleator indicated, the number of electrodes could be increased to four – two to carry the activating current, and two to pick up the current passing through the ground – in order to carry out both vertical and horizontal soundings more effectively. In the vertical process, the two middle electrodes are kept stationary, and their two outer counterparts moved apart in stages, in order to provide a picture of the underlying soil. Horizontal soundings, exploring the nature of the ground at a fixed depth below the surface, are obtained by moving the whole group of electrodes (at fixed distances from one another) along the ground. A dial, connected to the rods by cable, records the results.

By these methods of resistance survey, any likely ancient formation, such as a tomb or building, could be detected, and an estimate made of its depth. Then came a second stage, involving the use of a portable motor drill or probe, which bored holes in the soil, and brought up sample cores of soil for inspection. Next, when an empty space had been located by the probe, a third stage was launched: the lowering of a periscope. This device consisted of a tube from nine to fifteen feet long, with a pair of windows at its lower end, one for lighting up the tomb-chamber, and the other containing a camera to photograph whatever was revealed by illumination. By revolving the tube, a sequence of twelve pictures provided a complete photographic record of the chamber and its contents, thus enabling the excavators to decide which of the graves that had received this preliminary scanning deserved further attention.

By these means 450 tombs were examined within a period of 120 days. 'For comparison with previous work,' Lerici observed, 'it is sufficient to record that in the Tarquinii region it had previously taken the whole of the nineteenth century to record as many painted tombs as we have recorded in five years.'[4] At that juncture, in 1961, he quoted the discovery of 2,600 tombs at Tarquinii and 600 tombs at Caere. By June 1964 the figures had risen to 5,250 and 950 respectively. By now, the totals have multiplied yet further. These discoveries have been most timely, since every year deep ploughing devastates the archaeological picture of southern Etruria.

Lerici's methods represented the earliest stages of resistance surveying, which has been greatly developed subsequently. 'For some years,' wrote David Wilson in 1975, 'resistance surveying took second place to the magnetometer [Chapter 2, section 2], unless it was known that buildings or foundations would be encountered. But very recently there have been technical developments in the instruments for resistivity work which enable the archaeologists using the techniques to get away from the former disadvantages of lack of mobility and straight-line working... These developments include the production of a device rather like an electrified four-legged table, which is lightweight and highly mobile and in which the four metal legs can be used as the four electrodes of the early resistivity systems.'[5]

Yet even without these subsequent advantages the Lerici technique had produced conspicuous results. In particular, a number of the tombs he discovered contained important paintings: notably at Tarquinii. Instances could be quoted from many periods of Etruscan history and art. One is the Tomb of the Ship, of *c.*460–450. Another is the grave that is known as the Tomb of Giglioli, after the eminent archaeologist and Etruscologist of that name, the late Giulio Quirino Giglioli. This important Tarquinian tomb illuminates a twilight period, from the late third to the early second century BC, when the Etruscan city-states were losing or had lost their independence to the Romans, Tarquinii itself having succumbed after a war of 314–312 BC which resulted in an unequal 'treaty' or truce – revenge for the tradition that it was Tarquinii which had once imposed a royal house on Rome itself.

A feature of the paintings of this later, Rome-dominated period is the disappearance of the various themes of death and the afterlife which had been so characteristic of Etrurian tomb-paintings in the past. Instead, these subsequent pictures, like those in other, contemporary Tarquinian graves (notably the Tomb of the Shields and Tomb of the Festoons), represent trophies of battles. Such scenes had likewise appeared in reliefs on the walls of the Tomb of the Shields and Seats at Caere. Those Caeretan decorations, it is believed, were intended to recall the entrance-hall of an Etruscan house, and that may likewise be the purpose of the paintings in the Giglioli Tomb at Tarquinii. But the warlike designs in the Tomb of the Shields and Seats at Caere had dated from *c.*600, when that city, like Tarquinii, had been independent and powerful (see next section). To reproduce similar triumphant warlike themes in *c.*200, on the other hand, when the Etruscan world had come under the sway of Rome, was merely a nostalgic evocation of an ancient epoch that had disappeared for ever. Nor did such nostalgia remain unparalleled at Tarquinii, for there also came from there a group of Latin inscriptions of the first century AD (the *Elogia Tarquiniensia*) celebrating the military prowess which one of the city's families, the Spurinnas, had exhibited five or six hundred years previously.[6]

2 *Pyrgi: Etruscan History Recovered*

The Etruscan city-state of Caere (Cerveteri), a major political, naval and commercial power, possessed a number of ports on the Tyrrhenian Sea. One of them, Pyrgi (Santa Severa), eight miles from the city, yielded inscriptions which provide new evidence for Caere and the Etruscans in general. This new evidence is vital, for most of their history has virtually disappeared from the literary record, owing to the hostility of the Greeks and Romans and of their historians, who mention the Etruscans only at moments when they impinge on Greek or Roman developments. Even then the Greek and Roman writers tend to lump the highly individual, separate Etruscan city-states together as a single, amorphous unit.

Coastal currents have now, for the most part, eroded the harbour of Pyrgi, but excavations make it clear that it was the chief among Caere's ports. Valleys linked Pyrgi with metal-rich Mount Tolfa in the interior, and sea-voyagers intent on trade must have favoured its bay which, though small, supplied an anchorage protected from winds by a north-western promontory. On the landward side, Pyrgi was linked to Caere by a broad road, flanked by tombs crowned by substantial mounds. The road is likely to have been a Sacred Way, for a large shrine adjoined it; moreover, Pyrgi was a religious centre, as evidenced by its large, rectangular sanctuary area.

The sanctuary itself was probably very old, since the name 'Pyrgi', which is Greek and means 'towers', appears to go back to the Mycenaean epoch. Later, the precinct became one of the holiest places in all non-Greek Italy. The Greeks, in their own language, recorded its dedication to a goddess described alternately as Leucothea, a goddess of the sea, and Eileithyia, patron of child-birth. The Etruscans themselves, it would seem, named the same divinity as Uni (Hera, Juno, Astarte) – and indeed the Greeks, too, identified Eileithyia with Hera. The shrine was made the subject of a conference at Tübingen in 1979,[7] and subsequent excavations have been undertaken with the assistance of balloon-photographs and periscopes employing the Lerici technique (section 1 above).

In 1964 three thin rectangular sheets of gold were found in this sanctuary area. Each of the three sheets bears an inscription – one in the Punic (Carthaginian) language, a Semitic tongue that can be translated, and the other two in Etruscan, of which, although many words and forms are understood, the grammatical structure (particularly of the verbs) still remains partly obscure. At first it was hoped that the Etruscan texts might turn out to be exact translations of the Punic inscription – if so, we might have been in a position to break down the remaining unknown features of the Etruscan language, just as the Rosetta stone, in the British Museum, has led to the decipherment of Egyptian. Unfortunately, however, neither of the two Etruscan inscriptions has proved to be a word-for-word counterpart of the Punic rendering.

The Punic text reads as follows: 'To the Lady Astarte. This is the sacred place made and given by Thefarie Velianas, *mlkl* [king] over Kysry (Cisra, Caere), in the month of the Sacrifice of the Sun as a gift within the temple and the sanctuary (?), because Astarte has chosen by means of him in the three years of his reign...' The longer of the two Etruscan inscriptions approximately states: 'This is the temple (shrine?) and this is the place of the statue dedicated to Uni-Astarte... Thefarie Velianas has given them... three years... of the *zilath* [chief magistrate?]' The shorter Etruscan version reads: 'Thus has Thefarie Velianas dedicated [the temple?] he established the *cleva* [offering] in the month of Masan and there was the annual or anniversary sacrifice of the temple...'[8]

Even if the manifest differences between the Etruscan and Punic versions mean that our hopes of completely mastering the former language have been dashed, these plaques nevertheless illustrate the great contributions that epigraphy continues to make to history (cf. Chapter 4, section 2). The Punic inscription is the first in that language ever to have come to light on the mainland of Italy, while its two Etruscan counterparts constitute our first contemporary, official evidence from Etruria for the history of any of its city-states. The Punic text (as we have seen) and the shorter of the Etruscan renderings allude to the dedication by Thefarie Velianas of Caere, in the third year of his power, of sacrifices and a sacred place (or religious ceremony) to the Carthaginian (Phoenician) goddess Astarte, whose equation with Uni (Hera, Juno) is indicated (*Uniel Astres*). The other, longer Etruscan inscription lays down instructions concerning procedures connected with Thefarie Velianas's dedication.

The earliest ruler of any Etruscan city-state whose name is known to us from a contemporary source, he is described as a 'king', or 'reigning over' Caere (in the Punic version) and a *zilath* or supreme magistrate (Etruscan). In fact, he was probably a tough man who had seized autocratic power ('tyranny') in the city, like rulers in other parts of the Mediterranean world during this period of social and economic disturbances.

Thefarie Velianas's reverence for the goddess Astarte mirrors not only a religious sentiment but a political reference to his city's continuing association with Carthage. In *c.*535 the Caeretans and Carthaginians, in alliance, had fought the naval 'battle of Alalia' against the Phocaean Greeks, in order to drive them out of Corsica – an aim which, despite an indecisive outcome to the engagement itself, was to a large extent achieved. The alliance between Caere and Carthage seems, from these inscriptions, to have been maintained for some two further decades. Indeed, the earlier of two temples identified at Pyrgi ('Temple B'), which like the plaques dates from *c.*500, may very well be the actual building that Thefarie Velianas, according to one interpretation, recorded that he was dedicating.

These gold tablets from Pyrgi provide us with information which no surviving literary source has made available. In particular, they illuminate the Carthaginians' commercial interest in Etruscan ports. 'The international aspect', wrote H. H. Scullard, 'is important: a Punic element has been revealed at Pyrgi. This indicates trade between Carthage and Pyrgi (Punicum [Santa Marinella], quite close to Pyrgi, may have gained its name from a settlement of Punic merchants), and this at a time when the power of the Etruscans in central Italy was being threatened by the Greeks and Latins and they were relying on Carthage for help in the struggle. Further, it provides an appropriate setting for the first treaty which Carthage is said by Polybius[9] to have made with Rome in 509: the Polybian date for this, often questioned, will now seem more firmly anchored. Thus the inscriptions give us a hint of the position of one Etruscan city in the wider world as well as of the internal condition of Caere, where we should now perhaps picture a stronger Punic element mingling with the Greeks and Etruscans.'[10]

The Pyrgi tablets, then, have enabled us to recover a lost chapter of Etruscan history. Likewise, other archaeological evidence from the same country – for example, paintings from the François Tomb at Vulci – has made it possible to reconstruct a section of the abundant Etruscan mythology, legend and saga which the preoccupations of the Greek and Roman historians, directed elsewhere, had so effectively obliterated.

3 Orbetello and Prilius: Vanished Harbours

One of the contributions of recent research has been to show how greatly the coastlines of the Mediterranean area have changed throughout the centuries, a phenomenon which often requires ancient events to be reconstructed against an unfamiliar background. Nowhere has this occurred on a more radical scale, involving both encroachment and, conversely, withdrawal by the sea, than upon the western shore of Italy – where archaeology has to join forces with the physical and biological sciences to find out just what has happened.

A significant example is provided by Orbetello. This site may be the maritime Clusium (Calusium?) mentioned by Virgil[11] (he cannot be identifying the famous Clusium as this seafaring power, since it lies far inland). Orbetello stands on the coast of Etruria (Tuscany), at the neck of the jutting peninsula and promontory of Mount Argentarius (Argentario).

Today, after the massive erosion characteristic of this stretch of shoreline (as elsewhere in the Mediterranean, notably at Halieis, Chapter 2, section 4, and Caesarea Maritima, Chapter 6, section 3), the Argentario is joined to the mainland, on both its flanks, by a pair of sandbars, the Giannella to the west and the Feniglia to the east. These sandbars – isthmuses of silt raised by the continuing motion of the sea's waves – form the sides of a closed lagoon, upon the mainland bank of which stands the town of Orbetello, located upon a spit: that is to say, upon a third sandbar between the other two, but a sandbar which never fully developed or reached a substantial length.

In the earlier centuries of antiquity, however, the position was different. For one thing, the more westerly of the two lateral sandbars (Giannella) had by then hardly made its appearance, so that on that side the lagoon was open to the Tyrrhenian Sea. Secondly, the sea also contained openings on the other side, since the eastern sandbank (Feniglia) too, although already in existence, was pierced by two channels, which were apparently not closed up until Roman times. Until that time, therefore, Orbetello possessed a sea-lagoon which, while partially enclosed and thus enjoying adequate protection from the winds, at the same time opened out on both sides into the sea. In other words, the lagoon provided a convenient harbour, which was employed by ships bringing silver from Spain: and that is why the peninsula was known as the 'Argentarius'.

Indeed, the polygonal walls that have now been uncovered, similar to other fortifications revealed by air photography in the neighbourhood, suggest that this port dates back at least to Bronze Age times. In any case, there is firm archaeological evidence that Orbetello was an Etruscan centre at the end of the eighth century BC, when burial places were established just outside its periphery.[12] By *c.*550, the place enjoyed economic prosperity, declining after 500 only to become well-off again in *c.*350 before decadence set in once more after 300. Houses dating from the fifth to the third centuries have been uncovered.

Another find is a sphinx of volcanic stone, which shows the stylistic influence of the independent Etruscan city of Vulci, twenty-two miles to the east. Evidently it was to Vulci's territory that the port of Orbetello belonged, just as other Etruscan cities, too, sometimes possessed similar ports in outlying parts of their territories. But sight was lost of Orbetello's earlier shipping role when, after the closing-up of its lagoon by the two uninterrupted sandbars, its importance was transferred to the Roman colony of Cosa (Ansedonia) 4½ miles away (273 BC).

Twenty-two miles to the north-west of Orbetello was another sea-lagoon and port, on Lake Prilius. Once again, it has lost its function as a harbour, not because it has been sealed up and enclosed but because, on the contrary, it has disappeared completely, and become land – in direct contrast, therefore, to the coastline of, say, Dicaearchia (Puteoli, Pozzuoli), where land has vanished under the sea (Appendix II, iii).

Beside Lake Prilius stood the Etruscan city of Vetulonia, upon its three-spurred hill 1,130 feet high. Settled in the ninth century BC and reaching its greatest strength after 600, its power was served by a maritime trade, notably with Sardinia, provided by ships made of the timber from Vetulonian hillsides. Nowadays Vetulonia is nine miles away from the Tyrrhenian Sea; in ancient times, however, the water-level was higher, so that the sea-lagoon Lake Prilius came up close to the south-eastern limits of the city, which possessed harbours on its shores. The lagoon was fed by the Bruna river, upon whose waters boats brought down metals from the hinterland, and by another stream, the Umbro (Ombrone), of which Pliny the elder records the debouchment into the Tyrrhenian Sea.[13] Canals, too, may have connected the lagoon with these two rivers, and it was also linked directly with the sea by deep and navigable canals, which penetrated a sandbar separating the lagoon from the sea, and were augmented, as investigation shows, by an additional channel.

Remains of the buildings that stood along the banks of Lake Prilius can be detected. They date from the third and second centuries BC. The lagoon still existed in 52 BC, for Cicero, in that year, mentioned an island in the middle of its waters.[14] Indeed, Prilius still appears on Renaissance and later maps, though by then, like other Etruscan sea-lagoons, it had become almost land-locked by its sandbar – a malarial marsh. Silting at Orbetello eventually sealed off the harbour from the sea; silting at Prilius, on the other hand, as was mentioned above, obliterated the lake altogether and turned it into land, so that the harbours on what had been its shore became useless and were abandoned. At least one of them, however, can still be identified, at Badiola al Fango, now halfway between Vetulonia and the sea, where the road from the city joins an east-west thoroughfare. Moreover, other villages on what were once the banks of the lake still have Italian names that recall earlier maritime activity – Piscara a Mare (sea-fishery), Casa Galera (boat-house), Porto a Colle (hillside port), Porto alle Cavalle (mare's port). These names help to complete the archaeological evidence which testifies (in the absence of any literary record) to Vetulonia's maritime importance – an importance which was to suffer, apparently, a severe setback during the years around 500 BC. This interruption, it would seem, was due to another Etruscan city-state, Rusellae (Roselle), which had been established at the end of the eighth century, only nine miles away on the other side of what was then Lake Prilius. The two cities were visible to one another across its waters, which both had to use. Rusellae possessed its own port on the lake, perhaps at Terme di Roselle – and thus enjoyed its own access to the sea. But it was far too close for comfort to Vetulonia, whose soldiers its massive city-walls were no doubt erected to keep out. And this they succeeded in doing – perhaps after the two cities had come to blows[15] – for, as excavations of fifth- and fourth-century buildings suggest, it was Rusellae, for the time being, that proved the more effective survivor: its agricultural economy flourished, while Vetulonia was partly destroyed, or at least eliminated from power politics until about the third century BC – which is the date of a building discovered there in 1979. In *c.*241 BC, Rusellae having already been captured in 294, the Vetulonians succumbed to Rome.

4 Picentia (Pontecagnano): The Etruscan South

The Etruscan counter-presence and rivalry to the Greeks in Campania is illustrated by discoveries both in the north-western sector of the territory – for example at Capua (Santa Maria Capua Vetere, a competitor with Greek Cumae, Chapter 2, section 1), Cales (Calvi Vecchia, already strong in the seventh century BC), and Nola – and in its far south-eastern region, at Fratte di Salerno and Picentia (Pontecagnano).

Fratte di Salerno adjoined Salernum (Salerno) and Picentia – as the Romans later called the place; its earlier, Etruscan name is unknown. The exact location of the ancient town of Picentia has not yet been identified, but since 1977 some 3,000 tombs have been excavated in a cemetery which must have been close to its walls. The contents of these tombs confirm the statement of Pliny the elder that this piece of land (the Ager Picentinus) at one time belonged to the Etruscans.[16] For example, ornate swords found on the site originate from ninth-century Etruria. Indeed, such discoveries suggest that Picentia must have been one of the most substantial Etruscan centres in the area, possessing local native dependencies in the country round about.

Its earliest Iron Age graves, going back to the ninth century BC, resemble – as has been pointed out – those of Tarquinii (Tarquinia, section 1 above), which may, therefore, have been the Etruscan city-state which settled or resettled Picentia. The Etruscans were encouraged to colonize the region not only by its natural productivity but by the strategic position of Picentia itself on important thoroughfares leading both to the south and towards the interior of the country. Probably, too, there was a port in the neighbourhood, through which sea-links with Etruria were established, to supplement the more hazardous land-routes through Latium. The subsequent decline of Picentia was, in all likelihood, due to the rise of the Greek colony founded by Sybaris (Chapter 2, section 2) at Posidonia (Paestum), whose products influenced fourth-century deposits in the Picentine cemeteries.

The tomb-groups so far discovered in these cemeteries extend down to that period from the early Iron Age. One aspect which, as in south Russia, Sicily and elsewhere, is now receiving ever-increased attention is the relationship which such immigrants achieved, or failed to achieve, with the earlier populations which they found on the sites that they occupied (cf. Chapter 2, section 5; Chapter 4, section 3). Thus at Picentia, as a result of the excavations of the past fifteen years, David Ridgway observes that 'the profound cultural effect on the indigenous community can now be examined in much greater detail. As well as a notable increase in material prosperity (represented *inter alia* by imported and imitated pottery) new features include the addition of a monumental aspect to the inhumation burials and the introduction of a Greek type of cremation rite; this involves the deposition of burnt remains from the pyre, probably wrapped in a cloth, in a square cist [burial chamber] that may have been surmounted by a tumulus.'[17]

Ridgway speaks of 'Greek' rites, and at Picentia as at Cumae it is not yet easy to assess the relative proportions of Greek and Etruscan cultures in these burials. The Artiaco grave at Cumae displayed Etruscan contents but reflected Greek rites, and it is only to be expected that the Etruscan tombs at Picentia should not be exempt from Greek influences. Perhaps it is more profitable, at this stage, to regard both these burial places as examples of the 'princely tombs' that are found over a wide area of Italy. Early tombs at Lefkandi (Euboea) and Salamis (Cyprus) have been discussed elsewhere (Chapter 1, sections 1 and 2). Burials, with their tell-tale contents of various kinds, form a large part of archaeology's contribution to history, though they are not always easy to interpret. Jane McIntosh, discussing the point made by Lewis Binford that 'the form of disposal and the accompanying ritual... are frequently of symbolic significance within the community, giving expression to the position held by the dead person within the society...', says that 'recent ethnoarchaeological work [archaeological work in relation to ancient society], notably by Dr Ian Hodder of Cambridge University, indicates that the relationship between funeral arrangements and social structure are even more complex than Binford suggested. Religious beliefs, ideology and attitudes to death all play a part in determining details of funerary practices, rites and offerings, which do not therefore simply provide a mirror of social organization. Where social dimensions are expressed, they often reflect an idealized picture rather than the contemporary reality.'[18]

These points are relevant to the 'princely tombs' of Picentia. They date back to *c.*700 BC, not long after the tomb at Cumae. Thereafter, writes Martin Frederiksen, 'a whole series of similar tombs, that have become familiar as the "princely tombs", tombs of rulers or warriors . . . appear over the next fifty years in various localities in Etruria, and a number of others that lie in the peripheral areas of Etruscan influence . . . What surprises is the similarity, indeed the standardization, of the imported and prestige objects they contain . . . [But] it is probably premature to see these tombs as a *single* phenomenon, artistic or sociological; extending as they do from Vetulonia [section 3 above] to Pontecagnano [Picentia] . . . These tombs appear in a variety of social contexts, and show differences of rite and architecture in a number of local inflections . . . The significance of these tombs, which have no real precedents in the Villanovan [Early Iron Age Italian] cultures, remains to be fully understood . . . for the objects, which are oddly uniform in type yet internationally eclectic, are hardly explicable in terms of normal archaeological imitation. One recent account has appealed to the theories of economic anthropology, that we are dealing with what was a princely exchange of gifts, or a "chieftain's trade" . . . The explanation is attractive in part, but perhaps is not the whole story. Many of the gift-inscriptions ["X gave me as a gift to Y"] appear on relatively simple objects . . . These are more likely to be the normal gifts of the dead often found in Greek graves, where oil, honey and wine are quite frequent; alternatively, such gift-exchanges must have taken place at well below the social level of chieftains . . . As must be conceded, the full story has still to be told of the ways in which these great tombs, with their strongly Homeric colouring, spread out from the Campanian colonies so rapidly and so far through the Italian peninsula. To invoke the Greek aristocratic ethos, or the ideals of Homeric heroes, may be rather too romantic a solution; and we should remind ourselves that the tombs of the dead show us only a tiny part of the goods once possessed and employed by a whole society. An alternative solution is at least worth consideration: behind these lavish tombs there lies a fundamental lesson by the Greeks in primitive capital accumulation.'[19]

Frederiksen, like Ridgway, speaks of 'the Greeks'. But the great majority of 'princely tombs', as he remarked, were in Etruria or Etruscan-dominated areas – as were the tombs at Picentia. Greeks and Etruscans alike possessed contacts overseas. Thus many of the princely tombs of western Italy, like their earlier counterparts at Lefkandi, contain near-eastern goods, reflecting increased contacts with Asia and Egypt. A seventh-century silver-gilt bowl found at Picentia, for example, is of Phoenician origin. Faience [glazed terracotta] scarabs of Egypto-Phoenician type also make their appearance. An archaic burial, on the other hand, has yielded an Athenian Panathenaic amphora (in which prizes, consisting of oil, were stored for the four-yearly Panathenaea festival) attributed to the 'Eucharides painter'.

Elsewhere in Campania the Greeks and Etruscans were hostile rivals, but perhaps this was not the case at Picentia – or at least not all the time. After all, in north-eastern Italy, at Spina and Adria, they collaborated, and there were Greek quarters even in the city-states of Etruria itself, notably Caere (section 2 above).

5 Francolise and Settefinestre: Villa Farms

The economy of the ancient world was based on agricultural production. This is, of course, clear to prehistoric archaeologists, who have devised a hundred methods of studying the subject, but it also remains true of the Greco-Roman world, when the iron plough and other tools, made of the new metal, increased agricultural production on a revolutionary scale. 'The period of classical Greece', wrote F. M. Heichelheim, 'witnessed a rational differentiation of the various agricultural plants and their habits, of the different kinds of soil, and the appropriate manures, and production was stimulated by the growing demand for grain, meat and vegetables in towns... From Alexander to Augustus Mediterranean agriculture was improved by many inventions... The highest standard of ancient cultivation was reached in the Italian agriculture of the later Republic and early Principate. Big slave estates prevailed there, as long as prisoners of war were cheap. The varieties of plants, the rotation of crops, and the other methods of cultivation, amelioration, irrigation and manuring, book-keeping, the organization and division of labour, the buildings, tools, old and new machines were carefully selected from the technical as well as from the economic point of view.'[20]

Information about agriculture throughout this period has been provided in increasing abundance during recent years. Archaeologists influenced by the environmentally minded 'New Archaeology' (Appendix I) have been especially prominent, utilizing all the resources provided by air photography (Chapter 8, section 6), as well as working on the ground, examining the remains of agricultural activity by a variety of methods.

The second century BC was a time of increasing prosperity and pretensions among the landowners of Italy, whose properties included ever larger numbers of tenants and leaseholders. The younger Seneca described a villa built by Scipio Africanus the elder on his coastal estate at Liternum in northern Campania.[21] This residence, which was turreted, has not survived, but two others in the same region, at Francolise near Capua, have left remains of later Republican date. Their excavation has thrown light on the agricultural exploitation of the region during that period and in the first years of the imperial epoch that followed.

The village of Francolise occupies the western end of Mount Telefono, which is at the extremity of the Mount Maggiore massif. The site commanded a natural road-junction at the meeting point of the hills with the alluvial Falernian coastal plain. It was in convenient proximity to the Via Appia, and it enjoyed a fine panorama to the north, south and west. Nearby, what is left of the ancient villa-farms can be seen.

The Villa Posto stands less than a mile to the south-east of the village, upon gentle olive-growing slopes. Constructed between 120 and 80/75 BC, it was a working farm, the centre of an agricultural property. The original buildings, constructed of bluish-grey, locally quarried tufa, were grouped round a rectangular terraced courtyard which contained cisterns. On three sides of their exterior were lean-to porches, where crops, vehicles, farm implements and farm animals could be lodged. On the fourth side were residential quarters, including the dwelling of the resident bailiff, of which scanty ruins are preserved.

During the last quarter of the first century BC, the premises were enlarged, although the villa still remained relatively modest. The living quarters in the north wing were expanded by the construction of nine new rooms. At the same time, three new vaulted cisterns were installed to the north of the living areas, and a two-storeyed tower was erected beside the entrance. Subsequently, the middle years of the first century AD witnessed a third phase of building. At this stage, the courtyard was enlarged, the north-western part of the main wing was converted into a three-room bathing establishment, and the north-eastern section was transformed into an oil-processing area, housing two new oil-separating vats (there had been only one before) as well as an oil-press. In the later second century AD, however, the site was abandoned, perhaps because the estate was absorbed by a larger neighbour, though there was partial, temporary reoccupation some three hundred years later. Nowadays there is not much to be seen, but the site has greatly contributed to our understanding of the economy of rural sites.

The second villa at Francolise, the San Rocco, differed in that it was a residence as well as a farm. It stood on a limestone spur between the Posto and the village (which lies immediately to its west). The Villa San Rocco, like the Posto, experienced three successive phases of construction. The original plan, in the earlier part of the first century BC, was uncomplicated. This initial building, erected upon a terraced platform, consisted of living rooms grouped around an atrium, while agricultural installations were situated on a lower terrace to the south. Phase II (50–25 BC) (more impressive than the enlargements of the Villa Posto) provided an increase in size, luxury, privacy and symmetry, including the construction of a central peristyle court, with brick columns coated in fluted stucco, round which were grouped twenty-nine rooms. There was also a new, higher terrace to the north extending for the entire length of the rebuilt complex, and housing a parallel row of cisterns. Phase III (*c.* AD 50, until gradual decay and abandonment in the mid-second-century AD) incorporated a bathing-suite adjoining these cisterns. At this juncture, also, three rooms near the entrance were converted to accommodate vats for the separation of olive-oil.

Indeed it is these olive-oil institutions at the Villa San Rocco which contribute most extensively to our knowledge. Besides the vats, excavations have revealed oil-presses of two periods, a brick kiln, and a threshing floor. This Villa San Rocco was evidently the centre of a substantial property, of which oil appears to have been the principal product. Olives had already formed a staple Mediterranean crop for millennia. In ancient Italy, they had been introduced by Greek colonists in the south (Chapter 2, section 1), from which they gradually spread to other parts of the country. By the second century BC, olive-production was increasing on a massive scale.

Olive-trees do not produce for four or five years, and mature only after about eight. They may take thirty years to reach their optimum yield. Yet olive-groves were long-lived – a tree can last for centuries – and a single tree, at its best, could be relied upon to produce 110 pounds of edible fruit. Olive cultivation was well suited to the large estates of an absentee landowner, since the production of a cash-crop needed little additional effort except at harvest-time, when free labourers were hired to supplement the proprietor's slaves, and he could afford to wait for profitable returns.

In due course, as Varro describes, the processing of olives became a fine art, involving much technical expertise.[22] Cato the elder had advised on the different types of olive to plant in various grades of soil.[23] Virgil remarked that they could grow in even apparently barren earth, provided that drainage was available.[24] And Pliny the elder was acquainted with no less than fifteen especially good varieties of olive, and four types of press, worked by screws or beams.[25] Indeed, throughout the Mediterranean region, the olive-tree came to be regarded as a symbol of stability and prosperity. In addition to the various uses of its oil for culinary purposes, it was employed for the manufacture of scent, to anoint the body, as fuel for lamps, and in the performance of religious rites.

Oil, again, was one of the products of another villa-farm which likewise originated in the late Republic. This was at Settefinestre, in Etruria, situated on rising ground overlooking the Valle d'Oro beside the Tyrrhenian sea coast, about two miles from Rome's colony of Cosa (Ansedonia) – that is to say, within the territory of what was known as the Ager Cosanus. After a preliminary survey, excavations started in 1976.

The villa, constructed in about 75 BC, stood on the highest of three wide terraces, facing north-west, and dominating the region all around, like a medieval manor house. 'In the surrounding area', writes Anthony King, 'is a flat plain, bordered on one side by the sea and on the other by relatively inhospitable hills. The plain has the only fertile ground in the region, and for this reason has attracted settlements like villas, which are very common here and much rarer farther inland.

'The villa itself is built on artificial terraces in the side of a small hill in the middle of the plain. The lowest terrace was a private garden ... The front wall of the garden was built in the form of a miniature town wall, with watchtowers at intervals along it ... Very few contemporary town walls still survive, and so Settefinestre provides a valuable insight into the way in which Italian towns were fortified in the second century BC. The rear wall of the garden was also the base of the next terrace, upon which the residential quarters of the villa were built.'[26] Like the large houses around Pompeii, this residential sector was based on a peristyle court and atrium (further up the hill), round which were grouped numerous rooms. There were also bedrooms opening onto an L-shaped loggia, which extended on the garden side for the whole length of the north-west and south-east sides of the mansion.

The mud-constructed walls of the rooms were adorned with paintings of good quality. The remains of these pictures were discovered on the floors, which were littered with chunks of painted plaster that had fallen from the walls. The paintings, in the fashionable *trompe l'oeil*, or false perspective, architectural style ('Style 2'; see next section), date from the mid-first century BC, when the villa was built, as do the polychrome mosaics and marble inlays that decorate the floors. Under the buildings are two extensive cisterns, and barrel-vaulted corridors for storage space. These were linked to the ground-floor by stairs, and possessed access to the lower terrace through a row of arches.

The north-eastern part of the main building was an elaborate *villa rustica*, or farming section. As well as additional store-rooms, accommodation (including slave quarters), a small bath-suite and a communal lavatory, all surrounding a courtyard, these premises included a large barn or granary – fitted with architectural terracottas – which has prompted the tentative supposition that Settefinestre produced grain for sale quite far afield, perhaps as far as Rome itself.

Subsequently, however, perhaps at a time of general refurbishment in the late first century AD, Settefinestre went in for more complex diversification. One example of this process is provided by a well-preserved oil-mill, oil-presses and vats for oil storage. The oil-mill, lodged in its own courtyard, was operated by mules or donkeys walking round in circles – their worn tracks are still to be seen in the floor. About oil-production something was said above, in connection with Francolise. Settefinestre, however, also became notable for its production of wine, as is indicated by the presence of three wine-presses, from which grape-juice was fed through a plug-hole and drain into cellars where it could ferment in containers.

It had been Greek colonists in southern Italy who originally familiarized the peninsula with the cultivation of the grape, as of the olive. From *c.*350 BC onwards, this activity increased, and vines were trained on trees of various kinds (including olive trees) as well as on reeds, or attached to frames of forked stakes, sometimes fitted with horizontal cross-pieces. After 200 BC vine-growing, like olive-growing, was further extended, when landowners first distinguished between vintages, adopted varying grades of fermentation, and devoted increased scientific study to preservation methods. Pliny the elder differentiated between numerous kinds of wine and grape, proclaiming the supremacy of the national products with lyrical patriotism.[27]

Here in the *villa rustica* of Settefinestre the oil-mill and press were balanced by a row of three grape-presses and a vat. 'The [grape] presses operated', explains King, 'by using large stone weights mounted on wooden beams to press out gradually the juices from sacks of grapes. The liquid ran into a large fermentation tank or *lacus* where the sediment was allowed to settle out. The wine was then poured into *amphorae* for transportation elsewhere. It was a drink that would be thought heavy and bitter today, and since it continued to ferment in the *amphora*, must have become vinegary very quickly.'[28] Indeed, it is viticulture that was, or became, the primary enterprise of this agricultural centre, according to its excavators. As T. W. Potter observes, 'the emphasis upon wine production is of great interest, matching the evidence from the Campanian villas. Moreover, it is possible to make some rough guesses at the size of the production, since there are about a dozen large villas known in Cosa's territory, suggesting estates of about 500 *iugera* (125 hectares [308 acres]). Using figures cited by the ancient authors, this would mean that an estate like that of Settefinestre was producing in excess of 1.2 million litres [264,000 gallons] of wine a year, a very sizeable amount. By way of comparison, a great modern French chateau like Mersault in Burgundy farms 40 hectares [99 acres] and has in its cellars some 500,000 bottles and 2,000 huge casks.'[29] Wine from Settefinestre was shipped to many places in the empire, particularly the Gallic provinces.

Wine production was not all, however, for 'during the 1980 excavations,' reported Tim Tatton-Brown, who directed this Anglo-Italian project, 'we were able to look at a large area of the main farm buildings ... The most interesting discovery was of twenty-seven pigsties round a large open courtyard. This is the first time that they have been found at a Roman villa in Italy, though we knew all about them from the writings of Varro and Columella. It is clear that they were used for breeding sows and their piglets.'[30] Pork figured prominently in the Roman diet, as the literary authorities make clear; Pliny the elder, for example, writes of the matter in detail. 'Roman domestic pigs', K. D. White indicates, 'were smaller than the wild species. As the number of pig bones found at archaeological sites indicates, pigs usually made up between fifty and seventy-five per cent of the sample ... As well as keeping them for home consumption, farms would supply pigs to butchers in the local town, to be rendered into pork joints, hams, bacon and sausages.'[31]

The pigsty complex of Settefinestre, together with an extension to the slave quarters and a new set of baths, dates from the time of Trajan (AD 98–117). Although much work still remains to be done on the site, it has become clear that this villa-farm of Settefinestre must have been active and busy for a prolonged period, employing a good many slaves (the total resident population has been estimated as fifty-two). The owners were probably the distinguished family of the Sestii, since the initials LS have been found stamped on to local tiles, and SES is to be seen on many wine amphorae at Cosa and its port (and other sites). Yet the abundant oil-press provision suggests large quantity rather than high quality, and the whole labour-intensive farm, observed N. Purcell, with its adherence to the principles of Varro, Columella and Pliny, 'has a blueprint, buy-it-off-the-peg, doctrinaire feeling'.[32] Its importance to agricultural and economic historians, however, remains large. 'Settefinestre', K. Greene points out, 'provides an example of the potential of an integrated programme of fieldwork and excavation ... [And it also] helps to give a physical dimension to historical debates about the changing patterns of land management.'[33]

However, like its counterparts at Francolise, the place did not last throughout the imperial epoch, having apparently been abandoned and deserted by the 160s or 170s AD. During the early Middle Ages, however, the site was again employed as a farm. A skeleton dating from that period has come to light.

6 Oplontis: New Evidence for Roman Art

The Vesuvian cities and villas, creations largely of the second and first centuries BC, were, thanks to the eruption of Mount Vesuvius in AD 79, presented as a unique gift to future students. Their burial meant, as it were, that time had stopped suddenly, leaving an intact scene to await rediscovery from the eighteenth century onwards. For this reason, archaeologists have occasionally tended to deprecate concentration on such dramatic, peculiarly preserved sites, on the grounds that they leave no scope for the laborious, reconstructive, evolutionary processes which require the specializations of modern experts.[34] Yet these places inform us uniquely about the successive stages of Roman everyday life – and have done much, since they were first unearthed, to influence European tastes. Besides, these were the sites which first enabled archaeologists to find their feet. 'All other excavations and restorations', remarked Walter Leppmann, 'whether undertaken in Greece or Mesopotamia or Peru or Egypt or elsewhere, are essentially variations on a theme first played in the shade of Mount Vesuvius.'[35]

During recent years finds have continued to be made at Pompeii and Herculaneum, and something will be said about these when we reach the chronological moment of the eruption (Chapter 7, section 4). But that upheaval, of course, encapsulated buildings of much earlier dates – and not only at Pompeii and Herculaneum. For one development in our knowledge of those earlier times has been the recent revelation that the two famous towns can no longer be seen as the only centres which were overwhelmed by the catastrophe of AD 79. First of all, two villas at Stabiae were disinterred (with more to come), and then a villa at Oplontis as well.

Oplontis (Torre Annunziata), a short distance to the west of Pompeii, was buried by the eruption under almost six feet of dark-grey ash and pumice. What emerged, when this covering was lately removed, was the largest and most luxurious villa ever discovered, which has added an important chapter to our knowledge of Roman villas and art.

The name Oplontis is to be seen on two late Roman Itineraries and on the map known as the Peutinger Table – of thirteenth-century date, but reproducing fourth-century material – where the place is indicated as a station on the road between Pompeii and Herculaneum. In later times, it was known to have once been an ancient site, because many finds of Roman objects turned up at Torre Annunziata. Deep shaft samplings date back to 1839–40, but it was not until 1964 that substantial excavations took place at Oplontis. By now, more than fifty rooms have been unearthed, involving the clearance of 23,500 cubic yards over an area of nearly 2,300 square yards. Most of the principal residential block has been uncovered, together with the service quarters attached to it.

The northern part of this residential sector contained a large hall (*oecus*), lighted through an opening in the ceiling and facing a garden, which was entered between the columns of a gabled porch. To the south lay a series of rooms centring upon an atrium and terminating in a terraced platform that was flanked by a continuous portico and in ancient times opened onto the seafront. The west wing comprised another substantial hall, a dining-room, a kitchen, and baths. The servants' quarters lay to the east, grouped round an internal, 'rustic' peristyle with benches along its length, and leading on to an adjacent, sizeable farming complex. The mansion was adjoined by various gardens, which it has proved possible to reconstruct. They have contributed substantially to our knowledge of formal Roman gardening (cf. Chapter 7, section 1). The trees in the gardens of Oplontis included chestnuts, citrus, olive, apple, cypress, and poplar or plane. There were boxwood hedges, as well as ivy, oleander, myrtle, daisies, chrysanthemums and roses. The gardens were full of sculptures: among them were representations of a baby boy with a goose, a nude Venus unlacing her sandals, a pair of centaurs and a pair of their female counterparts, one playing the lyre, which served as fountains.

At the time of the eruption only the western wing was still inhabited. The principal portions of the residential area, on the other hand, stood empty (the only skeleton found was a cat's) since they were awaiting comprehensive redecoration and had therefore been denuded of their furnishings, fittings, and cutlery. These circumstances lent support to the supposition that the last owner of the villa had been Nero's wife Poppaea. The Poppaei were a well-known Pompeian family, and Poppaea is known to have possessed property in the area. Moreover, an amphora found in a communal latrine at the Oplontis villa bore the name of 'Secundus [freedman] of Poppaea'. Her death in AD 65, followed by Nero's in 68, may well explain why the villa lacked an occupant when Vesuvius erupted in 79.

The wide range of paintings found on the walls of this residence at times shows some independence of known Pompeian work. In the main, however, they provide an unequalled corpus of the various Pompeian styles – perhaps even superior to the Boscoreale paintings with which they invite comparison. Indeed, they form the largest and most complete cycle of Roman paintings still remaining on the site for which they were created. Pending redecoration, it is true, many rooms had been stripped of their murals as well as their contents, yet five still retained superb paintings of what is known as the Pompeian Second or Architectural Style, of the first century BC. These painted apartments were a niched and vaulted bedroom, a dining-room (*triclinium*) with adjoining kitchen, and the two large halls – one in the west wing (beside the dining-room and kitchen), and the other in the north wing.

In the first of these halls, the paintings of *c*.40 BC which covered the entire eastern wall depict lofty, yellow, fluted Corinthian colonnades in receding vistas, which, although this is not strict, single-viewpoint perspective, nevertheless provide an alluring impression of visual illusionism. The central feature of this composition, framed by the lateral double colonnades, is a Delphic tripod elevated on a slender round plinth and seen through a half-open gateway leading into a garden. The architectural motifs favoured by this Second Style are varied by small mythological scenes, and by lively, ornamental pictures showing peacocks, fishes, fruit and theatrical masks. The hall in the north wing had blue-studded doors painted upon its dark walls.

Portions of the building, however, were modernized some decades after these Second Style pictures were painted. This was the epoch of the Third Style – if such a term is really valid, since the style comprised a varied series of successive stages, from Augustus to Claudius. At Oplontis, Third Style paintings are to be seen in the bath suite to the west (especially the *calidarium*), and, unusually, they include red-painted ceilings. The decoration of the eastern peristyle belongs to a later phase still, shortly before the eruption.

Clearly, there is a great deal more still to come out of Oplontis: notably, the whole ancient town of that name – or holiday resort full of villas, if there was no real urban centre. However, these buildings lie buried under modern houses and apartments, and beneath a road, so that further excavation is impeded.

Five other places, too, which were, as we are told, likewise obliterated by the eruption have not yielded any trace. Probably they, once again, if ever excavated, would yield further valuable examples of paintings from the first centuries BC and AD. Meanwhile, however, the future of Vesuvius inspires fear, and disturbing tremors and movements of the earth and coast continue to manifest themselves in the neighbourhood (Appendix II, iii).

CHAPTER 6

THE AUGUSTAN EMPIRE

After Julius Caesar had completed the downfall of the Roman Republic, his grandnephew and adoptive son Octavian (the future Augustus) finally defeated his rival, Marcus Antonius – and Antonius's ally and mistress Queen Cleopatra VII of Ptolemaic Egypt – at the battle of Actium off the coast of Epirus (31 BC). The many commemorations of this establishment of Octavian's sole rulership of the Roman world included a monument at Nicopolis, founded beside the location of the victory, which recent discoveries have made it possible to reconstruct.

Augustus proved himself to be one of the greatest administrators of all time when he established the Principate, based on an overhaul of every political, social, economic and religious institution, within enlarged and systematically defended imperial frontiers. One of these frontiers, to the south-east, was the boundary of recently conquered Egypt, on whose military defences light has been thrown by excavations at a key frontier-post, Primis.

Another feature of Augustus's frontier arrangements, developed from the policies of the later Republic, was the maintenance of a string of client-kingdoms beyond the border-line, in which the rulers enjoyed autonomy combined with dependence in regard to imperial foreign and military policy. One of the foremost of these client-princes was Herod the Great of Judaea, whose activities have been illuminated by finds at the harbour-town Caesarea Maritima.

Rome itself was in a constant condition of reconstruction, expansion and embellishment (cf. Appendix II, iv), and one of the many features introduced by Augustus was a sundial, now made comprehensible by archaeological ingenuity.

1 *Nicopolis: Monument for Actium*

The triumvirate of Octavian (the future Augustus), Marcus Antonius and Lepidus, formed after the defeat of Julius Caesar's assassins Brutus and Cassius at Philippi in 42 BC, became, following the suppression of Lepidus in 36, a direct confrontation between Octavian in the west and Antonius in the east.

In 32, Octavian declared war – not indeed against his compatriot Antonius, but against Antonius's mistress and ally Cleopatra VII, the queen of Ptolemaic Egypt, who fought the ensuing war alongside her lover. With her help, Antonius brought up his army and navy to guard strongholds along the coast of western Greece. However, after Agrippa, Octavian's admiral, had succeeded in crossing the Ionian Sea in mid-winter, Antonius was cornered in the Gulf of Ambracia (Arta). At the naval battle of Actium (September, 31 BC), just outside the gulf, he tried to extricate his ships, but although both he and Cleopatra themselves succeeded in breaking out, only a quarter of their fleet was able to follow them. In the following year both met their deaths in Egypt, which then became a Roman possession under Octavian's personal control.

Although not a spectacular warlike operation in itself, the battle of Actium was hailed as one of the most decisive engagements ever fought, since it ushered in the imperial epoch, under western control. Octavian himself, as he gradually established the Roman Principate, celebrated the victory with unending propaganda, in which he was joined by the great Augustan writers and artists. One of his major celebrations was the establishment of 'Victory City', Nicopolis (Paleopreveza). It was founded upon the hilly isthmus of the Actium promontory at the northern extremity of the Gulf of Ambracia, where his headquarters camp had been located at the time of the battle. By one of the largest of such amalgamations ever recorded, Nicopolis was compulsorily settled by people brought in from towns and villages of many territories of north-western Greece.

The new city, writes B. de Jongh, is 'the most extensive Roman site in Greece . . . In conception and foundation it is Roman; more than any other Greek colony on Hellenic territory, however, it illustrates the continuity of Greco-Roman civilization . . . The whole isthmus is studded with remains of walls and foundations of Roman and early Christian edifices . . . It is a perplexing site, pastoral in character, though maritime, capable of producing a feeling of disorientation in the visitor.'[1]

The site of Octavian's camp, on what is now Michalitsi hill just beyond the village of Smyrtoula, was consecrated by Octavian, according to Suetonius, to Neptune and Mars. In addition – on the spot where his tent had been pitched during the battle – he built a commemorative monument. Dio Cassius refers to 'a foundation of square stones, adorned with the beaks of the captured ships'[2] – the bronze rams (*rostra*) attached to their prows in order to batter enemy vessels. This podium has been preserved, containing the stone sockets in which these rams or beaks were inserted; and recent discoveries and cleaning operations have enabled the whole monument to be reconstructed, in accordance with deductions about the sizes of the rams, derived from the dimensions of the best-preserved sockets.

These investigations have confirmed that the rams, in a long line, were inserted into a stone terrace, which was surmounted by an inscription celebrating the victory. Bulky fragments were found round about.[3] Since all the sockets into which the rams were lodged were cut carefully to fit the exact outlines of the rams, their sizes and shapes can be estimated. Twenty-three sockets have so far been found, but it seems that there were originally between thirty-three and thirty-five, and the same number, therefore, of rams – representing rather more than the tithe (tenth part) of the total number of vessels captured, which was the standard share dedicated to the gods. Some of these rams, William Murray and Photios Petsas conclude, were clearly, 'immense castings that must have weighed two tons or more . . . Until now we had no idea that the Greeks or Romans were capable of turning out such castings.'[4] Evidently, in order to stress the magnitude and glory of his victory, Octavian must have selected for his monument the rams belonging to the largest of Antonius's ships. Smaller ancient rams, which have survived elsewhere, include a specimen from a warship of Ptolemy v Epiphanes or vi Philometor of Egypt (204–167 BC) found at Athlit in Israel, weighing half a ton, and another in the museum at Bremerhaven – both of which helped in the reconstruction of the Athenian trireme (Chapter 3, section 1).

Just south of the monument at Nicopolis was the stadium, in which the Actia, quinquennial festivals founded by Octavian, were celebrated in honour of his victory, accompanied by mock sea-fights in the Gulf, re-enacting the battle of Actium.

On coins issued by the Latin colony at Nemausus (Nîmes) in Gaul, where some of Antonius's defeated seamen were settled – symbolized by the Egyptian crocodile that appears on these pieces – Octavian's head appeared together with a portrait of Agrippa.[5] Agrippa was shown wearing a crown formed of ships' prows (*corona navalis*) which had been invented by Octavian to honour Agrippa's earlier victory over Sextus Pompeius at Naulochus (36 BC), and now served again to celebrate his leading role at Actium. Later, after Octavian had become Augustus, he depicted his divine patron Apollo on his silver coinage and described him as 'Actian'.[6]

The later, local, bronze coinage of Nicopolis itself names the same god Leucates, after the adjoining island of Leucas, and pronounces itself, the City of Victory, to be *nauarchis*, mistress of the fleet.[7] Nicopolis enjoyed the rights of a free and federated community, and for two centuries was the principal urban centre of western Greece, becoming, in the later empire, the capital of the province of Old Epirus. The emperor Julian the Apostate (AD 361–3), inspired by pagan enthusiasm, renovated Nicopolis and revived the Actian Festival. However, Christianity was by then firmly established, and a number of early churches are to be seen on the site.

2 Primis (Qasr Ibrim): Egyptian Frontier

The frontiers of the Roman empire, as stabilized by successive rulers, were in some regions aligned to rivers, but elsewhere coincided with no natural obstacle, and required walls or fortifications, or at least garrisoned fortress centres. Later chapters will discuss the Rhine and Danube frontier areas, settlements close to Hadrian's Wall in Britain, and frontier posts in the east. In this section, mention will be made of a corner of the Roman world's long southern frontier zone, in north Africa.

When Octavian (the future Augustus) annexed Egypt from Cleopatra VII in 30 BC, the land he took over from her was later described by Josephus as naturally 'walled about on every side'.[8] Only at its southern extremity was there no better defined frontier than the First Cataract of the Nile, just beyond Syene (Aswan) and Philae (the centre of the worship of Isis). Further to the south, dominating the Middle Nile valley, lay the kingdom of the Aethiopians (Meroitic Nubians), ruled by a series of partially Hellenized monarchs bearing the title Katake (Candace). The northern part of their kingdom, described as the Triakontaschoinos, that is to say thirty *schoinoi* in width (a land measurement of fluctuating size according to Strabo,[9] but in this case covering about two hundred miles) reached as far as the Second Cataract at Buhen (Wadi Halfa). The northern sector of this Triakontaschoinos, more than eighty miles wide, was the Dodekaschoinos (twelve *schoinoi*) – traditionally Ptolemaic border territory in which, however, the Meroites had now established themselves.

After Rome's annexation of Ptolemaic Egypt and a rebellion in its southern region, one of the earliest duties of the first Roman prefect, the poet Gaius Cornelius Gallus, was to regulate this Dodekaschoinos frontier. First, he staged a military demonstration beyond the First Cataract, 'a region which' (he stated with a fatal boastfulness that was to lose him his emperor's good will) 'neither Roman nor Egyptian arms had ever reached.'[10] Then, at Philae, as a trilingual inscription recorded,[11] he received envoys of the Meroitic king, who was admitted to Roman 'protection' and instructed to appoint a governor or ruler (*tyrannos*) of the whole Triakontaschoinos, who would in fact be loyal to the Romans in the same way as the client–kings round other imperial frontiers (section

3 below). Akinidad, the crown prince of Meroe, was assigned this buffer protectorate, and three Roman auxiliary cohorts were stationed at the edge of his territory.

However, in 25 BC, after many of these troops had been withdrawn for an expedition to Arabia, the Aethiopians poured across the frontier, overpowered what was left of the garrison, and devastated Philae, Syene and its sister-town Elephantine (Abu). In return, Gaius Petronius, who was then prefect of Egypt, marched south, routed the Meroitic forces at Pselcis (Dakka), and stormed the hill-top fortress of Primis (Qasr Ibrim) in the southern part of the Triakontaschoinos, 120 miles south of Syene. He then moved onwards into the territory of the Meroites, sacked their northern capital at Napata (Gebel Barka, below the Fourth Cataract in the Sudan) returned to strengthen Primis, and left four hundred men there with supplies for two years. Soon afterwards, following renewed trouble, Augustus pushed the imperial boundary further south, annexing the rich market-town of Hiera Sykaminos (El-Maharraga).

Officially speaking, he relinquished at the same time the more remote, southern section of the Triakontaschoinos in exchange for a secure peace. This was arranged by a conference with a Meroitic delegation which visited him at Samos, and offered formal submission. The treaty should have meant that the Romans abandoned Primis, yet its excavations suggest that, in fact, it remained a Roman outpost, on the far side of, but in close touch with, what was the new frontier (like forts beyond the northern borders of the empire). This continued to be the situation until at least the end of the first century AD – and probably for much longer still, since one building at Primis has now been ascribed to the reign of Septimius Severus (AD 193–211), while the commander and senior officers of the legion stationed in Egypt (*Legio* II *Traiana Fortis*) are mentioned in a letter written from the fortress a little before AD 247.[12]

During the decades that lay ahead, however, nomadic Blemmyes in the eastern desert and Nobades (Nubians) west of the Nile launched repeated attacks on Rome's Egyptian province. Indeed, after the mid-third century, there is no further evidence of Roman official activity in any part of the Dodekaschoinos. Moreover, in *c.*297, while strengthening and stabilizing his armies and borders in general (Chapter 9, section 2), Diocletian accepted a frontier line at Syene near the First Cataract: though, once again, this withdrawal was not definitive, since there is evidence that Pselcis was still, in fact, occupied by a Roman garrison in the time of Constantine I the Great (306–337). Nevertheless, during the mid-fourth century, the armies of the eastern African empire of Axum not only swept up to the Fourth and possibly as far as the Third Cataract, but also created disturbed conditions considerably farther north as well. For when an imperial envoy,

Olympiodorus, visited Primis in *c.*420–1, he found it in the hands of the Blemmyes. In the mid-fifth century, however, both they and the Nobades were defeated and pushed back.

Primis (Qasr Ibrim) is now a barren island in Lake Nasser, an isolated hilltop eroded on the west by steep cliffs, its ruins a haven for snakes and scorpions. But before the construction of the High Dam (1960–9) the hill stood on the mainland, rising high and gaunt above the Nile and commanding views over the river and the desert approaches. The past centuries have left fifteen feet of débris on the uneven surface of the hill. Although much still remains to be done, the excavations of the 1980s have shown what Primis was like in ancient times, and have demonstrated that it was richer and more important than had been supposed. Its role in the Roman defence system has been clarified by the examination of ramparts on the southern side. Several hundred military boots and sandals have been unearthed, as well as several thousand pieces of cloth (a rarity among ancient discoveries). The religious significance of the place is also beginning to be understood. Numerous papyrus fragments have been found, in various languages, as well as extensive Meroitic material, throwing new light on Rome's southern neighbour and enemy.

3 Caesarea Maritima: Herod's Port

One of the most effective Roman governmental techniques was the employment of client-kings. These were monarchs who ruled over their own countries, outside the empire's official frontiers, and remained independent in their internal affairs, but were expected to conform with Roman policy – notably in regard to international concerns – and had to make their contribution to imperial defence. This *penumbra*, often extending, with decreasing degrees of direct dependency, far beyond the imperial borders, had been created during the Republic, when Pompey and Caesar and Marcus Antonius all developed such techniques. The same system then fulfilled an essential role in the administrative and political arrangements of Augustus.

In his time, one of the key client-monarchs was Herod the Great, king of Judaea (Israel, Palestine). Born in *c.*73 BC, he was the son of Antipater, from the southern region of the country, and became a Roman citizen in 47. Placed on the Judaean throne in 40 *in absentia*, and then, three years later, installed at Jerusalem by Marcus Antonius's troops, he managed to negotiate his way both through the jealousies of Queen Cleopatra VII of Egypt and through her subsequent downfall, with Antonius, at the hands of Octavian (the future Augustus) in 31–30. By steadfast loyalty he retained

Augustus's support for many years, until errors of judgment caused this goodwill to be forfeited shortly before the king's death in 4 BC.

Herod the Great was a grandiose builder, in the Hellenistic and Augustan tradition. His fortress-palace on the heights of Masada will be discussed elsewhere (Chapter 7, section 3), but he also built a great port at Caesarea Maritima, earlier known as the Tower of Strato, beside the Mediterranean Sea. Already incorporated in the Roman province of Syria for thirty-three years, this naval station was ceded by Octavian to Herod in 30 BC, and the port that Herod created there was one of his outstanding achievements. He began to construct it in 22 BC, and completed the project twelve years later, under the designation of 'Caesarea Beside the Augustan Harbour' – a name which gave twofold honour to his patron, who was Caesar as well as Augustus.

In recent years Caesarea has been the scene of two archaeological projects. One of these teams, the Joint Expedition to Caesarea Maritima (JECM), has been excavating the land site of the town since 1972, and the other, the Caesarea Ancient Harbour Excavation Project (CAHEP), was organized in 1980 to explore the port.

This port of Herod the Great was described by the Jewish historian Josephus. 'He noticed on the coast a town called Strato's Tower in a state of decay, but thanks to its admirable situation capable of benefiting by his generosity. He rebuilt it entirely with limestone and adorned it with a most splendid palace. Nowhere did he show more clearly the liveliness of his imagination. The city lies midway between Dora (Al-Tantura) and Joppa (Jaffa), and hitherto the whole of that shore had been harbourless, so that anyone sailing along the Phoenician coast towards Egypt had to ride the open sea when threatened by the south-west wind; even when this is far from strong, such huge waves are dashed against the rocks that the back-wash makes the sea boil up a long way out. But the king by lavish expenditure and unshakable determination won the battle against nature and constructed a harbour bigger than the Piraeus, with further deep roadsteads in its recesses.

'The site was as awkward as could be, but he wrestled with the difficulties so triumphantly that on his solid fabric the sea could make no impression, while its beauty gave no hint of the obstacles encountered. He first marked out the area for a harbour of the size mentioned, and then lowered into 20 fathoms of water blocks of stone mostly 50 feet long, 9 deep and 10 broad, but sometimes even bigger. When the foundations had risen to water-level he built above the surface a mole 200 feet wide; half this width was built out to break the force of the waves and so was called the Breakwater; the rest supported the encircling stone wall. Along this were spaced massive towers, of which the most conspicuous and most beautiful was called Drusium after Augustus's stepson.

'There was a row of arched recesses where newly arrived crews could land, and in front of these was a circular terrace forming a broad walk for those disembarking. The harbour-mouth faced north, as in that locality the north wind is the gentlest, and on either side rose three colossal statues standing on pillars; those on the left of ships entering were supported by a solid tower, those on the right by two upright stones clamped together, even higher than the tower on the other side.

'Adjoining the harbour were houses, also of limestone, and to the harbour led the streets of the town, laid out the same distance apart. On rising ground opposite the harbour-mouth stood Augustus's temple, of exceptional size and beauty; in it was a colossal statue of Augustus, no whit inferior to the Olympian Zeus which it was intended to resemble, and one of Rome comparable with the Hera of Argos. Herod dedicated the city to the province, the harbour to those who sailed these seas, and the honour of his new creation to Caesar Augustus: Caesarea was the name he gave it.'[13]

Herod employed the most advanced technological methods of his time to achieve this aim. Since there was no natural harbour along the coast, he 'defied nature' (as Josephus put it), by thrusting man-made breakwaters out into the open sea. Currents and strong seas, however, tended to fill the enclosed basin with silt and eventually to demolish even the heaviest construction. 'So Herod and his engineers provided an outer barrier on the harbour's southern flank, dropped large stones against the breakwaters to prevent undercutting and incorporated sluice gates to make the harbour self-flushing... Building this harbour was almost an act of showmanship... in which Herod went to extraordinary lengths to accomplish what appeared impossible.'[14]

The port that he built at Caesarea was said by Josephus to have surpassed even the Piraeus – and perhaps Herod was trying to rival Alexandria in Egypt. The harbour had its entrance on the north side, from which the wind blows least severely, and was protected by a sea-wall, and not merely by the one breakwater to which the historian referred, but by two – now submerged, but discernible in air photographs when the sea is calm and the sun bright. The southern breakwater extends from the shore for about 875 yards to the west and north of the small modern fishing jetty and anchorage. The ancient entrance channel penetrated the gap between this southern breakwater and its northern counterpart, which extended almost due west from the shore for about three hundred yards.

'Herod the Great', writes Kenneth Holum, 'imported Roman concrete into his kingdom and employed it extensively in building the harbour at Caesarea... [The excavators] also discovered parts of the wooden forms into which the builders had poured the concrete. The formwork had been constructed from large wooden base beams with uprights and horizontal planking inside and out. The elaborate carpentry included lap joints and mortising. To prevent collapse during pouring the builders had passed tie beams through the volume to be filled with concrete.

'The materials CAHEP excavated from this construction were sent to analytical laboratories, where carbon-14 analysis of wood samples produced a dating of 1,970 years BP ("before the present"), plus or minus seventy years, which is about right for Herod's reign. Botanists report that species of spruce, pine, fir and poplar are represented among the wood samples, and all are of European origin. The stone rubble, or aggregate, in the concrete came from local sources, but the mortar may contain *pozzolana* from Italy. It is reasonable to suspect that the materials and technology used at Caesarea came with Roman engineers Augustus sent to assist Herod's architects with the harbour project.'[15]

'Once at work CAHEP archaeologists use a number of devices developed especially for underwater exploration. An air probe is used to locate parts of the ancient harbour buried beneath the sea floor and to determine their shape, or profile... CAHEP divers use the air probe to trace the profile of structures concealed beneath the sea-floor. A jet of air introduced into an iron pipe quickly burrows into the sand until it encounters an obstacle. Depth beneath the sea-floor is then read from a metric scale on the iron pipe... A series of such measurements taken along a steel cable fixed at both ends produces a profile. If the decision is made to excavate, the archaeologist uses not a trowel but an air lift, a large-diameter, flexible hose that works much like a vacuum-cleaner. Compressed air sets up a flow of water that removes sand, mud, gravel, small stones, and other bottom debris – and that will suck up potsherds, coins and other artefacts as well, if the operator does not use it cautiously. One advantage of excavating underwater is the absence of muscle wear and tear in transporting heavy objects out of a trench. The diver uses an air-bag, filled from the breathing apparatus, which lifts objects to the surface with ease.'[16]

Designed on a grid pattern around a main street more than fifty feet wide, which was flanked by columns and floored with mosaics, this new Caesarea was equipped with all the appurtenances of a prosperous Greco-Roman city. Air photography and excavation have disclosed the site of Herod's royal palace and pool on a rock promontory. The remains of a theatre, too, have been found, with 4,000 seats, the earliest of its kind in Judaea. An amphitheatre and hippodrome, with 38,000 seats, have also been revealed, as well as temples, including a shrine dedicated to Rome and Augustus.

'Caesarea's archaeologists', comments Holum, 'are addressing questions about the phenomenon of urbanism in general. Why did ancient cities spring up? Was it by a natural process, or because ancient developers looked for some kind of profit in creating them? What emotional bonds linked citizens to one another, allowing them to inhabit the same city peacefully and constructively? What did cities need in order to prosper, and how sensitive were ancient governments – as opposed to modern ones – to these needs? How well did ancient cities withstand dramatic historical and environmental changes, like earthquakes or the rise of new religions and ideologies?'[17] With regard to this last point, the purely pagan institutions encouraged by Herod at Caesarea, deliberately demonstrating his allegiance to the Roman or Greco-Roman imperial world, make it easy to see why, although a professing Jew himself and aware of the need to placate stricter Jews, he nevertheless fell foul of them and their leaders.

Caesarea was not only a flourishing commercial centre but controlled a territory of which our knowledge is now extended by air photography (Chapter 8, section 6), and particularly by its use of the infra-red method. This reacts sensitively to varying degrees of water absorption so that it can detect changes in vegetation, for example, or the existence of buried features filled with disturbed soil, or the presence of ancient roadways. Infra-red film, as Holum writes, 'registers the heat emitted by living plants. Because dense plant growth depends on the amount of water available, and masses of subsurface stone hinder moisture from reaching root systems, infra-red photographs enabled JECM to 'see' ancient structures below ground level and subsequently place its trenches accordingly.' In a 'false colour' photograph which he appends, 'heat emitted by plants produces deep red . . . Zones of lighter coloration in an open field indicate ancient ruins beneath ground level.'[18] (Meanwhile, *remote* sensing techniques have further facilitated exploration from the air.)

The town of Caesarea also developed its own purple dyeing (*murex*) industry, and became first a royal customs post and then the capital of a newly created Roman province of Judaea. An inscription set up by Pontius Pilatus, the provincial prefect (his successors were known as procurators) from AD 26 to 36, has been found on the site,[19] and it was at Caesarea that St Peter baptized a Roman centurion and St Paul was imprisoned for two years. Local disturbances in AD 66 helped to trigger off the First Jewish Revolt or First Roman War (Chapter 7, section 3). But Caesarea, converted into a colony by Vespasian – who was proclaimed emperor there by its enthusiastic and mainly Greek population and who stationed two legions in the city – continued to flourish into Byzantine times.

4 Rome: The Imperial Sundial

Three monuments created by Augustus to form part of his magnificent Rome were designed to adorn the Field of Mars (Campus Martius), forming a single coherent complex. These were his Mausoleum, the Altar of Peace (Ara Pacis), and the Egyptian obelisk. This formed the indicator (*gnomon*) of a sundial, the Solarium or Horologium Augusti, which will be the subject of our present discussion.

The ancients had become adept at devising calendrical mechanisms (Chapter 4, section 4), and Augustus made his contribution by importing and erecting this obelisk and dedicating it to the Sun in 9 BC. 'The obelisk in the Campus', observed Pliny the elder, 'was put to use in a remarkable way by the divine Augustus so as to mark the sun's shadow and thereby the lengths of days and nights. A pavement was laid down for a distance appropriate to the height of the obelisk so that the shadow cast at noon on the shortest day of the year might exactly coincide with it. Bronze rods let into the pavement were meant to measure the shadow day by day as it gradually became shorter and then lengthened again. This device, which deserves to be carefully studied, was contrived by the mathematician Novius Facundus... He is said to have understood the principle from observing the shadow cast by the human head.'[20]

In 1792, the obelisk was taken away from its first Roman position and moved about 540 feet to the point at which it now stands, outside the modern Parliament building in the Palazzo Montecitorio. Since 1976, Edmund Buchner has investigated the remains that have made it possible to reconstruct the ancient purposes that it served. Augustus's experts arranged not only that it should provide a sundial, but also that, at the equinox, the shadow of the obelisk's tip should cross the hour line in a straight shadow track, and, towards sunset, should mount and enter the adjacent Altar of Peace – thus emphasizing a propagandist point. For in this way the obelisk, which, coming from Egypt, celebrated Augustus's conquest of that country from Marcus Antonius and Cleopatra VII (section 1 above), was deliberately linked with the altar dedicated to the imperial Peace which this conquest had brought about.

A further factor, too, was involved in the symbolism. The autumn equinox was Augustus's birthday, which according to an edict of his friend Paullus Fabius Maximus – probably datable to the very year of the dedication of the sundial – marked the inauguration of the civil year for the cities of the province of Asia (of which Fabius was governor). On the other hand the winter solstice, with which the sundial was also associated, was the day of Augustus's zodiacal sign, the Capricorn, which, for this reason, received prominent attention on contemporary coinage and other artefacts.

The sundial bore reliefs depicting Augustus and his family. However, recent excavations have revealed that this dial, as we have it today, is not the original monument of Augustus himself, but a subsequent restoration, nearly five feet above the Augustan dial, i.e. twenty-three feet beneath the present ground level – work apparently undertaken either by Domitian (AD 81–96) or by Hadrian (117–38), both of whom showed an interest in astrology and astronomy. The remains of this restoration have been found in a cellar. They consist of large travertine slabs, bearing markings of bronze which included Greek words, letters indicating the signs of the zodiac, and a network of marked-out lines comprising a vertical spine with horizontal bars corresponding to days, against which the shadow of the obelisk registered its marks. This restoration was prompted by a Tiber flood which had submerged and damaged Augustus's dial. At the same time, it served the purpose of correcting distortions resulting from certain calendrical shifts which had occurred some thirty years before Pliny wrote (and which invited his speculations).

Augustus's sundial, as now reinterpreted on the basis of these discoveries – for the later dial continued to employ his obelisk and probably his lettering as well – throws light not only on the horological and calendrical arrangements of the time but also on his urbanistic conceptions and the publicity that was associated with them. Furthermore, Buchner's investigations illustrate, in a special way, the means by which archaeological method can contribute to history. 'In 1976,' writes Antony Snodgrass, 'by means of a complex series of arguments, mathematical, astronomical and archaeological, [he] reached certain conclusions about the location, level, form and function of the gigantic horizontal network, some 160 by 75 metres [525 by 240 feet] in area, where the readings of the sundial were taken. He was working largely from a single archaeological datum: the known location and approximate height of the obelisk that had formed the pointer of the sundial.' Three years later Buchner was able to test these conclusions by a decisive find inside the cellar of a house. 'Here, at a depth of well over 6 metres [20 feet] below street level, was found a travertine block into which a nine-inch-high, bronze letter 'A' had been embedded in lead. Other letters soon followed, showing that the 'A' was the second letter of PARTHENOS – Virgo in the more familiar Latin form of the zodiacal calendar.'[21]

This is a rare example, adds Snodgrass, of an excavator being able to test a hypothesis and confirm its correctness. 'Where else but in the classical world can one dig a narrow hole twenty-one feet deep and find at the bottom almost exactly what one predicted?' This sort of investigation, he comments, is an example of the sort of particularistic work deplored by the more environmentally minded exponents of the New Archaeology

(Appendix I) but both approaches are necessary. For the many other archaeological activities that have been going on in Rome, see Appendix II, iv.

CHAPTER 7
THE POST-AUGUSTANS

The last chapter (section 3) said something about Herod the Great, a monarch of one of the client-states that formed a cordon outside the imperial frontiers. Another native supporter of the early emperors was Cogidubnus, within the province of Britannia, which had been annexed by Claudius.

These Julio-Claudian emperors were commemorated by statues and reliefs at Aphrodisias in western Asia Minor, of which the flourishing and long-lived sculptural school has now been much more fully understood, as a result of recent excavations. Further east, at Masada in Judaea, archaeology has proved valuable to military historians, who have used its findings to reconstruct the encampments and devices employed by the Romans in AD 73 to capture this fortress, the last to hold out against them in the Firs Jewish Revolt (First Roman War).

Six years later, in Italy itself, came the eruption of Vesuvius which destroyed the cities and other centres round the mountain. One of them was Oplontis (Chapter 5, section 6). But at Herculaneum, too, the recent discovery and investigation of skeletons has enabled this branch of archaeological studies to contribute to our knowledge of the epoch.

1 Noviomagus Regnensium (Fishbourne): Prince in a Province

Noviomagus Regnensium (Chichester in Sussex) was a town on the coastal plain below a spur of the South Downs, upon the River Lavant and about a mile from its estuary and harbour on the Fretum Gallicum (English Channel). It was the capital of the tribe of the Reg(i)ni or Regnenses. Excavations have shown that they had inhabited the place since the fourth or third century BC. Then, after the Roman landings in AD 43, which resulted in the creation of the province of Britannia, Noviomagus became a military fortress. Nevertheless, the local rulership of the tribal chief Tiberius Claudius Cogidubnus (*c.*43–75/80) was confirmed and supported by the Roman emperor Claudius and his successors, and it was at Noviomagus that Cogidubnus conducted his administration.

Most client-kings of Rome ruled over countries which, although under Roman protection and indirect control, were not in any Roman province and thus remained, technically, outside the Roman empire. Such, for example, had been the position of Herod the Great (Chapter 6, section 3). But the situation of Cogidubnus was different, and more unusual, though there are parallels from Syria and other regions, for he was permitted to remain chief of the Regnenses *inside* the Roman empire, presiding over a territory or enclave within one of its provinces. Moreover, in order to emphasize this dual position, he obtained from Vespasian (AD 69–70) the rank of imperial legate, while retaining his royal title as well. The status of King Prasutagus, of the tribe of the Iceni in East Anglia (the husband of Boudicca [Boadicea]), is likely to have received a similar definition. This interpretation of the British princes' status, combining that of a client-king and an imperial functionary, seems to have been an invention of Claudius, designed to associate local native personages with the new process of Roman government which, in Britannia, was now beginning to establish itself.

As early as *c.*AD 45, however, the Roman garrison had evacuated the fort of Noviomagus. At that juncture the place began to assume the lineaments of a town, which it has been possible, in part, to reconstruct by examining service trenches dug through modern streets. The successive stages of development include the building of a temple of Neptune and Minerva, erected, as an inscription records, in honour of the imperial family, by permission of Cogidubnus.[1]

Excavation has also now revealed the adjacent massive building complex and villa-palace of Fishbourne, commanding the head of the harbour which was becoming an important naval base. The first occupation, in about AD 43, had been intended to supply the granaries and storehouses required by the invading Roman army. But these edifices were replaced, some seven years later, by a private dwelling, constructed of wood and comprising two separate structures. At the same time work began on an adjacent villa, which was ready for habitation in the early 60s. Next, soon after 75 – at a time when construction was very active in Britain – the first steps were taken towards the replacement of this villa by the much more extensive palace whose remains can be seen today. It covers an area of ten acres, and offers us a concept of what Romanization could offer prominent collaborators, during the half-century that followed the invasion.

The grandeur of this mansion suggests that its owner must have been Cogidubnus himself. It would be hard to imagine anyone else residing in such state, so close to his capital. A Roman senator as well as a client-ruler, he was just the sort of man who wished to be surrounded by Roman civilization. For Cogidubnus had, no doubt, like other foreign princes, once resided in Rome, where he would have been groomed to become an apostle of the Roman way of life when he returned to Britain. His palace displays this attachment. Its architectural design (with courtyard in front of the hall and main rooms) was indeed of British and continental type, yet the style and construction methods and landscaping of the buildings echo the palaces of emperors at Rome.

Cogidubnus's mansion was built of stone (on a platform of stone and clay), some of which came from Britain, demonstrating that, within only two decades of the Roman conquest, the country's geology was well enough explored for several different varieties of British limestone and sandstone to be selected and crafted for specific sections of the edifice in accordance with their various qualities. The walls of the rooms, however, were covered with slabs and pieces of marble – sometimes formed into elegant patterns (*opus sectile*) – and a number of these had been imported from various western and eastern Mediterranean countries. Once more, comparison with major Roman palaces is invited, as it is again by the black and white mosaics decorating the floors, the earliest ever to have been discovered in Britain.

Imperial backing (and finance?) must surely have been available, to enable Cogidubnus to dwell in this unprecedented 'show-piece of Roman Britain, a *pièce de résistance*, a vivid testimonial to the sophistication and high style of the *ultimi Britanni* who found favour with Rome'.[2] The splendour of Cogidubnus's residence, as we saw, had come in stages. First, he seems to have lived in a relatively modest wooden house, and next in a villa of no great grandeur. Finally, however, this palatial residence was built for his use.

Its main area consisted of four wings extending round a central colonnaded courtyard, two hundred feet square. The courtyard was laid out as a formal garden containing fountains, trees and rows of flowering shrubs (planted in beds), round a central path bordered by hedges which were fashioned into a series of alternating rectangular and horizontal recesses. The wall-paintings from the 'House of Livia' at Prima Porta, now in the National Archaeological Museum at Rome, displayed a similar scene, but here it has been possible to reconstruct the garden's appearance from what was actually left on the ground. Indeed, Fishbourne provides one of the few pieces of surviving archaeological evidence for any Roman formal gardens in one of the provinces (for Italy, see also Oplontis, Chapter 5, section 6). Moreover, this was not the only garden at Fishbourne. There were also peristyle gardens in the east and north wings – probably once planted with shrubs, and perhaps with trees, and flanked by rows of rooms along one side. There was a kitchen garden, too, in the north-west corner, as well as perhaps a natural garden on the southern terrace.

The east wing, housing private apartments, was entered through a colonnaded entrance hall, approached by visitors from Noviomagus across a small bridge. On arrival they would see the main central garden on the other side of an ornamental pool. The pool was flanked by a suite of baths, which is so far little known, since it lies beneath a modern road. The west wing – probably the most important in the palace – stood at a slightly higher level. It contained another series of rooms including a large, square, apsed audience chamber, approached by a flight of steps from the main courtyard and originally roofed by a stucco vault. This complex was separated from the west front of the palace by a long, eighteen-foot-wide corridor terminating in apses at either end. It bears comparison with a similar feature in the palace of Domitian (Domus Flavia) on the Palatine Hill in Rome and may likewise have been an exercise area.

The twenty-three rooms of the north wing (probably guest accommodation) were arranged round two further colonnaded courtyards and flanked, at the eastern extremity, by an aisled hall. Much of the wing is now incorporated into a museum. Further to the north stood a complex of servants' quarters, workshops and farm buildings that have still not been traced in their entirety. The south wing of the palace is buried under the modern village of Fishbourne, but trenches have provided some indications of its plan. It was apparently adjoined by additional colonnades on both of its long sides, one looking out over the central port, and the other facing southwards towards the sea, where wharves and jetties were built to form a private harbour, approached by a navigable creek.

By the end of the first century AD – after Cogidubnus's princedom had been eliminated by incorporation into the Roman province – the palace was divided up into a series of separate units, for which new, separate bathing establishments were constructed, central heating (hypocausts) installed beneath several rooms, and polychrome mosaics laid out. Perhaps the owners were now Cogidubnus's heirs; or maybe some other local, or immigrant, family had moved in. By *c.*300 a further remodelling was taking place. At this juncture, however, the entire complex was demolished by fire – possibly caused by pirate raiders from the sea. As for the town of Noviomagus, it was protected by an earthwork – converted after AD 200 into a stone wall – and its fortifications were reinforced after naval attacks in 367. Whether, and to what extent, however, it survived the withdrawal of the Roman garrison, in 385 and 407, remains uncertain.

2 *Aphrodisias: School of Sculpture*

Aphrodisias (later Geyre) was a city in Caria (south-western Asia Minor), situated on a plateau, full of poplars and olives, about 1,800 feet above sea level on the western slopes of the Baba Dağı mountains, above the fertile valley containing the sources of the River Morsynus, a tributary of the Maeander (Büyük Menderes). In pre-Greek times the place was called Ninoe, probably derived from the Akkadian (Mesopotamian) moon-goddess Nin, who was subsequently equated with Aphrodite, from whom the Greek city took its name and its principal temple.

Aphrodisias, included in the Roman province of Asia, enjoyed cordial relations with the central government in the time of Sulla, dictator 81–79 BC (who extended his patronage to the city, since he venerated Aphrodite-Venus as his protector), and again under Julius Caesar (who claimed Aphrodite as his ancestress). During this first century BC the city was amalgamated with the neighbouring town of Plarasa.

Inscriptions of the period, found on the site, are abundant and informative. Octavian (the future Augustus) conferred privileges upon the city, and proclaimed the inviolability of the shrine of Aphrodite, the reconstruction of which was resumed under the influence of his freedman Zoilus, honoured by an allegorical frieze. During this and the following period Aphrodisias was a leading cultural centre. Writers born there included the novelist Charito (first century BC?), the medical author Xenocrates (of Neronian and Flavian date), and the Peripatetic (Aristotelian) philosopher Alexander, who taught at Athens and dedicated his book *On Fate* to the emperor Septimius Severus (AD 193–211) and his son Caracalla.

Numerous architectural remains have come to light at Aphrodisias, in addition to a vast harvest of epigraphy. Its outstanding distinction, however, lay in the field of sculpture, which forms such a vital element in classical archaeology (Chapter 3, section 3). Successive excavations have brought to light an unprecedented quantity of statues and reliefs. This output was made possible by the presence of some of the richest quarries in Asia Minor, lying less than two miles east of the city along the lower slopes of Baba Dağı. Exploited since the seventh and sixth centuries BC (and perhaps even longer) they produced excellent white and especially bluish-grey marble.

Work on the site of Aphrodisias was begun during the nineteenth century, and resumed in 1904–5, 1913 and 1937. It was not until 1961 and subsequent years, however, that further discoveries demonstrated the significance of this sculptural school and its output. Literary evidence on the subject is almost non-existent, but a large number of signatures of sculptors identify Aphrodisias as their city. These signatures appear on statues, bases, fragments and reliefs found in Greece, Italy and elsewhere, bearing witness, in some cases, to what may have been travelling workshops.

This versatile production included, in particular, portraits, at which Aphrodisias excelled. It also included genre groups, reliefs (which on occasion reflect current events), pedimental sculpture (notably a scene of Aphrodite's birth), and lavish architectural decoration decked out in polychrome. Aphrodisian art enjoyed a uniquely prolonged duration. I have chosen to discuss it in the present chapter, but it could equally well have been located in an earlier or much later section, for the school had already been flourishing in the first century BC, and was still producing some of its finest work in the years before and after AD 500.

All this became increasingly clear after work resumed in 1961. Activity was concentrated upon the Temple of Aphrodite, the Tetrapylon and the Odeon. Renewed investigation, too, has uncovered the luxurious Baths of Hadrian (AD 117–38), about which Kenan Erim, leader of the excavations, reported: 'A remarkable series of statuary, including several excellent portraits, was unearthed in the various rooms... Unusually handsome sculpture was also found in the excavation undertaken along the eastern extremity of the *palaestra* [wrestling-place] of the Baths, adjacent to the Portico of Tiberius.'[3]

And then later, in the 1970s, when the western and south-western ends of the same portico were cleared, a basilica (multi-purpose public hall) of the later third century AD, nearly 400 feet in length, came to light. 'The basilica was elaborately decorated and featured carved balustrades located in the intercolumniations of the upper storey over the eastern side. Many mythological scenes were depicted on these relief panels. The most interesting showed Semiramis of Babylon and her husband Ninus in Roman dress.' This picture alludes, as Erim points out, to the city's early name of Ninoe. 'An impressive statuary group', he adds, 'was also discovered in excavation east of the Odeon, where a habitation quarter with mosaic-paved rooms was recorded. The largest statue portrayed a colossal male figure in full military regalia, signed by "Apollonius Aster, son of Chrysippus".'[4]

Then, from 1979 onwards, further investigation gradually revealed the Sebasteion, a monumental zone dedicated to the cult of Augustus (in Greek, Sebastos) and his deified successors. 'The most stunning aspect of the complex was undoubtedly its lavish use of sculpture... Some showed mythological scenes [notably a relief of Prometheus liberated by Heracles]... Other larger reliefs portrayed Augustus [nude, accepting the bounties of the earth and command of the sea], other Julio-Claudian emperors, princes and princesses, crowning trophies and conquering nations... Fortunately several of the Imperial panels were identified by inscriptions... Thus one showed Claudius overwhelming Britannia, another Nero conquering Armenia, and a third Rome receiving the bounties of the earth (Ge). The Nero relief, as well as a few other ones, betrayed intentional damage, including erasure of the emperor's name, obviously signs of a *damnatio memoriae* [official posthumous condemnation]... Many of the reliefs portraying pagan gods were systematically hammered in Byzantine times.'[5]

The North Portico suffered even more seriously from Byzantine destruction. Nevertheless, it can be seen that its reliefs depicted the various peoples that were defeated or conquered by Augustus. The names of thirteen such peoples are recorded on surviving bases. Further inscribed bases bear the names not only of the Trojan Aeneas (celebrated by Virgil as the founder of the Roman state) and of his divine mother Aphrodite (described as the ancestress of Augustus, through the latter's adoption by Julius Caesar) but also of Augustus's grandsons and prospective heirs Gaius and Lucius Caesar, and of Drusus the younger the son of Tiberius (all three of whom died before they could succeed to the throne). Further Julio-Claudian portraits emerged in a newly discovered building adjacent to the North Portico, and inscriptions identified other busts as Pindar, Alcibiades, the philosopher Pythagoras (headless), and Apollonius (of Tyana) – the Neopythagorean philosopher of the first century AD – while an uninscribed head represents Alexander the Great.

In 1985, reports Erim, 'another series of remarkable finds made along the east end of the street [skirting the eastern façade of the Tetrapylon] added fresh evidence to the original approach of Aphrodisian artists to decorative sculpture... Over eighteen complete, or fragmentary, figural Corinthian revetment pilaster capitals [capitals of piers projecting from wall-coverings] were found... The subject matter of these capitals was occasionally repetitive, yet thoroughly beguiling and unusual. All featured child figures, *putti*, wingless Erotes [Cupids], pygmies or similar small-sized, chubby men. The most attractive among them was certainly the one showing an Eros in the process of throwing a stone at a snake threatening a fluttering owl in the acanthus leaves to the right... One of the new capitals seems to show what appears to be an opium poppy capsule in Eros's hands, which may be in the act of cutting it. If so, these would be among the earliest representations of opium poppy farming in our records.'[6]

The sculptural achievement of Aphrodisias stands comparison, in quality, with its counterpart at imperial Rome itself, with which it maintained close touch. Yet the Aphrodisian achievement is quite different, as a glance at the Roman Ara Pacis (Altar of Peace) shows. 'While Rome', comments Clara Valenziano, 'invests its spirals and garlands with shaded depths, the sculptors of Aphrodisias detach the decoration from its background, incise the outlines vigorously, accentuate contrasts of lighting; these statues were designed to live under an intense and ever-changing light of the sun. But beneath this style there also underlies a material consideration: the Greek marbles employed at Rome for official sculptures were white, compact and subtly grained, whereas the marbles of Aphrodisias were coloured and their grain was coarse, requiring in consequence a different sort of treatment, more summary, more unconstrained, almost baroque.'[7]

As long ago as 1943 Maria Squarciapino recognized that there was a distinctive, and in many ways independent, Aphrodisian school of sculpture, employing partly traditional, partly original methods.[8] Now, since all the subsequent discoveries, this claim has been confirmed, and indeed raised to an altogether new level. True, these sculptors were capable of making just copies, and making them well, and were not averse to imitating, in particular, some of the richly ornamental techniques which had been devised by their predecessors at other times and places. Yet the Aphrodisians, as Erim writes, 'were not mere copyists. Analysis of their methods has revealed a loose system of measurement and a reliance on the eye of the individual sculptor that makes it clear that they were never simply imitators. They were, rather, inspired interpreters of the past, in a way that a performing musician is the interpreter of a concerto or symphony. Their specific affinities were with Hellenistic sculpture, and particularly that of Pergamum, so the school can be regarded as the logical, and even the organic, continuation of Pergamene art.'[9]

While paying this careful attention to the work of other schools, the Aphrodisian artists nevertheless continued to display a certain technical homogeneity within their own ranks, reflecting proficiency based on longstanding perfectionist methods of training. Over the years, the number of sculptors the city produced was very large. For lately, not only has new evidence emerged for Aphrodisian artists already known, but also many additions have been many to the twenty known signatures, notably Alexander the son of Zeno, Apollonius Aster (see above) and Menodotus. And there must surely be made more names and works of art to come. Meanwhile, the sector of the town in which these men worked has been discovered, revealing trial pieces, unfinished works, rejects and tools.

Promoted to be the capital of a new province of Phrygia-Caria, Aphrodisias, under the threat of Gothic invasions in the 260s AD, began the construction of new walls, extending round a circumference of 12,000 feet. From the subsequent period, excavations have produced many fragments of the most important inscription of ancient times relating to economics, the Edict of Maximum Prices which Diocletian (284–305) promulgated and exhibited in provincial capitals.[10] Epigraphic examinations have also demonstrated, contrary to earlier assumptions founded on stylistic criteria, that a trio of Aphrodisian sculptors, Flavius Zeno, Flavius Andronicus and Flavius Chryseros, chiefly known for what is called the 'Esquiline Group' at Rome, are to be ascribed not to the Hadrianic or Antonine ages (second century AD), as had been supposed, but to an epoch two centuries later. Indeed, that much later period provided a whole portrait gallery of high local officials: including an outstanding head of Flavius Palmatus, governor-general of Asiana. Furthermore, a series of floor mosaics continued to maintain the distinction of Aphrodisias in that art as well.

From at least AD 325, the city was the seat of a bishopric – hence the defacement of pagan monuments – and at some stage it became the capital of Caria, which was detached from Phrygia to form a separate province.

3 Masada: Siege-Warfare

In AD 70 Jerusalem fell to Titus, the son of the Roman emperor Vespasian, and the First Jewish Revolt, or First Roman War, which had started four years earlier, was approaching its end. For the rebellious province of Judaea (Israel) had by now, for the most part, been regained by the Romans. Yet three important, powerful fortresses still held out. They were Herodium, Machaerus and Masada. The first two were reduced, probably late in 71 and in the summer of 72 respectively, by Sextus Lucilius Bassus, the first of a new and more senior series of imperial governors – of senatorial instead of merely knightly rank. Masada now stood alone.

Masada was a precipitous, isolated height rising 1,300 feet above the west coast of the Dead Sea. A small fort had been built there by a Jewish (Hasmonaean) monarch in the later second or early first century BC, and after Herod the Great had established himself on the throne as a Roman client-king (Chapter 6, section 3), he rebuilt this 'eagle's nest' as the southernmost of his chain of defensive stations – strongholds to control the countryside and serve as administrative centres. Excavations have added to the historian Josephus's description of this Herodian building. Combining the defences of a fortress with residential quarters, it showed how a Roman client–ruler could live in his own kingdom, just as grandly as another, Cogidubnus, lived in a Roman province (Chapter 7, section 1).

At the northern extremity of the boat-shaped plateau of Masada, three levels of rock terraces were utilized as the foundations of Herod's enlarged complex, and these structures were adorned with wall-paintings, of which those at the lower end are relatively well preserved. At the western end of the plateau rose a palace – with fine mosaic floors – comprising the king's personal quarters, additional domestic accommodation, and store-rooms. These apartments were grouped round a central court, which opened through a colonnaded entrance into the royal throne-room and audience chamber. Moreover, Masada also contained a public bath suite and a two-chambered edifice which has been identified as a synagogue – if the identification is correct, it is the earliest that has been traced. Twelve cisterns, fed by two aqueducts from seasonal watercourses (wadis), reflect Herod's efforts to deal with the problem of water supply.

Sextus Lucilius Bassus died before he could tackle the insurgents in Masada, and it was not until early in 73 that his successor, Flavius Silva, set up his headquarters in the neighbourhood. The besieged Jews inside the fortress totalled 967 persons, including women and children; perhaps 500 were fighting men. But the Romans were determined to exterminate them, so that none should be left at large (as had happened after the falls of Jerusalem and Machaerus) to rekindle the embers of revolt. Furthermore, a rapid conclusion was imperative, since the Roman army's supplies of food and water had to be brought in with considerable difficulty, from a distance (a task allotted to Jewish prisoners). Also, from May onwards the intense summer heat made the troops' position almost intolerable.

Flavius Silva, therefore, after setting up his headquarters to the east of Masada, promptly constructed a series of additional camps. That is to say, he planted a second large camp to the south-east of the main one, constructed six smaller camps as well, and then built a two-mile circumvallation to link the camps together and block possible escape routes. The outlines of all these camps are visible when looked down upon from Masada. Four small forts were also constructed to guard a mountain pass to the north. Since timber was unavailable, the material used for the building of these camps and forts was local stone. Their rubble walls averaged five feet in thickness and still stand about five feet high, which is probably about half their original height.

Inside the camps the soldiers were housed in semi-permanent barracks with similar rubble walls, two feet thick, and originally surmounted by tented roofs. The best-preserved of these walls are two feet high. Once again, this seems to be about half their initial height, which was sufficient to offer more headroom than an ordinary tent, thus providing greater coolness by day and warmth by night.

Each mess-unit (*contubernium*) was equipped with a triple couch (*triclinium*) of earth and stones, used both for sleeping and eating. The soldiers' cooking was performed on an external hearth in front of each unit, while baking was done over small fire-holes, which consumed a minimum amount of fuel. The *triclinium* in the tent of the commanding officer and provincial governor (*praetorium*) measured 20 × 26 feet. In front of his tent stood a dais and spaces for altars and standards, with guards' quarters beside them. Civilian settlements or encampments (*canabae*), including shops, were scattered over the surrounding hillsides. Another feature of the Masada camps was the provision of training facilities for the soldiers. These included scale models of various kinds of gateways and ramparts, designed to show them how to construct field encampments under siege conditions.

Thus archaeology – that is to say, its important military branch – shows us what the Romans' camps were like; and next it goes on to perform the same function in regard to the siege that now followed. 'In the study of warfare', comment the authors of *Past Worlds*, 'archaeology is circumstantial and is thus, to some extent, able to avoid the bias inherent in historical accounts written by victor and vanquished. It provides detailed information about military technology, on which written records are often vague or uninformative . . . Archaeology can also throw considerable light on the course of individual battles and military operations. The most common examples are sieges where the excavation of a city or fortress may encounter evidence of attack or destruction. In some cases these archaeological traces can be linked with a known historical event. The fortress of Masada in Israel . . . is a spectacular example.'[11]

Masada's excavation was led by the Israeli general and professor Yigael Yadin. His operations continued for eleven months, extending over two seasons in 1963–4 and 1964–5. Despite the inaccessibility of the place, its remoteness in the wilderness, and its harsh climate, the task was a privilege, he declared. This was 'because it had been the dream of every Israeli archaeologist to fathom the secrets of Masada; and because an archaeological dig here was unlike an excavation of any other site in antiquity. Its scientific importance was known to be great. But more than that, Masada represents, for all of us in Israel and for many elsewhere, archaeologists and laymen, a symbol of courage, a monument to our great national figures, heroes who chose death over a life of physical and moral serfdom.'[12]

This brings us into the domains of what may be called patriotic archaeology. It is true that many other excavations and projects are conducted with some thought for their national implications and advantages, but in some such projects the patriotic aim is dominant, and a primary motivation. Nor are they necessarily, on balance, the worse for that, since even if the resultant interpretations have to be taken with a grain of salt, at least the operations will have received full governmental encouragement, with all the financial benefits that then ensue. One example was Mussolini's determination to push ahead with the rediscovery of ancient Rome. Yadin's exploration of Masada, in particular his reconstruction of its capture, belonged to the same patriotic category – and was likewise backed by extensive resources.

When the time came for the Romans to press on with the siege, one whole legion was allocated to the complicated engineering tasks involved, which must have required at least a week, or perhaps two. The manning of the circumvallation, therefore, presumably fell instead to the auxiliaries (foreign non-legionaries) who customarily operated alongside legions – or instead of them – and who were no doubt stationed in the subsidiary camps. Some of these camps were planned solely as patrol forts, whereas others have gates opening towards Masada, and were intended to protect the circumvallation against possible sorties.

The defenders evidently expected an attempt by the Romans to scale the rock of Masada by the precipitous and tortuous 'snake-path' on its eastern side, or even up the cliffs to the south, for they amassed piles of small rocks above these points, to be rolled down upon the enemy soldiers as they clambered up. But the rocks were never launched, for what Silva did instead – following the example of Bassus at Machaerus – was to erect an earthen assault-ramp or siege-mound to bring his artillery up to the level of the fortifications. This could only be done on the west side, at the 'White Spur' (*Leuce*), a chalk ridge with a hummock at its foot. This ridge formed a slope against the rocky fortress and provided an emplacement for *ballistae* (engines for throwing projectiles).

The function of this Roman artillery was to cover the construction, and use, of the assault-ramp. This artificial ramp was 675 feet long, and 700 feet tall. It rose to a height of 225 feet, at an incline of one in three. The ramp was crowned, Josephus tells us, by a stone platform 75 feet wide and high; the ends of transverse logs can still be seen towards the summit of the ramp. On the hummock at its foot, an iron-plated siege-tower was constructed. It was 90 feet high, and must have been at least 20 feet wide, so as to find room both for a massive battering ram and for siege artillery, which would be jointly launched against the wall once the tower had reached the platform at the top of the ramp.

By April, AD 73, the tower, thus equipped, had been dragged up onto the platform, and the assault began. First of all, a shower of small stone cannon-balls, launched by the artillery, drove the Jewish defenders back from their wall. Then the ram, too, got to work with relentless, smashing force, and so the ramparts were breached. Behind their wall the Jews, when the ramp construction indicated where the attack was going to be made, had built a second, emergency defensive barrier of earth and timber.

How they did this, and the unexpected failure of the barrier, is described by Josephus. 'Even the engines were likely to find [this second wall] a tougher proposition: it was pliant and capable of absorbing the impetus of the blows owing to its peculiar construction. Huge baulks were laid lengthwise and fastened together at the ends: these were in two parallel rows separated by the width of a wall and with the space between filled with earth. So that the soil should not fall out as the height increased, they laid beams across the long baulks to secure them.

'To the enemy the rampart looked like a normal construction, but the blows of the engines falling on yielding earth were absorbed: the concussion shook it together and made it more solid. Seeing this, Silva decided that fire was the best weapon against such a wall, and instructed his men to direct a volley of burning torches at it. Being made mostly of wood, it soon caught fire: owing to its loose construction, the whole thickness was soon ablaze, and a mass of flame shot up. Just as the fire broke out, a gust of wind from the north alarmed the Romans. It blew back the flame from above and drove it in their faces, and as their engines seemed on the point of being consumed in the blaze they were plunged into despair. Then, all of a sudden, as if by divine providence, the wind veered to the south, and blowing strongly in the reverse direction carried and flung the flames against the wall, turning it into one solid blazing mass.'[13] Soon there was a yawning breach in the emergency wall, and well might Josephus add that God was indeed on the side of the Romans.

The next morning Silva's troops threw gangways across the breach and entered the fortress, which was then set on fire, as excavations have shown. Josephus tells how the rebel commander, Eleazar ben Yair, induced his men to kill themselves and their families so that no one should fall into Roman hands: only two women and five children survived to tell the tale.[14] What really happened, however, it has instead been suggested, was that Silva's soldiers, when they broke in, slaughtered everyone they could find, that the few who escaped this fate starved to death (hence the twenty-five skeletons of men, women and children found in the south cliff face), and that Josephus's version is a fabrication turning the final Jewish defeat into glory, and at the same time absolving the Romans – to whom he had defected – of the massacre of women and children.[15]

Finds dating from the last catastrophic day of the besieged garrison include arrows, a gold breastplate, religious and secular scrolls, fragments of pottery inscribed with personal names, pieces of fabrics and baskets, leather sandals, and a young woman's plaited hair. With all Jewish resistance now at an end, the Romans could bring permanent military arrangements for the province into force. As for Masada, Roman troops remained, for a few months, in a corner of Silva's headquarters camp, while preparing quarters for a new garrison.

4 Herculaneum: Skeletons

The eruption of Mount Vesuvius in Campania in AD 79 overwhelmed sites that have been uncovered only by recent excavations, notably Stabiae (Castellamare di Stabia) and Oplontis (Chapter 5, section 6). But the two famous Cities of Vesuvius – Pompeii and Herculaneum – have continued to add to their inexhaustible store of archaeological material. At Pompeii the new discoveries have been numerous. At Herculaneum, work has been devoted to the areas already excavated, but something else has happened there as well.

The town of Herculaneum – the Greek Herakleion or Heraklanon, now Ercolano beside Resina – stood about five miles from Neapolis (Naples) on the bay named after that city (in ancient times the Gulf of Cumae), upon a spur projecting from the lower slopes of Mount Vesuvius, beside the coast road. Cumae (Cuma) and later Neapolis exercised dominant influences upon the town, and then, still in early times, Italian peoples (Oscans, Etruscans and Samnites) had successively made their appearance. Shortly before 300 BC the Romans took over from the Samnites, whom they had defeated. During the Social War, however – the revolt of the Italians against the Romans (91–87 BC) – Herculaneum, along with Pompeii, joined the uprising. After the rebellion had been defeated, it was occupied by the forces of Sulla (89 BC), and was henceforward a Roman citizen community (*municipium*).

Although the population of Herculaneum probably did not exceed four or five thousand,[16] it became a successful holiday resort, its promontory being favourably placed to catch the south-western breezes. But its buildings suffered severely in an earthquake in AD 62, and were totally destroyed by the eruption of Vesuvius on August 24–25, AD 79. This monstrous eruption has now been reconstructed, with new findings, by Haraldur Sigurdsson. 'For nearly eleven hours', he concludes, 'the volcano hurled a column of pumice twelve miles into the stratosphere. Day became night as Pompeii took on more than six inches of ash and pumice an hour. Then, about midnight, the column collapsed for the first time, sending down the mountainside a glowing avalanche of superheated gases, pumice and rocks. The avalanche separated into a fast-moving surge – which blasted through Herculaneum, killing its residents – and a slower, ground-hugging pyroclastic flow [flow of fragmentary volcanic products]. Not until the fourth avalanche the next morning did a suffocating surge reach Pompeii.'[17]

Although closer than Pompeii to Vesuvius's summit, Herculaneum must have been spared the initial shower of ash and pumice, since only dustings of those substances are found on the site. No doubt, however, its inhabitants had already become alarmed when they first saw fiery cascades descending the mountainside – though they evidently had only the shortest notice of what was about to happen to them, since otherwise a baby would not have been abandoned in its crib, and a sick child in a bed. For, as Sigurdsson noted, the more rapid of the two halves of the avalanche obliterated Herculaneum very quickly, before Pompeii, and indeed in the middle of the previous night (which is why one of the fugitives was carrying a lamp). The first onslaught – the fast-moving surge – must have killed everyone in the town. They were already dead when the second half of the avalanche – the full heat of the pyroclastic flow – made its impact shortly afterwards.

Whether anyone at Herculaneum, sensing what was to come, managed to escape by sea we cannot tell. We do know, however, that just before the catastrophe some tried to do so, and actually reached the shore. 'Previously', writes J.J. Deiss, 'it had been thought that almost all the inhabitants of Herculaneum had been able to flee towards Naples (Neapolis) before the volcanic avalanche closed in. Now, from continuing excavations along the marina, it is known that hundreds of persons clustered on the waterfront in a desperate effort to escape by sea. There they were overtaken by a violent ground surge: winds of hurricane force combined with waves of volcanic matter hot enough to scorch or carbonize. Their bodies were sealed while they died of asphyxiation... The horror and pathos of these last moments can now be shared.'[18] For at the beach – now 500 yards inland – a boat was overturned by these convulsions. The boat has now been excavated, from beneath 75 feet of volcanic matter. It was underneath and beside its hull that the skeletons have been discovered.

The analysis of human remains has long been a feature of archaeology, and 'there is little doubt', says David Wilson, 'that the most successful study of man in archaeological terms has been the study of the disease-states of ancient peoples.'[19] Palaeopathology, the study of human bones found on ancient sites, enables significant conclusions to be drawn about age, state of health, social circumstances – including working and nutritional conditions – and life-expectation. Yet a complete Roman skeleton, points out Deiss, 'has proved one of the rarest of archaeological finds, chiefly because the Romans practised cremation after death'.[20] At Herculaneum, however, sudden catastrophe had prevented any possibility of orderly cremation. But there too, until recently, few traces of the people who lived at the town and were overwhelmed by the eruption of AD 79 had ever been found. Since 1982, however, after well over two hundred of their skeletons have been unearthed on what was then the sea-front – to which they had in vain fled – a remarkable opportunity has been offered for the physical characteristics and defects of ancient Italians to receive careful study.

Every technical expedient has been utilized to preserve these skeletons. Sara Bisel washed and dried the skeletons, dipped them, bone by bone, into an acrylic resin solution to prevent them from crumbling, and then put the bones together again. 'They came to me so well preserved', she writes, 'because they have been kept continuously wet by groundwater percolating through the volcanic soil. Perfectly sealed, they endured no temperature or humidity changes. For the earth that covered Herculaneum, moistened by the groundwater that flows down Vesuvius, has sealed and preserved the town far better than the pumice blanket that lay over Pompeii. The wet earth was what kept Herculaneum's skeletons in such good condition. For as the bodies decayed, the mud solidified around the bones, rather than leaving empty hollows as at ash-covered Pompeii.'[21]

Twelve skeletons, huddled in embraces, came from what has been described as 'the household in flight'. They included three adult men, whose ages have been estimated as thirty-five, thirty-one and twenty-five, and four females of about forty-two, thirty-eight, sixteen and fourteen. There were also five children. 'The three-year-old was wearing gold-and-pearl earrings. The five-year-old had cavities and an abscess.' The skeleton of a seven-month-old baby was discovered as well. 'It wore jewellery and was being cradled by the fourteen-year-old, who I suspect was a slave ... Scars on the upper shafts of her humeri ... means that she used those muscles for heavier work than she should have ... Grooves on her teeth indicate that she didn't get enough to eat when she was about eleven months old. She almost died either from illness or starvation.'

A man found next to the overturned boat has been described as the 'Helmsman'. The large crests on his bones, where the deltoid muscles [those of the shoulder that lift the upper arm] attached, show that he had done heavy work in his lifetime. The fusion of six of his middle thoracic vertebrae points to heavy strains on his arms and back. And his rotting teeth must have kept him in continual pain. Furthermore Herculaneum, adds Deiss, 'produced the only extant Roman soldier. He was well nourished, strong and tough, and carried carpentry tools. His forearms displayed a heavy muscle build-up, and he had the muscles for bareback riding. He had had a flesh wound in his left thigh, and three of his front teeth had been knocked out. He seems to have been well off; he wore not only a sword in a scabbard, but two elaborate belts, and carried three gold coins and some silver.'[22]

The 'Ring Lady' was a relatively tall woman of about forty-five, well nourished and wearing jewellery, but suffering from periodontal disease (disease of the soft tissues round the teeth). Another woman, 'Portia', whose skeleton was the first to be unearthed, 'had a great fall. She clearly landed on her face from some distance. There are roof tiles beneath her. Her thigh-bones were thrust up to her clavicles... Portia was about forty-eight, certainly not good looking. She had extreme buck teeth. Also, certain of her pelvic bones show rather unusual and unexpected changes. I do not like to make accusations across 2,000 years, but Portia's pelvic bones resemble those I once saw from a modern prostitute.'[23]

The men at Herculaneum, it has been concluded, averaged 5 ft 7 in. in height, the women 5 ft 1½ in. Out of twenty-six adults, five had suffered some trauma or injury. Moreover, in Portia's bones, and someone else's too, there was a high level of lead, and six more skeletons exhibited an excessive amount of the same metal. Lead water-pipes have been blamed in this connection, and, perhaps, the drinking of sweetened poor-quality wine (made from grape juice boiled down in lead vessels). This does not mean, however, as some have supposed, that the Roman empire subsequently fell because of excessive lead intake. After all, the empire lasted for many centuries, throughout which the Romans never stopped ingesting lead. So why, if lead had anything to do with it, did they not collapse much earlier?

The torrid, treacly flow of matter that engulfed Herculaneum later cooled and solidified into a compact layer attaining a height, at certain points, of sixty feet. This covering ensured the preservation of wooden frameworks, furniture, cloth and foodstuffs. Since the eighteenth century, together with Pompeii, Herculaneum has been gradually disinterred. But more than half of it still remains buried – including all its temples (unlike Pompeii, where they are so prominent). The rest still lies beneath the closely packed modern town of Resina, perhaps for evermore. On what was once the beach, too, there may be hundreds more skeletons remaining to be found. The second unearthing, however, of the Villa of the Papyri outside the town, after two centuries, is under way and likely to prove most important (Appendix II, ii).

CHAPTER 8

THE MIDDLE EMPIRE

In the aftermath of the Civil Wars of AD 68–9, of which one of the side-effects was a Gallo-German revolt, Vespasian rebuilt the bridge across the River Mosella at Augusta Trevirorum (Trier), as an investigation of the relative ages of tree-rings has now demonstrated. In his reign, in those of his sons Titus and Domitian (79–81, 81–96) and in those of their successors in the following century (Trajan, Hadrian, Antoninus Pius, Marcus Aurelius) the empire enjoyed a long period of prosperity, ensured by occasional defensive and offensive fighting along the enormous frontiers. The life of a garrison on Hadrian's Wall has been reconstructed with the help of an extensive array of letters written on wooden tablets discovered at Vindolanda (Chesterholm). In Britain, again, and elsewhere upon the northern frontiers and in the east, it has become possible to reconstruct what the soldiers ate. On the Danube, excavations at Novae (Stăklen) have cast light on one of the principal river ports which served the Danubian fleet, part of the network of flotillas that worked together with the Roman army to keep watch over the boundaries of the empire and move troops to wherever military operations were needed.

One of the archaeological aids to historical knowledge is papyrology. Significant discoveries in this field have included a Greek novel, the *Phoenicica* of Lollianus, which enables us to look at the development of Greco-Roman fiction in a new light.

Moreover, the story of this epoch can also be illustrated by another technique: air photography. Of all the archaeological methods that have advanced during recent decades, air photography is outstanding, and has evoked a vast literature. It could be illustrated from any of the periods and many of the countries listed in this book. But here preference will be given to the contributions made by aerial surveys of the Samara (Somme) valley of Gallia Belgica (Picardy, in north-eastern France). It is not only buildings that such surveys reveal, but entire environmental complexes and patterns, thus fulfilling the insistence of the New Archaeology that it is with these interactions that archaeological research should concern itself (Appendix 1). Yet buildings remain important, too, and discoveries at Cruciniacum (Bad Kreuznach in Germany) have thrown new light on an essential aspect of their functioning, namely the water supply that served their occupants.

1 *Augusta Trevirorum (Trier): Tree-Rings and Bridge*

Augusta Trevirorum, now Trier in western Germany, was situated at a point where the River Mosella (Moselle) widens, and where three routes divided to reach the Rhenus (Rhine) at Colonia Agrippinensium (Köln), Confluentes (Koblenz) and Moguntiacum (Mainz). The settlement at the place which later became Augusta Trevirorum had access to rich natural resources, and was protected from attack by mountain barriers.

It had originally belonged to the tribe of the Treviri (Gallic with a strong German admixture), which furnished cavalry to Julius Caesar but gave him a good deal of trouble. When Augustus divided the Gallic regions conquered by Caesar (Gallia Comata, 'long-haired', excluding the older southern Roman province of Gallia Narbonensis, founded in *c.*121 BC) into three provincial administrations, the town fell within Gallia Belgica. In due course – unlike other centres in the area – it came to assume a civilian character, and was the home of the *procurator*, who controlled the financial affairs not only of Belgica but also of the two frontier provinces of Upper and Lower Germany, created (out of military zones) by Domitian in *c.* AD 90. Augusta Trevirorum was, therefore, for a variety of reasons, a key point.

Aware of its advantages, Augustus had refounded it in 17/16 BC, and so it took on the name of Augusta Trevirorum – and became the oldest city in Germany. He also built a wooden bridge across the Mosella to that part of the town which lay on the west bank, a bridge which linked the Gallic interior to the Rhineland. Excavations of the bridge during recent decades, and subsequent analyses, have yielded information about the successive ancient stages of its construction, and corrected earlier views.

The method employed to reach these conclusions has been tree-ring chronology (dendrochronology, dendroarchaeology). The yearly growth of trees in spring, writes C. Renfrew, 'produces a series of annual tree-rings in the wood. By counting these rings on a tree-stump, the age of the tree at the time of felling can be computed ... The different annual rings vary a good deal in density and thickness, depending on climatic factors ... Over a number of years a distinctive pattern of thick and thin rings is built up in the tree, and this pattern can be picked out in the wood of different trees in the same region ... Using distinctive sequences, one can link tree with tree, and build up a continuous sequence of tree-rings extending just as far back as there is wood available from trees long dead.'[1]

When trees grow in a variable climate, that is to say, in certain years growth-rings thinner or thicker than average will be formed. After earlier preliminaries, it was shown in 1929 that this variation could be employed to determine the dates of wooden objects turned up by excavations. This was demonstrated in the south-western United States where, by matching the ring pattern of timbers originating from a limited area and therefore exhibiting the same climatic variations, it proved possible to construct a master-plot which carried back from the present to much earlier times. Any timber collected from one of the sites concerned could be dated by matching the rings against the plot.

This method was founded on the fact that trees add a growth ring for every year of their lives – large cells in early spring and early summer, small cells in late summer and autumn, no growth (standstill) during winter. By comparing a series of rings *from a tree of known date* with a series from an earlier, dead tree (of hitherto unknown date), it was found that ring patterns from the centre layers of the dated tree, and others from the outer layers of the undated tree, might show a correlation which could fix the period, even the year, when the felling and cutting of the older, undated tree had taken place. That is to say, the 'floating' date for that tree, which was all that could have been achieved before (i.e. a purely relative, subjective date based on the relationship between one tree and another) could be replaced by a precise, objective date anchored to specific years. And this type of deduction does not apply to America alone, since it has also proved possible to extend the technique to other parts of the world where seasonal climatic fluctuations are sufficiently extensive.

Dendrochronology has been extremely important in its use as a check and corrective to the system of radiocarbon (C14) dating that has dominated prehistoric archaeology in recent years. But in other respects, too, dendrochronological investigations have proved of enormous assistance – on the condition, it must be repeated, that some of the rings can be independently dated (and subject to other provisos as well: 'above all', observes Jane McIntosh, 'care must be taken to establish how the piece of wood being dated relates to the structure from which it derives. For example, timber may have been freshly cut to repair a centuries-old building; conversely, a new structure may incorporate old timbers.'[2] Romans, however, unlike many of their modern successors, generally used freshly sawn wood for construction purposes.)

A pioneer instance of the application of this method was provided by Novgorod the Great in Russia, where sequences have been produced going back to medieval times. The classical epoch, too, has also proved rewarding, a notable example being supplied by the bridge at Augusta

Trevirorum. Traces of its structures were found in 1921, and in 1959–64 canalizing operations in the river produced remains of wooden bridge-piles, now preserved in the Wood Archive (Holzarchiv) of the local Landesmuseum.

Dendrochronological study has been devoted to these remains, but without, until recently, anything more than 'floating' results (see above), owing to the absence of the sort of independent check that is required in order to produce a 'firm' dating. At first, the successive phases of the bridge's construction were dated to 18/17 BC (Augustan bridge built on pile foundations), AD 44 (Claudius), and AD 144 (Antoninus Pius). Since then, however, an independent, comparative dendrochronological check has moved the second of these dates from AD 44 (Claudius) to AD 71 (Vespasian). The breakthrough to this point was made possible in 1975 by studying a Frankish (Merovingian) chamber-tomb at Beerlegem in Belgium, south of Ghent.

More than two hundred tests have determined precisely what the history of the Trier bridge was. The oak post (10 x 12 in.) determining the initial date of 18/17 BC came to light in 1963, and was in perfect condition. This first bridge, of which the dating prompted the modern people of Trier to fix their bimillenary year in 1984, was of simple design, but construction techniques were already fairly well advanced. At the second stage, in AD 71 – the date which Beerlegem has been able to provide –the construction was a good deal more complex, and involved the use of stone piles. This Vespasianic rebuilding of AD 71, in all probability, was necessitated by the partial destruction of the first bridge during the rebellion of AD 69–70, one of the principal leaders of which was the Treviran chief Julius Classicus (this first bridge is mentioned in Tacitus's description of the revolt[3]). The third epoch of construction, in AD 144 under Antoninus Pius, comprised the erection, only a few yards upstream – of a stone bridge, for which the way was prepared by driving in wooden caissons (structures for keeping water out), of which specimens are preserved in the Landesmuseum. Antoninus's bridge was typical of the fine bridges which played such an effective part in Rome's communications system. Its substructures can still be seen supporting the busy modern bridge, so that this 'Römerbrücke' retains to this day its ancient function and character.

Augusta Trevirorum became a vital strategic, economic, industrial and cultural centre. Its time of greatest pre-eminence, in the fourth century AD, is still represented today by the most impressive Roman architectural achievements anywhere north of the Alps.

2 Vindolanda (Chesterholm): Writings on Wood

Vindolanda, now Chesterholm (Northumberland), was a fort for auxiliary non-Roman troops at the northern extremity of the province of Britannia. A section of its wall has been reconstructed to its original height of fifteen feet, with a two-storey turret. The fort was established by Cnaeus Julius Agricola, father-in-law of the historian Tacitus and governor of Britain from 78 to 83 – less than forty years after the annexation of the province – as part of his frontier defence system. A part-mounted Dalmatian auxiliary cohort seems, at first, to have been housed there. The army evacuated the fort, however, when the garrison was transferred to Hadrian's Wall, a mile to the north (122–6). But Antoninus Pius, who erected a more northerly wall (142), later reoccupied Vindolanda. Septimius Severus (193–211) rebuilt its fort, and it was again reconstructed in *c.* 300 by Diocletian's deputy emperor (Caesar) Constantius I Chlorus, to whose time most of the visible remains, covering 3½ acres, belong.

Since 1973, however, discoveries dating from the earlier periods of the place's history have also been made. For while digging a drainage ditch beneath the two civilian settlements outside the wall fort, archaeologists found by chance, between eight and fourteen feet down, the remains of the late first-century fort which had been built by Agricola.

The officers who lived in the fort, and their women and children whose possessions, in fragmentary condition, have come to light, seem not to have lived too badly, despite their geographical remoteness. There were central heating arrangements, and there were baths; civilians, including women, were allowed to use the military bath building. A sauna was constructed, and flush lavatories. A *mansio* – official posting station or hotel – housed travellers on imperial business. As regards the soldiers' eating habits, bones of hares and thrushes have come to light, and shells of oysters and mussels; on this subject more will be said below.

Moreover, the soil conditions of the site, upon which new layers of turf were deposited every time the Romans reconstructed the fort, have enabled fabrics, feathers, hair and insects to be preserved – and, particularly, objects made of leather. For example, there came to light a fine apron-pouch for tools, and numerous shoes – including a lady's elegant slipper, which, like other footwear found on the site, displays the maker's stamp. Nearly three-quarters of these shoes have a Roman, metropolitan appearance, while the rest seem to have been made on the spot. The site has yielded a quantity of evidence for local leather-working, not just manufacture, but also de-hairing and tanning with the assistance of excrement and urine, the remains of which were detected spread over the floor (cf. section 7 below).

Perhaps the most important finds at Vindolanda, however, are portions of wooden writing tablets coming from this early, pre-Hadrianic stratum. They were found in a large wooden edifice, perhaps the *praetorium* (commander's residence). Wood is preserved only in especially favourable circumstances. 'That the tablets were preserved at all', write A. K. Bowman and J. D. Thomas, 'was due to the fact that the soil conditions in that part of the site were such that very little organic deterioration had taken place; traces of chlorophyll could still be seen in some of the bracken and gorse pods.'[4]

Rapidly treated, since they were fragile and soon faded on exposure to the air, these fragments of wood, when photographed under infra-red light (chapter 6, section 4), displayed traces of inscriptions. Some of the fragments were thin, wafer-like slices on which a reed or quill pen, and carbon ink (vegetable gum mixed with water and soot), had been employed for the writing. But most of the tablets were thicker, and had been carved out to create a surface which was treated with wax and then written upon with iron pens (*stili*).

Most of these Vindolanda tablets measured about $4\frac{1}{2} \times 3\frac{3}{4}$ in. The writings detected on their surface proved to be in cursive script, without standard spelling, or word division, or punctuation. Given the difficulties presented by this sort of script, and the defective condition of the tablets, their decipherment has been hard. When it was completed, however, there emerged a large number of texts. Attributable to the years between AD 85/90 and *c.* 130, and in most cases between 95 and 105, they comprised both private letters and official correspondence relating to military affairs – the work of no less than six hundred hands.

'Some 1200 documents have been found so far,' Robin Birley, director of the Vindolanda Trust, has written to me, 'of which 200 are stylus tablets with a few legible addresses and so far unreadable multiple texts. Of the remaining 1000, written in ink, the majority are small fragments of shredded material. Some 200, however, are either complete or have substantial surviving texts. There are a number of different categories: incoming mail to prefects [commanders of auxiliary units or camp commandants], wives of prefects, officers and men; draft letters with corrections, by prefects; a *pridianum* [see below] and a variety of daily reports by *optiones* [adjutants] to the prefect; requests by soldiers for leave or travelling expenses; lists of stores – food, clothing and equipment – issued to a variety of soldiers; daily work schedules; accounts and receipts; intelligence reports; a child's writing exercise; and a variety of miscellaneous items.'[5]

A letter, addressed to a certain Cerialis who may have been the commanding officer of the fort, appears to be a letter of recommendation, composed on behalf of a new recruit or young officer. A further communication refers to goods brought to, or bought for, the recipient, including sandals, woollen socks (or felt slippers) and two pairs of underpants. The writer also requests that his greetings should be conveyed to a number of people and to 'all your fellow-soldiers'. Another letter, which is, unusually, written on both sides of a piece of wood, may have been the first draft of which a fair copy was subsequently made and dispatched. Addressed to a certain Crispinus, it expresses the hope that he will satisfy the writer's high expectations. Views about the conditions of military service are added.

A recently discovered 4-page, 45-line letter on birch or alder wood (not the more usual lime), the longest Roman letter ever discovered, comes from a certain Octavius. From somewhere unknown, he addresses his friend Candidus at Vindolanda, complaining that an expected consignment of 5,000 bushels of grain has failed to arrive. 'I need money for this,' he writes. 'Unless you send me some money, at least 500 *denarii* [silver pieces], I shall lose what I have paid out of my own pocket, that's about 300 *denarii*, and I shall be financially embarrassed. So please send me some money as quickly as you can.' Octavius then asks for some cattle-hides at present located at Cataractonium (Catterick) also to be dispatched. 'I would already have fetched them,' he says, 'but I didn't want to cause difficulties for the mules as the roads are bad.' Perhaps this letter was written during the winter. 'One would hope', remarked David Thomas, the papyrologist who with Alan Bowman translated many of the Vindolanda tablets, 'that in London [Londinium] and Colchester [Camulodunum] the roads would be much better, but up here, where they had conquered only twenty years previously, they were just getting the roads in.'

A senior officer's wife sends a message to another, whom she addresses as 'sister'. The writer is Claudia Severa, who invites Lepedina to her birthday party, 'to make the day more enjoyable for me because of your arrival, if you come'. This is the earliest known example of writing in Latin by a woman. There are also tablets that offer enlightenment about the administration of the garrison. One, consisting of seven leaves, of which three are complete, offers forty-five short lines of text. They begin with records of minor payments for some religious purpose (which is unusual, since on the whole religion – like fighting, and the emperor – is a subject absent from these letters). But the main part of the document is a requisition for food and drink, of a variety of kinds. Wine is specified, of differing qualities, including *acetum*, sour wine, a soldier's regular drink. Beer, too, is mentioned, and so is pork-fat and fish-sauce. Much is also said about barley, which was apparently intended not as human food (it was a primitive diet for delinquents) but as animal fodder. Another, smaller, tablet refers to foodstuffs once again, listing spice, goat's meat, piglet, ham, venison, grain, flour and salt. Local discoveries include duck feathers and cabbages: see next section, where it is also suggested that the consumption of meat was not always reserved for special occasions, as had been thought.

New finds include the *pridianum* to which Birley referred – a periodical strength report (on a specially prepared thin slice of oak-wood). It records that more than a dozen soldiers stationed at Vindolanda were suffering from pink-eye (conjunctivitis). They belonged to a cohort of Tungrians (Germans) from north-eastern Gaul (Gallia Belgica); it was nominally 750 strong, but only 270 were present at Vindolanda, and ten per cent of them were ill. Other types of official correspondence also appear, including accounts and daily work schedules. In addition, there are applications to go on leave – often to the larger military centres, such as Pons Aelius (Newcastle). Daily reports from junior officers to their commandant appear as well. At Vindolanda everything was listed and itemized, down to the last vinegar bowl and salt cellar. A letter that appears to be an intelligence report refers, in derogatory fashion, to the natives as *Brittunculi*, 'little Brits', commenting that they rely excessively on cavalry, do not use swords, and fail to take up fixed positions to throw javelins.

At some stage, for a reason unknown, the files of the commanding officer's quarters were evidently deposited in a rubbish dump. A number of the documents seem to have been ripped up by their recipients, and others were found in drainage areas, suggesting that they had been flushed away. Since only eight per cent of the surface of Vindolanda has so far been excavated, many thousands of additional tablets, of historical importance, no doubt still await discovery.

Not many other parts of the empire were wet enough to preserve writings on wood. True, other examples had been found elsewhere (including a few in Britain), but such earlier finds lacked the bulk and significance of those from Vindolanda. A number of tablets from Egypt, for instance, are too scattered, in both location and date, to invite any comprehensive view; whereas documents from Pompeii and Dacia (Rumania) lack variety (being concerned with auctioneering and sale transactions respectively). The Vindolanda texts, on the other hand, not only come from a single place and a single relatively brief period, but contain very varied material.

They throw light on the miltary organization of the camp during the years before and after AD 100 – a period for which no literary evidence exists. Indeed such evidence for Roman Britain as a whole is very scanty. But even if it was available, it would not be like the Vindolanda letters, for the fortuitous and day-to-day nature of these communications, sometimes written by quite humble persons, distinguishes them from the sort of thing that ancient writers provide. It distinguishes them, too, from the pronouncements provided by that better-known branch of epigraphy, comprising inscriptions on stone (Chapter 4, section 2). Such pronouncements committed to stone are, inevitably, more public and formal, whereas the Vindolanda letters reveal the private personalities and habits of Roman army men and their wives. They also add to our knowledge of the development of Latin writing – and of the Latin language as well, since these documents use the Latin which was being employed by ordinary Romans, different in many respects both from what we find in our classical authors, and from inscriptions engraved on stone.

3 The North and Wadi Fawakhir: A Soldier's Diet

As the authors of *Past Worlds* observe, 'availability and distribution of different types of food has had a powerful influence on the ways in which human societies have organized their annual round of everyday activities. The study of food is a critical element in the understanding of these societies and their development.'[6] Direct evidence may survive in different forms: animal bones (a branch of zooarchaeology), plant remains in a variety of contexts (palaeobotany), remains of shellfish, desiccated or fossilized excrement (coprolites), occasionally surviving prepared foods, implements and pots involved in their preparation, and representations of such activities and of the foodstuffs themselves in contemporary visual art. Thus food archaeology is essential to the prehistorian, but relevant to the classical archaeologist as well. Knowledge about Roman foods has been provided partly by discoveries at Pompeii and Herculaneum and partly by numerous other excavations of villas and farms in various parts of the empire, among which Francolise and Settefinestre have been singled out here (Chapter 5, section 5). Moreover, recent excavations, not only at Vindolanda, as we have just seen, but also, for example, at Betthorus as well, (Chapter 9, section 2), have identified the diet which supported the Roman soldiers in their marches and campaigns and conquests that created the empire.

Although it is sometimes believed that these soldiers did not usually eat meat except at festivals and feasts (for which deductions were made from their pay), it seems more accurate to suppose that they ate it, roast or boiled, at all times, whenever supplies were obtainable.[7] The bones of the domesticated ox are most frequently found. Sheep – and to a lesser extent goats – are also represented, and pork or ham was popular. Poultry, too, formed part of the diet. Roman soldiers ate fish as well, and liked fish sauces; and they were partial to sea-food.

Grain, however, served as their basic foodstuff – wheat, that is, not barley, which was a punishment diet. Grain had to be ground to form flour, and could be made, most obviously, into bread. But it was also employed as the basis of soups, porridge, and various forms of pasta. Campaign 'iron rations' took the form of hard biscuits known as *buccellati* (from *buccella*, a small mouthful). Each Roman soldier got through about a third of a ton of grain each year, occupying half a cubic yard of space in camp granaries – as excavations have shown. Every Roman fort in Britain had sufficient supplies to last a year, and in the third century the daily consumption of the British frontier forces was $33\frac{1}{2}$ tons. Cheese, salt and olive oil were also welcomed.

'Fruit', indicates David Breeze, 'included blackberries, strawberries, bilberries and cherries, while vegetables (most commonly beans and lentils) and nuts were also eaten. Both beer and wine were drunk. There were fixed times for the meals, which were probably a light breakfast and a main meal in the evening. While in theory each soldier was issued with his own food from the granaries, it seems probable that those soldiers in each barrack room who were off-duty cooked for those on duty. The cooking was carried out in hearths and ovens set into the rear of the ramparts. There were no communal messes in Roman forts so it seems probable that the troops either ate in the open or in their barrack rooms.'[8]

When on the march they were heavily laden, carrying – in addition to their military equipment – rations for three days, as well as a bronze food-box or mess-tin, a kettle or boiling pan, a spit, and perhaps a portable hand-mill. However, although a soldier baked his own bread, over hot stones or embers, and was sometimes encouraged to augment his meat by hunting, he did not have to do everything for himself. Army units often possessed grazing lands of their own round their forts, and there were soldiers known as *pecuarii* who looked after the animals. Indeed, a large number of men were occupied, permanently or temporarily, with the collection, distribution and payment of foodstuffs. The commander took overall responsibility for these operations – extorting or requisitioning or compulsorily purchasing supplies from civilians whenever necessary – and their logistics and efficiency were impressive. In many regions, soldiers were better fed than the local populations.

Elsewhere in this book it has been, and will be, customary to fasten and concentrate on single, individual sites or regions to illustrate archaeological operations that have contributed to history. In Rome's northern frontier provinces, however – when we continue to consider this question of military diet – it is necessary to depart from such an arrangement, since the evidence is spread widely over a number of different locations. Even within a single country our information comes from a variety of sources. This is the case, for example, in Britain. Graham Webster recorded his own findings at Waddon Hill in Dorsetshire. Here, bones were not particularly numerous. 'Cattle and sheep were present, but very little pig. Bird bones included doves and pigeons and a fair amount of fowl ... What was interesting and unusual was the quantity of fish bones, probably of the Giant Wrasse, which is today considered to be virtually inedible on account of its large number of bones.'[9] The Giant Wrasse – of which five teeth were discovered – although rather bony and nasty to eat, was probably chosen because of its resemblance to the Mediterranean Parrot Wrasse. Waddon Hill yielded 40 fragments of cattle, 49 of sheep or goat, 3 of pig, 4 of horse, 101 of hare (some, no doubt, the products of hunting for sport), 1 of fox, 1 of mouse, 450 of birds (including mallard, wader, rock dove or domestic pigeon, redwing, bantam, raven), 50 of fish, 1 of snail. Remains of shellfish, too, came to light, including both natural and cultivated oysters. The site also produced cockles and *venerupis*, a sort of clam.

At Viroconium Cornoviorum (Wroxeter), 220 pounds of animal bones have been recovered from the midden. Most of the meat consumed was beef, but a number of sheep and pig bones have also been discovered. There was one red deer to every eight cattle. Shellfish, obviously, was more available to units stationed near the sea, for example at Alauna (Maryport) and Arbeia (South Shields). Perch was eaten at Deva (Chester), and cod at Hod Hill. At Vindolanda (where letters cast additional light on what was eaten and drunk, see last section) duck feathers have been discovered, and cabbages were grown. The soldiers at Newstead consumed hazelnuts; and so did those at other centres, including Bar Hill, where walnuts also appeared, and Holt and Castleshaw, where sloes formed an additional part of the diet. The auxiliaries at Caersws ate cherries and blackberries. Wheat has been found at a number of centres, barley at Bremetennacum (Ribchester), and both at Newstead. At Bearsden on the Antonine Wall, where a Roman defensive ditch served as a cesspit, soldiers' excrement was found to include wheat fragments from bread or other farinaceous foods. 'In a store-hut in the military annexe,' records R. W. Davies, 'dated to the Flavian era and lying south of the fortress of Caerleon [Isca Silurum], the carbonized remains of various grains and other vegetable matter were discovered: cultivated barley and also a little wild barley, spelt, rye and wheat, while both cultivated and wild oats were found, apparently as weeds rather than food, and also lentils, horsebeans and various weeds. Most of these weeds were not indigenous to Britain, and so must have been imported with the cereals. Dr Helback has concluded that the Romans probably intended to sow the lentils and rye, but that the grain was to be malted to make beer (*cervesa*). Clearly beer must have been a popular drink for the Roman troops; a discharged marine of the *classis Germanica* [German fleet] set himself up to supply beer to the military market towards the end of the first century.' Beer was not the only drink, however – a high-class white wine, Aminean, found its way to Isca Silurum as well.

Evidence also comes from the German frontier region. 'Recent analysis of vegetable matter recovered from the legionary fortress of Novaesium (Neuss),' continues Davies, 'which is mostly dated to the first century and often to before AD 69, has revealed a clear picture of the military diet. Quantities of wheat, barley, wild oats (probably used as fodder, as was hay and some other crops) were found, as well as broad beans, beans, lentils, garlic, and various salt plants (sorrel, nipplewort [a yellow-flowered weed]), plus grapes and elderberries and hazelnuts. Particularly noteworthy were four plants that had been deliberately introduced into Germany by the Romans: rice, chickpea, olive and fig.

'However, perhaps the most interesting finds came from the camp hospital (*valetudinarium*) [see also section 4 below]. In addition to five medicinal plants, the remains of lentils, garden peas, and figs were discovered, all prescribed by medical authorities for a diet for invalids. Earlier excavation in the hospital had revealed evidence for a sick diet of meat, eggs and oysters. This confirms the statements of Vegetius that not only was poultry to be kept for the benefit of the sick but that they were to be brought back to health by means of an appropriate diet. This included wine; not a few barrels of special wine were imported from outside the local customs zone to the legionary fortress at Aquincum (Budapest).'[10]

Elsewhere on the German frontier, Vindonissa (Windisch in Switzerland) has provided varied food remains. The oysters discovered there came either from Lusitania (Portugal) or the Fretum Gallicum (English Channel). Fish-bones were accompanied by a hook, with which catches were made in the River Arura (Aare) beside Vindonissa. Some of the wine drunk by the garrison there came from Surrentum (Sorrento) – it was 'very old', *pervetus* – and other wine came from Messana (Messina; formerly Zancle), while a third variety may have been a sort of fruit cocktail. For the Vindonissa legionaries ate numerous kinds of fruit – apples, pears, plums, cherries, peaches, grapes and elderberries. Their vegetables included beans, peas, lentils and carrots, as well as various nuts (sweet chestnuts, walnuts, hazelnuts and beechnuts).

At the other end of the empire, remote Wadi Fawakhir in the Eastern Desert of Upper Egypt, upon the road from Coptos (Qift) to the Mare

Erythraeum or Sinus Arabicus (the Red Sea), has proved particularly informative. There, just north of the village of Bir Fawakhir, remains of the stone huts of a Roman gold-miners' camp stretch as far as the eye can see. The investigation of mines often yields significant archaeological results. In the land of Egypt it was proverbial, among the other nations of the near east, that gold was as dust. The terrible working conditions of the Nubian mines have gained notoriety from the pages of Diodorus Siculus,[11] and conditions in these mines of the Upper Egyptian desert are unlikely to have been any better.

Here, however, as the Roman watch-towers along the road still remind us, we are concerned not with the mining community, but with the auxiliary troops who guarded its zone. They wrote letters, many of which have been discovered, on *ostraca*, potsherds or fragments of pottery. In the classical epoch of Greece, potsherds had not been habitually employed for writing, except as voting tablets at Athens. But after Alexander the Great's conquest of Egypt the custom grew apace in that country, and Upper Egypt thenceforward remained at all periods the most abundant source of inscribed *ostraca* – to be found in rubbish-mounds and the ruins of houses.

The number of soldiers' letters on *ostraca* discovered at Wadi Fawakhir amounts to nearly a hundred, if not more. They are almost exclusively concerned with food. It might seem that their description here, in a book concerned with the discoveries of the last three decades is cheating, since most of these letters were published in 1942. But it was R. W. Davies, some twenty-eight years later, who read them correctly and accurately. Their Latin is noteworthy, like that of the letters at Vindolanda (Chapter 8, section 2), and so is the information with which they provide us.

'Valerius wrote to Julius about the purchase of barley. Lupercus had sent straw to Licinius and hoped to receive oil in return, and had also sent a salad plant called purslane. Rufus had sent Silvanus oil. Someone said that he had received eight slices of salted fish but that Clemens had not received one *artab* of barley, a jar of mustard, or three *matia* of onions, but that the writer had in fact received a bundle of cabbages. Another anonymous person wrote to Terentius and Atticus that he had received a bunch of radishes (a type used as a purge or emetic) and was sending gourds and citron.

'Antonius Proculus wrote to Valerianus to say that he had been hunting all species of wild animals and birds and had sent his catches to him via Cerealis; on the back of this letter gardening is mentioned. Someone and Apollinarius wrote to Priscus to acknowledge receipt of a bundle of cabbage (a different type) and a bunch of eating-grapes. Someone sent an empty bag with apologies for not having found anything to put in it, while someone else asked for fodder to feed his horse, plus half an *artab* of something and condiments. Thermouthis asked Orion to draw the other half *artab* of corn from the granary, add half a *mation* to it, and send it to Menandros. Longinus had received several *matia* of mustard, and asked a friend to buy him half a *congius* of radish-oil and the same amount of something else.

'Castor Chesthotes asked his friend to give the soldier Papirius, who delivered the letter, as much wine as he wanted and also some little sacks, presumably with food inside them. Harbekis had received kidney-beans and probably other vegetables; Capito was sending Silurius Priscus five *artabs* of something; Parabolus asked Zosimes and Schyras to send an *artab* of barley. Papirius sent six obols to Demetrius in payment for vegetables that had been sent. Turanis asked his father Antonius to get him an *artab* of barley; reference is also apparently made to tunny fish (small ones) and the herb all-heal. Someone wrote to Niger mentioning a wine-measure and a sucking pig, Valerius mentioned an *artab* of barley and coconuts, an anonymous person cabbage and perhaps flat fish, while Germanus is apparently mentioned in connection with vegetables, and someone else in connection with cooked fish.

'The most interesting of the letters are a set of five from Rustius Barbarus to his friend Pompeius. In a fragmentary one he mentions bread and a basket, in another bread and salt. However, the other three are better preserved:

' "Rustius Barbarus to Pompeius, greetings. Why on earth haven't you written back to me, if you received the loaves? I sent you 15 loaves by Popilius and Dutuporis and also 15 loaves – and a jar – by Draco, the carter. You used up four *matia*! I sent you 6 loaves by Thiadices, the trooper, who said he could take them. Please get some weights – as beautiful as possible – made for my personal use and write to me so that in payment for them I can make you some bread or send you the money, whichever you prefer. I want you to know that I am getting married. As soon as I am, I'll write to you straight away to come." '

' "Rustius Barbarus to Pompeius, greetings. First of all I pray that you are in good health. Why do you write me such a nasty letter? Why do you think I am so thoughtless? If you did not send me the green vegetables so quickly, must I immediately forget your friendship? I am not like that, or thoughtless either. I think of you, not as a pal, but as a twin brother, the same flesh and blood. It's a term I give you quite often in my letters, but you think of me in a different light. I have received bunches of cabbage and one cheese. I have sent you by Arrianus, the trooper, a box, inside which is one cake and a *denarius* (?) wrapped in a small cloth. Please buy me a *mation* of salt and send it to me without delay, because I want to bake some bread." '[12]

5.3a View of Orbetello and the Argentario, showing the two lateral sandbars closing the lagoon which in ancient times was a harbour opening onto the sea.

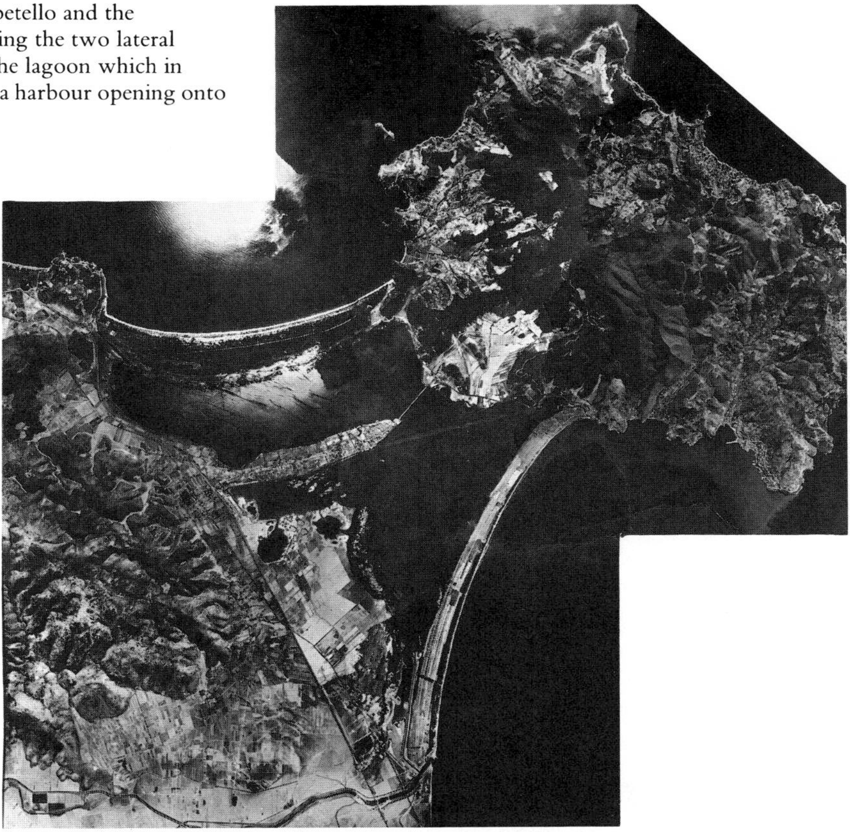

5.3b View from Vetulonia towards Rusellae (Roselle) in Etruria, overlooking the plain of the River Bruna. In ancient times the plain was a sea-lagoon.

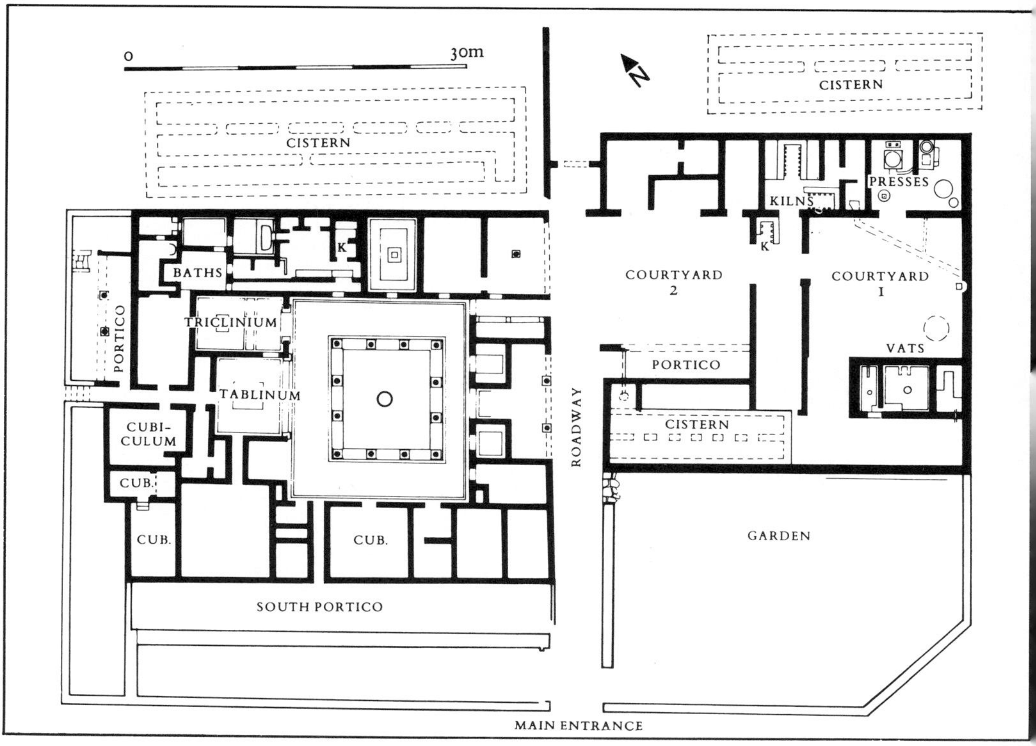

0 30m

CISTERN

CISTERN

PRESSES

KILNS

K

BATHS

K

COURTYARD 2

COURTYARD 1

PORTICO

TRICLINIUM

VATS

PORTICO

TABLINUM

CISTERN

CUBI-CULUM

ROADWAY

CUB.

CUB.

CUB.

GARDEN

SOUTH PORTICO

MAIN ENTRANCE

5.5 Plan of the villa-farm at Francolise, northern Campania, dating from the 1st century BC.

5.6 Architectural wall-paintings of the Pompeian 'Second Style' at the huge villa of Oplontis, c. 40 BC. The villa was destroyed by the eruption of Mount Vesuvius in AD 79.

6.1b Silver *denarius* of Octavian (Augustus) with AEGVPTO CAPTA, celebrating the annexation of Egypt (of which the crocodile is the emblem) from Cleopatra VII, 28 BC.

7.3b Brass *sestertius* of Vespasian (AD 69–79) celebrating the suppression of the First Jewish Revolt (IVDAEA CAPTA).

9.1 Bronze coin of Macrinus (AD 217–18) at Byblus (Phoenicia), indicating how coins (in stylized fashion) can reveal the appearance of ancient buildings; in this case the temple of Aphrodite.

9.2b Billon *follis* of Diocletian (AD 284–305) who reorganised the army and defences of the empire, taking the east as his own sphere. The mint is Heraclea (Perinthus) in Thrace, and the type the Genius of the Roman People.

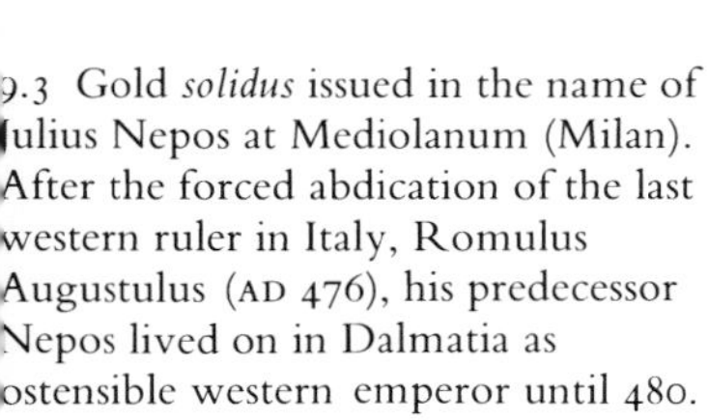

9.3 Gold *solidus* issued in the name of Julius Nepos at Mediolanum (Milan). After the forced abdication of the last western ruler in Italy, Romulus Augustulus (AD 476), his predecessor Nepos lived on in Dalmatia as ostensible western emperor until 480.

6.3 Aerial view of the harbour of Caesarea Maritima in Judaea, built by Herod the Great (37–4 BC).

6.1a Reconstruction of the monument of Octavian (Augustus) at Nicopolis in Epirus incorporating the bronze rams of Marcus Antonius' ships which he had captured at Actium in 31 BC.

6.4 Part of the sun-dial created by Augustus, and restored by Domitian or Hadrian, at Rome.

7.1 Model of the palace of Cogidubnus at Noviomagus Regnensium (Fishbourne) as it was in AD 75.

7.2 Bust of the goddess Aphrodite, patron of the city of Aphrodisias, dedicated by a certain Theodorus.

7.3a The hill of Masada, the last fortress to resist the Romans in the First Jewish Revolt (First Roman War), AD 73. The ramp up which the Romans dragged their victorious siege tower is seen on the right.

7.4a Skeletons found at Herculaneum. These were people who had tried, in vain, to escape from the eruption of Vesuvius by boat.

7.4b Skeleton of a man about 45 years old (the so-called 'Helmsman'), recently found near the boat at Herculaneum. His bones had been distorted by over-work and inadequate food, and his teeth were bad.

8.1 Tree-ring indicating, according to dendro-chronological comparisons, the rebuilding of the Roman bridge at Augusta Trevirorum (Trier) in AD 71.

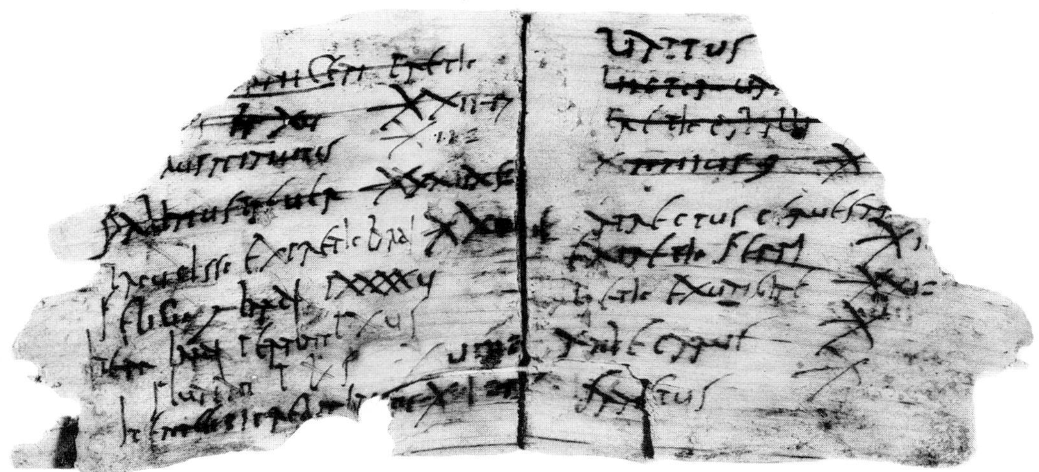

8.2 An example of the inscribed wooden tablets found in abundance at the Roman military fortress at Vindolanda (Chesterholm), near Hadrian's Wall. It is an account for the supply of goods (varying from horses to pork fat) to certain named soldiers, c. AD 120.

8.6 A large Roman villa at Estrées-sur-Noyes, south of Samarobriva (Amiens): one of the many achievements of air photography in this area.

8.5 A papyrus fragment of Lollianus' *Phoinicica* (*Phoenician Tale*), c. AD 200, which casts new light on the history of the Greek novel.

9.2a Reconstruction of the late Roman military fortress at Lejjun (Jordan).

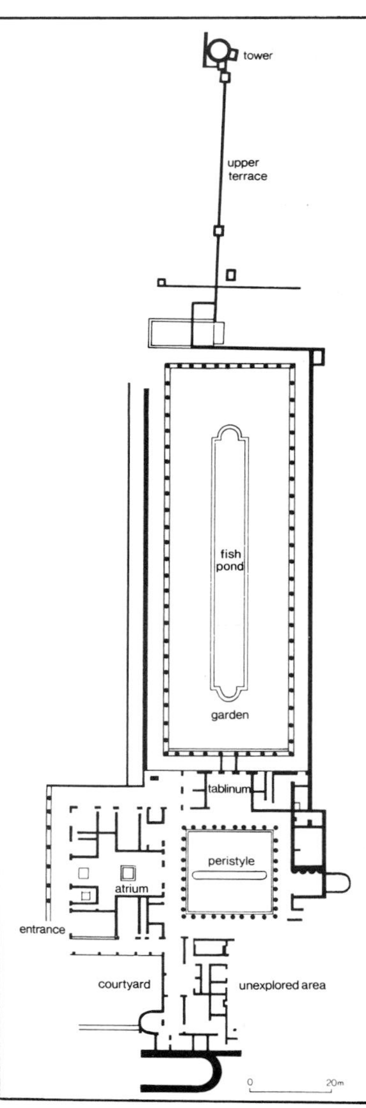

App II (ii) The Villa of the Papyri outside Herculaneum, found to contain an immense quantity of papyri and bronze statues. This plan was produced before the site was covered over again in the later eighteenth century. Its re-excavation is eagerly awaited.

App II (iii) The Portus Julius, built by Agrippa between Puteoli (Pozzuoli) and Baiae (Baia), and in lakes behind them, upon the Gulf of Cumae (Bay of Naples). As a result of seismic movements the harbour constructions, like many other ancient buildings in the area, now lie under the sea.

4 Novae: Danubian Legionary River Port

Moesia was originally the land of the Moesi, a Thracian tribe living south of the River Danube (in eastern Serbia, Yugoslavia). Later the name was extended to the entire territory south of the Danube from between its tributaries the Margus (Morava) and Drinus (Drina) as far as the Euxine (Black) Sea – thus including also the northern section of Bulgaria and the Rumanian part of the Dobrogea (Dobruja).

In 30–28 BC Marcus Licinius Crassus, a general of Octavian (shortly to become known as Augustus), advanced this Roman frontier to the Danube, along the whole length of Moesia. After various initial steps the region became a fully fledged province under Tiberius in AD 15, though it was grouped together with Macedonia and Achaea (Greece) under a single governor (*legatus Augusti propraetore*) until 44. In 86 Domitian divided the province into two, Upper Moesia (Malvensis) to the west and Lower Moesia to the east, with their boundary on or near the River Ciabrus or Cebrus (Tsibritsa). After Trajan's Second Dacian War in 105/6, both provinces were enlarged by the addition of trans-Danubian annexes adjoining the newly conquered territories in Dacia (Rumania). Moesia prospered and later became the homeland of Roman officers and emperors. After the abandonment of Dacia by Aurelian (271) the name of the evacuated territory was (confusingly) transferred to the Moesian provinces, of which the frontiers were redrawn.

By the third quarter of the first century AD, or perhaps even as early as AD 15, the governor of Moesia had begun to command a river fleet, the *classis Moesica*. One of its principal Danube ports was Novae (Stăklen) in Lower Moesia (now northern Bulgaria). Novae occupied a low, uneven plateau bordered on the north by the Danube and on the east by its tributary the Novas or Noas (Noes), from which the place had taken its name. The fortress of Novae, adjoining an old Thracian site, was perhaps founded by the Romans in *c.* AD 30 and became the headquarters first of one legion (45/6, the Legio VIII Augusta) and then, some years later, of another (69/70, the Legio I Italica). Novae owed its significance not only to its position on the river, controlling one of its easier crossings, but also to two important roads from western and eastern Thrace which both terminated at the town. Under Domitian's reorganization (in connection with his Dacian War, 85/9), the river-fleet, now known as the *classis Flavia Moesica*, was assigned to Lower Moesia. Moreover, a tribune of the Legio I Italica was regularly appointed by the governor of that province to command groups of vessels in the northern waters of the Black Sea, stationed in the ports of Tauris (Crimea) and elsewhere.[13]

In AD 101 Trajan, in order to fight his First Dacian War – in which

Lower Moesia bore the brunt of the Dacian king Decebalus's onslaught – probably disembarked at Novae after proceeding down the river with a troop-carrying flotilla. When his campaigns were over, the Legio I Italica remained at Novae, but the headquarters of the fleet was probably at Noviodunum (Isaccea), near the mouth of the Danube.

A civilian habitation subsequently developed round the fortress of Novae, and under Marcus Aurelius (161–80) the place attained Roman citizen rank as a *municipium*. It was an importation centre for pottery from the west, and re-exported much of what was brought in, sending the cargos on to central Europe across the Danube. It was, however, relatively defenceless when the river froze over every year between December and February, and received damaging blows from the Gothic king Kniva (251), twice more in the fourth century – during the civil war between Constantine I and Licinius (*c.* 316), and from the Visigoths (376/8) – and then again in the fifth century. In the early 470s it became the temporary residence of Theoderic the Ostrogoth, subsequently king of Italy.

Excavated by joint Polish and Bulgarian expeditions since 1960, Novae has a claim to be the most thoroughly investigated Roman headquarters in eastern Europe. Excavations in recent years have uncovered much of the legionary camp. The wooden and earth walls are datable to Domitian's Dacian War, while stone walls were constructed under Trajan in *c.* AD 100. Under the Severan dynasty (193–235), extensive reconstruction was undertaken. A fortified area of 64 acres has been traced; its basic plan is rectangular, but it has been adapted to benefit from the lie of the land.

While the west gate is the most vivid reminder of Novae's importance, a good idea can also be obtained of the *principia*. The *principia* was the administrative centre of legionary camps, a large complex of buildings with a central courtyard (the commander's quarters were removed to a separate unit, his *praetorium*). Such *principia* generally possessed architectural façades, large cross-halls with a tribunal at one end (serving as a court of justice, and for the swearing-in of officials) and a range of offices for headquarters staff. Adjacent to the *principia* of Novae was a shrine or chapel of standards (*sacellum*) which has been uncovered along with the soldiers' bank (*aeraria*) that stood beside it.

The military hospital (*valetudinarium*) has also been investigated, with some difficulty since there were successive stages of reconstruction and altered lay-out. It can be compared with similar hospitals at other legionary centres, notably Carnuntum (Petronell), Vetera (Xanten), Novaesium (Neuss, see last section), Isca Silurum (Caerleon) and Inchtuthil (in Scotland). *Valetudinaria* were large buildings with an internal courtyard and a continuous circulating corridor, carefully planned to isolate wards and ensure quietness. They included casualty reception centres, and rooms for administrative staff and storage. 'The medical service in the army', writes Graham Webster, 'was remarkable for its apparently modern ideas.'[14] The numerous lamps found in the *valetudinarium* at Novae were probably imported.

The excavators of the fortress have also brought houses, shops and workshops to light, and have located streets, one of which reveals two successive levels. East of the *principia* structures that have been unearthed include a heterogeneous complex of colonnades, interiors and courtyards of second- and third-century date. After the Gothic devastations of 251 the town was rebuilt on a larger scale than before. During the civil war of *c.*316, however, the *principia* was destroyed, and the original fortress abandoned. The demolition of the wall, too, seems to have started in this century. The civilian settlement, though, enjoyed a subsequent recovery, aided by strengthened fortifications, sections of which have now been disinterred. Christian churches of the fifth and sixth centuries have also been identified, including an episcopal basilica.

5 Egypt: Novel on Papyrus

Although this book has mentioned inscriptions on stone, gold leaf, wood and potsherds (*ostraca*), and could also have discussed the employment of wax for the same purpose, the normal writing material of the ancient world from the classical period onwards was the marsh plant named papyrus. 'Civilization,' said Pliny the elder, 'or at the very least human history, depends on it.'[15]

To prepare it to receive writing, a piece of papyrus was first sliced vertically into thin strips, each of which was overlaid crosswise by a further strip. The next step was to stick these two layers together (by means of the plant's natural gum) into a single long slice, averaging between 8 and 9 inches in width and between 20 and 30 feet in length. A reed pen and carbon ink were employed to inscribe the writing on the surface in vertical columns, and the papyrus was then rolled up upon a stick of wood. In order to peruse its contents, it was held in the left hand and unrolled with the right hand, each part being rolled up again once its study had been completed. Rolls were normally made up of 20 sheets, though totals up to 50 or 70 are known. In libraries, they were lodged inside rows of pigeon-holes, identified by labels attached to their covers.

The papyrus plant grew in a number of places, but in Egypt most abundantly of all. This Egyptian variety, alone, was manufactured into paper, which has been described as the country's greatest legacy to posterity. Moreover, although there are a number of exceptions – including, especially, the huge collection found in the Villa of the Papyri at

Herculaneum (Appendix II, iii) – it is in Egypt that the greatest numbers of surviving ancient papyri have been discovered, and especially in areas south of the Nile delta, where the rainless climate permitted their survival. Their condition, however, is frequently fragmentary, because the find-sites have often been casual rubbish heaps and gutted buildings, deserted when the irrigation level receded (before the construction of the Aswan Dam).

The first rediscoveries of papyri were made in the eighteenth century, and since then more than thirty thousand papyrus texts of various sizes have been published. Many of these papyri, covering an enormous range of public and private material, have contributed greatly to our historical knowledge. In particular, they have caused literary history to be rewritten at a number of points.

One such papyrus, for example, has revealed a hitherto unknown sort of Greek novel. While the Hellenistic Greeks favoured short stories of a sex-orientated, ironical type known as the 'Milesian Tales', the novels that they simultaneously launched upon the Mediterranean world were of a different character. For these novels generally featured love of a more middle-brow and saccharine nature – so familiar from today's best-sellers – melodramatically separating earnest heroes from their coy heroines, only to reunite them in a sentimental, happy ending. Such were the *Ninus Romance*, *The Dream of Nectanebus*, *Joseph and Aseneth*, forerunners of Achilles Tatius's *Leucippe and Clitophon*, Heliodorus's *Aethiopica* and Longus's *Daphnis and Chloe* of Roman imperial times. It has long caused some surprise, therefore, that the two Latin novels that have come down to us, Petronius's *Satyricon* and Apuleius's *Metamorphoses* or *Golden Ass*, of the first and second centuries AD respectively, are by no means middle-brow and starry-eyed. On the contrary, unlike their Greek counterparts, they are sophisticated, literary, and often prurient (even Apuleius's famous *Cupid and Psyche* is very far indeed from the naiveté it professes). How is it that these Latin novels seem to deviate so fundamentally from what might have been expected to be their Greek prototypes?

A papyrus has now furnished what seems to be the answer: that there was a whole genre of Greek novels, now otherwise lost, which bore a far greater resemblance to the sharp productions of Petronius and Apuleius than to the sentimental Greek novels that have come down to us. One such papyrus, or rather the series of its fragments which survive, is at Köln.[16] It came from Egypt, and the fragments were studied and published in 1968 and 1972. They form part of a hitherto unknown Greek novel, the *Phoenician Tale* (*Phoenicica*) by Lollianus. The papyrus dates from *c.* AD 200. But even if the novel itself, which it transcribes, was written as late as that, it may well go back to an earlier tradition – earlier than

Apuleius or even Petronius, both of whom may have been familiar with this tradition, which is so much closer to their own ways of thinking than to those of previously known Greek novelists. One of the fragments of the *Phoenicica*, it is true, describes the ritual murder of a child, which somewhat reminds us of a scene written by Achilles Tatius; but a further fragment deals with sexual initiation, and another with some macabre goings-on regarding corpses, in terms which could scarcely have been employed by Achilles Tatius, but which would not have seemed strange to Petronius or Apuleius, writers to whom, indeed, Lollianus has now been explicitly compared.

The same is true of the author of a further unknown novel, of which a passage known as the *Iolaus* fragment has likewise been deciphered on an Egyptian papyrus, from Oxyrhynchus. The *Iolaus* fragment is a mixture of prose and verse – like the *Satyricon* of Petronius (and a third new Egyptian papyrus, the *Tinouphis*) – and includes vigorously coarse obscenities which could easily have occurred in the Latin works but never in the standard starry-eyed Greek novels. In the words of Graham Anderson, 'Iolaus belongs, as its first editor tentatively suggested, to something like a Greek *Satyricon*. The net is closing.'[17]

And what are the prospects of future discoveries of papyri, and will warnings that their supply may be almost exhausted prove more justified, in time to come, than they have been hitherto? Finds of new papyri, writes E. G. Turner, 'continue to be made. Two observations may help us to judge the chances of their continuing. First, the new high dam at Aswan [Syene] and the progress of irrigation technique must inevitably bring a rise in the water-table throughout Egypt, not merely south of or in the neighbourhood of Aswan. Undetected texts that may still be lurking underground in irrigated areas cannot but be jeopardized thereby. Second, manuscripts in graves or hiding-places in the desert fringing the Nile valley will still await a finder. Texts preserved in this way are normally completer and more extensive than those recorded from open sites, even if Homer and Menander are the authors they are most likely to contain. To locate such cemeteries and hiding-places will be like looking for a needle in a haystack; but the prize is of infinitely greater value than the proverbial needle, and perhaps new techniques of search can be developed, comparable to those now employed by Dr Lerici in Etruria [Chapter 5, section 1]. This possibility apart, the mounds of the villages around the former Lake Moeris [the Fayyum] – perhaps even of Elephantine – should be finally cleared. Outside Egypt it is time for work to be resumed vigorously at Herculaneum [cf. above, and Appendix II, ii].'[18]

6 The Samara (Somme) Valley: Air Photography

Air photography, which has already come to our attention a number of times in this book, heads the archaeological methods which have yielded historical results during recent years, providing new data at an ever-increasing pace.

This type of photography is, simply, an extension of the principle that a camera held over the head, or raised on a scaffold, clarifies the relationship between one detail and another, owing to its elevated viewpoint. Air photographs can be taken either at a high or low altitude. Vertical photographs from a high level prove especially useful when prints of adjoining scenes are studied stereoscopically to bring out their relief. The results are convertible to a map by photogrammetry, the art or science of obtaining accurate measurements from photographic records of this kind. Such high-level methods can often supplement, or replace, arduous and time-consuming detailed planning in the field. For archaeological purposes, however, low-level obliques are more frequently employed. They produce improved versions of ground views, and are less difficult to interpret than their high-level counterparts.

With the aid of the infra-red technique (Chapter 6, section 3) and numerous electrical, magnetic and sonic instruments, air photography can perform many functions. First, it permits sites to be comprehended at a single glance, enabling their individual details to take integral shape within their larger whole. Moreover, air photographs provide evidence of topographical changes over the centuries. And they discover sites, and types of site, that were hitherto completely unknown. By such means, they make it possible for excavators to concentrate on sites that are usefully typical, or interestingly atypical, or located in key positions. They also help national and regional authorities to decide what objects and areas need to be included in conservation policies. Furthermore, as Graham Shipley points out, this type of survey 'informs us, as excavation cannot, about rural settlement and agriculture throughout the whole territory of an ancient town.'[19] It thus fits in with the New Archaeologists' desire to shift attention from individual sites to environmental patterns of settlement and landscape (Appendix 1).

There are various particular ways in which photographs taken from the air explain features and objects which, at ground level, are invisible or incomprehensible. For one thing, such photography, when undertaken in low sunlight, produces informative shadow-marks. And then again, ancient buildings, even if completely razed down to the level of the landscape, often show up in air photographs because of the different soil which has become established on top of their skeletal remains, with the result that the crops or vegetables growing in that soil also display differences, perceptible from the air. Thus, cereals grow to a greater height, and ripen later, above pits cut in buried ditches, and, conversely, grow shorter, as well as yellowing earlier, over hard ancient material such as road surfaces or the foundations of walls.

'This now extensively used procedure', sums up P. E. Cleator, 'relies on the fact that subsoil, once it has been disturbed, can never be restored to its former condition. As a result, vegetation which roots itself in an otherwise unnoticeable filled-in ditch will, because of the higher moisture content of the replaced earth, exhibit a stronger growth than that of adjacent foliage. Conversely, where an ancient roadway has once existed and has become grassed over, the poorness and lack of depth of the topsoil will tend to inhibit plant development. In England, these phenomena had been observed and commented upon as long ago as the sixteenth century ... But what was not fully appreciated at this time, or, indeed, until several centuries later, was the extent to which the visibility of these so-called crop- and parch-marks was governed, not only by the nature of the soil and the type of vegetation it supported, but also by seasonal considerations, by climatic conditions, by the position of the sun, and, above all, by the location of the viewer ... Repeated photographing of a particular area of countryside, at different times of the day and year, and from varying heights and angles, may be necessary before the presence of suspected markings can be confirmed.'[20] The patterns of settlement that thus emerge often throw light on social and economic changes which the literary sources have not disclosed.

Although these techniques were substantially developed by O. G. S. Crawford in Britain during the 1920s, it was in the 1960s and 1970s that they reached their culmination. Here attention will be concentrated on the achievements of French air photography in the valley of the River Samara (Somme), centring upon Samarobriva (Ambiani, Amiens in Picardy). Operating in an area packed with ancient remains, or outlines, which became visible from the air, Roger Agache, writes K. Greene, 'discovered a remarkable number of sites. For example, to the east of Amiens along the valley of the River Somme, four Roman roads enclose a diamond-shaped block of land around 618 square miles in area. After researches up to April 1976, it was known to contain ten villa complexes whose remains exceed 656 feet in length, 128 smaller villas and 39 probable villa sites. In addition, there were seven extensive and 243 smaller sites with Roman masonry foundations, and 127 further traces of sites which were probably occupied in the Roman period ... The countryside also contained demonstrably non-agricultural buildings – 15 temple or religious sanctuary sites and one theatre ... The dominant impression ... is of a fully occupied rural landscape containing an impressive range of settlements ranging from native farms with traditional round timber houses to spectacular complexes of villas and associated buildings, some of great architectural distinction.'[21]

Agache himself wrote: 'We have undertaken 750 flying hours, spread over sixteen years, in all seasons and all weathers ... The Somme basin is the first region of France to become the object of such systematic investigations, for these flyovers have covered every sector, whatever its type of terrain.'[22] Although flying in summer and winter alike, he paid special attention to the photography of ground denuded during the winter months, upon which anomalies of soil and humidity could be seen. It was mainly in winter that ploughing revealed the sites of Gallo-Roman structures, by bringing to the surface chalk rubble from the tops of buried walls and foundations.

It has thus been possible to delineate in detail the plan of building after building (of various dates), ranging from large complexes 900 feet long and nearly 400 feet wide – the residences of prosperous owner-occupiers – down to much more diminutive establishments. This mass of material raises problems of historical interpretation, but offers enlightenment not only regarding the buildings themselves but about their environment as well, leaving no doubt that the Somme basin was densely settled and farmed under Roman imperial rule, and became the scene of heavy capital investment.

Moreover, as Agache reminds us, 'the Somme is far from being a privileged sector from the point of view of land and soil conditions. The possibilities of aerial survey are equally great, if not a good deal greater, in a number of other parts of France.' Meanwhile, he also has a lot to say on the manner in which deep ploughing and other culprits inflict fatal destruction on such remains of the past. This rural annihilation, of course, requiring urgent rescue archaeology (see notes on the Introduction), occurs on both sides of the Channel. Yet there are technical differences between the ancient Gallic scene, as revealed by this photography, and its counterparts disclosed by aerial activity in Britain. 'Here [in Gaul]' observes R.J. Fowler, 'we see much that is familiar from the English landscape ... Yet the idiosyncrasy of insular field archaeology is emphasized by the absence from the Somme basin of causewayed enclosures, cursuses, henges, and pit alignments; while the Somme landscape itself possesses an extra confusing overlay in the form of bomb and shell craters and the saw-edge skeins of military trenches. Further, the twentieth-century martial mind apparently had a penchant for placing its establishments on Gallo-Roman sites.'[23]

The techniques employed for these aerial surveys of the Somme valley have now been augmented, and in part superseded, by newer methods (Chapter 6, section 3). They remain important, though, as the products of a pioneer enterprise, both in their own right and as inspirations of what was to happen afterwards elsewhere, and will, we hope, happen again in the future.

7 *Cruciniacum (Bad Kreuznach): Water Supply*

The ordinary people in the cities of the Roman empire were not favoured by what would now be regarded as a satisfactory water supply.

In the capital, despite its magnificent aqueducts, no water whatever reached tenement buildings. Such water as they could get (not enough, incidentally, to put out fires) had to be brought by water-carriers. If a tenement happened to be placed suitably for the purpose, the sewage from its ground floor (only) could be discharged down into one of the city's drains, or, more frequently, into its cess-trenches (one of which, investigated by an intrepid archaeologist in 1892, was found to be neither deep enough, nor proof against seepage). The stinks emanating from these trenches, and the consequent health risks, are evident. Moreover, residents on the upper floors did not even possess these limited facilities, but employed chamber pots and commodes, which they emptied into a vat placed under the well of the staircase. Alternatively, a male could relieve himself into the receptacles that the fullers (cleansers and thickeners of cloth) lined up in the street in front of their shops, hoping to use the urine for their work (cf section 2 above). Or he could make his way to public latrines, consisting of groups of two-handled jars, once again in the streets.

Those who could afford it, on the other hand, availed themselves of Rome's famous, marble-adorned – though to most modern tastes embarrassingly gregarious – lavatories in the public Baths which were such a feature of Rome's civilization. Running water served these baths, and flowed beneath their lavatories. Running water was also piped into the richest town houses (equipped with their own private baths), whose occupants did not, therefore, have to undergo the sanitary horrors of the tenements.

Nor did the owners of the very numerous villas in the Roman and provincial countryside have to submit to such unpleasantnesses. For many of these country mansions, like the more imposing of the town houses, had private bathing establishments of their own. At Pompeii, for example, 'all houses, except the poorest, had water-pipes fitted with taps – though running water was not to be expected in bedrooms ... In the Villa of the Papyri outside Herculaneum, the garden fountains were supplied by a remarkable system of hydraulic pipes ... At the House of the Neptune Mosaic [at Herculaneum] there was a pipe down to a sewer; and elsewhere, the pipes led down, if not to a sewer, at least to a trench.'[21] The atrium courts of the houses, though occasionally roofed over, were more frequently provided with a skylight furnished with terracotta gutters or drain-pipes which poured the rainwater from the sloping roof into a catch-basin (*impluvium*) below.

At Ostia, the fountain in the central courtyard in the many-storeyed Diana Block was fed by the public aqueduct and available for common use, including laundry needs and cooking. In Britain (where we also have information about the water-supplies to towns), the more affluent homes and farms used surplus water to flush their drains. But the water arrangements that have now become most completely understood are at a villa in Germany, at Cruciniacum (Bad Kreuznach) in the Roman province of Germania Superior.

Cruciniacum was situated between Bingium (Bingen) and Borbetomagus (Worms), in the lower part of a valley leading off from the valley of the Ellerbach, which joins the Nahe, a tributary of the Rhine. Its peristyle villa is the grandest so far known to us in Germania Superior, although it is not recorded by any extant ancient literary authority and the name of its ancient owner remains unknown. The villa was nearly square, measuring 77 × 88 yards, and covering an area of 6,377 square yards. It was erected shortly after AD 150, on a site which had already been occupied. Although the four-winged villa possessed outbuildings for farming purposes, its use was not primarily agricultural but residential.

Its existence has been known for quite a long time; a mosaic of a gladiatorial scene (dating not from the period of original construction, but from the middle of the third century AD), was discovered there in 1893, and then another of the same period, representing Oceanus, came to light in 1966. Since 1975, excavations have been resumed – and it is now that Cruciniacum has made its specific contribution. For these new investigations have revealed how the water-supply of the villa was organized. The arrangements included a clay pipe feeding (from an unidentified source) a four-arched, pyramid-roofed, water reservoir, which lay outside the main residence but possessed ready access to the kitchen. In addition a lead pipe carried water to a fountain (with a hexagonal basin) in the large apsed room at the centre of the villa's southern front.

Underneath the building ran a vaulted canal, nearly 3 feet wide and 3½ feet high. Its multiple purpose was to siphon off the overflow from the fountain, to dispose of sewage and to carry away unused water that was left over in the reservoir outside the villa, rainwater collected in the stone gutter round the outer wall, and the water that gathered in the valley after rainfalls. The canal deposited these contents in the River Ellerbach.

The original villa at Cruciniacum did not have a long life. In *c.* AD 260–75 it was burnt, probably in the course of Frankish incursions. In the fourth century, however, the building was reconstructed, with impressive fortifications but inferior living conditions. Not long afterwards it was evacuated once again, probably at the time when Valentinian I (364–75) constructed a fortress of his own nearby (though this has also been dated to Constantius II, 337–61). The adjacent necropolis, though, remained in use until after the fall of the western empire, when the Franks had asserted their control of the territory.

CHAPTER 9

THE LATER EMPIRE

The reign of the north African Septimius Severus (AD 193–211) has often been seen as marking a dividing line between the empire's relatively tranquil prosperity of the second century and its conclusive loss of peacefulness and living standards in the third.

But that picture, although true in so far as Severus saw that a tougher and more militarized régime was needed in order to cope with Rome's growing problems, is nevertheless oversimplified. In many ways, with more or less subtle variations, the empire went on as before. Its abundant coinage, for example, continued. The immensely varied designs (types) which appear on such pieces make an inestimable contribution to history, and investigation of them develops year by year. In the present chapter, third-century coins of Byblus (Jebeil) in Phoenicia will be cited as examples of this numismatic phenomenon.

By the time of Diocletian (AD 284–305) the crisis had become graver still, and he sought to meet the needs of his era by far more comprehensive measures than any of those undertaken by Severus. For one thing, he appreciated that the empire could no longer be ruled by a single man, but that four rulers were needed (two Augusti, and two Caesars acting as their deputies). Secondly, he multiplied the number of provinces. And thirdly, he reorganized the army. Archaeologists have lately thrown light on these arrangements by excavations at the frontier station of Betthorus (Lejjun in Jordan).

Constantine I the Great (AD 306–37) once more brought the Roman world under a single ruler. But in 364 its territories were again divided, and the geographical separation between western and eastern empires that now occurred became (except for the briefest of breaks) permanent. The destinies of the two dominions proved extremely different. The eastern régime, based on Constantinople (formerly Byzantium, which has earned it the name of the Byzantine empire), survived – with a short disruption in the thirteenth century – until 1453. The western realm, on the other hand, which was governed first from Mediolanum (Milan) and then after 404 from Ravenna, suffered more severely from external threats and internal dislocations, and broke up piecemeal into German kingdoms as early as the fifth century. One of the German states comprised Italy itself, and the abdication of the emperor Romulus 'Augustulus' (476) is commonly considered as marking the end of this western empire. At this point, however, we return to the coinage with which this chapter began. For it has been established that his immediate predecessor at Ravenna, Julius Nepos, compelled to leave Italy in the previous year, continued to reign as western emperor in Dalmatia until 480, with the ostensible approval both of the eastern emperor and of the German monarch who now ruled in Italy.

1 Byblus: Buildings on Coins

Coins should not be divorced from archaeology (see Introduction); on the contrary, they should be seen as a vital branch of the subject and a uniquely diversified archaeological source. But 'in order to interpret the significance of ancient coins,' I have suggested, 'we have to forget many features of our modern currency ... If governments had no press and radio (or even postage-stamps) to advertise their achievements and intentions, might they not be forced to advertise them on coinage instead? That is what ancient governments did ... [Their coins] were noted by thousands of people – sometimes hundreds of thousands. This can be said with confidence, because Greek and Roman governments planned and designed them in such a way that no other conclusion can be drawn.'[1]

Something has been said elsewhere of what modern forms of technical analysis, and the examination of coin-finds, can achieve in increasing our historical understanding of Greek coinages (Chapter 4, section 5; Chapter 3, section 5). As for Roman imperial coins, their obverses were planned to make the numberless peoples of the empire familiar, in every possible way, with the personality and appearance and names and titles of the reigning emperor, in addition to his wife and relatives and heir and forebears. This looks odd today, and the reverse types of these pieces, too, differ equally from the reverses of modern coinages in that they were continually changed, implying, presumably, that people did indeed look at them: 'What is most surprising to us is the immense variety of these reverse designs ... How very strange it would seem [today], in almost any state, if its coinage began to announce the themes of successive new governments with great promptitude, and then *altered its message from year to year and month to month as policies shifted.*'[2]

The messages of these innumerable reverse types of Roman imperial coins were not limited to politics, however. They also provided, for example, a mass of evidence concerning religion and myth and patriotic legend, by no means all of it yet digested or interpreted: The last time that I ever spoke with the late Professor H. J. Rose, whose understanding of Roman religious institutions was unrivalled, he expressed the view that the most promising avenue for future studies of this subject was the coinage. Furthermore, religion, as well as other considerations, prompted the Roman authorities to depict temples on their coinage, and these representations have added to our knowledge of the appearance and structure of such buildings, as well as of the works of art that they contained.

Yet the coinage of Rome itself and of other imperial mints, massive though it was, constituted only a limited proportion of the currencies of the empire as a whole. For extraordinarily abundant and varied, too, were the issues of numerous individual cities, known as the 'Greek imperial' series. 'The Romans were faced with a mighty currency problem. Not even Alexander the Great had been offered the task – and the political and economic advantage – of supplying coinage to so large an area of the civilized world. For centuries the Roman emperors provided their vast heterogeneous empire with sufficient coinage for its needs; and they rarely made the mistake of sacrificing efficiency to uniformity. So there was a bewildering multitude of different monetary arrangements in different regions, and, in any one area, many different sorts of coins could co-exist ... Great quantities of base-metal token-coinage were issued by local (not imperial) authorities at hundreds of different centres. Cities all round the Mediterranean coasts had for a long time issued their own coins ... [and] under Augustus not less than 300 towns in the Roman Empire struck their own bronze coinage. Later this number considerably increased, and with various fluctuations in number and bulk these city-issues continued during the first three centuries of the imperial regime. No historian can effectively study any Roman emperor's reign unless he has a good knowledge of the local coinages issued in all parts of the empire during that reign ... [though] he can, at present, only with the utmost difficulty obtain that knowledge ... Many coins are still unpublished ... Attempts to compile empire-wide descriptions of local coinages for any given period have so far been extremely rare ...'[3] I attempted the task for the reign of Augustus,[4] and the British Museum's Department of Coins and Medals has embarked on a similar, more ambitious plan for an extensive subsequent period.

The obverse types of all these multitudinous issues provide insight into the local communities' interpretations of successive emperors' titles and portraits and families, while their reverse types – with which we shall be concerned here – supply a mass of diversified evidence. Any single mint may well offer a host of different designs and these possess, for the most part, a local significance, referring to the internal history, religion, mythology, economics, social life, topography, art and architecture of the city that issued them.

Although the most abundant city-coinage come from western Asia Minor, 'the issues of Syrian towns were particularly varied and longlived ... Many problems are raised by the multiplicity of the chronological systems which they employ. They are also ill-preserved, wretchedly inartistic [not always], often rare nowadays, and extremely hard to interpret.'[5] Reference has just been made to their depictions, among much else, of local architecture, and it is this aspect that may be singled out as an example of the information to be gained from these local Syrian and Phoenician issues.

'Hundreds of thousands of coins', rightly observed Michael Rostovtzeff, 'have revealed to us not only the external appearance of many ancient cities but also the main features of every aspect of their life – their walls, streets, gates and public and private buildings.'[6] This is information that either supplements the literary sources or reveals structures of which those sources (and excavations) tell us nothing. True, the pictures on the coins are subject to stylizations and conventions – including the map-like opening-out of the design to present a ground plan, and the bringing forward of a statue in a temple so that it can be seen within the portico – but these conventions can be recognized and interpreted. And there is a contrary, more positive side of the picture as well: these coins delineate certain aspects of architectural detail with a careful exactness that permit an accurate reconstruction.

The study of architecture on coins goes back to T. L. Donaldson's pioneering *Architectura Numismatica* of 1859 (reprinted 1966), but has developed on a notable scale during the past three decades. Thus Martin Price and Bluma Trell are able to write that there is an 'enormous variety of buildings for the very existence of which the coins are now the only evidence. Even when a building has been excavated, the coins are often the only evidence for the superstructure, the part most vulnerable to act of God and man ... Each artist had a different view of the three-dimensional building which he was transferring to the two-dimensional plane of a miniature relief sculpture ... One artist will emphasize the general appearance of the façade of the building; another will put it in its natural setting, on top of a mountain or in a wooded grove; another will give details of the superstructure, or of the column capitals, or of the cult image ... Carefully delineated architectural details should particularly be noted, such as the sculptured drums at the base of the columns of the Temple of Artemis at Ephesus ... and the great stairway in front of the temple of Jupiter at Heliopolis (Baalbek). All these can be checked against the existing remains of the buildings. The die-maker could show, in a manner that would baffle the modern photographer, parts both of the interior and of the exterior of a building.'[7]

Heliopolis was just one of the Syro-Phoenician centres at which these architectural types occur on local bronze coinage. Another was Byblus (Jebeil). A coastal city of Phoenicia at the foot of Mount Libanus (Lebanon), Byblus was already inhabited in the fourth millennium BC, and described as the oldest city in the world by Philo of Byblus (AD 64–141), who claimed to be drawing on the work of Sanchuniathon, a Phoenician of the later second millennium before the Christian era. Before and after the time of Sanchuniathon, Byblus had played a leading part in the development of the alphabet. Subsequently, it became dependent, in turn, on the Persians, Alexander the Great, the Seleucids, and the Romans. It was a major centre of weaving, and exported a good deal of cloth.

Remains of the ancient city of Byblus include walls and paved streets, a basilica, an apsed fountain building (*nymphaeum*) containing statues, and a habitation centre of the second century AD containing mosaics. A theatre, too, has been located, and this likewise possessed a mosaic pavement, depicting Dionysus (Bacchus).

Bronze coins of the city, issued under the Roman emperor Macrinus (AD 217–8) – a Mauretanian who reigned briefly after helping to murder Caracalla – show another building,[8] of unusual architectural character (although partially paralleled at Heliopolis). To the left stands a gabled edifice (with an altar in the front of its porch), adjoining a large porticoed courtyard, reached by steps, which the artist has opened up in order to display what, in fact, lay hidden within: a balustraded, horned altar surmounted by a lofty conical stone (baetyl). What is shown here is no doubt the famous shrine of Aphrodite at Byblus, where the death of Adonis, whom the goddess loved, received its principal celebration, extending over eight days, according to literary tradition. 'I saw at Byblus', declared Lucian, 'the great sanctuary of Aphrodite, in which they celebrate the ritual of the death of Adonis . . . First of all they weep for Adonis, as if for a corpse, but on the next day they pronounce that he is alive.'[9] Despite its fame, this shrine has not yet been located by archaeologists, though they have found what may have been one of its forerunners, the Bronze Age 'Temple of the Obelisks' of *c.*2000 BC, containing a number of sacred baetyls. Also from about that date is the holy place of Nini-Zaza at Mari on the Euphrates, where a single baetyl stood in the centre of a courtyard, as on this coin of Macrinus issued at Byblus more than two millennia later.

2 *Betthorus (Lejjun): Late Rome's Eastern Frontier*

In 64/63 BC Pompey the Great converted Syria, formerly the centre of the Seleucid kingdom, into a Roman province, with supervisory powers over numerous city-states and client-kingdoms. During the early Principate, however, these kingdoms were gradually suppressed (or brought inside the empire) and the province was extended north-east to the upper Euphrates. Septimius Severus, after eliminating a rival contender for the throne (AD 193–5), divided this province into two, Syria Coele and Syria Phoenice. Emperors from the Syrian city of Emesa (Homs) ruled at Rome from 218 until 235, and then a temporarily independent Emesan state, controlling most of the near east, was suppressed by Aurelian in 273. Meanwhile the former kingdom of the Nabataeans, in north-western Arabia, had long become a separate province, under the name of Arabia Petraea (from 106 or 111/112).

Beyond the eastern frontier, which Syria and Arabia adjoined and guarded, extended the only major power among all Rome's neighbours, the state of the Parthians. The Parthian régime, however, was overthrown in AD 224/9, and succeeded by the even more formidable kingdom of the Sassanian Persians. For over half a century, aerial exploration has made it possible for us to form a picture of the methods adopted by successive emperors to protect this sensitive frontier – and, above all, to push it forward when possible. To the east, the border was secured by the River Euphrates, which was too broad and rapid to cross and was commanded by hills studded with fortresses (*castella*).

During the third century AD, however, these arrangements had to be amplified in face of the growing Persian threat, and it was Diocletian (284–305) who took the required steps. His measures formed part of a complete reconstruction of the empire's military system necessitated by increased pressures on the eastern and northern frontiers alike. The number of troops under arms was substantially augmented, and the army was divided into two branches: the *comitatenses*, 'soldiers of the retinue', who were a mobile field force, and the *limitanei*, 'men of the borders'. These *limitanei*, maintained by annual drafts of Roman conscripts, as well as by numerous Germans and other non-Romans, manned defences of a more elaborate nature than ever before, on all the confines of the empire.

Nowhere were such defences more formidably reinforced than in the near east, where Persian invasions had compelled new ways of thinking. In effect, Diocletian transformed the organization of the frontier from a flexible, and to some extent offensive, character into a defensive line that was fixed and unchangeable. The destruction wrought by the Persian Wars provided a vacuum which his new military works were designed to fill. In Syria, the nucleus of his improved communications system, feeding the defence line, was a road, the *strata Diocletiana*, which extended from Damascus to Sura on the Euphrates, after crossing the desert by way of Palmyra, and was protected by numerous strong points.

Farther south, too, in the province of Arabia Petraea – even though this territory, so far, seemed fairly remote from the Persian menace – the frontier was likewise radically strengthened. This is illustrated by recent excavations at Lejjun, east of the Dead Sea. This is identified with the ancient Betthorus,[10] and proves to be the only known late legionary fortress built on a virgin site and not disturbed by significant later occupation. This garrison fortress, datable to *c.*AD 300, measures about 15 acres in extent (only about a quarter of the size of earlier counterparts elsewhere), and apparently accommodated about 1,500 soldiers (as against 5,000 in the earlier camps).

That was probably the strength of the Legio IV Martia, perhaps formed by Diocletian himself from which Lejjun took its modern name; the unit doubled the strength of the Arabian garrison, hitherto consisting of a single legion. Betthorus was the fortress which, supported by a network of smaller forts and watch-towers (between six and twelve miles apart), was given the task of blocking invaders or raiders from the desert – most immediately, no doubt, Arabian nomad tribesmen, though Persian forces, too, might always appear in the vicinity. In normal times of peace, the frontier force also devoted its time to regulating traffic between desert nomads and sedentary cultivators.

In 1980 a survey team of the American Central Limes Arabic project recorded fifty sites along the desert fringe. These were mostly nomad camps, but then in 1982, out of 130 sites visited along the frontier (at three of which soundings were undertaken), at least one half proved to be watch-towers of earlier construction that were rehabilitated and occupied by the Romans, forming a system of signal and observation posts.

'In an effort', records S. T. Parker, 'to see just how successful such a network of lookout posts might have been, members of the Project undertook a bold experiment ... Staff members manned fourteen forts and watchposts known to be contemporary with the Lejjun legionary occupation and extending from north to south over a thirty-five kilometre [twenty-two mile] stretch of the frontier. Using smoke and mirror signals by day and torch signals by night, the teams stationed at these outposts communicated messages ... Even though the daylight signalling met with mixed results, it was a haunting reenactment, especially at night when the pinpoints of torchlight lit up at distances of ten kilometres [six miles], appearing and disappearing as they transmitted vital messages. By such means had the Romans forewarned their fellows that Saracens were approaching, bent on destruction.[11]

Betthorus stands twenty miles east of the Dead Sea upon the Moabite plateau, in a region drained by valleys containing artificial channels and seasonal streams (wadis) that debouch into the Dead Sea. One of the shallower valleys is the Wadi Lejjun, which was selected to house the fortress of Betthorus, largely, no doubt, because of the presence of a perennial spring. The general plan and many features of Betthorus were already known in the nineteenth century, and the first air photographs date from the 1930s. But the further excavations and air photography during the last ten years (with the fifth and final campaign in 1989) have revealed much more. The fortress is now seen to be a rectangular complex, rebuilt in Diocletian's time of locally quarried limestone, chert (a flint-like quartz) and basalt, and extending over an area of eleven acres.

Within its periphery the *principia* or headquarters building (cf. Chapter 8, section 4) gave access to a central courtyard, which was surrounded by an arcaded portico with a tiled roof. The north and south walls of the *principia* were pierced by flanking entrances, between which a hall (*basilica*) may have stood. Its southern entrance was adjoined by a staircase leading up to an elevated, apsed platform, from which the commander could address some of his officers or troops. The western section of the *principia* contained administrative offices and a chapel housing the legionary standards, closed by an iron gate or grill.

An excavated barracks block illustrated the lives of the rank-and-file soldiers of the frontier army during these later years of the empire. It contained two rows of eighteen rooms extending along either flank of a central wall. The westernmost rooms on each side were rather larger than the others, and presumably intended for soldiers of higher rank. The other rooms seem to have housed eight soldiers apiece. Each room was roofed by limestone arches supporting basalt roof-beams, and beside the block lay a courtyard which (to judge from the contents of pits) was employed for the preparation of meals.

Diet (cf. Chapter 8, section 3, on the food eaten by soldiers) was most commonly mutton or goat, with some chicken, beef and pork as well. Other foods included barley, dates, grapes, olives and lentils. The principal fuel was dung, but wood, reeds and sedges were also used. A complex water-supply system included a dam, six mills and a number of channels. The garrison also operated a metalworking industry. Outside the fortress was a civilian settlement which provided housing and services for soldiers' families, discharged veterans, and merchants. A building in this area was probably a hotel for visitors (*mansio*).

The huge towers in the enclosure wall of the fortress have also been examined. 'The fort', writes Parker, 'was, given the likely size of the Fourth Mars Legion, an example of overkill, so massively is it fortified. Its projecting towers are characteristic of the Late Empire, when the Roman army shifted from essentially offensive tactics to defensive ones: the projecting towers permitted enfilading missile fire to be directed at attackers attempting to scale or undermine the walls ... At Lejjun [Betthorus] such [platforms for artillery] are clearly anomalous since the nomadic Arab tribes who constituted the local enemies were extremely mobile and had no siege capability. Either the Roman architects were simply following a standardized plan employed all over the empire, or the Roman command was worried that the Sassanid Persians, who were a major threat to Syria and Mesopotamia and who possessed a sophisticated siege capability, might strike this far south.'[12]

Betthorus was demolished during the fourth century AD, by raiders or an earthquake. It was subsequently rebuilt, with smaller interior rooms. However, in the time of the Byzantine emperor Justinian I (AD 527–65) the camp was finally dismantled, together with the rest of the territory's defence system. As pressure multiplied on other frontiers, the Arabian garrisons had been gradually weakened by the transfer of troops to more urgently threatened regions, until in *c.*530, as an economy measure, Justinian abolished many of the frontier units altogether, and handed over their functions to native Arabian dependants; an earthquake in 551 completed the process. What Justinian could not have foreseen was the rise of the Moslems, whose armies, when they arrived in the territory early in the following century, found that there was no longer any fortified Byzantine frontier to stand in their way.

3 Mediolanum (Milan): The Last Western Emperor

Numismatists – whose other researches have been discussed elsewhere (Chapter 3, section 5; Chapter 4, section 5; Chapter 9, section 1) – have now reminded us that the last western Roman emperor was not Romulus 'Augustulus', to whom, when he was forced to abdicate by the German Odoacer in AD 476, tradition has assigned this role, but Julius Nepos, who reigned on in Dalmatia until he was murdered there in 480.

In *c.*468 Nepos had succeeded to his father Nepotianus's command as Master of Soldiers in Dalmatia, a country in which the military command owed formal allegiance to the eastern (later Byzantine) empire – separated from the west since 364, and permanently since 395 – but in practice obeyed no imperial master. Nepos had married into the family of the eastern emperor Leo I, who helped him to secure the western throne from Glycerius (sent, on abdication to Salonae [Solin] as its bishop), so that Nepos took Glycerius's place at the western capital, Ravenna. His accession was confirmed by the Roman senate and by some measure, at least, of popular support, and brought Dalmatia back temporarily to western rule.

Nepos gave his principal military post, the Mastership of Soldiers at the Ravenna headquarters, to Orestes, formerly secretary to Attila the Hun. But when Nepos lost Gaul to Euric the Goth, (to his great discredit), Orestes decided to replace him on the western throne by his own son Romulus 'Augustulus'. With this aim, Orestes led a force to attack Ravenna, whereupon Nepos, having reigned in Italy from June 474 until August 475, made his escape by sea and withdrew to his princedom of Dalmatia. The emperor of the west, therefore, was now Romulus. Not for long, however, since in the following year a mutiny broke out among the east German troops in Italy, who wanted land for themselves, and found a leader in one of Orestes's German officers, Flavius Odoacer (Odovacar). Odoacer soon compelled Romulus to abandon the throne (relegating him to a villa at Misenum in Campania), and his troops proceeded to declare him king: thus Italy, like other parts of what had been the western Roman empire, was henceforward a German kingdom.

Before long the eastern emperor, now Leo's son-in-law Zeno, received two deputations. One was from Odoacer, who urged formal recognition for himself in the west – in return for which he was prepared to acknowledge Zeno's titular imperial supremacy. The other deputation came from Nepos in Dalmatia, who reminded Zeno of their marriage connection, urged sympathy for his predicament as a refugee (pointing out that this had once been the fate of Zeno himself), and appealed for support to regain the western throne. Odoacer's application was granted, and he was awarded the rank of patrician of the empire. As for Nepos, however, Zeno reminded Odoacer, and the senate of Rome, that they had originally received him from the east but had treated him badly, and gave instructions that they should take him back as their formal suzerain in Italy.

What happened next is revealed by the coinage. Although Odoacer, one may assume, took no steps to invite Nepos back to Italy, he accorded him the recognition that the eastern emperor had requested. This can be seen from the gold pieces issued in Nepos's name by the mint of Mediolanum (Milan). On the obverse the *solidi* (units) show his full-faced bust, with spear and shield, inscribed D(*ominus*) N(*oster*) IVL(*ius*) NEPOS P(*ius*) F(*elix*) AVG(*ustus*). On the reverse is a figure of Victory carrying a long cross, with the inscription VICTORIA AVGGG. (*Augustorum*, i.e. of the three *Augusti*, who were presumably, in the first place, Nepos and Leo and Nepos's or Leo's wife). These *solidi*, however, can be divided into two chronologically distinguishable categories on the basis of stylistic considerations (despite the frequent, but not always justified, numismatic criticism of such criteria as unduly subjective). The first of these two categories is stylistically analogous to the gold issues of other western emperors of the immediately preceding years. The second and later category, on the other hand, is close to pieces bearing the heads of Zeno, and belongs to the period when Nepos had returned to Dalmatia.

J. P. C. Kent, who has noted the distinction between these two categories at the mint of Mediolanum, sums up their differences as follows:

'1: *Solidi* of good style and *tremisses* with small-spiked wreath struck in the name of Nepos only. I attribute these to January–August 475.

'2: *Solidi* of poor style and *tremisses* with large spikes, in the names of Nepos and Zeno. They share one group equally, but in another Zeno is dominant. This was doubtless that current at Nepos's death in May 480.'[13] (These last issues, with their careful lettering but poor style, bear a marked resemblance to German issues of the period.)

The conclusion is, then, that the first category belongs to the period of Julius Nepos's rule in Italy (475), and the second category to the subsequent epoch (476/7–480), the period when he had gone back to Dalmatia but was, at least officially and superficially, recognized as western emperor by Odoacer, who was now the German king of Italy but issued these coins in Nepos's name. Odoacer also struck pieces in the name of Zeno, both at Mediolanum and at Ravenna, and in his own name at his capital Ravenna. But some of the gold *solidi* bearing the name of Nepos also display the mintmark AR, indicating that they were issued at Arelate (Arles) in southern Gaul. This has given rise to the supposition that in that country, as in Italy, Nepos maintained vestigial, ostensible sovereignty, though it must, in practice, have been subject to the rulership of Euric the Visigoth, who was, effectively, in control of Gaul.

As for Nepos himself, his death in Dalmatia (480) came when he was assassinated by two members of his staff at his country house near Salonae (Solin) – perhaps at the instigation of his predecessor Glycerius, who was now, as we have seen, the local bishop. The last Roman emperor of any part of the west had now ceased to rule – there was subsequently no western emperor until Charlemagne's coronation in 800 – and after Nepos's death Odoacer crossed over from Italy into Dalmatia, supposedly to inflict vengeance upon Nepos's assassins, but in reality (although he continued to coin in Zeno's name) to take the Italian peninsula over and make it part of his own kingdom. In 488, however, Zeno authorized the Ostrogoth Theoderic to suppress Odoacer, which was achieved after a four-year campaign.

EPILOGUE

I have included in this book only a few out of the many recent discoveries in the field of classical archaeology relating to history; but I hope, nevertheless, that this selection, however inadequate, demonstrated that the contributions made by archaeology to Greek and Roman historians during the past three decades have been massive, novel and varied – in fact, indispensable, for every chronological phase of the ancient world.

These advances have included the application of new techniques. Among them, the exploration of underwater sites and shipwrecks has been conspicuous. Air photography, too, has developed into an increasingly revealing science. The magnetometer and potentiometer and many other mechanisms have been brought into play to see what lies underground, and every kind of chemical analysis has been applied to the metals and other objects that come to light. The study of tree-rings (dendrochronology) has furnished dates. The investigation of skeletons has enabled the physical characteristics of those who lived in the ancient world to be reconstructed, and the examination of food remains has led to new conclusions about their diet.

More or less orthodox excavation of urban architectural sites and burial places, too, has likewise transformed our knowledge of the ancient world, especially in areas where other forms of record are deficient at important epochs: for example upon the islands of Euboea and Cyprus, in Campania and Macedonia, on the Black Sea coast and the banks of the Danube, and in even remoter regions of classical expansion such as Afghanistan. In some cases these excavations have provided checks or new viewpoints in regard to the literary evidence, and amplifications or contradictions of mythology and legend. Many of the new discoveries harmonize with the taste for wider environmental and agricultural pictures that has characterized the New Archaeology (Appendix 1). Furthermore, peripheral branches of archaeology have also proved invaluable to historians. They have been able, for example, to make deductions from discoveries of inscriptions, coins, sculpture, papyri, jewellery and scientific objects and installations.

Such are the finds that have taken place during the past few years. But the future will yield even more, since all these types of archaeological contributions to history are on the increase – and other methods of investigation, too, will be found. Activity is intense, and if another book on this subject comes to be written in ten years' time it will surely contain a great deal of new material, including not only new finds (some of them on sites which can already be forecast or guessed at, others at unexpected locations), but also techniques which, at this juncture, are still embryonic or undeveloped or even non-existent and unimagined. Archaeology as an aid to Greek and Roman history has longlasting, continuing achievements to its credit. But they are nothing, it can be predicted, in comparison with those that lie in the future. 'Archaeology', writes George F. Bass, 'can play a key role in the expansion of the historical sciences and in providing a new understanding of the world in which we live. Whatever course archaeology takes, one thing is clear – the archaeology of the twenty-first century will bear little relation to contemporary practice ... Sixty years from now, technical advances still unimagined will be routine.'[1]

MAPS

1 GREECE

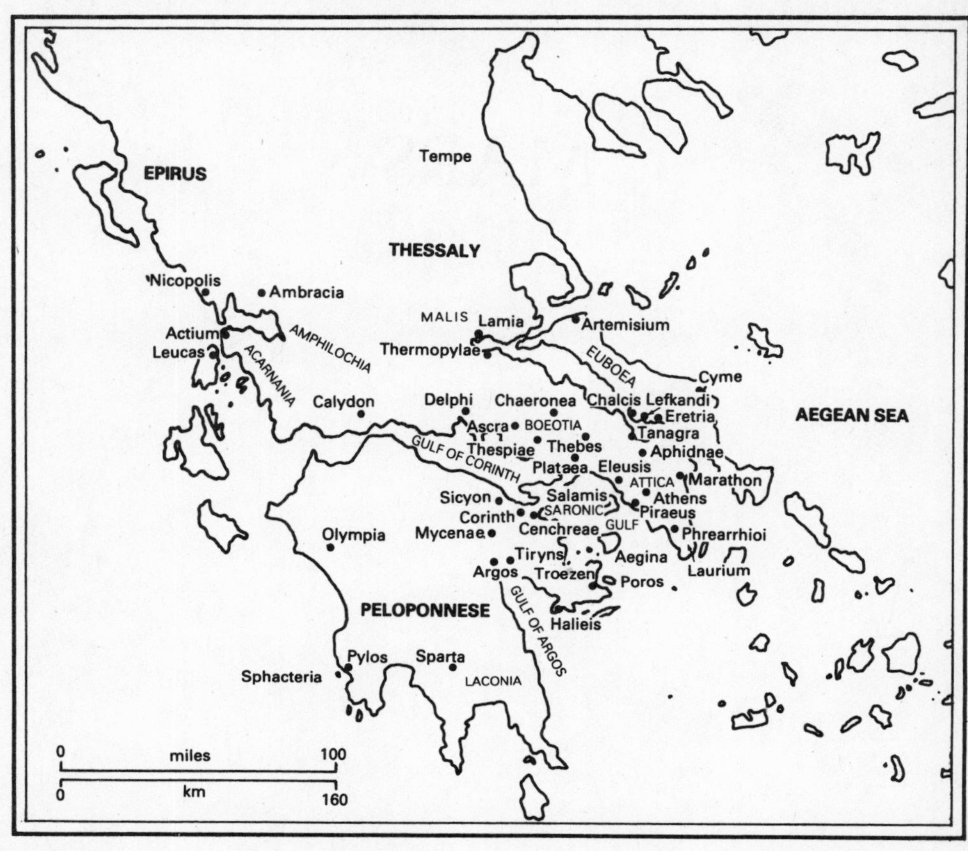
EPIRUS
Tempe
THESSALY
Nicopolis
Ambracia
MALIS
Lamia
Artemisium
Actium
Leucas
AMPHILOCHIA
ACARNANIA
Thermopylae
EUBOEA
Cyme
Calydon
Delphi
Chaeronea
Chalcis
Lefkandi
Eretria
AEGEAN SEA
Ascra
BOEOTIA
Tanagra
Thespiae
Thebes
Aphidnae
GULF OF CORINTH
Plataea
Eleusis
ATTICA
Marathon
Sicyon
Salamis
Athens
Corinth
SARONIC
Piraeus
Olympia
Mycenae
Cenchreae
GULF
Phrearrhioi
Tiryns
Aegina
Argos
Troezen
Poros
Laurium
PELOPONNESE
GULF OF ARGOS
Halieis
Pylos
Sparta
Sphacteria
LACONIA
0
miles
100
0
km
160

2 MACEDONIA AND BEYOND

River Borysthenes
River Ingul
SCYTHIA
River Hypanis
River Tyras
CALLIPIDAE
Olbia
Berezan
LAKE MAEOTIS
Cimmerian Bosphorus
TAURIS
Panticapaeum
Tyras
Carnuntum
Aquincum
ILLYRICUM
Noviodunum
DACIA
R Drinus
Istrus
DALMATIA
Drobeta
BLACK SEA
Salonae
Ratiaria
River Danube
R Margus
Novae
LOWER MOESIA
R Ciabrus
UPPER MOESIA
THRACE
Thracian Bosphorus
R Haliacmon
R Axius
Hadrianopolis
MACEDONIA
Byzantium (Constantinople)
Pella
Philippi
Sindus
Amphipolis
R Lydias
Thessalonica
Aegae
PIERIA
THERMAIC GULF
AEGEAN SEA
0 miles 300
0 km 500

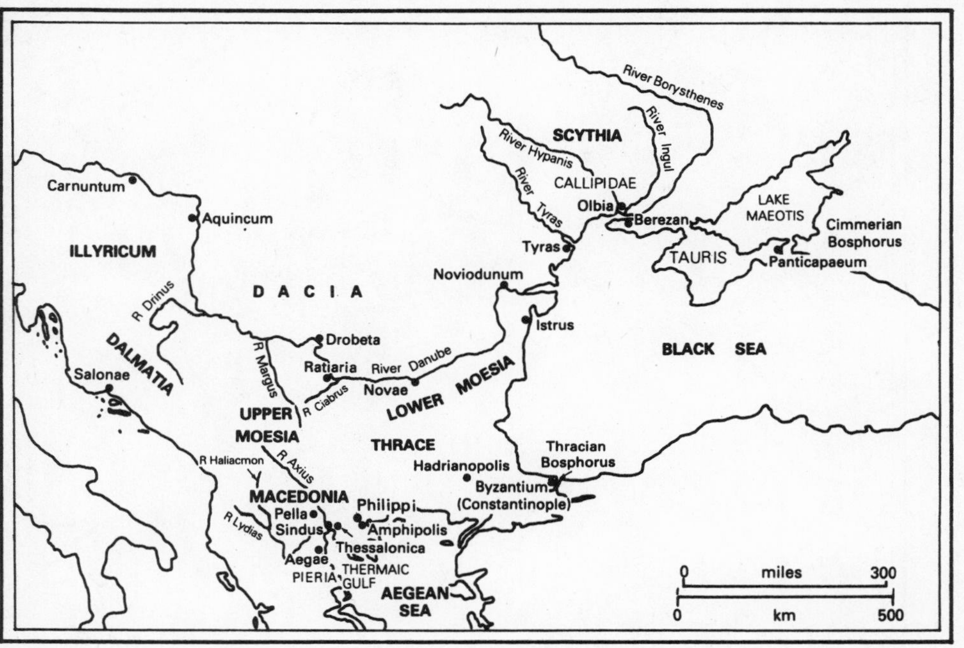

3 ASIA MINOR AND THE ISLANDS

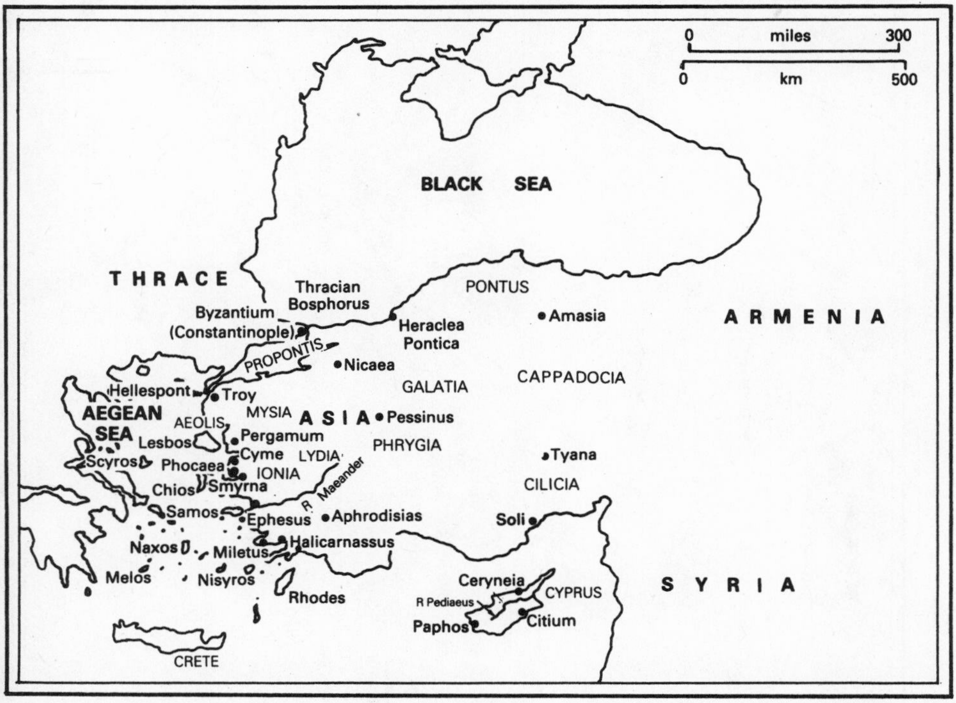

0 miles 300
0 km 500
BLACK SEA
THRACE
Thracian Bosphorus
PONTUS
Byzantium (Constantinople)
Heraclea Pontica
Amasia
ARMENIA
PROPONTIS
Nicaea
GALATIA
CAPPADOCIA
Hellespont
Troy
AEGEAN SEA
MYSIA
AEOLIS
ASIA
Pessinus
Pergamum
Lesbos
Cyme
LYDIA
PHRYGIA
Tyana
Scyros
Phocaea
IONIA
Chios
Smyrna
R Maeander
CILICIA
Samos
Ephesus
Aphrodisias
Soli
Naxos
Miletus
Halicarnassus
Melos
Nisyros
Rhodes
Ceryneia
CYPRUS
SYRIA
R Pediaeus
Paphos
Citium
CRETE

4 SYRIA AND FARTHER EAST

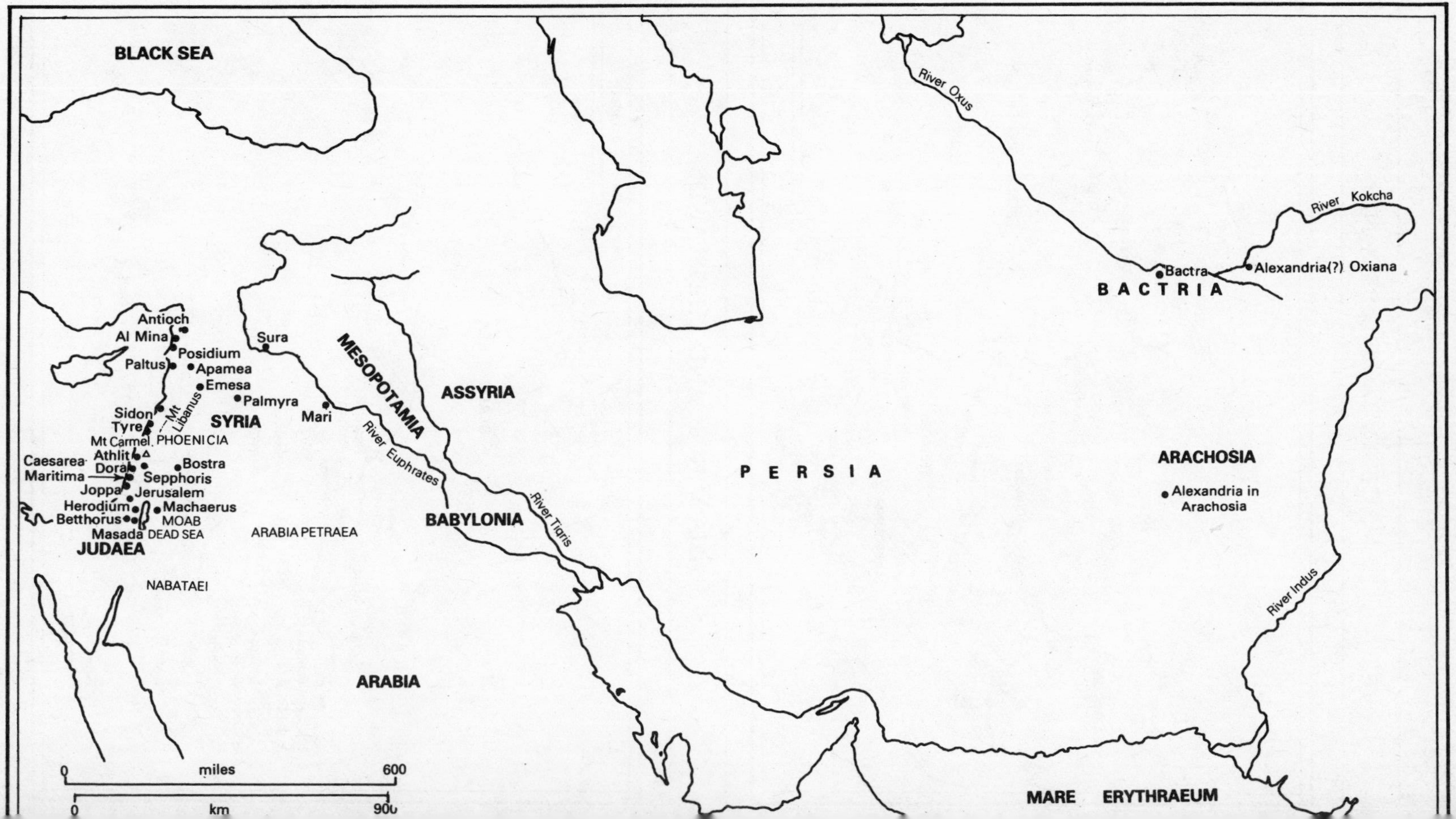

BLACK SEA
River Oxus
River Kokcha
Bactra
Alexandria(?) Oxiana
BACTRIA
Antioch
Al Mina
Posidium
Paltus
Apamea
Emesa
Sura
MESOPOTAMIA
ASSYRIA
Palmyra
Mt Libanus
Sidon
Tyre
SYRIA
Mari
Mt Carmel
PHOENICIA
Athlit
Caesarea Maritima
Dora
Bostra
Sepphoris
Joppa
Jerusalem
Herodium
Machaerus
Betthorus
MOAB
Masada
DEAD SEA
JUDAEA
River Euphrates
River Tigris
BABYLONIA
ARABIA PETRAEA
PERSIA
ARACHOSIA
Alexandria in Arachosia
NABATAEI
River Indus
ARABIA
0 miles 600
0 km 900
MARE ERYTHRAEUM

5 EGYPT

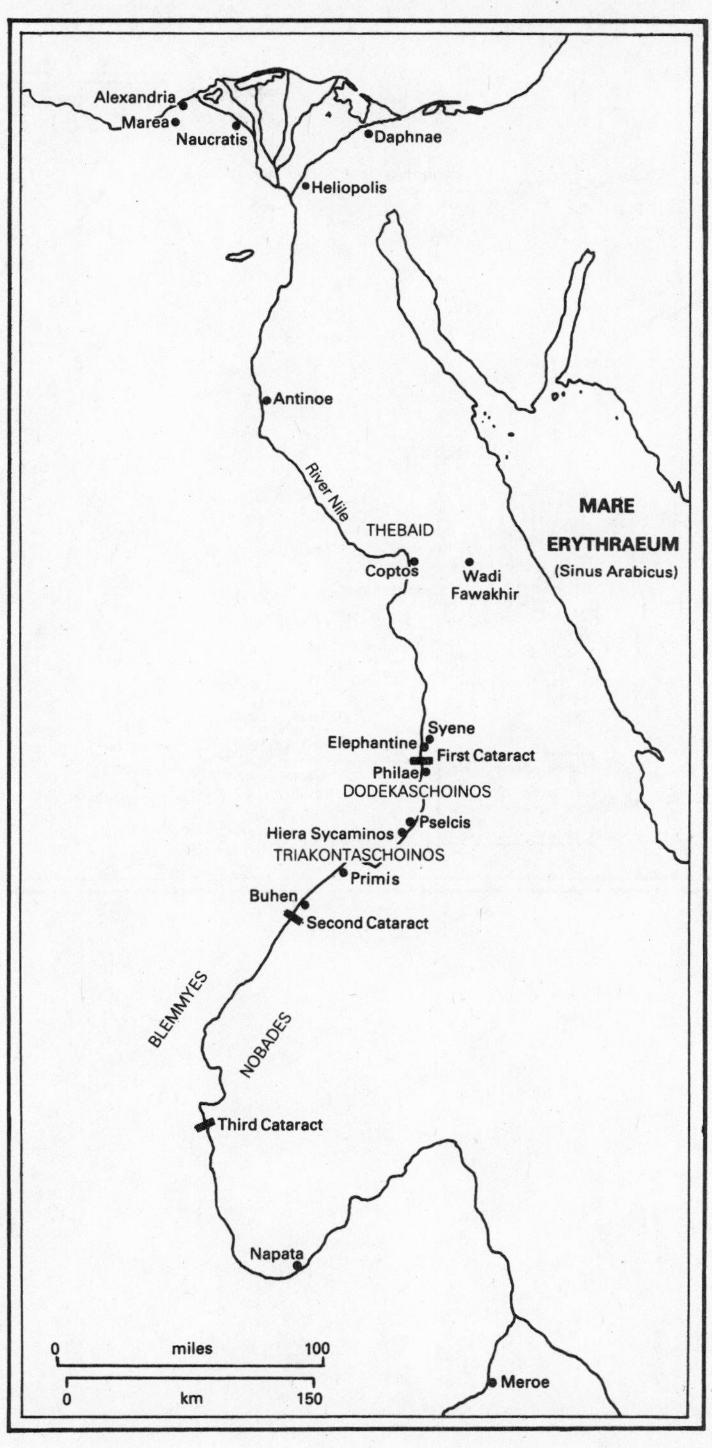

Alexandria
Marea
Naucratis
Daphnae
Heliopolis
Antinoe
River Nile
THEBAID
Coptos
Wadi
Fawakhir
MARE
ERYTHRAEUM
(Sinus Arabicus)
Syene
Elephantine
First Cataract
Philae
DODEKASCHOINOS
Pselcis
Hiera Sycaminos
TRIAKONTASCHOINOS
Primis
Buhen
Second Cataract
BLEMMYES
NOBADES
Third Cataract
Napata
Meroe
0
miles
100
0
km
150

6 NORTHERN AND CENTRAL ITALY

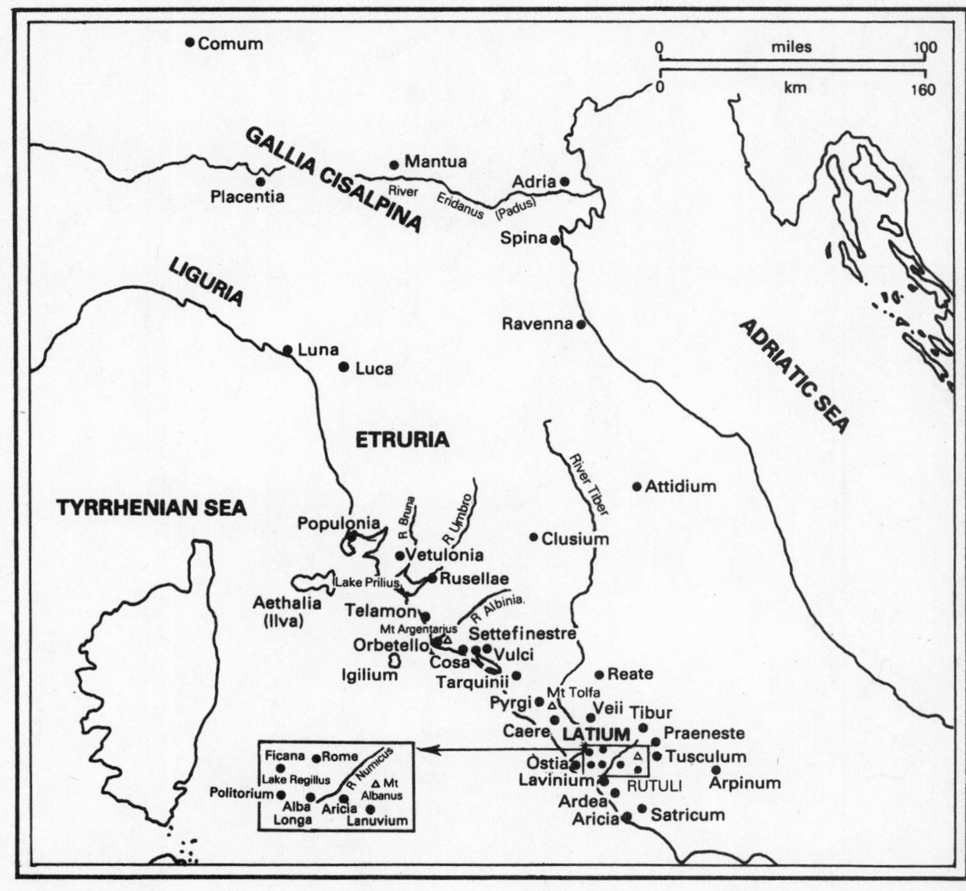

7 SOUTHERN ITALY AND SICILY

8 GAUL AND GERMANY

9 BRITAIN

Bar Hill
River Bodotria
Bearsden
Bridgeness
Antonine Wall
River Clota
River Clota
0 miles 50
0 km 80
Hadrian's Wall
Vindolanda
Pons Aelius
Maia
R Tinea
Segodunum
Corstopitum
Arbeia
River Ituna
Alauna
Cataractonium
Bremetennacum
Castleshaw
Cawthorne
Lindum
Deva
Holt
CORNOVII
Viroconium
ICENI
Verulamium
Camulodunum
Venta Silurum
Isca Silurum
Frocester Court
Londinium
Durobrivae
Hod Hill
REGNENSES (REGNI)
Waddon Hill
R. Lavant
Noviomagus
FRETUM GALLICUM
OCEANUS
BRITANNICUS

APPENDIX I

ARCHAEOLOGY AND THE CLASSICS

The classical historian obviously needs the archaeologist – who provides the only means of investigating more than ninety-nine per cent of the human past. The two disciplines are independent but complementary and inextricably interactive. Even if descriptions of archaeology as the 'handmaid of history' now seem too subservient, it *is* part of history, even though it employs materials and techniques of its own.[1]

For one thing, it is not belittling classical archaeology, or relegating it to the role of a mere auxiliary, to recall that it supplements, on thousands of occasions, what is told us by the Greek and Roman historians, who, despite their literary gifts, inevitably left gaps and ambiguities (Chapter 2, section 6). For example, it has been those historians who taught the world, with fateful effects, that history is mainly political and military. And it has been up to the archaeologists to fill the picture out with other themes: social, economic, agricultural, technological, industrial, pathological, dietetic, and related to patterns of settlement and the landscapes by which those environmental patterns were sustained. That is to say, it is one of the archaeologists' functions to handle matters affecting the broad masses of the population, and to lay down and evaluate quantitative assessments regarding such matters.

These tasks are carried out with the aid of new methods adopted during the past three decades – displaying a fresh, sharp awareness of how such methods can yield fruitful generalizations. But it has not been an easy business. Indeed, at times it has looked, as Colin Renfrew declares, like 'a challenge and a struggle – a sustained struggle to devise meanings and interpretations which can be related to the finds, the data, in a coherent and justifiable way ... This struggle for meaning has always been and remains the fundamental challenge of archaeology.'[2]

Archaeologists, during these recent years, have continually asked themselves, and have continually been asked by others, whether what they profess is a science or a humanity. But the answer does not matter all that much – except in a university, where it has to be decided to which Faculty they belong – because they have to fulfil, and are in a position to fulfil, *both* purposes and functions alike. As regards their scientific role, the relationship of archaeologists with the natural sciences, and their closeness to those sciences, has intensified in recent decades, during which they have taken to the laboratory in no uncertain fashion. They have also come far closer to the social sciences as well. 'The shift, as I see it,' observes Renfrew, 'is from artefacts to talk of societies.'[3]

P. Rahtz expands the point. 'Archaeology is the study of material culture in its relationship to human behaviour – the physical manifestation of man's activities ... It is not a science like biology or chemistry, though it uses scientific methods and adopts scientific attitudes. It has been described as a cultural science ... [for it] finds increasingly common ground with anthropology, philosophy, sociology and politics. It is really aiming at the same thing – the understanding of humans – by utilizing the special method of the interpretation of human residues.'[4] Archaeology seeks to achieve such understanding, that is to say, by considering, as systematically as possible, the relationship between material culture *and behaviour*.

This makes archaeology a social science – but it also makes it history (whether or not one regards history as one of the social sciences). For as Mortimer Wheeler observed, 'the archaeologist is digging up, not things, but people'[5] – people as elements of society, and people, persons, as part of history, which is what archaeology is all about. Stuart Piggott formulated this indissoluble connection between archaeology and history. 'Archaeology', he wrote, 'is in fact a branch of historical study ... What is needed in the application of archaeological techniques to historical studies is in fact all the expertise devised for the examination of non-literate, prehistoric peoples (including the cooperation with the natural scientists), further combined with a cooperation between the archaeologist and those working in the humanistic disciplines involved in, for instance, philology and history ... The additional sources [available in the historical field] ... demand a further interdisciplinary comprehension by the archaeologist. With such a cooperative approach, the application of archaeological techniques to historical societies can in fact amplify the strictly literary record in many directions.'[6]

And the sort of history with which archaeology is particularly concerned is *ancient* history, in which the story of the Greeks and Romans plays such a leading part. 'Nowhere', wrote Antony Snodgrass, 'are the distinctive assets and liabilities of archaeology as a source shown up so conspicuously as in Greek and Roman history. While the decisive theoretical battles of archaeology have long been fought out on other fields and between bigger battalions, it is in the closer encounters of classical archaeology that the more continuous attrition of empirical testing takes place. The experience has not had much influence on wider archaeological thought, but it has revealed certain assets on the part of archaeological evidence in an historical context; four of these, which I would single out, are its independence, its directness, its experimental character, and its unlimited potential for future extension.'[7] And, unlike the prehistorians, classical archaeologists also possess the advantage that their theories and data can be tested against the written record and the place.

This somewhat bewilderingly multidisciplinarian vocation of the archaeologist, reflected, as Snodgrass observes, in 'decisive theoretical battles', can be summed up by the phenomenon of the New Archaeology. This was a product of the 1960s and 1970s, which reacted against the more romantic or woolly aspects of the study in earlier days, and preferred processes (hence its alternative name 'processual') to individuals.

As Andrew Sherratt records, 'it was in Britain (closely followed by the Netherlands and Scandinavia) in the mid-1960s that new thinking took place, largely oriented to America, and to anthropology. Like much else in that assertive decade, it proclaimed itself as 'New' archaeology; and in its attempt to create a methodology of an independent discipline – and to answer questions beyond those traditionally asked by historians – it did indeed bring a new dimension to research.

'The context of this movement was an expanding economy and a rapidly increasing university population, in an optimistic and anti-authoritarian atmosphere in which science was the model of success. It coincided with technical advances such as radio carbon dating, rapid microchemical analysis, and the computer; but its main novelty was an interest in generalization and theory, building models in the manner of ecology and economics and using the language of systems analysis. In a subject where "models" had hitherto implied scale replicas of Stonehenge or Scandinavian girls in Bronze Age dress, its impact was startling. The ecological emphasis had a direct influence on fieldwork, bringing to notice classes of evidence previously thrown out with the dirt – animal bones, carbonized seeds, pollen grains and beetle wings – which were now seen as crucial for *reconstructing ancient environments*. It lifted attention from individual sites to patterns of settlement and the landscapes which sustained them, and so raised basic questions of economics and demography.'[8]

Thus the New or Processual Archaeology advocated building up 'a body of central theory capable of synthesizing the general regularities within its date'. Yet it has now become widely accepted that such aspirations and claims were overdone. This is because some of its exponents – not always admitting that they, too, like historians, cannot always command objectivity – replaced their original questioning methods by laying down too many dogmatically unchangeable general laws. Today, therefore, by way of despairing reaction, archaeology has sometimes seemed to be breaking up into fragments, and failing to define, or losing, its identity. Thus its practitioners have passed, some like to say, into a new 'post-processual' stage; or, in the words of those who wish to avoid jargon, they have become mature enough to make room for the diversity and controversial uncertainty which are both required and inevitable in a subject whose tests often cannot be repeated, and whose variables elude tight control.

These fierce battles over matters theoretical were fought out in archaeological fields unconnected with Greece and Rome: that is to say, in the fields of prehistoric archaeology. Yes, comments B. A. Sparkes, 'Only distant gunfire from the archaeological revolution seems to have been heard in the camp of the classical archaeologists.'[9] True, in the course of these gigantic discussions, the classical archaeologists have not always received, or even wanted to receive, a great deal of notice. Moreover, the number of these 'new' techniques and methods that they have utilized is not entirely impressive, as Snodgrass has now insisted further.[10] In consequence of such inadequacies, a *new classical archaeology* is demanded.[11]

Yet this may not be necessary: after all, classical archaeologists – as this book has shown – have used *some* of the new methods. And indeed those they have found it possible to use have (along with traditional or novel applications of older methods) contributed largely to the fact that archaeology, in recent years, has virtually transformed classical and historical studies. For during this period, points out Graham Shipley, 'there has been something of a change in the intellectual origins of Greek archaeologists. A classical education is still common, but many now come from ancient history, pure archaeology, sociology, and the experimental and earth sciences. Partly as a consequence of these changes, there has been an increase in fruitful cooperation between all these disciplines ... It is probably fair to say that perceptions of Greek history between the eighth and first centuries BC have almost completely altered in the past sixty years. Archaeology is mainly responsible for this.'[12]

APPENDIX II

A FEW TASKS FOR THE FUTURE

The next few years, as has already been suggested, are likely to see many new archaeological developments contributing still further to our understanding of ancient history. Here mention will be made of just four sites or areas, all in Italy – though other Italian projects could also have been mentioned, and the list might also have been extended to include every other single country where the Greeks and Romans settled. The present Appendix, then, is merely a brief and more or less random selection, intended just to show the sort of enterprise from which archaeological contributions to history are at the present time, hoped for.

(i) Lavinium: Archaeology and Myth

One function of archaeology is to throw light, not merely on literature as a whole (Chapter 2, section 6), but on literary mythology in particular. It can corroborate, elucidate, and amend the myths. Of this the ancients were already very conscious, since large sections, for example, of Athenian tragedies were devoted to explaining and announcing the foundation of cults, a task which often arose because of the existence of sites or buildings, ruined or intact, which seemed mysterious and in need of such an explanation.

Latium provides illustrations of this complex relationship between archaeology and mythology, in both of which the territory is so rich. But the illustrations are sufficiently enigmatic and inconclusive to warrant relegation to an Appendix – at this stage at least, pending further elucidations. The territory of Latium, the southern part of what is now Lazio, extends over a well-watered, undulating region of western Italy from the River Tiber down to the borders of Campania. At the beginning of the first millennium BC the prehistoric inhabitants of the region were joined or superseded by groups of mixed race later known as the Latins, who were descended from people connected with the Mycenaean civilization, and spoke an Indo-European language. These immigrants formed small communities, gradually amalgamating into larger city-states, and uniting into confederations for religious purposes, centred upon the Alban Mount, Africia (Ariccia), Ardea and Lavinium (Pratica del Mare), and undergoing varying degrees of Etruscan influence from north of the Tiber (cf. Campania, Chapter 5, section 4).

Lavinium, seventeen miles south-east of Rome, belonged to one of these Latin Leagues, and became its federal sanctuary during the sixth century BC. It is also mentioned in Polybius's description of the first treaty between Rome and Carthage (508 BC).[13] Proximity to the sea gave Lavinium early contacts with the Greek world, which endowed its cults with a Greek rather than an Etruscan character. According to mythical tradition, the town had been created towards the end of the second millennium BC by Aeneas, a fugitive from the Trojan War, who named his foundation after his wife Lavinia, daughter of Latinus who was king of the Latins. It was from Lavinium, according to this tradition, that Aeneas's son Ascanius, three decades later, became the founder of Alba Longa, from which, after a long line of Alban kings, Romulus and Remus established Rome itself, traditionally in 753 BC.

These were fictitious refinements upon simpler ideas: the idea, for example, that Aeneas had founded Rome, not Lavinium. The subsequent version, making him the founder of Lavinium instead, was partly prompted by difficulties in establishing a satisfactory mythical chronology which did not leave an uncomfortable gap in Roman history. His foundation of Lavinium thus became canonical. He chose the site, we are told, because he had been instructed – while in Epirus, on his way to Italy – to establish his settlement at the location where he would see a sow with thirty young (the sow being a tribal or civic badge of the Latins and other Italian peoples). When he arrived in Italy, near this point on the Tyrrhenian coast, the god of the River Tiber warned him in a dream that the fulfilment of the portent was imminent. The next morning it duly appeared. In fact, however, the whole story of Aeneas's disembarkation in this area was stimulated, or even brought into existence, by the fact that a place in the region (near Zingarini, between Lavinium and Ardea) bore the name of *Troia* – round which myths relating to the Trojan War were obviously likely to accumulate.

Aeneas's burial place near Lavinium, beside the River Numicus (or Numicius), was also shown to visitors, although others said that the tomb belonged to his father Anchises (who was more generally believed, however, to have met his death in Sicily). In relation to this grave, Aeneas was given the surname of 'Indiges'. The Indigites were ancestors who received worship, and the monument beside the Numicus had apparently, at first, been the shrine of some divine ancestor or other (whose name was subsequently lost sight of). But the building underwent various reconstructions, the last phase of which corresponds conveniently to a reference by Dionysius of Halicarnassus to a tumulus erected in Aeneas's memory by the Latins after a battle against the Rutuli – fought not far from Lavinium:[14] doubtless this structure was thus identified with the tumulus.

There was also a tradition that Aeneas had brought his household gods (Penates) to Lavinium from Troy, on their way to a permanent abode in the Roman Forum. The devotion of the Romans, in historic times, to this cult of the Penates, lodged in their midst, helped to encourage the story of Aeneas's migration from Troy and its apparent explanation of how the Penates had arrived in Rome. The Romans, eager to stress the glories of their own alleged Trojan ancestry, made a point of declaring that their own Penates were the same as the Trojan gods brought by Aeneas to Lavinium – and that it was from Lavinium that they had come to Rome.

The link was stressed after 338 BC, when the Romans absorbed what was now the sole Latin League, and entered into new relations with its individual members, including Lavinium, which had remained loyal to them during the preceding Latin revolt. It was apparently at this juncture that certain Romans decided to project this association back in the mythical past by enhancing the Lavinian rites as a symbol of the antique Roman-Latin link. An inscription found at Tor Tignosa,[15] close to Lavinium, has been interpreted, though without universal agreement, as calling Aeneas 'Lar', which later meant 'household god', but originally seems to have signified (like Indiges) a revered ancestor – in this case, an ancestor of the Roman people. The inscription is apparently of the third century BC, and harmonizes with the belief that the national role of Aeneas was magnified after Rome's suppression of the Latin League in 338.

Excavations have now revealed much of Lavinium. 'The landscape itself', wrote their director Ferdinando Castagnoli, 'has been preserved relatively untouched in its rustic simplicity and in its wide open spaces, and it is still possible to gaze from the gentle heights on which the city was placed at the sea and at those shores where sailors landed, bringing with them the first objects of a much more advanced civilization, the Greek, and marvellous tales of gods and heroes. Something still remains of the fascination which has been destroyed in the Roman Campagna, and this is an extraordinary circumstance if one thinks of the sudden industrial transformation of so many other ancient cities, such as its neighbour Ardea....'[16]

The remains which this landscape has preserved confirm Lavinium's leading role among the early religious centres of Latium. One extra-urban sanctuary was found in 1959 to display thirteen carefully aligned altars of substantial size, extending in date from the sixth to about the second century BC. A bronze inscription of *c*.500 BC, discovered on this site, alludes to the worship of the Dioscuri (Castor and Pollux),[17] who were identified at Lavinium with the city's Penates, and were believed by the Romans to have brought them divine aid at the legendary battle of Lake Regillus (*c*.496 BC). Bronze statues of young men and women (*kouroi* and *korai*) have also come to light. A second sanctuary, farther to the east, provides rich and varied material which likewise goes back, in part, to a sixth century origin. This material included a votive deposit consisting of a number of large statues, ranging in date from that century to the years preceding 300. At least four of these statues – mostly belonging to the later stages of this time-span – represent the goddess Minerva (Athena Tritonia), fully armed. They were probably buried when her temple on the site was destroyed.

A recent rescue excavation between this sanctuary of Minerva and the modern town of Pratica del Mare has revealed the foundation of round, oval and rectangular huts, dating from the eighth to the mid-seventh century BC, interspersed with children's burials. On the same site two substantial votive deposits have been found, serving some cult that has not yet been identified, and containing many miniature impasto (thickly coloured) vases. The latest material in the earlier deposit, dating back to about the mid-sixth century BC, provides an upper date for the city walls, which cut through the deposit.

As the Romans grew in power, Lavinium declined, but after their war with the Latins (338) – in which, as we saw, the town had maintained a pro-Roman attitude – it was granted a privileged, formally independent status, corresponding with its status as a venerated religious centre, in which the myths associated with its past still remained so very much alive. It is this mythology which makes the recent discoveries significant. Yet, here as so often, the relation between archaeology and myth, although insistent, remains enigmatic. 'From recent excavations', writes T.J. Cornell, 'we can begin to form some picture of Iron Age Latium (*c*. tenth to seventh centuries BC) in terms of settlement patterns, social structures, forms of production and economic exchange, the beginnings of urbanization, and so on. But such material data can neither confirm nor refute literary accounts which contain a mixture of pseudo-ethnography and erudite conjecture, interwoven with myths, folk-tales and local traditions ... Archaeology can act as a positive check on the sources only in the sense that it can indicate elements which might unconsciously reflect historical reality; in a negative sense it can help to illustrate and explain the distortions and secondary elaborations that took place in the formation of the historiographical tradition.'[18]

Here at Lavinium, however, in relation to the cult and myth of Aeneas, we are not much further forward. 'The excavations undertaken at Lavinium and its neighbourhood,' writes Nicholas Horsfall, 'which have had such brilliant results, have left the problem of the development of the Aeneas legend in the greatest uncertainty. For the fifth century BC one could hope for illuminating correspondences with the Greek texts; but not so ... It is certainly not easy to integrate the Aeneas legend with the data offered by the monuments brought to light at Lavinium ... The 'heroon of Aeneas' seems to be a fourth-century BC transformation of a seventh-century tumulus, equipped with rich furnishing, but the identification with the sanctuary set up to *Pater Indiges* (Aeneas) according to Dionysius of Halicarnassus is problematical ... Efforts have been equally made to identify Aeneas in epigraphic texts coming from Lavinium and its neighbourhood: years ago an inscription on a cippus from Tor Tignosa was very confidently read as LARE AENIA, but it is not to be found any longer, and a definitive reading has not been arrived at.'[19] Although, however, doubts on this subject still persist, it does seem probable that the inscription refers, in some form or other, to Aeneas and a cult devoted to him, and that it should be dated to the third century BC. About earlier ages, therefore, it is uninformative.

About the failure of archaeology and literature invariably to speak the same language something was said in connection with Naucratis (Chapter 2, section 6). As Cornell has reminded us, the same applies to the relationship between archaeology and myth. These reservations are highlighted by the discoveries at Lavinium, where, as we have seen, there is no certainty that a 'heroon' of Aeneas has been discovered after all – or (although this is more likely) that the lost inscription read as LARE AENIA referred to Aeneas, as has been supposed. Thus anyone who expected the excavations to yield a confirmation of, or commentary on, the Aeneas legend will be disappointed – until or unless something more turns up.

(ii) Herculaneum: Villa of the Papyri

One of the most magnificent Roman country-houses ever to have been discovered was the 'Villa of the Papyri' on the slopes of Mount Vesuvius, just outside the western end of Herculaneum, where it covered an area of some 40,000 square yards. Already buried by the eruption of AD 79 (Chapter 7, section 4), the area was reburied under sixty-five feet of lava in 1631. But then digging operations between 1738 and 1765, penetrating into this hardened volcanic mass, disclosed a wealth of statues and papyri. The statues, found in the house and garden, can be seen in the National

Archaeological Museum at Naples. Among them are seven marble statues and fifteen marble heads, and the most important single collection of ancient bronzes that has ever been discovered, including eighteen figures of various sizes, and thirty-two portrait busts.

The 1,803 papyri that also came to light belonged to the first ancient library that had ever been found, representing an immeasurably important contribution to papyrology (Chapter 8, section 5). Lying on wooden shelves, the papyri looked like small black bricks or lumps of charcoal, but they turned out to be rolls which had been carbonized – turned into solid lumps – by a combination of water, damp, decomposition and the hardening of the surrounding tufa deposit.

During the early endeavours to unroll and decipher these rolls, many ceased to exist: some were destroyed in the vain attempt to read them, others were thrown away, and others just fell to bits. By the mid-nineteenth century, however, 341 had been unrolled, and 195 deciphered and published. The others, which still remain to be dealt with, include 800 in the National Library at Naples: while a few are to be seen in the same city's National Archaeological Museum. Since a large number of the deciphered papyri contained writings by the Epicurean philosopher Philodemus of Gadara (*c.*110 – *c.*40–35 BC), it has been supposed that the Villa dei Papiri belonged to his patron Piso (Lucius Calpurnius Piso Caesoninus), father-in-law of Julius Caesar – though this has been contested.

In 1765 the excavations of the villa came to an end because of the lethal exhalations of carbonic gas which emerged from its depths. At this juncture, all the tunnels and vents were closed, and the site was abandoned. The galleries were no longer propped up nor the air-shafts kept clear, so that the ground fell in and the villa disappeared from view, as though excavations had never taken place. Indeed, it disappeared so completely that no one even knew exactly where it was. Fortunately a plan of the lay-out had been drawn up at the time of the excavations by the engineer Karl Weber, the only man at the time who possessed any idea of how archaeologists should proceed. His plan reveals how the villa, originally an atrium-style farmhouse, later incorporated an extensive peristyle with gardens and pools, and displayed a belvedere at the end of a long promenade overlooking the sea.

Yet a substantial amount of this dwelling had remained unexcavated, and is still waiting to be disinterred from beneath its earthen covering. For example, the living quarters – with their paintings, furniture, statues and jewellery – were never discovered. Nor were the kitchens, workshops, servants' quarters, garden sheds and boathouses that must have been needed to serve such an opulent residence. Moreover, even in the sections already excavated, there is still, no doubt, much more to be found. Now, after

220 years, the effort to find what this grandest of all villas has still kept hidden from us has been revived. Excavations recommenced in 1987, preliminary reports were published, and since then the work has been carried even further. 'I myself went underground', Carlo Knight has written to me, 'and reached the border of the *piscina* (swimming pool).'[20] The first two Latin texts (containing fragments of Lucretius) have now been discovered, and the next few years should yield remarkable results.

(iii) Puteoli: Movements of Earth and Shore

Reference has been made elsewhere to Lake Prilius on the Etruscan coast, which has disappeared as the sea receded (Chapter 5, section 3). Conversely, many parts of the Greek and Roman worlds around the Mediterranean are now under water. This is what happened, for example, to parts of the harbour cities of Halieis and Caesarea Maritima (Chapter 2, section 4; Chapter 6, section 3). It has also happened to Puteoli, the Greek Dicaearchia and now Pozzuoli.

Puteoli was a coastal city of Campania (south-western Italy) in the bay of the same name forming the north-western part of the Gulf of Cumae (Bay of Naples, called after the city [Neapolis] which lies seven miles to the west). Dicaearchia, 'city where justice reigns', was believed to have been founded in *c.*521–520 by refugees from Samos who had earlier gone to Cumae. The Samnites occupied Dicaearchia in 421, and in *c.*338–334 it came under the control of the Romans, from whom, after successfully resisting Hannibal in the Second Punic War, it received a citizen colony (194). Thereafter, under the name of Puteoli, it became the principal port of Rome. Sulla and Cicero were among those who possessed villas in its fashionable neighbourhood, and Augustus added new drafts of colonists. Despite the rise of Ostia to supersede it as Rome's busiest harbour, Puteoli retained much of its importance. By *c.* AD 200, however, land ownership had replaced overseas trading as the source of the largest local incomes. Before 300, signs of stagnation were apparent, and fifth- and sixth-century devastations at the hands of German marauders compelled the inhabitants to move elsewhere.

The remains of numerous buildings, in an upper and lower town alike, testify to Puteoli's importance. But the task of the archaeologist is complicated by the natural phenomenon of bradyseism or slow earthquake. This takes the form of a series of gradual, not always very noticeable, earth tremors. Over the years, the tremors at Puteoli have taken the form of a sometimes almost continuous series of minor earthquake shocks, numbering more than four thousand in 1983 alone. Since then, a hundred more bradyseismic tremors have been hitting the town every day. These have caused alarm among its 80,000 inhabitants, many of whom have evacuated the town.

It stands within the Phlegraean Fields (from the Greek *phlegein*, to burn), an ancient *caldera* or volcanic explosion-pit 7½ miles across. The Phlegraean Fields erupted on a mammoth scale some 36,000 years ago. Some of their thirteen low craters (*fumaiuoli*) still emit jets of steam, and there are volcanologists who fear that a new eruption may be brewing beneath the soil. Trouble of this kind has been experienced before. In 1538, for example, the town of Tripergole, beside Pozzuoli, was obliterated by a series of shocks and replaced by a volcano, Monte Nuovo, 450 feet high.

Just off the coast, as well, two large underwater fields of *fumaiuoli*, some fifty-four yards across, have now been discovered (1984). The magma (subterranean molten rock) moving beneath Pozzuoli is heating the ground-water offshore, as fields of bubbles indicate, and the muddy sea-bottom seems to be boiling. Although, over a long period, the Phlegraean Fields themselves have become less eruptive, this extension of the underground magma might eventually set the process in reverse, causing a vaporization of the offshore water which would result in an explosive blow-out not only under the sea but also upon the adjacent coastland. This prognosis will become more pessimistic still if some of the rising magma mixes with the steam, as happened in the Phlegraean Fields in *c.*1800 BC (when a new volcanic centre, the Astroni craters, came into existence).

Meanwhile there remains a second, interrelated problem raised by the continuous process of bradyseism. This consists of the falls and rises of the land level in relation to the sea. Thus in the early 1970s the ground rose 5½ feet in three years, before subsiding a little thereafter. And in the two years 1983 and 1984 a further rise of 3½ feet occurred. This is not an unprecedented process: In the years immediately preceding the obliteration of Tripergole in 1538, the ground-level had risen 23 feet within only a few years. Afterwards, however, a slow subsidence followed – and over the centuries and millennia falls have been much more considerable than rises.

Falls of the ground-level mean rises in the sea-level, and much of busy ancient Puteoli, including the entire port, has been submerged in the course of the centuries. The discovery of numerous statues under water reminds us how very much still lies beneath the sea. Moreover, air photographs have begun to tell the same story for the whole region of the coastland of Puteoli, the Ripa Puteolana, extending across this part of the Bay of Naples. Submerged villas, swimming pools, baths, porticos and gardens have been identified in this area, and their underwater excavation is a task for the future.

One of the best indices of bradyseism in this region is provided by the remains of the colonnaded Market of Puteoli, built in Flavian times (AD 69–96) and repaired in the following century – also known, wrongly, as the 'Serapeum' from a statue of the Egyptian god Serapis that was found there when excavations began in the 1750s. The years that followed, however, formed one of the periods when the ground-level subsided, until in 1919 and 1933 the Market's pavement was 515 and 673 feet under water respectively. Subsequently the ground-level rose again, so that the central rotunda of the building stood once more on dry land. Whether, and when, in the future, the level will go up or down it is impossible to tell. In either case, as we saw above, these bradyseisms and the eruptions to which the region is subject are interrelated. For when the magma moves about below the earth and sea, and forces the land surface up and down, this is an activity which can trigger off eruptions. And meanwhile the hot *fumaiuoli* discovered off the Puteoli shoreline might have this effect of reawakening the whole enormous *caldera*. Scientists, writes Rick Gore, 'begin to fear that a new eruption of unpredictable magnitude is brewing beneath Puteoli ... As magma moves below, it forces the land surface up and down in an earthquake-triggering action. Today's fear comes from a speedup of this activity.'[21] Nature may well, therefore, take a hand in uncovering the extensive remains in the area, at present buried beneath the land, and, particularly, beneath the sea. In 1989, investigations have concentrated on the underwater volcano Marsili Seamount, a hundred miles south-west of Naples, of which the continual activity affects the whole area.

(iv) Rome

I have discussed the Augustan (and later) sundial at Rome because it illustrated questions relating to archaeological methods (Chapter 6, section 4). But it would be wrong to end this book without some further reference to the superlative, unending archaeological productivity of the ancient imperial city, which has been witnessing unremitting investigation in recent years. Nevertheless, I place this reference in an Appendix, because it is in the next few years, the immediate future, that the results and fruits of all this activity are likely to become fully apparent.

To give an idea of the breadth of the current and recent activities that generate such hopes, I will quote from a letter of 9/12/88 sent to me by Henry Hurst, in which he listed the following recent and current archaeological events in the imperial metropolis: 'In the Forum [Romanum] itself (a) a major reinterpretation of the archaic levels ... (b) Andrea Carandini's excavation between the House of the Vestals and Arch of Titus, where remains of very early (8th century BC) walling, perhaps defining an original Palatine *pomoerium*, have been found, and much evidence for later periods, (c) at the risk of immodesty my own excavation in the area of Santa Maria Antiqua, which has pretty certainly revealed the extension to the imperial palace made by Gaius (Caligula), (d) various other smaller excavations ... Then, outside the Forum itself, Clementina Pannella's work on the Baths of Trajan and Porticus Liviae; ... On the area by the Arch of Constantine and Meta Sudans another stretch of the Domus Aurea; Carlo Pavolini's work on an insula block on the Caelian Hill. And now work in the Fori Imperiali [Fora of Augustus, Nerva and Trajan], just started. And many others!'

And many others, too, no doubt, to come.

REFERENCES

PART I: THE GREEKS

CHAPTER 1: THE DARK AGE

1 J. N. Coldstream, *Geometric Greece*, 1979 ed., p. 42.
2 *Ibid.*, p. 52.
3 J.J. Coulton in M. Grant and R. Kitzinger (eds.), *Civilization of the Ancient Mediterranean*, III, 1988, p. 1657.
4 M. Popham, E. Touloupa and L. H. Sackett, *Antiquity*, 56, 1982, p. 173.
5 A. M. Snodgrass, *An Archaeology of Greece*, 1987, p. 161.
6 V. Karageorghis, *Cyprus: From the Stone Age to the Romans*, 1982, p. 130.
7 Homer, *Iliad*, 23, 170–176.
8 Homer, *Odyssey*, 7, 162, etc.
9 *Ibid.*, 23, 195ff.
10 A. M. Snodgrass, *Archaic Greece*, 1981 ed., p. 76.
11 *Op. cit.*, p. 350.
12 Hesiod, *Works and Days*, 141–2.
13 I. Morris, *Antiquity*, 62, 1988, pp. 754f., 758.

CHAPTER 2: THE ARCHAIC GREEKS

1 M. W. Frederiksen, *Archaeological Reports*, 1976/7, p. 44.
2 *Id.* in D. and F. R. Ridgway (eds.), *Italy Before the Romans*, 1979, p. 277.
3 Herodotus, v, 44–47, Heraclides Ponticus, fragment 49, Phylarchus, fragment 45, Diodorus Siculus, XII, 9–10.
4 P. E. Cleator, *Archaeology in the Making*, 1976, p. 68.
5 D. R. Wilson, *Science and Archaeology*, 1978 ed., pp. 192ff.
6 F. Rainey, *Illustrated London News*, 8/12/62, p. 931.
7 O. H. Bullitt, *The Search for Sybaris*, 1971, pp. 110f.
8 A. Bullock in P. Throckmorton (ed.), *History from the Sea*, 1987, p. 7.
9 P. Throckmorton, *Shipwrecks and Archaeology*, 1970, p. 174, and *History from the Sea*, 1987, p. 8.
10 G. F. Bass, *Princeton Encyclopedia of Classical Sites*, 1976, p. 832.
11 *Past Worlds: The Times Atlas of Archaeology*, 1988, p. 36.
12 M. Bound, *Archeologia Viva*, 4, 12, 1985, pp. 64f.
13 M. H. Jameson, *Hesperia*, 38, 1969, p. 332.
14 *Id.*, *Marine Archaeology* (Proceedings of the 23rd Symposium of the Colston Research Society, Bristol University, 1971), 1973, pp. 219f.
15 *Id.*, *Hesperia*, *op. cit.*

16 *Id., Marine Archaeology, op. cit.*, p. 220.
17 *id., National Geographic Society Research Reports*, 14, 1982, p. 364; cf. B.V. Head, *Historia Numorum*, 2nd ed., 1911, p. 443.
18 *Past Worlds, op. cit.*, p. 36.
19 A. Farkas, *From the Lands of the Scythians*, p. 20.
20 W. G. East, *The Geography Behind History*, 1965 ed., pp. 118ff.
21 J. G. F. Hind, *Archaeological Reports*, 1983/4, p. 80.
22 *Ibid.*
23 Herodotus, IV, 53f.
24 Polybius, IV, 38.
25 Herodotus, IV, 78–80.
26 S. C. Humphreys, *Anthropology and the Greeks*, 1983 (1978), p. 117.
27 Herodotus, II, 154.
28 Strabo, XVII, 18, 801–2.
29 Herodotus, II, 178.
30 A. M. Snodgrass in M. Crawford (ed.), *Sources for Ancient History*, 1983, pp. 145ff.
31 Thucydides, VI, 2, 6.
32 A. M. Snodgrass, *An Archaeology of Greece*, 1987, p. 61; cf. p 5.
33 D.Clarke, *Analytical Archaeology*, 1978 ed., p. 12.

CHAPTER 3: THE CLASSICAL GREEKS

1 Thucydides, I, 13.
2 J. S. Morrison in P. Throckmorton (ed.), *History from the Sea*, 1987, p. 49; cf. J. S. Morrison and J. F. Coates, *The Ancient Trireme*, 1986, p. 40 (cf. p. 38 n. 8).
3 J. F. Coates, *Archaeology*, March/April 1988, p. 29.
4 J. M. Camp, *The Athenian Agora*, 1986, p. 15.
5 H. Thompson in R. A. Wertime, *Archaeology*, Nov./Dec. 1988, p. 43.
6 T. L. Shear jr, *Archaeological Reports*, 1981/2, pp. 7, 9.
7 Pausanias, I, 154: Synesius, *Epistulae*, 135.
8 J. M. Camp, *op. cit.*, p. 215.
9 A. M. Snodgrass, *An Archaeology of Greece*, 1987, pp. 1, 3, 134.
10 G. Foti in A. Busignani, *The Bronzes of Riace*, 1981, p. 14 n. 1.
11 Diogenes Laertius, VIII, 46, Pliny the elder, *Natural History*, XXXIV, 59.
12 J. Barron, *An Introduction to Greek Sculpture*, 1981 ed., p. 89.
13 M. Andronikos, *The Times*, 14/12/88, p. 36.
14 A. W. Johnston and M. A. R. Colledge in K. Branigan (ed.), *Atlas of Archaeology*, 1982, p. 6.
15 M. Andronikos, *Illustrated London News*, May 1978, p. 58.
16 J.J. Pollitt in M. Grant and R. Kitzinger (eds.), *Civilization of the Ancient Mediterranean*, III, 1988, p. 1762.
17 H. W. Catling, *Archaeological Reports*, 1982/3, p. 44.
18 P. MacKendrick, *The Greek Stones Speak*, 1981 ed., p. 368.
19 Strabo, VII, fragment 23.
20 Livy, XLII, 51, 2.
21 S. C. Humphreys, *Anthropology and the Greeks*, 1983 ed., pp. 112, 119.

22 R. J. A. Talbert, *Timoleon and the Revival of Greek Sicily 344–317 BC*, 1974, pp. 146ff.
23 C. Kraay, *Greek Coins and History*, 1969, p. 54.
24 R. J. A. Talbert, *op. cit.*, pp. 163, 165; cf. Diodorus Siculus, 16, 83, 1.

CHAPTER 4: THE HELLENISTIC GREEKS

1 P. Levi, *Atlas of the Greek World*, 1980, p. 191.
2 L. Robert, *Comptes-Rendus de l'Académie des Inscriptions*, 1968, p. 416.
3 J. Barnes, *Oxford History of the Classical World*, 1986, p. 366.
4 S. Sherwin-White, *History Today*, 33, December 1983, p. 47.
5 Herodotus, VII, 144.
6 F. G. H. Millar in M. Crawford (ed.), *Sources for Ancient History*, 1983, pp. 80, 82.
7 A. G. Woodhead, *The Study of Greek Inscriptions*, 1981 ed., pp. 3f.
8 R. Meiggs and D. M. Lewis (eds.), *A Selection of Greek Historical Inscriptions*, 1969, no. 23, C. W. Fornara (ed.), *Archaic Times to the End of the Peloponnesian War*, 1983 ed., pp. 54f., no. 55, R. J. Lenardon, *The Saga of Themistocles*, 1978, pp. 69f., O. Murray, *Early Greece*, 1980, pp. 274f.
9 Diodorus Siculus, XVIII, 10.
10 Aeschines in Demosthenes, *On the Embassy*, 303.
11 O. Murray, *op. cit.*, pp. 275f.
12 *Id.* pp. 276ff.
13 N. G. L. Hammond, *Journal of Hellenic Studies*, 102, 1982, p. 93.
14 A. R. Burn, *Persia and the Greeks*, 1984 ed., p. xvi; cf. pp. 351, 359f., 364, 377f.
15 E. M. De Juliis, *Gli ori di Taranto in età ellenistica* (1984/5), 1987 ed.
16 Strabo, VI, 3, 1.
17 E. M. De Juliis, *op. cit.*, p. 23.
18 D. de Solla Price, *Transactions of the American Philosophical Society*, 64, 7, 1974.
19 J. G. Landels in M. Grant and R. Kitzinger (eds.) *Civilization of the Ancient Mediterranean*, I, 1988, p. 348.
20 M. Grant, *From Imperium to Auctoritas*, 1969 ed. (1946), p. 493 etc.
21 *Survey of Numismatic Research 1978–84* (International Numismatic Commission), II, 1986, pp. 961ff.
22 D. R. Walker, *The Metrology of the Roman Silver Coinage*, I, 1976, p. 139.
23 M. Crawford, *Sources for Ancient History*, 1983, p. 221.

PART II: ITALY AND THE ROMAN EMPIRE

CHAPTER 5: ETRUSCAN AND REPUBLICAN ITALY

1 G. M. Dennis, *The Cities and Cemeteries of Etruria*, 1848, p. 335, rev. ed. 1883 (1878), p. 396 (reprint 1968).
2 P. E. Cleator, *Archaeology in the Making*, 1976, p. 68.
3 C. M. Lerici, *Studies in Conservation*, VI, 1, 1961 in C. W. Ceram (ed.), *The World of Archaeology*, 1968 ed., p. 484.
4 *Id.*, p. 483.
5 D. R. Wilson, *Science and Archaeology*, 1978 ed., p. 196.
6 M. Torelli, *Elogia Tarquiniensia*, 1975, M. Grant, *The Etruscans*, 1980, pp. 135f.

7 *Die Göttin von Pyrgi*, Tübingen, 1981.
8 M. Pallottino, *Testimonia Linguae Etruscae*, 1968 ed., pp. 109f., nos 873–877, M. Grant, *op. cit.*, pp. 152f.
9 Polybius, III, 22.
10 H. H. Scullard, *The Etruscan Cities and Rome*, 1967, p. 104.
11 Virgil, *Aeneid*, X, 166–9, 655.
12 M. Cristofani, *Gli etruschi sul mare*, 1983, p. 38, *id.*, *Dizionario della civiltà etrusca*, 1985, p. 195, indicates the early seventh century.
13 Pliny the elder, *Natural History*, III, 51.
14 Cicero, *In Defence of Milo*, 24, 74.
15 *Archeologia*, March 1988, p. 6.
16 Pliny the elder, *Natural History*, III, 70.
17 D. Ridgway, *Archaeological Reports*, 1981/2, p. 68.
18 J. McIntosh, *The Archaeologist's Handbook*, 1986, p. 160.
19 M. Frederiksen in D. and F. R. Ridgway (eds.), *Italy Before the Romans*, 1979, pp. 292ff.
20 F. M. Heichelheim, *Oxford Classical Dictionary*, 1970 ed., p. 29.
21 Cato the elder, *On Agriculture*, 14, Seneca the younger, *Epistles*, 86.
22 Varro, *On Rural Affairs* (*De Re Rustica*), I, 24, 1f.
23 Cato the elder, *op. cit.*, 6.
24 Virgil, *Georgics*, II, 179ff.
25 Pliny the elder, *Natural History*, XV, 13–18.
26 A. King, *Archaeology of the Roman Empire*, 1982, p. 79.
27 Pliny the elder, *Natural History*, XIV, 8.
28 A. King, *op. cit.*, pp. 79f.
29 T. W. Potter, *Roman Italy*, 1987, p. 108.
30 T. Tatton-Brown, *Illustrated London News*, Archaeology 2967.
31 K. D. White in M. Grant and R. Kitzinger (eds.), *Civilization of the Ancient Mediterranean*, I, 1988, p. 257.
32 N. Purcell, *Journal of Roman Studies*, 78, 1988, p. 196.
33 K. Greene, *The Archaeology of the Roman Economy*, 1986, p. 84.
34 L. R. Binford, *In Pursuit of the Past*, 1988 ed., p. 32.
35 W. Leppmann, *Pompeii in Fact and Fiction*, 1968, p. 49.

CHAPTER 6: THE AUGUSTAN EMPIRE

1 B. de Jongh, *Companion Guide to Mainland Greece*, 1979, p. 369.
2 Suetonius, *Augustus*, 18, 2, Dio Cassius, 51, 2, 2.
3 V. Ehrenberg and A. H. M. Jones (eds.) *Documents Illustrating the Reigns of Augustus and Tiberius*, 1955, p. 57 no 12.
4 W. Murray and P. Petsas, *Archaeology*, Sept./Oct., 1988, pp. 28–55.
5 M. Grant, *The Six Main Aes Coinages of Augustus*, 1953, pp. 10ff.
6 *Coins of the Roman Empire in the British Museum*, I, 1923, p. 18 no 95.
7 B. V. Head, *Historia Numorum*, 1911, p. 321.
8 Josephus, *Jewish War*, IV, 610.
9 Strabo, XVII, 1, 24, 804.
10 Dessau, *Inscriptiones Latinae Selectae*, 8995.
11 *Corpus Inscriptionum Latinarum*, III, 14147.

12 *Oxyrhynchus Papyri*, 1511.
13 Josephus, *Jewish War*, III, 408–414 (tr. K. G. Holum etc).
14 K. G. Holum, *Archaeology*, May/June 1988, p. 45.
15 K. G. Holum, R. L. Hohlfelder, R. J. Bull, A. Raban, *King Herod's Dream: Caesarea on the Sea*, 1988, p. 101.
16 *Ibid.*, pp. 94ff.
17 K. G. Holum, *Archaeology*, *loc.cit.*
18 *Id.* (etc.), *King Herod's Dream*, *op.cit.*, pp. 35–37.
19 E. M. Smallwood, *The Jews under Roman Rule*, 1976, p. 167, n. 79.
20 Pliny the elder, *Natural History*, XXXVI, 72f.
21 A. Snodgrass, *An Archaeology of Greece*, 1987, pp. 27f., 31.

CHAPTER 7: THE POST-AUGUSTANS

1 E. Sammes in D. E. Johnston (ed.), *Discovering Roman Britain*, 1983, p. 110.
2 A. G. McKay, *Houses, Villas and Palaces in the Roman World*, 1975, p. 190.
3 K. Erim, *Archaeological Reports*, 1970/1, p. 51.
4 *Ibid.*, 1978/9, p. 75.
5 *Ibid.*, 1984/5, p. 90.
6 *Ibid.*, *Anatolian Studies*, 1986, p. 178.
7 C. Valenziano, *La Repubblica*, 10/8/85.
8 M. Squarciapino, *La scuola di Afrodisia*, 1943.
9 K.Erim, *Aphrodisias: City of Venus Aphrodite*, 1985, p. 151.
10 H. Dessau, *Inscriptiones Latinae Selectae*, 642.
11 *Past Worlds: The Times Atlas of Archaeology*, 1988, p. 44.
12 Y.Yadin, *Masada*, 1966, p. 13.
13 Josephus, *Jewish War*, VII, 315.
14 *Ibid.*, 323–388.
15 M.Smith in E. M. Smallwood, *The Jews under Roman Rule*, 1976, p. 338.
16 J. J. Deiss, *Herculaneum*, 2nd ed., 1985, p. 33.
17 H. Sigurdsson in *National Geographic Magazine*, 165, 5, 1984, p. 576.
18 J. J. Deiss, *op. cit.*, pp. xiif.
19 D. R. Wilson, *Science and Archaeology*, 1978 ed., p. 244.
20 J. J. Deiss, *loc. cit.*, cf. p. 190.
21 S. Bisel, *National Geographic Magazine*, *loc. cit.*, pp. 587, 595ff.
22 J. J. Deiss, *op. cit.*, p. 193.
23 S. Bisel, *op. cit.*, p. 600.

CHAPTER 8: THE MIDDLE EMPIRE

1 C. Renfrew, *Before Civilization*, 1976 (1973), pp. 77f.
2 J. McIntosh, *The Archaeologist's Handbook*, 1986, p. 135.
3 Tacitus, *Histories*, IV, 77.
4 A. K. Bowman and J. D. Thomas, *The Vindolanda Writing Tablets*, 1974, p. 6.
5 Letter from R. Birley, 3/10/88.
6 *Past Worlds: The Times Atlas of Archaeology*, 1988, p. 38.
7 R. W. Davies, *Britannia*, II, 1971, p. 138.
8 D. Breeze (ed.), *The Frontiers of the Roman Empire*, 1986, p. 54.
9 G. Webster, *The Roman Imperial Army*, 1969 ed., pp. 255f., n. 9, cf. *Proceedings*

of the Dorset Natural History and Archaeological Society, 86, 1965, pp. 142–4.
10 R. W. Davies, *op. cit.*, pp. 133f.
11 Diodorus Siculus, III, 12.3–13.3
12 R. W. Davies, *op. cit.*, pp. 134f.
13 *Corpus Inscriptionum Latinarum*, VIII, 619.
14 G. Webster, *The Roman Imperial Army*, 1969 ed., p. 195.
15 Pliny the elder, *Natural History*, XIII, 68.
16 A. Henrichs, *Die Phoinikika des Lollianos: Fragmente eines neuen griechischen Romans*, 1972.
17 G. Anderson, *Ancient Fiction: The Novel in the Graeco-Roman World*, 1984, p. 158.
18 E. G. Turner, *Greek Papyri: An Introduction*, 1980 ed., pp. 40f.
19 G. Shipley, *History Today*, 38, May 1988, p. 53.
20 P. E. Cleator, *Archaeology in the Making*, 1976, pp. 69f.
21 K. Greene, *The Archaeology of the Roman Economy*, 1986, p. 116.
22 R. Agache, *La Somme pré-romaine et romaine*, 1978, p. 35.
23 R. J. Fowler, *Antiquaries Journal*, lii 1972, p. 368.
24 M. Grant, *Cities of Vesuvius*, 1971, p. 122.

CHAPTER 9: THE LATER EMPIRE

1 M. Grant, *Roman History from Coins*, 1968 ed. (1958), p. 11.
2 *Ibid.*, p. 16.
3 *Ibid.*, p. 73.
4 *Id.*, *From Imperium to Auctoritas*, 1969 ed. (1946).
5 *Id.*, *Roman History from Coins*, op. cit., p. 74.
6 M. Rostovtzeff, *Social and Economic History of the Roman Empire*, rev. ed. (P. Fraser), 1957, vol. 1, p. 139.
7 M. J. Price and B. L. Trell, *Coins and their Cities*, 1977, pp. 15, 17, 19.
8 *Ibid.*, pp. 150–3.
9 Lucian, *On the Syrian Goddess*, 6.
10 G. W. Bowersock, *Journal of Roman Studies*, 61, 1971, p. 237.
11 S. T. Parker, *Archaeology*, Sept./Oct. 1984, p. 39.
12 *Id.*, p. 38.
13 J. P. C. Kent, *Corolla Memoriae Erich Swoboda Dedicata*, 1966, pp. 149f.

EPILOGUE

1 G. F. Bass, *Archaeology*, 42, 1989, pp. 105, 51.

APPENDICES

1 P. E. Cleator, *Archaeology in the Making*, 1976, p. 17.
2 C. Renfrew in L. R. Binford, *In Pursuit of the Past*, 1988 ed., p. 7.
3 *Id.*, *Before Civilization*, 1976 ed., p. 277 (referring to prehistoric archaeology).
4 P. Rahtz, *Invitation to Archaeology*, 1985, p. 1.
5 R. E. M. Wheeler, *Archaeology from the Earth*, 1954, p. 13.
6 S. Piggott, *Approach to Archaeology*, 1959, pp. 1, 110.
7 A. Snodgrass in M. Crawford (ed.), *Sources for Ancient History*, 1983, p. 137.
8 A. Sherratt, *Times Literary Supplement*, 12/9/86, p. 1006.

9 B. A. Sparkes, *Greece and Rome*, 1988, p. 221.
10 A. Snodgrass, *An Archaeology of Greece*, 1987, pp. 6, 19, 14.
11 J. Boardman, *Antiquity*, 62, 1988, p. 297.
12 G. Shipley, *History Today*, 38, May 1988, pp. 49–52.
13 Polybius, III, 22.
14 Dionysius of Halicarnassus, I, 64, 4–5.
15 G. Dury-Moyaers, *Enée et Lavinium*, 1981, pp. 240ff.
16 F. Castagnoli, *Vergilius*, 13, 1967, p. 4.
17 S. Weinstock, *Journal of Roman Studies*, 1960, pp. 112ff.
18 T. J. Cornell, *Acta of the XIIth International Congress of Classical Archaeology* (3/9 September 1978), 1979, pp. 190f.
19 N. Horsfall, *Enciclopedia Virgiliana*, II, 1985, pp. 223f.
20 Letter from Carlo Knight, 13/9/88.
21 R. Gore, *National Geographic Magazine*, 165, 5, 1984, p. 617.

NOTES

Introduction

Visible history. The term 'the visible past' is used by J. McIntosh, *The Archaeologist's Handbook*, 1986. Henry James wrote of the 'palpable, imaginable, visitable past'.

Rescue archaeology. Undertaken to protect or save sites or areas endangered by modern industrial development – e.g. air pollution, traffic vibration (microseismicity), construction work – or by agriculture (e.g. ploughing), or flooding for reservoirs or natural disasters such as movements of the earth (earthquakes, bradyseisms, volcanic eruptions), as well as other threats mentioned in the text. See P. Rahtz, *Rescue Archaeology*, 1974, P.J. Watson, S.A. Le Blanc, C.L. Redman, *Archaeological Explanation*, 1984, pp. 242ff. ('contract' archaeology), D.R. Wilson, *Science and Archaeology*, 1978 ed., pp. 286ff., H. Mytum and K. Waugh (eds.), *Rescue Archaeology – What's Next?*, 1987. For the methods and urgency of conservation see J. M. Cronyn, *Elements of Archaeological Conservation*, 1989, G. Ulbert and G. Weber, *Konservierte Geschichte?*, 1985, G.F. Bass, *Archaeology*, January/February 1989, pp. 52, 105. Sometimes rescue archaeological projects produce new discoveries, e.g. recently at Herculaneum (Chapter 7, section 4), at Lavinium (Appendix II, i) and at the Haliacmon (Aliakmon) Barrage in Macedonia (3rd century BC temple tomb).

Fringe branches. For art, see Chapter 3, section 3. A. Snodgrass, in M. Crawford (ed.), *Sources for Ancient History*, 1983, p. 142, excludes epigraphy from archaeology. For more detailed discussions of classical and other archaeology, see notes on Appendix I.

Hazards of archaeological work. J.L. Allen and A.St.J. Holt, *Health and Safety in Field Archaeology*, 1986.

PART I: THE GREEKS

CHAPTER 1: THE 'DARK AGE'

1 Lefkandi: The Not So Dark Age

Dorian Invasions. M. Grant, *The Rise of the Greeks*, 1987, pp. 2f.

Lelant(i)on. Ancient name of Lefkandi? *Ibid.*, p. 114.

Greek burials. E. Vermeule in M. Grant and R. Kitzinger (eds.), *Civilizations of the Ancient Mediterranean*, II, 1988, pp. 993ff. (and bibliography). See also section 2, and Chapter 5, section 4.

The Lefkandi Centaur. Illustrated in M. Grant, *The Rise of the Greeks*, 1987, between p. 208 and 209.

Phoenicians and Greeks. *Ibid.*, pp. 355f. n. 16; and s.v. in index.

Textiles. M. Grant and R. Kitzinger, *op. cit.* s.v. in index.

Horses in woman's tomb. 'Rain seepage during the winter (1981/2) had rotted some of the bones ... Further cleaning was difficult due to the extremely friable state of the bones which had to be consolidated as far as possible with polyvinol and acetone as uncovered ... Since, despite consolidation, the bones continued to disintegrate, major bones were coated in paraffin wax and left *in situ* as requested by the Ephorate,' H. W. Catling, *Archaeological Reports*, 1982/3, p. 13.

Crete. M. Grant, *The Rise of the Greeks*, 1987, pp. 193ff.

2 Salamis in Cyprus: Homeric Analogies?

Mycenaean survivals. 'Tomb 3' at Salamis seems reminiscent of Mycenaean beehive-*tholos* styles.

Post-Mycenaean. For the earliest phase (Cypro-Geometric I), see V. Karageorghis, *Cyprus*, 1982. pp. 114–22.

Salamis tombs. Only the large *dromoi* (ante-chambers) have been found intact. The burial chambers were looted long ago.

Chariots in tombs. The wooden parts have crumbled away, but have left impressions on the soil.

Cauldrons. For their Syrian origin see M. Grant, *The Rise of the Greeks*, 1987, p. 336, n. 44, p. 355, n. 11.

'Tomb 79' was employed again in the Greco-Roman period.

Sword. A fine sword found in 'Tomb 3' has a broad silver border soldered onto the iron with copper.

Date of Homer. Poems in final form *c.* 750/700 BC, M. Grant, *op. cit.*, p. 140.

Cenotaph of Nicocreon (?) contained fragments of lifesize statues made of unbaked clay but hardened by fire. Other pyres show clay figurines and fruit offered in honour of the dead.

CHAPTER 2: THE ARCHAIC GREEKS

1 Pithecusae (Ischia) and Cumae: The West

Mycenaeans. Also on the island of Vivara, between Pithecusae (Ischia) and Prochyta (Procida), D. Ridgway, *Archaeological Reports*, 1981/2, p. 66.

Pithecusae. A necropolis of the seventh and/or sixth century BC has now been discovered at Panza, *Archeologia*, February 1988, p. 6.

Cumae. City-walls of mid-sixth century date have been identified, M. W. Frederiksen, *Archaeological Reports*, 1976/7, p. 45.

2 Sybaris: The Magnetometer

Magnetometer. See E. K. Ralph, *Archaeometry*, 7, 1964, pp. 20–7, *ibid.* (etc.), *Geoexploration*, 6, 1968, pp. 109–22. The current is transmitted back from a bottle to an instrument and there registered on dials. The resulting figures are plotted to reveal the anomalies in field strength. (A bleeper was subsequently found to be less costly, and a differential fluxgate gradiometer (J. C. Alldred, *Archaeometry*, 7, 1964, pp. 14–19) capable of more rapid operation). In preparation for the employment of the proton magnetometer, recourse was had to a mechanical probe such as had been employed in Etruria (Chapter 5, section 1). Pioneer use of the magnetometer was made at Durobrivae (Rochester) and Londinium (London).

Rubidium is a rare chemical element of the alkali metal group – the most reactive of all metals except caesium. The way in which it transmits light is sharply affected by magnetism.

Caesium (cesium). The first element discovered by the use of the spectroscope. Its principal value is in photo-electric cells and it is extensively used in the pick-up tubes of television cameras (though caesium 137 is a lethal contaminant). On the use of caesium magnetometer followed by ground-penetrating radar, see B. Bevan, *M.A.S.C.A. Newsletter* (Philadelphia), December 1975, pp. 1ff. On the Subsurface Interface Radar system of electromagnetic investigation, F. Berg and H. Bruch, *P.A.C.T.* (Strasbourg), 7, 1982, pp. 285ff.

Viewfinder. This new digital read-out made it possible to operate the instrument with much greater speed.

Sybaris strata. Diagram in J. B. Ward-Perkins, *Landscape and History in Central Italy*, 1963, p. 3.

Earthquake at Sybaris. The shoreland subsided with a pronounced landward tip.

Campaigns of 1960s. For aerial reconnaissance experiments made with remote-sensing devices (infra-red aerial film and scanning, cf. Chapter 6, section 3), F. Rainey, *American Journal of Archaeology*, 1969, pp. 262, 265.

Croton. Eclipsed by Taras in the mid-fifth century, cf. Chapter 4, section 3.

Drainage. At nearby Metapontum the well-point system (used also at Sybaris) was introduced, and the ancient drainage system was employed to dry out deep levels.

3 Igilium (Giglio): Shipwrecks

Origins of underwater exploration. In 1854 Adolphe Morlot, with a glass-fronted bucket over his head, employed a pick and a butterfly net to recover remains from the bottom of Lake Lemannus (Geneva).

'Treasure'. Referred to by Throckmorton, this is an indirect allusion to the once prevalent, but now much condemned, idea that the purpose of underwater archaeology is to search for valuables.

Pottery. Its classification and quantification is especially important for shipwrecks (e.g. the Euonymus [Dattilo] wreck off northern Sicily [1985], a hundred feet down, in which black-glazed ware was found (see note below); cf. also the merchant vessel of 415–385 found off Porticello di Trada in S.W. Italy, C.J. Eiseman and B.S. Ridgway, *The Porticello Shipwreck*, 1987). Pottery is also of significance at Ostia, where a new extension of the National Servizio Tecnico per l'Archeologia Subacquea has been established. The atomic absorption analysis of pottery (by archaeometrists) may assign provenances on the basis of distinctions that the eye cannot detect; the firing of pottery "fossilizes" the earth's magnetic field as it was at the moment of cooling. In areas where the variations of the earth's magnetic field is known [Chapter 2, section 2], it is possible to date a pottery sample by fitting it to the known curve', K. Branigan (ed.), *Atlas of Archaeology*, 1982, p. 234. Cf. *ibid.* p. 235 on thermoluminescence: 'based on the principle that ceramics contain small amounts of radioactive material, absorbed since the pottery was fired, which on heating is released in the form of light. By measuring the amount of light it is possible to find the length of time since the mineral crystals of the pottery were last heated, and thus the date it was made' (G. F. Bass, *Archaeology*, January/February 1989, pp. 51 ff., believes that thermoluminescent dating [M. J. Aitken, etc, *Nature*, 219, 1968, pp. 442–5] will greatly develop.) See also K. Greene, *The Archaeology of the Roman Economy*, 1986, p. 15 n. 4, R. Franchi, *Archeologia Viva*, 10, 1985, pp. 77f., *History Today*, 38, May 1988, pp. 50ff., M. Millett (ed.), *Pottery and the Archaeologist* (London Conference 1977), 1979, P. Rice (ed.), *Pots and Potters: Current Approaches in Ceramic Archaeology*, 1984, A. G. Orphanides, *Radioanalytical Techniques in Archaeology: Pottery and Raw Clay Analysis*, 1985, D. S. Peacock, *Pottery and Early Commerce*, 1977 (referring to ceramic petrology, the examination of the minerals in the clay), M. Vickers (ed.), *Pots and Pans*, 1986, P. M. Rice, *Pottery Analysis: A Sourcebook*, 1987, C. C. Kolb, *Ceramic Ecology Revisited*, 1988.

The Ceryneia (Cyrenia) Shipwreck. After a mound of amphoras came to light in 1967, nearly a hundred feet below the surface, it took eight years to raise, preserve and reassemble the vessel, which proved to contain a great variety of objects. The ship was constructed in the early fourth century BC, was patched up at least twice, and sank in *c.*300–260. Most of the amphoras came from Rhodes, a major source of wine production and perhaps the vessel's home port. Some amphoras, too, had originated from Samos, and millstones from another Aegean island, Nisyros. 10,000 fresh almonds came from Cyprus, off which the ship was wrecked. Hazelnuts, pistachios, olives, figs, garlic, grapes and sprigs of dried herbs have also been found – as well as iron spearheads, and a marble pedestal (of a statue) with a basin for sacrificial pleas for divine protection. A reconstructed copy of the ship was made at Perama in Attica in 1985, shipped to the United States, and taken back first to Greece and then to Cyprus. See also M. L. Katzer in P. Throckmorton (ed.), *History from the Sea*, 1987, pp. 55–59, *id.*, *National Geographic Magazine*, 1974, pp. 618–625, *ibid.*, 1985, pp. 71–101, J. R. Steffey, *American Journal of Archaeology*, 89, 1985, pp. 71–101, P. A. Gianfrotta, *Archeo* 39, 1988, pp. 122ff. At the time of its discovery this was the best-preserved ship known, *Illustrated London News*, June 1974, pp. 69ff. For the fourth century BC wreck beside Dattilo (a rock in the Euonymus [Panarea] group of the Liparaeae [Lipari] islands off north-eastern Sicily), see M. Bound, *Archeologia Viva*, September/October 1989, pp. 56ff.

'Plemmirio C'. *International Journal of Nautical Archaeology*, 1989. I am grateful to Mr David Gibbins for his letter of October 4th 1988 on the Plemmyrium (Plemmirio) wrecks.

4 Halieis: Underwater Site

Halieis site. I owe gratitude to Professor Michael H. Jameson for information on this subject. He led the expeditions on behalf of the University of Pennsylvania, with which the University of Indiana was later associated.

Pumping. For the disadvantages of the 1967 method, and further particulars of the 1968 device, M. H. Jameson, *Marine Archaeology* (Proceedings of the 23rd Symposium of the Colston Research Society, 1971), 1973, p. 221.

Balloon. Previously employed at Sardis in Lydia (Asia Minor), *Archaeology*, January 1967, pp. 67f., October 1967, pp. 273f. At a height of 3,300 feet more than 1½ square miles can be covered. Another lift device is the airfoil (kite), which does not need hydrogen (or helium), and can contend better against winds.

Shallow water excavation techniques. Also utilized at Cenchreae, J. W. Shaw, *American Journal of Archaeology*, 71, 1967, pp. 227ff.

Radiocarbon dating of Temple of Apollo. On this method see note on Chapter 6, section 3. Pottery also contributed to this dating, cf. note on Chapter 2, section 3.

Laconian temple. Its *acroterion* (above the pediment) was ornamented with a disc.

Underwater Methods. Mention should be made of the Asherah, a two-man submarine equipped with stereoscopic cameras, G. F. Bass, *Archaeology Beneath the Sea*, 1975, pp. 113ff., P. Throckmorton, *Shipwrecks and Archaeology*, 1969, pp. 205f., and the unmanned underwater Argo which takes sonar images of the sea and releases the remote-controlled robot Jason, and of the teleguided ROV, M. Bound, *Archeologia Viva*, September/October 1989, pp. 60f.

5 Olbia: The Greek North-East

Photography. For air photography see especially Chapter 8, section 6. For underwater sites, see last section.

Olbia: upper town. A gymnasium of the late fourth and third centuries has also been located.

Berezan letter. English translation and interpretation in J. G. F. Hind, *Archaeological Reports*, 1983/4, p. 80.

Berezan. A. J. Graham, *Cambridge Ancient History*, III, 3, 2nd ed., 1982, p. 125, does not agree with Hind's view that Berezan is significantly earlier than Olbia.

Stones of Aegean origin found at Jagorlik and Berezan, M. Grant, *The Rise of the Greeks*, 1987, p. 274.

'Helleno-Scythians'. Later described as *mixellenes*, half-Greeks: W. Dittenberger, *Sylloge Inscriptionum Graecarum*, 3rd ed., 1915–24, p. 495.

Cimmerian Bosphorus. The field systems of Chersonesus (Sevastopol) in Tauris (Crimea) are particularly clear, A. W. Johnston and M. A. R. Colledge in K. Branigan (ed.), *Atlas of Archaeology*, 1982, p. 65.

6 Naucratis: Archaeology against History?

Pelusiac sites and Marea. Not identifiable with certainty. Additional Sites in north-eastern Nile delta, E. D. Oren, *Acta of the XIth International Congress of Classical Archaeology* (London, 1978), 1979, p. 199.

Herodotus and Archaeology. See also Herodotus versus epigraphy in Chapter 4, section 2.

CHAPTER 3: THE CLASSICAL GREEKS

1 Corinth and Athens: The Trireme

Corinthian supremacy. M. Grant, *The Rise of the Greeks*, 1987, pp. 73ff.

Character of trireme. The ancient authorities settle the length of oars of the trireme, its system of command, the leather gaskets installed in the lowest oar-ports, etc. Some help is also obtained from the Athenian navy yard's official records, and from harbour slips. Underwater archaeology has furnished information about the hull's structure and shape. Mr Thomas C. Gillmer writes to me on 12/6/89 that there are some details of the reconstruction with which he does not agree.

1987 launching. The co-sponsors were the Hellenic navy and Britain's Trireme Trust. The application of archaeo-ergonomics (the science of making the job fit the worker, applied to ancient times) to the crew's rowing techniques showed where the design was weakest; and biomechanical evaluation of the rowers and their oars, pivot pins and beam spacings were also employed.

2 Athens: The Painted Portico

Athenian Agora. Before 1931 it was mostly covered by housing. On the 'Prison of Socrates', see J. M. Camp, *Illustrated London News*, June 1976, pp. 87ff.

Porticos (Stoas). The ancient name of the South Portico is unknown. At the southern end of the Royal Portico is a slotted base on which some of the city's statues were displayed. The Portico of Zeus was decorated with sculptures on its *acroteria* (lower extremities, as well as vertex, of the pediment). In the Portico of the Herms, (not located), three stone herms (busts of Hermes on a pedestal) were set up in 330 BC. The Portico of Attalus II of Pergamum (159–138 BC) has been reconstructed as a museum (1953–6).

Doric and Ionic Orders. M. Grant, *The Rise of the Greeks*, 1987, pp. 23f.

Painting of Marathon. The uncertainty about who was the painter is strange, seeing that it was probably the most famous picture at Athens.

Academy and Lyceum. Schools of Plato and Aristotle respectively.

Eleusinian Mysteries. M. Grant, *op. cit.*, pp. 45f.

Cynics and Stoics. *Id.*, *From Alexander to Cleopatra*, 1982, pp. 234ff., 244ff.

Heruli. A Germanic people originating from Scandinavia, a branch of whom appeared in the Black Sea area and in AD 267 sacked Athens, Corinth, Sparta and Argos.

Alaric I. King of the Visigoths, he led his people southwards from Lower Moesia in AD 395, devastated Greece before invading Italy in 401, sacked Rome in 410, and died in the same year.

Slavs. Began their migration after the middle of the 5th century AD. One group overran Greece in *c.*580.

3 Riace: Peak of Classical Sculpture

Classical art-history. The complaint of R. Bianchi Bandinelli, *Mélanges offerts à K. Michalowski*, 1966, p. 262, that there was too much obsession with classification, dating and attribution is queried by A. Snodgrass, *An Archaeology of Greece*, 1987, p. 133. G. F. Bass, *Archaeology*, January/February 1989, pp. 55, 103, believes that the interpretation of classical art by archaeological methods (not the same as art history) will develop further.

Balloons. For their archaeological use see especially Chapter 2, section 4.

Analyses of bronze statues. The XRF (X-Ray Fluorescence Spectrometer) analyses metal (and paint) – studying elements rather than components – and displays the date on a screen. On archaeometallurgy see also V. di Cesare, *Archeologia Viva*, 3, 7–8, 1984, pp. 65ff. (bibliography on p. 71). In 1989 the Riace statues have been returned to the laboratory in order to extract the earth introduced at the time of fusion, so as to stop sweating.

Pythagoras of Rhegium. A. Stacchi identifies the sculptor of both Riace bronzes as Pythagoras, and believes that both represent the hero Euthymus of Locri Epizephyrii. A statue of marble from Asia Minor found at Motya (Mozia) in western Sicily in 1979 (Marsala Museum), perhaps representing a charioteer, has been tentatively ascribed to Pythagoras.

Cresilas. A Roman copy of his bust of Pericles is in the British Museum, M. Grant, *The Classical Greeks*, 1989, plate 19.

4 Aegae (Vergina) and Pella: Macedonia Revealed

Tomb of c.500 BC contained an iron model of a cart resembling one found in a cemetery at Sindus near Thessalonica (Salonica).

Paintings of Persephone and Hades. The same theme is found on the panel or seat-back of a carved marble throne found over the tomb (*c.*500 BC), and at Panticapaeum (Kerch), T. A. S. Tinkoff-Utechin, *Bulletin of the Institute of Classical Studies* (London), 26, XXVI, 1979. For the story, M. Grant, *Myths of the Greeks and Romans*, 1986 ed., pp. 126, 131 (Demeter).

Royal character of Great Tomb. A torque of gilt silver found in the tomb may be a royal diadem, M. Andronikos in K. Branigan, *Atlas of Archaeology*, 1982, p. 70.

Eucleia. Sometimes identified with Artemis.

Eurydice. (1) mother of Philip II, (2) wife of Philip III Arrhidaeus (see next note). H. W. Catling, *Archaeological Reports*, 1982/3, p. 44, accepts the identification with the former.

Tomb of Philip II? Or of his feeble-minded or epileptic son Philip III Arrhidaeus (d. 317 BC), the half-brother of Alexander III the Great? For recent discussions of this still-disputed question, see A. J. N. W. Prag, J. H. Musgrave and R. A. H. Neave, *Journal of Hellenic Studies*, 104, 1984, pp. 60ff. (on the skull), E. A. Fredricksmeyer, *American Journal of Archaeology*, 1987, pp. 99f., W. M. Calder III, *ibid.*, pp. 102f. For a reconstruction of Philip's disfigured face, S. Lloyd, *Ancient Turkey*, 1989, p. 132, and comment.

The Great Mound. Perhaps heaped up by the Macedonian King Antigonus II Gonatas (276–239 BC) after the monuments had been shattered by the Gaulish soldiers of Pyrrhus of Epirus (274–3) (as Plutarch, *Pyrrhus*, 26, 11f., reported), since Greeks would have been unlikely to perform such an action.

Aegae royal palace. Partially cleared in 1861, 1937 and 1963.

Hippodamus. Adapted Greek urban planning to 'grid-iron' scheme, notably at Piraeus and Thurii (on the site of Sybaris).

Pella. Cybele was the great mother-goddess of Asia Minor, whose worship was centred upon Pessinus (Balhissar). By the fifth century BC she was known in Greece. See also below, Chapter 4, section 1. A circular sanctuary outside Pella, from which many objects have been recovered, is believed to have been dedicated to Demeter and Persephone, with a parallel cult of Artemis and Poseidon, H. W. Catling, *Archaeological Reports* 1981/2, p. 36.

Rape of Helen. Theseus was said to have kidnapped Helen, when she was twelve, from Sparta, to be his bride, and to have locked her up at Aphidnae, from which she was rescued by her brothers Castor and Polydeuces (the Dioscuri).

5 Syracuse: Archaeology and Economics

Suppression of autocrats by Timoleon. Hicetas of Syracuse, Mamercus of Catana, and Hippon of Messana (Zancle), were put to death, but Andromachus of Tauromenium was spared because it was he who had invited Timoleon to Sicily.

Prosperity. Trade is now a fashionable subject for archaeologists once again, A. Snodgrass and C. Chippindale, *Antiquity*, 62, 237, December 1988, p. 725.

Hiero II more important than Timoleon? M. von Sydow in R. J. A. Wilson, *Archaeological Reports*, 1986/7, p. 111.

Coin finds. For their historical significance see M. Crawford, *Sources for Ancient History*, 1983, pp. 187ff., P. Grierson, *Numismatic Chronicle*, 1965, pp. 1ff, 1966, pp. 1ff. For the application of trend surface analysis to such finds, I. Hodder and C. Orton, *Spatial Analysis in Archaeology*, 1979 (1976), pp. 172ff., 181ff.

CHAPTER 4: THE HELLENISTIC GREEKS

1 Alexandria (or Seleucia) Oxiana (Aï Khanum): The Farthest Greek East

Mountains above River Kokcha. Rubies and rock crystal as well as *lapis lazuli*.

Greco-Bactrian rule. Eucratides (*c.* 170–145 BC) probably ruled at Aï Khanum (renamed Eucratidea?), and it may have fallen at the end of his reign, P. Bernard, *Scientific American*, January 1982, p. 153. Remains of a local mint have been located on the site, also square bilingual coins of Agathocles Dikaios have come to light at Aï Khanum. For other coins found there see W. W. Tarn, *The Greeks in Bactria and India* (1984 ed. by F. L. Holt), pp. ixf., n. 23 (bibliography). Bactrian and Indo-Greek coins display the portraits and names of unknown or scarcely known monarchs, M. Grant, *From Alexander to Cleopatra*, 1982.

Cultural 'fusion' theories questioned. The more simplistic kind of 'diffusionist' theory has also come under a cloud (under the influence of the 'New Archaeology', Appendix 1), D. Wilson, *Science and Archaeology*, 1978 ed., pp. 303f.,

K. Branigan, *Atlas of Archaeology*, 1982, p. 235, though such wholesale rejections have been queried. For acculturation on the eastern edges of Alexander's empire see *Acta of the* XIth *International Congress of Classical Archaeology* (Berlin 1988). R. Lane Fox, *Oxford History of the Classical World*, 1986, p. 347, distinguishes between the policies of Hellenistic kings and those of cities (less collaborative) regarding cultural intercourse with natives. For Greco-Asian mixtures of sculptural techniques at Aï Khanum see P. Bernard, *op. cit.*, p. 158.

2 *Troezen: Inscriptions and History*

Marathon. Recent discoveries and discussions underline the importance of battlefield archaeology, D. M. Lewis in A. R. Burn, *Persia and the Greeks*, 2nd ed., 1984, pp. 606f., E. Vanderpool, *Hesperia*, 35, 1966, pp. 93ff., *id.*, *American Journal of Archaeology*, 70, 1966, pp. 329ff. Cf. Chapter 7. section 3, on the archaeological evidence for siege-warfare.

Persian revenge in 480. Especially against Athens and Eretria, which had helped the Ionian cities to revolt against Persia. On the expedition of Xerxes I see now N. G. L. Hammond, *Cambridge Ancient History*, IV, 2nd ed., 1988, pp. 518–91.

Thessaly in 480. M. Grant, *The Rise of the Greeks*, 1987, pp. 127f.

Leonidas's death at Thermopylae. His mountain-flank, inadequately protected by 1,000 Phocians, was turned by an enemy force guided by a Greek collaborator, Ephialtes of Malis. He had dismissed most of the non-Spartans in his force (except the men from Thespiae in Boeotia).

Epigraphy. Not to be excluded from archaeology (see note on Introduction).

Reserves about epigraphy. Cf. also J. C. Mann, *Journal of Roman Studies*, 75, 1985, pp. 204ff: inscriptions do not provide information about the total population, but only about the people who used them.

Pittheus. Mythical founder of Troezen (named after his brother), visited by King Aegeus of Athens.

Patronymics and deme. Absent from inscriptions until *c.*350 BC, C. W. Fornara (ed.), *Translated Documents of Greece and Rome*, I, *Archaic Times to the End of the Peloponnesian War*, 2nd ed., 1983, p. 55 n. 1.

Manning of the two hundred ships. These arrangements indicated in the 'Troezen decree' are hard to believe. They presuppose that no measures had yet been adopted to train crews, that no trierarchs (citizens nominated to organize and defray such preparations) had been appointed – and that the crews would be created by dividing the total number of citizens and aliens 'into two hundred companies'. This is an administrative step far more in keeping with the fourth century than with the emergency of 481/480 (cf. J. B. Bury and R. Meiggs, *A History of Greece*, 4th ed., 1975, p. 530, n. 3). Cf. also A. R. Burn, *Persia and the Greeks*, 2nd ed., 1984, pp. 366ff.

Other anachronisms. (1) The Troezen decree provided for 100 ships to go to Artemisium, whereas according to Herodotus, 8, 1–2 and 14, there were 127. The discrepancy can be accounted for in various ways, but the 'Decree' may have adjusted the figure in the light of what became known after the battle, R. J. Lenardon, *The Saga of Themistocles*, 1987, p. 71. (2) Directions for the evacuation of Athens before the fall of Thermopylae are unlikely, though just credible (J. B. Bury and R. Meiggs, *op. cit.*, p. 529 n. 3, A. R. Burn *op. cit.*, p. 368. (3) Reservations about the return of the ostracized (sent away to Salamis pending an Assembly decision) do not look authentic (*op. cit.* p. 530 n. 3 and p. 368).

Lettering of 'Decree'. The lettering seems appropriate to a third-century date, A. R. Burn, *op. cit.*, p. 364 and n. 1.

Revolt of 323 BC against Macedonia. The Lamian War, led by the Athenians who mobilized other Greek city-states, but failed to make headway against Antipater, governor of Macedonia and 'general of Europe', and were then, like other states, forcibly converted from allies to subjects.

Aeschines quoted alleged (fictitious) decrees of Themistocles and Miltiades during a tour of the Peloponnese designed to gain support against Phillip II of Macedonia (before the king 'bought' him, as Demosthenes asserted. *On the Embassy*, 303; cf. A. R. Burn, *op. cit.*, pp. 359 and 241). It was from this epoch that a definitive text of the Themistocles decree became established (quoted by Plutarch and Aelius Aristides, A. R. Burn, *op. cit.*, p. 351 n. 40).

Themistocles's reputation eclipsed: M. Grant, *The Classical Greeks*, 1989, pp. 12f.

Details in decree that seem to go back to a fifth-century date. (1) General colouring of language, *ibid.*, p. 371. (2) A few specifically fifth-century terms, R. Sealey, *A History of the Greek City-States 700–338* BC, 1976, p. 214. (3) Ships filled 'up to the number of a hundred men': complicated argument in O. Murray, *Early Greece*, 1980, p. 277. Thus 'there remains the possibility that parts of [the decree] rest on genuine tradition', according to J. B. Bury and R. Meiggs, *op. cit.*, p. 530 n. 3, cf. N. G. L. Hammond, *Journal of Hellenic Studies*, 102, 1982, pp. 75ff. (more strongly); but see text.

Oracle of Delphi. The Pythia (priestess) had first advised flight to the west, but then produced a more ambiguous but still basically defeatist oracle, Herodotus, VII, 142, O. Murray, *op. cit.*, pp. 271f.

3 Taras (Taranto): Jewellery

Milan exhibition (1984–5, *Gli ori di Taranto in età ellenistica*): goldwork from provinces of Taranto, Bari, Brindisi and Foggia. Such work, before Hellenistic times, had been abundant only in the northern Black Sea area (Chapter 2, section 5).

Taras: foundation and early history. M. Grant, *The Rise of the Greeks*, 1987, p. 348 n. 8.

1979, 1980 finds. Near new Tribunale and in Via Dante respectively. Two burial pits in the centre of the town: Via Principe Amedeo.

Terracotta figurines. Many represent the mythical local heroes Taras and Phalanthus.

4 Rhodes: Calendar-Calculator from Anticythera

Gamma rays. Among the shortest waves of the electromagnetic wave spectrum, they resemble X-rays, but tend toward higher penetration as well as frequency;

with high energy and no electrical charges, they can penetrate thick pieces of metal (or concrete).

Gears of the mechanism were cut from a sheet of bronze two metres thick, and the gear teeth were cut at the same angle, so that any one would mesh with any other. The complex gearing was operated by a drive shaft.

Astronomical motions were indicated by letters inside and outside.

Geminus. Writer of textbooks on mathematical subjects and astronomy, with special reference to the zodiac and the calendar. Simplicius, *On Aristotle's Physics*, 291–2 D, quotes from Geminus's epitome of the *Meteorologica* of Posidonius (*c.*135–*c.*51/50 BC), who was born at Apamea (Qalaat Al-Mudik) in Syria but settled at Rhodes (on which see M. Grant, *From Alexander to Cleopatra*, 1982, pp. 108ff).

Rhodian catapult. P. Levi, *Atlas of the Greek World*, 1980, p. 137. See also Chapter 7, section 3 (note), on ancient *ballistae*.

Date of wreck. Radiocarbon (C14) date (see Chapter 6, section 3 and note) of a piece of wood from it: Elizabeth Ralph in P. Throckmorton, *Shipwrecks and Archaeology*, 1969, p. 159, 'concluded that the tree that formed the plank had absorbed its C-14 between 260 and 180 BC . . . If large logs were used, the particular sample which was dated may have come from the centre of a log and would therefore have been earlier than the cutting of the tree by an amount equal to the age of the tree.'

Advanced ancient Greek technology. E.g. Rhodian catapult (see last note but one), and ship's gear for oscillating water-pump (Tunisia), G. Kapitän, *International Journal of Nautical Archaeology*, 12, 1983, pp. 145–153.

5 Alexandria in Egypt: Debasing the Coinage

Numismatics. For its various historical relevances see Chapter 3, section 5, and Chapter 9, sections 1 and 3.

Chemical analysis. On its techniques in relation to coins see G. F. Carter, *American Numismatic Society Museum Notes*, 33, 1988, pp. 91ff. Debasement analyses are also useful for the detection of forgeries, ancient and modern: *Survey of Numismatic Research 1978–1984*, 1986, pp. 970, 977 (bibliography).

Computers. In 1977 the Commission Internationale de Numismatique appointed a sub-committee on the computerizing of data relating to coins.

Ptolemaic kingdom. Established by Ptolemy I Soter (304–283/2 BC), annexed by Rome on the death of Cleopatra VII (30 BC; see Chapter 6, section 1).

Ptolemy XII Auletes. His full designation was Ptolemaios Theos Philopator Philadelphus Neos Dionysos. On the debts he owed to Romans see M. Grant, *Cleopatra*, 1972, pp. 16ff.

PART II: ITALY AND THE ROMAN EMPIRE

CHAPTER 5: ETRUSCAN AND REPUBLICAN ITALY

1 Tarquinii: Potentiometer, Periscope

Potentiometer. Sensitive to the difference between solid soil and empty underground space, so that e.g. a damp pit offers less resistance, and foundations of dry stone more resistance, than the surrounding soil. Spacing between the rods is varied according to conditions. When they are spaced equally, features up to a depth equal to their spacing (separation) can be detected. Work could be speeded up by the introduction of a fifth rod, moved up ready to become the first in the next reading.

Motor drills. Concepts borrowed from Sybaris, Chapter 2, section 2. For various types see F. Rainey, *American Journal of Archaeology*, 1969, pp. 264f. The older versions were slow and difficult to operate, especially in thick clays.

Subterranean exploration. A recent technique is sonic detection, beaming sound-waves into the earth, so that the study of their reflections provides detailed information about what lies beneath the surface.

Tarquinii and Rome. The Roman kings Tarquinius Priscus (traditionally 616–579 BC) and Tarquinius Superbus (534–510 BC) were said to have come from Tarquinii, the former having been the son of an emigrant from Corinth.

2 Pyrgi: Etruscan History Recovered

Leucothea. Identified with Ino the daughter of Cadmus, transformed into a sea-goddess.

Eileithyia. Identified with Hera or Artemis, or with the daughter of the former or partner of the latter.

Carthage. M. Grant, *Guide to the Ancient World*, 1986, pp. 153ff.

Alalia. *Id.*, *The Etruscans*, 1980, pp. 148ff.

Pyrgi. The 1985 excavations focused on a zone to the south.

François Tomb at Vulci. M. Grant, op. cit., pp.169ff.

3 Orbetello and Prilius: Vanished Harbours

Ancient name of Orbetello. Did the Etruscans call it Cusa? *Ibid.*, p. 168. This Etruscan ethnic seems to be echoed by the adjacent, later, Roman colony Cosa, M. Cristofani, *Dizionario della civiltà etrusca*, 1985, p. 195. For Clusium (Calusium) as a coastal town, distinct from the city in the interior, see A. J. Pfiffig, *Ost Jahreshefte*, 58, *Beiblatt*, 1988, pp. 190ff. In 1988 an Etruscan settlement, probably a colony of Vulci, was found four miles from the coast in the Albinia (Albegna) valley, near Settefinestre (Chapter 5, section 5).

Eighth-century BC burials at Orbetello: in the Serpentario area. Fifth- to third-century houses: Doganella site. Ports in Etruscan cities' outlying territories: Telamon and Populonia, belonging to Rusellae and Vetulonia respectively.

Prilius lagoon open to sea. V. Melani and M. Vergari, *Roselle*, 1974, p. 23, H. H. Scullard, *The Etruscan Cities and Rome*, 1967, pp. 61, 140, M. Grant, *The Etruscans*, 1980, pp. 184f., M. Cristofani, *Gli etruschi sul mare*, 1983, p. 39. At Cosa, on the same coast, the sea level has risen only between two and three feet since antiquity.

4 Picentia (Pontecagnano): The Etruscan South

Greeks and Etruscans. D. Ridgway, *Early Italy and the Etruscans, Cambridge Ancient History*, IV, 2nd ed., 1988. Craniological analyses at Picentia by F. Salvi, *Studi etruschi*, series 3, 52, 1984 (1986), pp. 185ff., 303ff.

Ethnoarchaeology: the reconstruction of cultural systems by archaeological means. Discussed by P.J. Watson, S. A. LeBlanc and C. L. Redman, *Archaeological Explanation*, 1984, pp. 259ff.

Princely tombs. Also at Attidium (Fabriano), Rome, Praeneste (Palestrina) and Politorium (Castel di Decima).

5 Francolise and Settefinestre: Villa-Farms

Roman agriculture. A conference on Roman agriculture in the Mediterranean area was held in January 1988 by the British, French and Spanish schools at Rome.

Villas. For the term and its definition see D. E. Johnston, *Roman Villas*, 1979, pp. 6ff., J. F. Drinkwater, *Roman Gaul*, 1983, pp. 161f., 164, 174, 184 n. 60, K. Greene, *The Archaeology of the Roman Economy*, 1986, p. 89. The Falernian plain (Ager Falernus) is a promising area because it contains villas unencumbered by later remains. For the archaeobotany of an Etruscan villa-farm, Tartuchino, see *Proceedings of the British School at Rome*, 1988 (2nd season).

Villa Posto. Before excavation the cisterns were visible on a high rectangular platform.

Villa San Rocco. Its remains were first noted shortly before the Second World War.

Olives. The intercultivation of wheat and hay with vines and olives was common, as now. Going over to olives, therefore, did not (as was believed) mean waiting for fifteen years without income.

Valle d'Oro. Originally divided into small plots for colonists in the third century BC.

Settefinestre. Miniature round turrets (with dovecotes) alternate with buttresses. Much construction was of triumviral date (third quarter of first century BC). The *villa rustica* included guest-rooms and accommodation for the bailiff (*vilicus*). There was a twenty-seat latrine in one corner of the oil-mill courtyard.

Owners. They were not necessarily the actual traders, but were a high-status family which employed the estate as a centre for commercial exploitation.

Amphorae with SES from Cosa were shipped up the north-west coast of Italy, into southern Gaul (and up the valley of the River Rhodanus [Rhône]) and north-east Spain.

6 Oplontis: New Evidence for Roman Art

Stabiae. A. G. McKay, *Houses, Villas and Palaces in the Roman World*, 1975, M. Grant, *Cities of Vesuvius*, 1971 (indices s.v.), *Pitture e stucchi di Stabiae* (exhibition) 1989, A. de Franciscis, *The Buried Cities of Pompeii and Herculaneum*, 1979 (1968), p. 127.

Oplontis. In the Via dei Sepolcri in the centre of the modern Torre Annunziata. Unknowingly discovered by Colonel Robinson in 1834.

Oplontis baths contained *frigidarium*, *tepidarium*, fountain, and under-floor and intramural heating.

Redecoration planned in AD 79: defective marble pillars were laid out for repair. A pile of red earthenware oil-lamps in one room was evidently temporary. The eruption of 79 also caused much jewellery to be left behind.

Second Style: approximately of the last three-quarters of the first century BC, R.J. Ling in M. Grant and R. Kitzinger (eds.), *Civilizations of the Ancient*

Mediterranean, 1988, pp. 1774ff; cf. M. Grant, *Cities of Vesuvius*, 1971, pp. 149–152. At Oplontis five rooms decorated in this style survive.

Third Style: F. L. Bastet, *Proposta per una classificazione del Terzo stile pompeiano*, 1977, R. J. Ling, *op. cit.*, pp. 1777ff., M. Grant, *op. cit.*, pp. 152–4 (see also bibliography). One painting at Oplontis shows Heracles (Hercules) in the Garden of the Hesperides, with a poet playing a lyre.

Boscoreale paintings. M. Grant, *Cities of Vesuvius*, 1971, p. 149.

CHAPTER 6: THE AUGUSTAN EMPIRE

1 Nicopolis: Monument for Actium

Amalgamation. Settlers were brought into Nicopolis from Ambracia, Amphilochia (including Amphilochian Argos), Acarnania (including Calydon), Aetolia, Leucas.

Athlit ram: J. R. Steffy, *Mariner's Mirror*, 69, 1983, pp. 229–47 (quadrireme or quinquereme).

Sextus Pompeius. Second son of Pompey the Great; outlawed 43 BC, occupied Sicily, defeated at Naulochus (36), executed at Miletus in Ionia (western Asia Minor).

Actian Festivals. Nicopolis was sometimes known as Actia Nicopolis (Dessau, *Inscriptiones Latinae Selectae*, 2080). The supervision of the Actian Games was entrusted to the Spartans.

Temples of Apollo. Dio Cassius seems to have been wrong in supposing there was a temple of Apollo on the tent site, cf. W. M. Murray and P. M. Petsas, *Archaeology*, September/October 1988, p. 32. But Octavian rebuilt his shrine on the Actium promontory.

Contributions to Nicopolis. One of those who contributed to its construction was the client-king Herod of Judaea (Chapter 6, section 3), M. Grant, *Herod the Great*, 1971, p. 103.

2 Primis (Qasr Ibrim): Egyptian Frontier

Isis. For this Egyptian, Hellenized goddess see M. Grant, *From Alexander to Cleopatra*, 1982, pp. 227ff.

Dodekaschoinos. Incorporated into the civil administration of the Thebaid (Upper Egypt), possibly as early as Augustus, certainly by the time of Domitian (AD 81–96).

Papyri found at Qasr Ibrim. Bibliography in E. G. Turner, *Greek Papyri: An Introduction*, 1980 ed., p. 200. For papyri see Chapter 8, section 5.

Meroe and Axum. Meroe's northern region continued to flourish in the third and fourth centuries AD, though its southern territories waned. In *c.*320–50 the country was devastated by the ruler of Axum (in Tigre), which became Christian in the first half of the fourth century under Ezana, who was the first Axumite monarch to call himself King of Aethiopia. Eight days journey from Axum was its east African port of Adulis, which is fairly inaccessible but demands excavation.

3 Caesarea Maritima: Herod's Port

The Tower of Strato is now seen to have had two harbours, one to the north and one to the south.

Partial explorations of Caesarea Maritima in 1951, 1959–63.

Zeus of Olympia and Hera of Argos. M. Grant, *The Classical Greeks*, 1989, pp. 95f., 88.

'Augustan harbour'. Herod's nomenclature for his projects repeatedly honoured Augustus. Its flanking tower was named after the emperor's stepson Drusus the elder (died 9 BC).

Herod's harbour. Many vaulted buildings (*horrea*) for storing grain were found along the shore. One is datable to the reign of Herod the Great by ceramics.

Carbon 14 (radiocarbon). One of the basic chronological devices of modern archaeology, though of only limited value to classical archaeologists. All living things contain both Carbon 12 as well as traces of radio active Carbon 14, in a fixed proportion to each other. After an organism dies, its C14 begins to decay. Since it does so at a fixed rate, the approximate date of the death of the organism can be calculated by measuring the amount of C14 left. C. Renfrew, *Before Civilization*, 1976 ed., pp. 53, 280ff., etc., P. Cleator, *Archaeology in the Making*, 1976, pp. 183ff., D. R. Wilson, *Science and Archaeology*, 1978 ed., pp. 75ff., D. Miles in K. Branigan, *Atlas of Archaeology*, 1982, pp. 16f., R. E. Taylor, *Radiocarbon Dating: An Archaeological Perspective*, 1987. Carbon 14 datings have been amended by dendrochronology (Chapter 8, section 1).

Pozzolana (pit-sand): a finely pulverized volcanic product found at Puteoli (Pozzuoli; see Appendix II, iii), the basis of the all-important Roman discovery of concrete. M. Grant, *The World of Rome*, 1960, pp. 268ff.

Finds now go to the museum at Kibbutz Sdot Yam.

Amphitheatre. Discovered by air photography (see Chapter 8, section 6), and then explored by aerial infra-red photography (see note below).

Hostility of Jews to Herod the Great in his last years: M. Grant, *Herod the Great*, 1971, pp. 205ff.

Aqueduct had two channels, the eastern one probably Herodian, and the western one dating from Hadrian (AD 117–38).

'False colour' infra-red photography. 'False colour' refers to the accentuation of specific features in red, pink, blue, yellow, etc., which are not natural colours but serve to emphasize contrasts. For false colour satellite imagery from high altitudes see *Past Worlds: The Times Atlas of Archaeology*, 1988, p. 282.

New devices for aerial exploration include (1) airborne oceanographic Lidar, a laser device which makes profiles of the earth's surface, (2) synthetic aperture radar which beams energy waves to the ground and records the energy reflected, (3) thermal infra-red multispectral scanners, which use six channels to measure the thermal radiation given off by the ground (radiation from ultra-violet and visible light, and infra-red wave-bands), (4) ground-penetrating radar (see note on Chapter 2, section 2). (5) Remote sensing techniques (see next note). See also D. R. Wilson, *Air Photo Interpretation for Archaeologists*, 1982, p. 21, D. Metz, *Archaeology*, July/August 1983, pp. 68f., 77.

Remote sensing techniques, using digital instruments, collect data well beyond the visible, optical range, H. J. Ebert, *Advances in Archaeological Method* *and Theory*, VII, 1984, pp. 293–362, T. Sever and J. Wiseman, *Remote Sensing and Archaeology: Potential for the Future*, 1985, P. Sheets and T. Sever, *Archaeology*, 41, 1988, pp. 28ff., D.N. Riley, *Air Photography and Archaeology*, 1987, p. 58 (cf. p. 140 for the rapid development of these techniques).

4 Rome: The Imperial Sundial

The Augustan calendar. On Augustus's modifications of the calendar of Julius Caesar, see M. Le Roy, *Initiation à l'archéologie romaine*, pp. 162ff., E.J. Bickerman, *Chronology of the Ancient World*, 1980 ed., p. 47. Equinoxes: *ibid.*, pp. 51, 58. Solstices: *ibid.*, pp. 51f, 55. Augustus renamed the month of 'Sextilis', calling it *mensis Augustus* because it was on August 1st 30 BC that he had entered Alexandria after the defeat of Marcus Antonius and Cleopatra VII.

Domitianic or Hadrianic sundial was located exactly on top of its predecessor, since the obelisk had not yet been moved.

CHAPTER 7: THE POST-AUGUSTANS

1 Noviomagus Regnensium (Fishbourne): Prince in a Province

Princedom of Cogidubnus. For Syrian parallels to its intra-provincial status, see D.C. Braund, *Rome and the Friendly King*, 1983, p. 113. The territory of Cogidubnus's princedom was fragmented, *ibid.*, p. 84; it is uncertain if it contained a Roman garrison.

Marbles in Cogidubnus's palace came from Luna (Carrara), the Pyrenees, the Garumna (Garonne) valley, Gallia Lugdunensis, Scyros and Asia Minor. They could have been acquired from a single, central stockpile where materials of various origins were stored.

Plants, trees. For the (wavering) distinction between archaeobotany (the study of botanical remains from archaeological sites) and palaeobotany and palaeoethnobotany, see S. Champion, *Dictionary of Terms and Techniques in Archaeology*, 1980, pp. 8, 87.

Roman gardens in Britain. Remains of a garden have also been discovered at Frocester Court Villa, Gloucestershire, D. E. Johnston, *Roman Villas*, 1983 ed., pp. 12, 20, 34f.

2 Aphrodisias: Schools of Sculpture

Temple of Aphrodite. Its construction in its final form was perhaps started early in the first century BC. On her imperial cult there see J. M. Reynolds, *Studii Clasice* 24, 1986 (*Festschrift D. M. Pippidi*), pp. 109ff. For the temple, G. E. Bean, *Turkey Beyond the Maeander*, 1989 (1971), pp. 190ff. For her bust, K. M. Erim, *National Geographic Magazine*, 141, 6, June 1972, p. 777.

Zoilus frieze. He is attended by Demos, Polis, Time (Honour), Andreia (Courage), Aion (Time), Rhome (Strength – or Rome) and Mneme (Memory). This was one of the earlier finds.

Aphrodisian work in Italy: Aristeas and Papias signed sculptures of old and young centaurs of which copies were found at Hadrian's Villa at Tibur (Tivoli; Capitoline Museum, Rome). Another Aphrodisian sculptor, Antonianus, signed a relief depicting Hadrian's friend Antinous from Lanuvium (Lanuvio). For the 'Esquiline Group', see text.

Sebasteion sculptures: R. R. R. Smith, *Journal of Roman Studies*, 77, 1987, pp. 88–138, *ibid.*, 78, 1988, pp. 50ff.

Finds at Aphrodisias. Now preserved in a local museum.

Travelling 'workshops'? The arch and other Severan buildings at Lepcis Magna are stylistically close to Aphrodisian work, J. M. C. Toynbee, *The Art of the Romans*, 1965, p. 75. Severus may also have imported masons from Aphrodisias for his arch at Rome, R. Brilliant, *Roman Art*, 1974, p. 68.

Portraits. Often on *imagines clipeatae* (marble representations of shields). There are also busts of barbarians and priests (crowned) and magistrates, some of late styles.

Tetrapylon (elaborate monumental gateway). Excavated in 1963, reconstructed 1970 and 1983–4.

Odeon. Excavation started in 1963.

Decorative sculpture at Aphrodisias also included garland friezes and garland sarcophagi.

Greek influences. The panels decorating the Sebasteion echo certain fifth century BC traditions.

Edict of Diocletian. A second inscription of the same period, relating to currency and coinage, has also been found, G. E. Bean, *Turkey Beyond the Maeander*, 1989 (1971), p. 197.

Fourth century AD. Some time before AD 400 Aphrodisias was damaged by an earthquake, *Anatolian Studies*, 1985, p. 179.

Asiana, comprising western Asia Minor, was one of the twelve *dioceseis* (groups of provinces) established by Diocletian (AD 284–305) under *vicarii* (governors-general).

3 Masada: Siege-Warfare

First Jewish Revolt (First Roman War). See now M. Goodman, *The Ruling Class of Judaea: The Origins of the Jewish Revolt against Rome* AD 66–70, 1987, M. Hengel, *The Zealots*, 1989.

Hasmonaeans (Maccabees): the Jewish dynasty which ruled Judaea from the time of Judas Maccabaeus (166–160 BC) until the death of Antigonus (37 BC).

Masada paintings on terrace imitated panelling in stone and marble. Similar paintings are found at Herod's other centres, e.g. Caesarea Maritima and Herodium.

Camp design. See also Chapter 8, section 4, Chapter 9, section 2.

Cooking arrangements. See also Chapter 8, section 2.

Training facilities. Cf. evidence from Cawthorne in Yorkshire.

Patriotic archaeology. Yadin's attitude was shared by Moshe Dayan, who declared that it was through archaeology that he understood his people, R. Rahtz, *Invitation to Archaeology*, 1985, p. 25. See also 'Archaeology and Politics' in *Archaeological Review from Cambridge*, 5, 1, 1986. G. F. Bass, *Archaeology*, January/February 1989, p. 102 stresses the need for internationalization to counteract geopolitical nationalism.

Siege artillery. See J. Coles, *Archaeology by Experiment*, 1973, p. 128, on the mathematics of *ballistae*.

4 Herculaneum: Skeletons

Pompeii. After an earthquake in 1980 had caused collapses, the installation of an electrical cable near the Forum in 1981 enabled 85 military engineers and 36 architects to undertake a topographical, stratigraphical and structural survey. Sites: Houses of Gaius Julius Polybius (excavation began in 1966), Marcus Fabius Rufus, the Ceii, Sallust; tomb of Marcus Obellius Firmus; vineyard inside Pompeii; necropolis just outside; Large Palaestra (vegetation control by Round Up, a natural modified amino-acid) etc. Yet only 10% of all excavated material at Pompeii has survived, though another 10% is, to some extent, documented. However, much of Pompeii is 'Archaeologically still largely unintelligible' (J.J. Wilkes, *Times Literary Supplement*, 7–13/4/89 (cf. Chapter 5, section 6) *Rivista di Studi Pompeiani*, I, 1987, II, 1988, *Progetto Pompeii: Stralcio* (exhibition), 1988. See G. Gullini, *Archeo*, 42, August 1988, pp. 24–37 (Progetto Pompei), W. Jongman, *The Economy and Society of Pompeii*, 1988, L. Richardson, *Pompeii: An Architectural History*, 1988.

Herculaneum. A Convegno Internazionale was held to celebrate the 250th anniversary of excavations in 1988. Systematic work on the *palaestra* began in 1968, and restoration of the Suburban Baths in 1971. There has also been recent work on the Decumanus Maximus.

Vesuvian region. Specialists with image processors, scanning devices and an IBM computer have been reading, mapping and collecting digitized images. A new programme was announced at a press conference, *Archeologia*, 26, 3, March 1987, pp. 1–6.

Samnites. Four Oscan-speaking tribal states in the southern Apennines; M. Grant, *History of Rome*, 1979 ed., pp. 52ff.

Destruction of Herculaneum by ignimbrite (misinterpreted as mud), C. Vita-Finzi, *Archaeological Sites in their Setting*, 1978, p. 92.

Boat and skeletons were discovered when work was started, in 1980, on an emergency trench along the shore, to divert surplus water from the Suburban Baths. This, then, is an example of rescue archaeology leading to new discoveries (see note to Introduction). Although now made of fragile charcoal, the boat has proved informative about the construction of such vessels. Goldwork and aromatic substances have also been found.

Palaeopathology: D. R. Wilson, *Science and Archaeology*, 1978 ed., pp. 244–50, J. McIntosh, *The Archaeologist's Handbook*, 1986, p. 114, *Past Worlds: The Times Atlas of Archaeology*, 1988, pp. 42f.

Dentistry of skeletons. The flaws indicated here were exceptional – and the Helmsman (see below) was also in poor dental condition – since teeth, on the whole, proved to be excellent. Lesions were relatively few, and caries absent owing to the lack of refined sugar – though there has been an overall increase in caries since Neolithic times, except during the epoch of the collapse of the Roman empire, D. R. Wilson op. cit., pp. 246f.; nearly 90 rotten teeth have now been found in a dentist's surgery in the Forum Romanum, *Archaeology*, July/August 1989, p. 34.

Helmsman. A misnomer, since his body did not arrive at the shore with the boat.

Soldier at Herculaneum. For military diet see Chapter 8, section 2.

Injuries. Roman medicine was good at dealing with fractures and dislocations.

Lead intake. Lead was no major threat or factor in the subsequent decline of the Roman empire, cf. J.J. Deiss, *Herculaneum: Italy's Buried Treasure*, 2nd ed., 1985, pp. 191f. Aside from decompression chambers in public water distribution systems, lead pipes were concentrated in upper-class houses and public baths. Lead in the water of masonry aqueducts was negligible, because the pipes were coated internally with calcium (from mountains rich in limestone, as is still the case today at Rome).

CHAPTER 8: THE MIDDLE EMPIRE

1 *Augusta Trevirorum (Trier): Tree-Rings and Bridges*

Dendrochronology. The rings on the trees are caused by variation in climate linked to the annual rotation of the earth round the sun. The technique has been employed in connection with eruptions (which stamp trees sharply), and extended to many new fields (including wood used for 14th–17th century paintings). For C14 dating (deeply affected by dendrochronology, which shows the incorrectness of the assumption that the amount of C14 in the atmosphere has remained constant throughout time) see Caesarea Maritima, Chapter 6, section 3, note to Chapter 4, section 4, and bibliography to the present section.

Bridge. I am grateful to Diplom Forstwirt Mechthild Neyses, author of *Holz macht Geschichte* (*Holz aktuell*, 5, 1985, pp.67f.) for writing to me on 14/3/89 on this subject. Dredging operations in the Mosella have also provided new evidence for another bridge (dating back to the pre-Roman second century BC) between Stadtbredimus and Palzern, E. M. Wightman, *Rome and the Treveri*, p. 16.

Franks (Merovingians): i.e. Salian Franks; extended rule to Ripuarian Franks and Alamanni under Clovis I (AD 481–511).

Oak-post 18/17 BC. Cracks developed subsequently. On the quality of Trier oak see H. Cüppers, *Die Trierer Römerbrücken*, 1969, pp. 136ff.

Bridge of Antoninus Pius. Its 9 piers (2 embedded) were no longer on wooded piles but on solid stone foundations. Alterations were effected in *c.* AD 185. The modern bridge overlaying it escaped destruction in 1945.

Other ancient bridges. Remains of a wooden bridge have been found at Amphipolis in Macedonia, *Illustrated London News*, August 1978, p. 48.

Augusta Trevirorum was made an honorary colony by either Augustus or Claudius (AD 41–54). It was a centre of pottery manufacture, and possessed a school of sculpture. A third public bath-house was found in 1986/7. For the city's great significance in the later empire, M. Grant, *Guide to the Ancient World*, 1986, pp. 89f.

2 *Vindolanda (Chesterholm): Writings on Wood*

Hadrian's Wall (AD 122–6). From Segodunum (Wallsend) on the Tinea (Tyne) to Maia (Bowness) on the Ituna (Solway).

Antonine Wall (AD 142–5). From Bridgeness on the Bodotria (Forth) to Old Kilpatrick on the Clota (Clyde).

Writing tablets at Vindolanda. More have been found in 1985 in the *praetorium* (general's residence, see Chapter 7, section 3 and note). A child's writing exercise displayed a line of Virgil (*Aeneid*, IX, 473).

Extrication and preservation. For the difficulties see A. K. Bowman and J. D. Thomas, *The Vindolanda Writing Tablets*, 1974, p. 6.

Meat. Vindolanda is one of a number of sites in the western empire where the increased size of cattle is evident from bones, S. Applebaum in J. Wacher (ed.), *The Roman World*, II, 1987, p. 517. *Ibid.*, p. 516 on zooarchaeology, cf. J. McIntosh, *The Archaeologist's Handbook*, 1986, pp. 106f. Hunting wild boar, deer, etc, was extensive in Roman Britain, but not universal in other lands, where most of the meat came from domesticated animals.

Auxiliary cohorts. The *praefectus* of the 1st Tungrian cohort was named Priscinus. The 8th Batavian cohort, of which the *praefectus* was Flavius Cerealis, was also at Vindolanda. Both cohorts had fought under Agricola at Mons Graupius (Bennachie?) in AD 83 against the Caledonian tribesmen. There are also new references to the 9th Batavian cohort, and a reference to the 3rd. For auxiliaries see M. Grant, *The Army of the Caesars*, 1974, pp. xxii, 56f., and index (s.v.).

3 The North and Wadi Fawakhir: A Soldier's Diet

Roman soldiers. On their physique see Chapter 7, section 4.

Porridge. A slang name for Greeks at Rome was 'eaters of porridge', which was despised by the Romans.

Buccellato. Still the name of a popular form of loaf (cake) at Lucca.

Granaries contained mill-stones for grinding.

Mines. See now J. F. Healy in M. Grant and R. Kitzinger (eds.), *Civilizations of the Ancient Mediterranean*, II, 1988, pp.779ff., A. Woods in J. Wacher (ed.), *The Roman World* II, 1987, pp. 611ff. For new discoveries at Laurium in Attica see S. Mitchell, *Archaeological Reports*, 1984/5, pp. 106ff.

Ostraca. J.G. Milne, *Oxford Classical Dictionary*, 1970 ed., p. 762 (bibliography).

Measures. A *mation* was estimated by H. Brugsch, *Thesaurus Inscriptionum Aegyptiacarum*, V, p. 1501 at $\frac{1}{12}$ of an *artab(a)*, but this is uncertain (V. Wilcken, *Griechische Ostraka aus Ägypten und Nubien* (1899), pp. 751f) An *artab* contained 116 pints. A *congius* contained nearly 6 pints.

4 Novae: Danubian Legionary River Port

Novae in Lower Moesia as distinct from another Novae (Chezava) in Upper Moesia.

River Ports also at Drobeta (Turnu Severin), Ratiaria (Arčar) and Oescus (Ghighen), all excavated. For Oescus, see also next note but one. For Ratiaria see now A. Fol, *Archeologia Viva*, 8, NS.6, 1989, pp. 22–31.

Classis Moesica: inadequate depiction on Trajan's Column at Rome, J. S. Morrison, *The Ship*, 1980, p. 49. For the column see L. Rossi, *Trajan's Column and the Dacian Wars*, 1971, F. Lepper and S. Frere, *Trajan's Column*, 1988.

Legion at Novae. A second legion was at another river port, Oescus, only fifty-six miles away. In AD 69 two of three Moesian legions were at Oescus (?) and Novae, R. Syme, *Journal of Roman Studies*, 49, 1959, p. 32.

Scythian fleet detachment. (N.Black Sea). *Under praepositus vexillationibus Ponticis aput Scythia(m) et Tauricam, Corpus Inscriptionum Latinarum*, VIII, 619. There was also a detachment of the fleet at Istrus (Histria in Rumania).

Sacellum. Its second stage dates from late Severan times (nearly 3rd century AD).

Lamps. Bronze casting also took place locally.

5 Egypt: Novel on Papyrus

Recently discovered Greek papyri up to 1977: E.G. Turner, *Greek Papyri: An Introduction*, 1980 ed., p. 197, supplemented by I. Gallo, *Greek and Latin Papyrology, 1986*. A profitable source has been Antinoe in Egypt, on which Professor Giovanna Merici wrote to me on 10/12/88: see M. Manfredi, *Atti del* XVII *Congresso Internazionale di Papirologia (Naples)*, I, 1984, pp. 85–96. For papyri from Wadi Fawakhir, see Chapter 8, section 3, and for a reverse trace at Aï Khanum Chapter 4, section 1.

Papyrus of Lollianus's *Phoenicica*. Professor Klaus Maresch informs me that the place in Egypt where it was found is unknown.

Achilles Tatius is now tentatively attributed to the late 2nd century AD, T. Hägg, *The Novel in Antiquity*, 1983, p. 42.

6 The Samara (Somme) Valley: Air Photography

Early air photography. For exploratory endeavours in 1891, 1920 and 1921 see D.R. Wilson, *Science and Archaeology*, 1978 ed., p. 190.

Photogrammetry. First used in 1850, more systematically since 1920: UNESCO *Courier*, February 1960, in C.W. Ceram (ed.), *The World of Archaeology*, 1968 ed., pp.488ff. The camera can be mounted on a rigid frame, and moved along so that it takes overlapping vertical photographs.

Environmental surveys. For environmental archaeology see also note on Appendix 1.

Soil differences indicating ancient sites were commented on by William Camden, *Britannia*, 1772, quoted by P.E. Cleator, *Archaeology in the Making*, 1976, p. 69.

Air photography in 20th century. Especially in military zones, e.g. Italy, Syria, Tunisia. The Air Photography Unit of the Royal Commission on the Historical Monuments of England possesses four million air photographs. See the journal *Aerial Archaeology* since 1977, and, for new techniques, note on Chapter 6, section 3.

Samara valley. Gaps between known sites are filled by woods that probably conceal further ancient buildings.

Gaul. Here, 'rural studies' essentially means 'villa studies', J.F. Drinkwater, *Roman Gaul*, 1983, p. 162. For definition of villas, see above, note on Chapter 5, section 5.

Cursuses: elongated but more or less rectangular enclosures.

Henges: more or less circular enclosures, normally with the bank outside the main ditch. Late Neolithic and Bronze Ages.

7 *Cruciniacum (Bad Kreuznach): Water Supply*

Rome's water supply. For statistics see M. LeRoy, *Initiation à l'archéologie romaine*, 1965, pp. 39ff. For conditions, J. Carcopino, *Daily Life in Ancient Rome*, 1956 ed., pp. 49–54.

Pompeii. Earlier houses had wells.

Herculaneum. At the Forum Baths the lavatory was flushed from the cold plunge.

Impluvia, to contain rainfalls, were retained at the Vesuvian cities to supplement the abundant supply from the water mains that was developed, probably because rainwater was softer than aqueduct water, e.g. for laundering, A. G. McKay, *Houses, Villas and Palaces in the Roman World*, 1975, p. 49.

Ostia. *Ibid.*, pp. 93–5, J. Carcopino, *op. cit.*, pp. 50–3.

Roman towns in Britain. The water arrangements at Lindum (Lincoln), Verulamium (St Albans), Venta Silurum (Caerwent) and Viroconium (Wroxeter) are referred to by A. G. McKay, *op. cit.*, p. 200.

Cruciniacum. For its size and date, *Die römische Peristylvilla (Kreuznach)*. For a plan, G. Rupprecht, *Mainzer Zeitschrift*, 75, 1980, p. 223, to whom I am grateful for information and material relating to the site.

Previous occupation. There was a crossroads settlement from the time of Augustus, in which many curse tablets, of lead, have been found in tombs, H. Bullinger in R. Stillwell (ed.), *Princeton Encyclopaedia of Classical Sites*, 1976, p. 248.

Oceanus, son of Uranus (heaven) and Ge (earth), was, in Homer, the river encircling the whole world, and subsequently conceived of as (a) the cosmic power, (b) 'ocean' in a geographical sense.

Destruction, reconstruction, evacuation. G. Rupprecht, *op. cit.*, p. 226.

Fortress of Valentinian I or Constantius II? See H. von Petrikovits, *Journal of Roman Studies*, 61, 1971, pp. 186, 189, 218.

Necropolis. H. Bullinger, *loc. cit.*

Late Roman villa palaces. The excavation of Piazza Armerina (Philosophiana) in Sicily came a little too early for inclusion in this book: see now A. Carandini, A. Ricci, M. de Vos, *Filosofiana: The Villa of Piazza Armerina*, 1982.

CHAPTER 9: THE LATER EMPIRE

1 *Byblus: Buildings on Coins*

Coin portraiture. P. Brucen, *Coin Portraits as Tools of Research* (in press).

'Greek imperial' is an inadequate designation for all the local bronze coinages of the empire (silver issues were very few) because citizen communities (colonies and a few *municipia*) in the east used the Latin language on their coins; and so did the citizen communities in the west, until the reign of Gaius (Caligula; AD 37–41).

Philo and Sanchuniathon. M. Grant, *History of Ancient Israel*, 1984, p. 22.

Mosaics in Byblus house. Meleager and Atalanta; Acme and Charis.

Macrinus. M. Grant, *The Roman Emperors*, 1985, pp. 123ff.

Adonis was believed to have died at Aphaea, at the sources of the River Adonis, in the mountains above Byblus.

2 Betthorus (Lejjun): Late Rome's Eastern Frontier

Syria. The Roman province included Smooth Cilicia until AD 73.

Emperors from Emesa. Elagabalus (AD 218–22) and Severus Alexander (222–35).

Independent Emesan state. Under Zenobia and her son Vaballathus Athenodorus (271–73).

Adjacent states absorbed. In addition to the Nabataean kingdom, Herod's Judaea, too, had become a province even earlier (from AD 6, with an interval from 41–4). It became known as Syria Palaestina in 135, after the Second Jewish Revolt.

'Limes' hard to define: B. Isaac, *Journal of Roman Studies*, 78, 1988, pp. 125ff.

Eastern legionary camps are rarely discoverable because they were normally within cities in these urbanized areas. But see Primis, Chapter 6, section 2.

Diocletian apparently conducted a campaign against the Arabs (Saracens: D. Graf and M. O'Connor, *Byzantine Studies*, IV, pp. 52–66) in 290, but few details are known. If the Legio IV Martia was not his creation, it could have been Aurelian's (270–75).

Arabian frontier fortresses. Two large *castra*, seven *castella* and several watchtowers, mainly east of the Dead Sea. Soundings were taken at Qasr Bishr, Rujm Beni Yasser and Khirbet El-Fityan (1½ miles north of Betthorus).

Eleven acre fortress at Betthorus. For a normal-sized British legionary fortress, four times larger, cf. Vindolanda, Chapter 8, section 2.

Wall-towers. There were 20 U-shaped interval towers projecting 36 feet from the walls, 92 feet apart. Circular angle towers stood 36 feet high. The wall contained four gates.

Persian threat. After the destruction of the eastern emperor Valens by the Visigoths at Hadrianopolis (Adrianople, Edirne) in AD 378, Persian (Sassanian) pressure elsewhere may have drawn away some of the troops from the Arabian frontier.

3 Mediolanum (Milan): The Last Western Emperor

Last western emperors: M. Grant, *The Roman Emperors*, 1985, pp. 322ff, 332ff.

Julius Nepos's wife: the niece of Aelia Verina, the wife of the eastern emperor Leo I.

Abdication of Romulus 'Augustulus'. His father Orestes had been killed at Placentia (Piacenza) and his uncle Paullus at Ravenna.

Zeno's first reign was in 474–5 and he had been temporarily expelled by Basiliscus in 475–6.

Stylistic criteria. Defended by M. Grant, *The Six Main Aes Coinages of Augustus*, 1953, pp. 62ff.

Julius Nepos's issues at Mediolanum. Between (1) and (2) J. P. C. Kent, *Corolla Memoriae Erich Swoboda Dedicata*, 1966, pp. 149f. places an intermediate group struck for Basiliscus and Romulus (Nov. 475–Sept. 476).

Julius Nepos's issues at Ravenna. See J. P. C. Kent, *op. cit.*, pp. 148f. (Arelate p. 147, Rome p. 148); for coinage in Zeno's name *ibid.*, p. 150.

APPENDIX I: ARCHAEOLOGY AND THE CLASSICS

Classical and other archaeology. Some of the recently developed techniques have little relevance to a historical period (J. Boardman, *Antiquity*, 62, 237, December 1988, p. 297), i.e. relate principally to prehistory (G. Daniel, *The Idea of Prehistory*, 1964 ed., especially Chapter 7: Prehistory and the Historians; *id.*, *The First Civilizations*, 1971 ed., p. 23), so that recent archaeological convulsions have, to a large extent, passed the classicists by. This is partly because the New Archaeology (see below), uninterested in literary and linguistic backgrounds, tends to neglect classical archaeology of which the mental attitudes are so different (A. Snodgrass, *American Journal of Archaeology*, 89, 1985, p. 37). However, classical archaeologists, too 'are criticised for being too narrow ... but asking a classical archaeologist why he has not totally adopted the 'new archaeology' is like asking a composer why his string quartet does not sound like an opera: he did not intend to write an opera' (G. F. Bass, *Archaeology*, January/February 1989, p. 102.) All the same, the cleavage is damaging (S. C. Humphreys, *Anthropology and the Greeks*, 1983 (1978), p. 129, cf. S. Dyson, *Bulletin of the American Schools of Oriental Research*, 242, 1981, pp. 7–13. The protohistorical Bronze Age provides a link, A. M. Snodgrass, *op. cit.*, pp. 31ff.

Ancient history and archaeology. On the transformation of the former by the latter, cf. G. Shipley (on the Greeks), *History Today*, 38, 1988, pp. 49ff. So many terms have recently been invented to describe archaeology's links with quite other disciplines (see below) – archaeometry, archaeomagnetism, archaeometallurgy, archaeoastronomy, *Archaeonautica*, *Archaeophysika*, archaeobiology, archaeobotany, archaeography, archaeozoology, archaeogemmology, archaeoergonomics, ethnoarchaeology, zooarchaeology, geoarchaeology, dendroarchaeology (not to speak of a host of words starting with palaeo-) – that we may one day be forced to coin the term 'archaeohistory' to re-emphasize archaeology's long-established, permanent and inseparable links with history. C. and S. Hawkes bore witness to these links by naming a new series *Archaeology into History* (1973; cf. *Greeks, Celts and Romans*, p. xiii). Nevertheless, the data used by historians and archaeologists are not identical, D. L. Clarke, *Analytical Archaeology*, 1978 ed., p. 12, A. M. Snodgrass, *An Archaeology of Greece*, 1987, pp. 36ff., 38, 41ff, 62. It is partly for this reason that communications between historians and archaeologists (as between classical and other archaeologists) seem inadequate to S. C. Humphreys, *Anthropology and Greeks*, 1983 ed., p. 112. The relationship between the two disciplines is likewise discussed by I. Hodder, *Reading the Past*, 1986, pp. 11, 77, 91f., 140, cf. *Symbols in Action*, 1982. On archaeology vs. literary history see also above, Chapter 2, section 6, and Chapter 4, section 2.

Natural and social sciences are favoured by two different, distinguishable types of archaeologist, L. R. Binford, *In Pursuit of the Past*, 1988 ed., p. 15. But although the journal *Archaeometry* concentrates on archaeology as a natural science (cf. also E. A. Slater and J. O. Tate (eds.), *Science and Archaeology* [Glasgow Conference, 1987], 1988), and G. F. Bass (*Archaeology*, January/February 1989) envisages a far greater role for scientific methods, 'the exactitude of the mathematical or physical sciences is rarely achieved' (T. B. Jones, 1967, quoted by P. E. Cleator, *Archaeology in the Making*, 1976, p. 16).

As regards the social sciences, K. Greene, *The Archaeology of the Roman Economy*, 1986, p. 9, stresses that sociology and anthropology have changed the terms of our approach to the past (and recently [cf. the text] history itself has often been treated as a sort of social science – the link of the social sciences with the humanities being stressed when the former are called the 'human' sciences). Indeed, O. G. S. Crawford asserted (in 1953) that 'archaeology is merely the past tense of anthropology', and C. Runnels, *American Journal of Archaeology*, 1985, pp. 523f., maintains that good archaeology has always been social archaeology. For this aspect see J. L. Bintliff and C. F. Gaffney, *Archaeology at the Interface*, 1986.

The 'New Archaeology'. D. R. Wilson, *Science and Archaeology*, 1978 ed., pp. 308ff., L. R. Binford, *In Pursuit of the Past*, 1988 ed., pp. 7ff., 15f., 106ff. (cf. S. R. and L. R. Binford [eds.], *New Perspectives in Archaeology*, 1968), I. Hodder, *Reading the Past*, 1986, index, ss.vv. New Archaeology, processual archaeology – which seeks to deduce laws from a study of the variables that cause cultural change, P. J. Watson, S. A. Le Blanc, C. L. Redman, *Archaeological Explanation*, 1984, pp. viii, xi, 15, 58–60, 266, etc., etc. For its original questioning methods, C. Renfrew in L. R. Binford, *op. cit.*, p. 8. Archaeologists of this type have applied systems theory (see next note) and information theory (I. Hodder, *Reading the Past*, 1986, and C. Renfrew, *Approaches to Social Archaeology*, 1984, indices, s.v. information), and stress adaptive processes (e.g. population increases, resource utilization, social complexity: see also next note) and statistical methods (bibliography in I. Hodder and C. Orton, *Spatial Analysis in Archaeology*, 1979 [1976], p. 10), T. Madsen (ed.), *Multivariate Archaeology*, 1988, assisted by computerization, M. A. Cooper and J. D. Richards, *Current Issues in Archaeological Computing*, 1985, S. P. Q. Rahtz, *Computer and Quantitative Methods in Archaeology*, 1988. For the computerization of numismatic evidence, see above, note on Chapter 4, section 5.

Environmental archaeology. The 'New Archaeology' has sometimes been equated with this (M. Shackley, *Using Environmental Archaeology*, 1985), and with ecological study. A single site does not adequately represent the whole system, hence the 'systems theory', which seeks to establish relationships and the rules underlying them (P. J. Watson, etc., op. cit., pp. 67ff.: bibliography of its advocates and critics). The model environmental survey is that of Melos, C. Renfrew and J. M. Wagstaff, *An Island Polity*, 1982, K. Greene, *Archaeology of the Roman Economy*, 1986, pp. 101, 135. On the theoretical background see J. Bintliff, D. A. Davidson, E. G. Grant (eds.), *Conceptual Issues in Environmental Archaeology* (Oxford symposium 1985), 1988. The remark of L. Mumford, *The City in History*, 1961, p. 571, that cities are more interesting than the countryside now has, for environmentalists, an old-fashioned ring, though cities are important from an anthropological point of view, cf. J. Rykwert, *Idea of a Town: The Anthropology of Urban Form in Rome, Italy and the Ancient World*, 1976, G. Audring, *Zur Struktur des Territoriums griechischer Poleis in archäischer Zeit*, 1989.

Changing shape of archaeology. New forms probable, D. R. Wilson, *Science and Archaeology*, 1978 ed., p. 317. For the defects of earlier archaeology, see D. Miles in K. Branigan (ed.), *Atlas of Archaeology*, 1982, pp. 19f., and for the limits of the subject as a whole, K. Greene, *The Archaeology of the Roman Economy*, 1986, pp. 9f., 71. The various branches of archaeology do not always take enough account of each other; nor is archaeology, any more than history, always 'objective'. So it has suffered a 'loss of identity', *Antiquity*, 62, 237, December 1988, p. 295, and 'a new paradigm is needed', C. Renfrew, *Before Civilization*, 1976 ed., p. 19 (cf. pp. 272ff.). This need for reassessment, in the present 'post-processual' phase, was the theme of the World Archaeology Congress at Southampton (1986) and the First Joint Archaeological Congress in 1989 *American Journal of Archaeology*, 93, 3, 1989, pp. 429ff.), and is the keynote of the series *One World Archaeology* (1989–), edited by P.J. Ucko (*id.*, *History Today*, 39, March 1989, p. 11); cf. *Archaeology and Planning* (Council of Europe Florence Colloquy 1985), 1987, M. Shanks and C. Tilley, *Reconstructing Archaeology: Theory and Practice*, 1988. P. Courbin, *What is Archaeology?*, 1989 (1982), on the other hand, wants to put the clock right back and restrict archaeology to its traditional techniques of excavation and classification (which he sees as its real sources of progress during the past thirty years), leaving to others the interpretation of the 'facts' that it produces. For quite other concepts of present and future developments, see I. Hodder, *Reading the Past*, 1986, pp. 146–71, 173f., 177, *id.*, *Symbolic and Structural Archaeology*, 1982, P.J. Watson, etc., *op. cit.* pp. xi, 269ff. (ideational, structural, cognitive and Marxist archaeology: cf. D.K. Washburn [ed.], *Structure and Cognition in Art*, 1983). However, 'current philosophical debates over the ultimate purpose of archaeology will rage on', G.F. Bass, *Archaeology*, January/February 1989, p. 51.

APPENDIX II: A FEW TASKS FOR THE FUTURE

(*i*) *Lavinium: Archaeology and Myth*

Latium. Important recent excavations at Ficana, Politorium (Castel di Decima), Satricum (Borgo Montello): M. Grant, *Guide to the Ancient World*, 1986, pp. 251, 514, 565f.

Greeks and Etruscans in Latium. There were rival traditions of many city foundations, C. Ampolo, *Dialoghi di archeologia*, 8, 1, 1974–5, p. 161.

Aeneas's point of arrival near Lavinium later transferred to Tiber mouth, F. Castagnoli, *Enciclopedia Virgiliana*, III, 1987, p. 149.

Indiges: J. Scheidt, *ibid*, II, 1985, pp. 946f.

Penates: lodged in the Roman Forum within the shrine of the national protectress Vesta.

Lavinium after 338 BC: E.T. Salmon, *The Making of Roman Italy*, 1982, pp. 55, 195, n. 255.

Castor and Pollux inscription. N. Horsfall, *Enciclopedia Virgiliana*, II, 1985, p. 224.

(*ii*) *Herculaneum: Villa of the Papyri*

Papyri in the villa. Most of them were found in the library. Surviving papyri from this site were displayed in a 1979 exhibition in the National Library at Naples, where there has been a Centro Internazionale (Officina) per lo studio dei papiri ercolanesi since 1969.

Decipherment. 'The best that could be done', wrote E.G. Turner, *Greek Papyri: An Introduction*, 1980 ed., p. 18, 'was to break through the crust and detach single thicknesses of the original, reconstitute the pieces, and copy them by holding them obliquely to the light so that the iridescence of the ink might stand out from the blackened background.' For restoration techniques, see A. Fackelmann, *Bulletin of the Institute of Classical Studies* (London), 17, 1970, pp. 144–7, M. Gigante, *Archeo*, 6, 19, 1985, p. 10.

Proprietor of the villa. Appius Claudius Pulcher has also been suggested, M. R. Wojcik, *La Villa dei Papiri ad Ercolano: Contributo alla riconstruzione dell'ideologia della nobilitas tardo-repubblicana*, 1986, *id.*, *Annuario della Facoltà di Lettere a Perugia*, 17, 1, 1978–80, pp. 357–68.

New excavations. B. Conticello and A. De Simone, *Cronache Ercolanesi*, 17, 1987, and since then more has been cleared (including most of the *gruta derecha*, the subterranean tunnel dug by 18th century archaeologists), offering a new impression of the sculpturally decorated Library. See also bibliography to Appendix II (ii).

(iii) Puteoli: Movements of Earth and Shore

1980 earthquake: brought to light the Capitolium (hitherto regarded as a temple of Augustus).

Bradyseisms. R. F. Paget, *Journal of Roman Studies*, 58, 1968, p. 154, A. Maiuri, *The Phlegraean Fields*, 1958, pp. 24ff. These movements are often quite local, W. Bray and D. Trump, *Dictionary of Archaeology*, 1970, p. 41.

Volcanic eruptions can be dated relatively by tephrology, the mineralogical identification of different ash layers, and (at times) absolutely by radiocarbon dating (cf. above, Chapter 6, section 3).

Market of Puteoli. A. Boethius and J. B. Ward-Perkins, *Etruscan and Roman Architecture*, 1970, p. 298. Borings in the columns produced by marine molluscs are evidence for localized submergence followed by re-emergence, C. Vita-Finzi, *Archaeological Sites in their Setting*, 1978, p. 53.

Port of Puteoli. The mole of Gaius (Caligula) has now come to light, *Archeologia*, June/July 1988, p. 27.

Underwater buildings off Puteoli (the Ripa Puteolana): A. de Franciscis, *Archaeology*, May/June 1967, p. 211, *National Geographic Magazine*, 165, 5, 1984, p. 621. The village of Baiperate once existed in the area that is now submerged.

Marsili Seamount volcano: investigated by robot-submarine equipped with telecamera providing readings via satellite.

BIBLIOGRAPHY

I ANCIENT

(*a*) *Greek*

ACHILLES TATIUS, of Alexandria, before AD 200 (?). Novelist; author of *Leucippe and Clitophon.*

AESCHINES, of Athens, *c.*397–322 BC. Orator and politician.

ALEXANDER, of Aphrodisias, early 3rd cent. AD. Peripatetic philosopher, commentator on Aristotle.

APPIAN, of Alexandria, 2nd cent. AD. Historian.

ARISTIDES, AELIUS, of Mysia, AD 117/129–81 or later. Orator and man of letters.

CHARITO, of Aphrodisias, 1st cent. BC (?). Novelist, author of *Chaereas and Callirhoe.*

DEMOSTHENES, of Athens, 384–322 BC. Orator and politician.

DIO CASSIUS, of Nicaea (Iznik), late 2nd and early 3rd cent. AD. Historian.

DIODORUS SICULUS, of Agyrium (in Sicily), 1st cent. BC. Historian.

DIOGENES LAERTIUS, 3rd (?) cent. AD. Historian and biographer.

DIONYSIUS, of Halicarnassus (Bodrum), later 1st cent. BC. Rhetorician and historian.

EUSEBIUS, of Caesarea Maritima, *c.*AD 260–340. Bishop and ecclesiastical historian.

HELIODORUS, of Emesa (Homs), 3rd cent. AD. Novelist; author of the *Aethiopica.*

HERACLIDES PONTICUS, of Heraclea Pontica (Ereğli), *c.* 388–315 BC. Platonic philosopher, physicist, astronomer.

HERODOTUS, of Halicarnassus (Bodrum), *c.*480–*c.*425 BC. Historian.

HESIOD, of Cyme (Namurtköy) and Ascra, 8th cent. BC. Epic poet.

HOMER, probably born on Chios and worked in Smyrna, 8th cent. BC. Epic poet.

JOSEPHUS, FLAVIUS, of Jerusalem, AD 38–after 93/4. Jewish historian.

LONGUS, perhaps of Lesbos, 2nd cent. AD. Novelist; author of pastoral *Daphnis and Chloe.*

LUCIAN, of Samosata (Samsat), *c.*AD 120/5–180. Satirical popular philosopher.

PAUSANIAS, of Magnesia beside Sipylus (Manisa), 2nd cent. AD. Travel writer.

PHILO, of Byblus (Jebeil), AD 64–141. Writer on Phoenician religion and customs.

PHILODEMUS, of Gadara, *c.*110 – *c.*40/35 BC. Epicurean philosopher and poet.

PHYLARCHUS, of Athens, 3rd cent. BC. Historian.

PLUTARCH, of Chaeronea, before AD 50–after 120. Philosopher and biographer.

POLYBIUS, of Megalopolis, *c*.200–after 118 BC. Historian.

STRABO, of Amasia (Amasya), *c*.63 BC–at least AD 21. Geographer and historian.

SYNESIUS, of Cyrene, *c*.AD 370–413. Christian Neoplatonist.

XENOCRATES, of Aphrodisias, 2nd half of first cent. AD Author of books on medicine, plants and gems.

(*b*) Latin

APULEIUS, of Madaurus (Mdaourouch) in N. Africa, 2nd cent. AD. Novelist; author of the *Metamorphoses* (Golden Ass).

CATO THE ELDER, of Tusculum, 234–149 BC. Historian, rhetorician, writer on agriculture.

CICERO, of Arpinum, 106–43 BC. Orator, rhetorician, philosopher, poet.

HORACE, of Venusia (Venosa), 65–8 BC. Poet.

LIVY, of Patavium (Padua), 64/59 BC–AD 12/17. Historian.

PETRONIUS ARBITER, probably Titus Petronius Niger, consul *c*.AD 61. Novelist; author of the *Satyricon*.

PLINY THE ELDER, of Comum, AD 23/24–79. Writer on history, military science and language, and of encyclopaedic *Natural History*.

SENECA THE YOUNGER, of Corduba, 4 BC/AD 1–AD 65. Philosopher, scientist, letter-writer and satirist.

SUETONIUS, of Pisaurum (Pesaro) or Hippo Regius (Annaba), *c*.AD 69-after 121/2. Biographer and writer on miscellaneous themes.

TACITUS, of northern Italy or southern Gaul, *c*.AD 56–before or after 117. Historian and writer on oratory.

VALERIUS ANTIAS, early 1st cent. BC. Annalistic historian.

VARRO, of Reate (Rieti), 116–27 BC. Encyclopaedic writer (including *De Re Rustica [On Rural Affairs]*) and librarian.

VEGETIUS, late 4th or early 5th cent, AD. Writer on military affairs.

VIRGIL, of Andes (near Mantua), 70–19 BC. Poet.

II MODERN

General Works

Reference should also be made to *Archaeological Reports* (Society for the Promotion of Hellenic Studies and British School at Athens) and to the journals indicated in the foregoing Notes.

P. Barker, *Techniques of Archaeological Excavation*, 1988 (1987)

G. F. Bass, 'The Great Tradition Looks Ahead' in *Archaeology*, January/February 1989, pp. 51f., 104f.

W. R. Briers, *The Archaeology of Greece: An Introduction*, rev. ed., 1987

L. R. Binford, *Debating Archaeology*, 1989

J.Bintliff (ed.), *Extracting Meaning from the Past*, 1988

K. Branigan, *Archaeology Explained*, 1988 (1973)

K. Branigan (ed.), *The Atlas of Archaeology*, 1982
R. H. Brill (ed.), *Science and Archaeology*, 1971
D. R. Brothwell and E. Higgs (eds.) *Science in Archaeology*, 2nd ed., 1969
K. R. Butzer, *Archaeology as Human Ecology*, 1982
C. W. Ceram (ed.), *The World of Archaeology*, 1966
S. Champion (ed.), *Dictionary of Terms and Techniques in Archaeology*, 1980
J. G. D. Clark, *Archaeology and Society*, 1957
D. L. Clarke, *Analytical Archaeology*, 2nd ed., 1980 (1971)
P. E. Cleator, *Archaeology in the Making*, 1976
J. Coles, *Archaeology by Experiment*, 1973
P. Courbin, *What is Archaeology? An Essay on the Nature of Archaeological Research*, 1989 (from French original of 1982)
M. Crawford (ed.,) *Sources for Ancient History*, 1983
G. E. Daniel, *A Short History of Archaeology*, 1981
G. E. Daniel (ed.), *Towards a History of Archaeology*, 1981
G. E. Daniel and C. Chippindale (eds.), *The Past Masters: Eleven Modern Pioneers of Archaeology*, 1989
L. De Paor, *Archaeology: An Illustrated Introduction*, 1969
M. I. Finley, *Ancient History: Evidence and Models*, 1985
P. M. Fischer, *Applications of Technical Devices in Archaeology*, 1980
C. Flon (ed.), *World Atlas of Archaeology*, 1985
P. Fowler, *Approaches to Archaeology*, 1977
L. Gernet, *The Anthropology of Ancient Greece*, 1981
Z. Goffer, *Archaeological Chemistry*, 1980
M. Grant (ed.), *Greece and Rome: The Birth of Western Civilization*, 1986 (1964)
M. Grant and R. Kitzinger (eds.), *Civilization of the Ancient Mediterranean*, 1988
K. Greene, *Archaeology: An Introduction*, 1983
K. Greene, *The Archaeology of the Roman Economy*, 1986
I. Hodder, *Reading the Past*, 1986
I. Hodder (ed.), *Archaeology as Long Term History*, 1986
I. Hodder and C. Orton, *Spatial Analysis in Archaeology*, 1987 (1976)
P. Horden and M. Purcell, *The Mediterranean World: Man and Environment*, 1989
S. C. Humphreys, *Anthropology and the Greeks*, 1983 (1978)
R. E. Jones and H. W. Catling (eds.), *New Aspects of Archaeological Science in Greece*, 1988
D. R. Keller and D. W. Rupp (eds.), *Archaeological Survey in the Mediterranean Area*, 1983
A. King, *The Archaeology of the Roman Empire*, 1982
R. Layton (ed.), *Who Needs the Past?*, 1989
M. Le Roy, *Initiation à l'archéologie romaine*, 1965
J. McIntosh, *The Archaeologist's Handbook*, 1986
P. MacKendrick, *The Greek Stones Speak*, 2nd ed., 1981
P. MacKendrick, *The Mute Stones Speak*, 2nd ed., 1983
B. Orme, *Anthropology for Archaeologists*, 1989
C. Orton, *Mathematics in Archaeology*, 1982
Past Worlds: The Times Atlas of Archaeology, 1988
P. Phillips (ed.), *The Archaeologist and the Laboratory*, 1985

S. Piggott, *Approach to Archaeology*, 1965 ed.
P. Rahtz, *Invitation to Archaeology*, 1985
C. Renfrew, *Approaches to Social Archaeology*, 1984
M. Rowlands, M. Larson and K. Kristiansen (eds.), *Centre and Periphery in the Ancient World: New Directions in Archaeology*, 1987
M. B. Schiffer (ed.), *Advances in Archaeological Method and Theory*, 1986
M. Shanks and C. Tilley, *Social Theory and Archaeology*, 1987
A. Sherratt, *Cambridge Encyclopaedia of Archaeology*, 1980
G. Shipley, 'On Second Thoughts: Greek Archaeology from Schliemann to Surveys' *History Today*, 38, May 1988, pp. 49ff.
A. M. Snodgrass, *An Archaeology of Greece: The Present State and Future Scope of a Discipline*, 1987
S. Stanley, *Method and Theory in Historical Archaeology*, 1977
S. Stanley, *Research Strategies in Historical Archaeology*, 1977
B. R. Trigger, *A History of Archaeological Interpretation*, 1989
P. J. Ucko (ed.), *One World Archaeology*, 20 vols (projected), 1989–
C. Vita-Finzi, *Archaeological Sites in their Setting*, 1978
J. Wacher (ed.), *The Roman World*, I–II, 1987
P. J. Watson, S. A. Le Blanc, C. L. Redman, *Archaeological Explanation: The Scientific Method in Archaeology*, 1984
D. R. Wilson, *Science and Archaeology*, 1978 (1975)

PART I: THE GREEKS

CHAPTER 1: THE 'DARK AGE'

1 *Lefkandi: The Not So Dark Age*

R. Chapman (etc.), *The Archaeology of Death*, 1981
J. N. Coldstream, *Geometric Greece*, 1977
V. Desborough, *The Greek Dark Ages*, 1972
I. Morris, *Burial and Ancient Society: The Rise of the Greek City States*, 1987
M. R. Popham, *Lefkandi* I, 1979, 1981
M. R. Popham and L. H. Sackett (eds.), *Excavations at Lefkandi 1964–6: A Preliminary Report*, 1968
M. R. Popham, L. H. Sackett and P. G. Themelis (eds.), *Lefkandi I: The Iron Age Settlements: The Cemeteries*, 1980 (Plates 1979)
M. R. Popham, E. Touloupa and L. H. Sackett, 'The Hero of Lefkandi' in *Antiquity* 56, 6, 1982, pp. 169ff.

2 *Salamis in Cyprus: Homeric Analogies?*

A. De Cesnola, *Salaminia*, 2nd ed., 1984
J. N. Coldstream, *Geometric Greece*, 1977
V. Karageorghis, *The Archaeology of Cyprus* (13th J. L. Myres Memorial Lecture), 1987
V. Karageorghis, *Cyprus: From the Stone Age to the Romans*, 1982
V. Karageorghis 'Cyprus' in J. Boardman and N. G. L. Hammond (eds.), *Cambridge Ancient History*, III, 3, 2nd ed., 1982, pp. 57ff.
V. Karageorghis, *Excavations in the Necropolis of Salamis*, I–IV, 1967–78

V. Karageorghis, *Salamis in Cyprus: Homeric, Hellenistic and Roman*, 1969
V. Karageorghis, *The Archaeology of Cyprus*, 1988
J. Pouilloux (etc.), *Salamine de Chypre* IV, *Anthologie Salaminienne*, 1973
V. Tatton-Brown, *Ancient Cyprus*, 1987
H.J. Watkin, *The Development of Cities in Cyprus from the Archaic to the Roman Period*, 1989

CHAPTER 2: THE ARCHAIC GREEKS

1 Pithecusae (Ischia) and Cumae: The West

G. Buchner, *Pitecusa, scavi e scoperte 1966–1971: Atti del* XI *Congresso Internazionale di Preistoria e Protoistoria Mediterranea* (Taranto), 1971, 1972
G. Buchner and D. Ridgway, (eds.), *Pithekoussai*, I, *La Necropoli*, 1980
F. Fedele and G. Guadagno, *Campania archeologica*, 1984
M.W. Frederiksen, *Campania*, 1984
A.J. Graham, *The Western Greeks* in J. Boardman and N.G.L. Hammond (eds.), *Cambridge Ancient History*, III, 3, 2nd ed., 1982, pp. 163f.
M. Grant, *The Rise of the Greeks*, 1988
L.H. Jeffery, *Archaic Greece: The City-States c.700–500* BC, 1976
W. Johannowsky, *Problemi relativi a Cuma arcaica*, 1975
A.G. McKay, *Cumae and the Phlegraean Fields*, 1972
D. Ridgway, 'The First Western Greeks' in C. and S. Hawkes (eds.), *Greeks, Celts and Romans*, 1973
R.V. Scherder, 'Ancient Cumae' in *Scientific American*, 209, 6, 1963, pp. 108–21
A. Snodgrass, *Archaic Greece*, 1980
F. Uliano, *Cumae: il tempio di Apollo e il dromos: strutture egeo-micenee*, 1984
A.G. Woodhead, *The Greeks in the West*, 1962

2 Sybaris: The Magnetometer

(For the magnetometer, see Notes)
O.H. Bullitt, *The Search for Sybaris*, 1969
T. De Santis, *Sibaritide a ritroso del tempo*, 1960
K. Fabricius, 'Sybaris: Its History and Coinage' in *Actes du Congrès Internationale de Numismatique*, II, 1953, pp. 65ff.
P.G. Guzzo, *Archeologia e territorio della Sibaritide* in M.G.M. Costagli and L.T. Perna (eds.), *Studi di antichità in onore di Gugliemo Maetzke*, pp. 203ff.
P.G. Guzzo, *Le città scomparse della Magna Grecia*, 1982
P.G. Guzzo, *Scavi a Sibari* II, *Annali del Seminario di Studi del Mondo Classico, Archeologia e Storia Antica* (Istituto Universitario Orientale, Napoli, III), 1981
F.G. Rainey, 'The Location of Archaic Greek Sybaris' in *American Journal of Archaeology*, 73, 1969, pp. 261–73
F.G. Rainey and C.M. Lerici, *The Search for Sybaris 1960–1965*, 1967
A.G. Woodhead, *The Greeks in the West*, 1962

3 Igilium (Giglio): Shipwrecks

G.F. Bass, *Archaeology Beneath the Sea*, 1975
M. Bound, 'Uno scavo eroico' in *Archeologia Viva*, 5, 1, 1986

International Journal of Nautical Archaeology, 12, 2, 1983

K. Muckelroy, *Maritime Archaeology*, 1978

A.J. Parker, 'Shipwrecks and Ancient Trade in the Mediterranean' in *Archaeological Review* (Cambridge), 3, 2, 1984, pp. 99–113

A.J. Parker, 'The Mediterranean: An Underwater Museum' in *The Courier* (UNESCO), 1987, pp. 8f.

E. Riccardi, *Techniche di lavoro subacqueo per l'archeologia*, 1988

A. Rosso, *Introduzione all'archeologia dell'acque*, 1988

P. Throckmorton, *Shipwrecks and Archaeology: The Unharvested Sea*, 1969

P. Throckmorton (ed.), *History from the Sea*, 1987

4 Halieis: Underwater Site

N. C. Flemming, 'Classical Harbours and Relative Changes of Sea-level' in *Acta of the XIth International Congress of Classical Archaeology* (London, 1978), 1979, pp. 253f.

M. H. Jameson, 'Excavations at Halieis 1973–1974' in *Archaiologikon Deltion*, 29, 1973–4, pp. 261–4

M. H. Jameson, 'Halieis at Porto Cheli: Marine Archaeology' in *Proceedings of the 23rd Symposium of the Colston Research Society, Bristol University* (1971), 1973, pp. 219–29

M. H. Jameson in *Phoros: Tribute to B. D. Meritt*, 1974, pp. 67–75

M. H. Jameson, 'The Excavation of a Drowned Greek Temple' in *Scientific American*, 231, 1974, pp. 110–19

M. H. Jameson, 'The Submerged Sanctuary of Apollo at Halieis in the Argolid of Greece' in *National Geographic Society Research Reports*, 14, 1982, pp. 363–7

W. Rudolph, 'The City of Halieis: Aspects of Pre-Classical and Classical Town-Planning on the Greek Mainland in Acta' (see above, Flemming), pp. 197f.

J. D. Whittlesey, 'Tethered Balloon for Archaeological Photos' in *Photogrammetric Engineering*, February 1970, pp. 181–6

J. H. Young, *A Migrant City in the Peloponnese: University of Pennsylvania Museum Expedition*, 5, 1963, pp. 2–11

5 Olbia: The Greek North-East

E. Belin de Ballu, *Olbia*, 1972

R. Drews, 'The Earliest Greek Settlements on the Black Sea' in *Journal of Hellenic Studies*, 96, 1976, pp. 18f.

From the Lands of the Scythians (New York), n.d.

M. Grant, *The Rise of the Greeks*, 1988

L. Kopeikina, 'Die Besonderheiten der Entwicklung der Siedlung auf Berezan in der archäischen Epoche' in *Acta of the XIth International Congress of Classical Archaeology* (London, 1978), 1979, p. 198

L'oro di Kiev (Florence), 1987

V.T. Paschuto and A.P. Novosel'zew, *Die ältesten Quellen zur Geschichte der Völker auf Territorium der UdSSR*, 1 (Herodotus) 1982; Strabo in preparation

B. Piotrovsky, L. Galamina and N. Grach, *Scythian Art*, 1987

T. Talbot Rice, *The Scythians*, 3rd ed., 1961

J. Vinogradov, *Olbia: Xenia* 1, 1981

A. Wasowicz, *Olbia pontique et son territoire*, 1975

6 Naucratis: Archaeology against History?

M. M. Austin, *Greece and Egypt in the Archaic Age*, 1970
T. F. R. G. Braun, *The Greeks in Egypt* in J. Boardman and N. G. L. Hammond (eds.), *Cambridge Ancient History*, III, 3, 2nd ed., 1982, pp. 32ff.
M. Grant, *The Rise of the Greeks*, 1988
A. M. Snodgrass, 'Archaeology' in M. Crawford (ed.), *Sources for Ancient History*, 1983, pp. 144ff.

CHAPTER 3: THE CLASSICAL GREEKS

1 Corinth and Athens: The Trireme

G. F. Bass, *The History of Seafaring*, 1973
L. Casson, *Ships and Seamanship in the Ancient World*, 1986 (1971)
J. F. Coates and S. McGrail (eds.), *The Greek Trireme of the Fifth Century: Discussion of a Projected Reconstruction*, 1984
V. Foley and W. Soedel, 'Ancient Oared Warships' in *Scientific American*, 244, 4, 1981, pp. 116–29
P. Lipke, 'Trials of a Trireme' in *Archaeology*, March/April, 1988, pp. 22–9
F. Meijer, *A History of Seafaring in the Ancient World*, 1986
J. S. Morrison, *The Ship: Long Ships and Round Ships*, 1980
J. S. Morrison and J. F. Coates, *The Athenian Trireme: The History and Reconstruction of an Ancient Greek Warship*, 1986
J. S. Morrison and R. T. Williams, *Greek Oared Ships*, 1968
F. Welsh, *Building the Trireme*, 1988

2 Athens: The Painted Portico

J. M. Camp, *The Athenian Agora*, 1986
Short Guide to the Agora, rev. ed., 1983
H. A. Thompson, *The Athenian Agora: A Short Guide*, 1980
H. A. Thompson and R. E. Wycherley, *The Agora of Athens*, 1972
The Athenian Agora, 1976
J. Travlos, *Bildlexikon zur Topographie des antiken Athen*, 1989
R. E. Wycherley, *The Stones of Athens*, 1978

3 Riace: Peak of Classical Sculpture

J. Barron, *An Introduction to Greek Sculpture*, 1981
J. Boardman, *Greek Sculpture: The Classical Period*, 1985
A. Busignani, *The Bronzes of Riace*, 1981
G. Foti and F. Nicosia, *I bronzi di Riace*, 1981
M. Grant, *The Classical Greeks*, 1989
C. C. Mattusch, *Greek Bronze Statuary: From the Beginnings Through the Fifth Century* BC, 1989

4 Aegae (Vergina) and Pella: Macedonia Revealed

Ancient Macedonia (IVth International Symposium, Thessalonica, 1983), 1986
M. Andronikos, *The Finds from the Royal Tomb at Vergina: Treasures of Ancient Macedonia*, n.d.
M. Andronikos, 'The Tombs at the Great Tumulus at Vergina' in *Acta of the IXth International Congress of Classical Archaeology* (London, 1978), 1979, pp. 39ff.
M. Andronikos, *Vergina: The Royal Tombs and the Ancient City*, 1984
K. Branigan, *The Atlas of Archaeology*, 1982
J. Crossland and D. Constance, *Macedonian Greece*, 1982
N. G. L. Hammond and J. G. Griffith *History of Macedonia*, II, 1979
D. Leakey and N. Efstratiou, *Archaeological Excavations in Central and Northern Greece*, 1980
P. Petsas, *Pella*, 1964
J. L. Wynne-Thomas, *Proud-Voiced Macedonia*, 1979

5 Syracuse: Archaeology and Economics

M. Grant, *The Classical Greeks*, 1989
P. Grierson, *Numismatics and History*, rev. ed., 1951
G. K. Jenkins, 'A Note on Corinthian Coins in the West' in H. Ingholt (ed.), *Centennial Publication of the American Numismatic Society*, 1958
C. M. Kraay, *Greek Coins and History: Some Current Problems*, 1969
L. R. Laing, *Coins and Archaeology*, 1969
M. Sordi, *La Sicilia dal 368/7 al 337/6 a.C.*, 1983
M. Sordi, *Timoleonte*, 1961
R. J. A. Talbert, *Timoleon and the Revival of Greek Sicily*, 1974
M. Thompson, O. Mørkholm, C. M. Kraay (eds.), *An Inventory of Greek Coin Hoards*, 1973

CHAPTER 4: THE HELLENISTIC GREEKS

1 Alexandria (or Seleucia) Oxiana (Aï Khanum): The Farthest Greek East

F.R. Allchin and N. Hammond, *The Archaeology of Afghanistan*, 1978
W. J. Ball and J.-C. Gardin, *Archaeological Gazetteer of Afghanistan*, 1982
P. Bernard, 'Ai Khanoum' in *Bulletin de Correspondance Hellenique*, 1965, pp. 604–57
P. Bernard, 'An Ancient Greek City in Central Asia' in *Scientific American*, 247, 1982, pp. 148–59
P. Bernard, *Fouilles d'Ai Khanoum*, I-V, 1973–86
S. K. Eddy, *The King is Dead: Studies in the Near Eastern Resistance to Hellenism*, 1961
M. I. Finley, *Atlas of Classical Archaeology*, 1977
F. L. Holt, *Alexander the Great and Bactria*, 1988
F. L. Holt, 'Discovering the Lost History of Ancient Afghanistan: Hellenistic Bactria in the Light of Recent Archaeological and Historical Research' in *The Ancient World*, 9, 1–2, 1984, pp. 3ff.
A. Kurt and S. Sherwin-White (eds.), *Hellenism in the East*, 1989

R. Lane Fox in J. Boardman (etc., eds.), *Oxford History of the Classical World*, 1986, pp. 340, 343, 347
P. Levi, *Atlas of the Greek World*, 1980
L. Robert, 'De Delphes à l'Oxus' in *Comptes Rendus de l'Academie des Inscriptions*, 1968, p. 416
W. W. Tarn, *The Greeks in Bactria and India*, 3rd ed. (F. L. Holt), 1984

2 Troezen: Inscriptions and History

J. Boardman (etc., eds.), *Cambridge Ancient History*, IV, 2nd ed., 1989
A. R. Burn, *Persia and the Greeks*, 2nd ed. (D. M. Lewis), 1984
J. B. Bury and R. Meiggs, *A History of Greece*, 4th ed., 1975
B. F. Cook, *Reading the Past: Greek Inscriptions*, 1987
N. G. L. Hammond, 'The Expedition of Xerxes' in *Cambridge Ancient History*, IV, 2nd ed., 1988, pp. 518–91
N. G. L. Hammond, 'The Narrative of Herodotus, Book VII, and the Decree of Themistocles at Troezen' in *Journal of Hellenic Studies*, 102, 1982, pp. 75ff.
R. J. Lenardon, *The Saga of Themistocles*, 1978
F. Millar, *Epigraphy* in M. Crawford (ed.), *Sources for Ancient History*, 1983
O. Murray, *Early Greece*, 1980
R. Thomas, *Oral Tradition and Written Record in Classical Athens*, 1989
A. G. Woodhead, *The Study of Greek Inscriptions*, 2nd ed., 1981

3 Taras (Taranto): Jewellery

M. De Juliis (ed.), *Gli ori di Taranto in età ellenistica*, 1986; and *Materiali e suggerimenti per la didattica di una ricerca archeologica*, 1988
M. Grant, *From Alexander to Cleopatra*, 1982
R. Higgins, *Greek and Roman Jewellery*, 2nd ed., 1980
Il Museo Nazionale di Taranto, 1983
Jewellery Through 7,000 Years, 1976
J. Ogden, *Jewellery of the Ancient World*, 1982

4 Rhodes: Calendar-Calculator from Anticythera

R. S. Brumbaugh, *Ancient Greek Gadgets and Machines*, 1975 ed.
W. K. C. Guthrie, 'The Revolution of the Mind' in M. Grant (ed.), *Greece and Rome: The Birth of Western Civilization*, 1986 (1964), p. 86
J. G. Landels, 'Engineering' in M. Grant and R. Kitzinger (eds.), *Civilization of the Ancient Mediterranean*, I, 1988, pp. 323ff.
D. J. De Solla Price, 'An Ancient Greek Computer' in *Scientific American*, 200, 9, 1959, pp. 60ff.
D. J. De Solla Price, 'Gears from the Greeks' in *Transactions of the American Philosophical Society*, 64, 7, 1974
J. J. Thorndike (ed.), *Mysteries of the Past*, 1977
P. Throckmorton, *History from the Sea*, 1987
P. Throckmorton, *Shipwrecks and Archaeology*, 1969
G. D. Weinberg (etc.), 'The Antikythera Wreck Reconsidered' in *Transactions of the American Philosophical Society*, 55, 3, 1967
K. D. White, *Greek and Roman Technology*, 1984

5 *Alexandria in Egypt: Debasing the Coinage*

E. Bevan, *A History of Egypt under the Ptolemaic Dynasty*, 1967 (1927)
N. L. Brooke (etc.), *Studies in Numismatic Methods presented to P. Grierson*, 1983
M. Grant, *Cleopatra*, 1972
E. T. Hall and D. M. Metcalf (eds.), *Methods of Chemical and Metallurgical Investigation of Ancient Coinage*, 1972
Metallurgy in Numismatics, I, 1980, II, 1988
W. A. Oddy (ed.), *Scientific Studies in Numismatics*, 1980
Scientific Techniques in Numismatics, M. Price (etc., eds.), *A Survey of Numismatic Research 1978–1984*, II, 1986, pp. 961ff.
H. Volkmann, *Cleopatra*, 1958
D. R. Walker, *The Metrology of the Roman Silver Coinage*, I 1976

PART II: ITALY AND THE ROMAN EMPIRE

CHAPTER 5: ETRUSCAN AND REPUBLICAN ITALY

1 *Tarquinii: Potentiometer, Probe, Periscope*

M.Cristofani, *Dizionario della civiltà etrusca*, 1985, pp. 286ff.
M. Grant, *The Etruscans*, 1980
C. M. Lerici, *Alla scoperta delle civiltà sepolte: I nuovi metodi di prospezione archeologica*, 1960
C. M. Lerici, *The Lerici Periscope* in C. W. Ceram, *The World of Archaeology*, 1968 ed., pp. 481ff.
C. M. Lerici (etc.), *Prospezioni archeologiche*, III, 1968
M. Moretti, *Tarquinia*, 1974
L. C. Vanoni, 'Recenti interventi a Tarquinia della Fondazione Lerici: Prospezioni Archeologiche' (II Congresso Internazionale Etrusco, Florence) in *Comunicazioni Scientifiche* 1985, pp. 69ff.

2 *Pyrgi: Etruscan History Recovered*

G. Colonna, *Pyrgi: scavi del santuario etrusco 1959–1967*, 1973
M. Cristofani, *Gli etruschi sul mare*, 1983
M. Grant, *The Etruscans*, 1980
Le lamine di Pyrgi (Tavola rotonda internazionale, Rome), 1968
M. Pallottino, *Etruscologia*, 6th ed., 1968
M. Pallottino, *Testimonia Linguae Etruscae*, 2nd ed., 1968, pp. 109f., nos 873–876
V. Protani, *Pyrgi e il Castello di Santa Severa*, 1988
H. H. Scullard, *The Etruscan Cities and Rome*, 1967

3 *Orbetello and Prilius: Vanished Harbours*

E. C. F. Bird and P. Fabbri (eds.), *Coastal Problems in the Mediterranean Sea*, (Symposium 1982), 1983
P. Bocci Pacini, 'Orbetello' in R. Stillwell (ed.), *Princeton Encyclopaedia of Classical Sites*, 1976, p. 653
M. Cristofani, *Dizionario della civiltà etrusca*, 1985 (Orbetello, Rusellae, Vetulonia)
L'Età del Ferro nella Etruria marittima, 1965
M. Grant, 'The Ports of the Etruscans' in B. A. Marshall (ed.), *Vindex Humanitatis:*

Essays in Honour of J. H. Bishop, 1980, pp. 1–16
A. Raban (ed.), 'The Archaeology of Coastal Changes' in *Proceedings of the First International Symposium on Cities of the Sea, Past and Present* (Haifa), 1988
T. G. Schmiedt, *10th Congress of the International Society of Photogrammetry*, 1964, p. 19
T. G. Schmiedt (ed.), *Il livello antico del Mar Tirreno: testimonianze dei resti archeologici*, 1972
F. H. Thompson (ed.), *Archaeology and Coastal Change*, 1980

4 Picentia (Pontecagnano): The Etruscan South

B. D'Agostino, *Pontecagnano: Enciclopedia dell'arte antica classica e orientale*, Supplement, 1970
B. D'Agostino, *Tombe principesche dell'orientalizzante antico da Pontecagnano*, 1977
M. Frederiksen, *Campania*, 1984
M. Frederiksen, 'The Etruscans in Campania' in D. and F. R. Ridgway (eds.), *Italy Before the Romans*, 1979
M. Grant, *The Etruscans*, 1980

5 Francolise and Settefinestre: Villa-Farms

(see also Chapter 8, section 2)

G. Bazin, *Les fouilles de la ville de Settefinestre* in *Archéologie*, 154, 1981, pp. 54–62
P. von Blanckenhagen, M. A. Cotton, J. B. Ward-Perkins, *Two Roman Villas at Francolise, Provincia Caserta: Interim Report on Excavations 1962–1964* in *Proceedings of the British School at Rome*, 33, 1965, pp. 56ff.
J. Boardman, 'The Olive in the Mediterranean' in *Philosophical Transactions of the Royal Society*, Series B, 275, 1976
A. Carandini, 'Il vigneto e la villa del fondo di Settefinestre nel Cosano' in *Memoirs of the American Academy in Rome*, 36, 1980
A. Carandini, *Settefinestre: una villa schiavistica nell'Etruria romana*, I–III, 1985
M. A. Cotton, *The Late Republican Villa at Posto, Francolise*, 1979
M. A. Cotton and G. Métraux, *The San Rocco Villa at Francolise*, 1984
J. M. Frayn, *Subsistence Farming in Roman Italy*, 1979
K. Greene, *The Archaeology of the Roman Economy*, 1986
D. E. Johnston, *Roman Villas*, 1983 (1979)
A. King, *The Archaeology of the Roman Empire*, 1982
K. S. Painter (ed.), *Roman Villas in Italy: Recent Excavations and Research*, 1980
J. Percival, *The Roman Villa: An Historical Introduction*, 1988 (1976)
J. Percival, 'The Villa in Italy and the Provinces' in J. Wacher (ed.), *The Roman World*, II, 1986
T. W. Potter, *Roman Italy*, 1987
P. J. Reynolds, *Ancient Farming*, 1987
M. S. Spurr, *Arable Cultivation in Roman Italy 200 BC–200 AD*, 1986
K. D. White, 'Farming and Animal Husbandry' in M. Grant and R. Kitzinger (eds.), *Civilization of the Ancient Mediterranean*, I, 1988, pp. 218ff.

6 Oplontis: New Evidence for Roman Art
(see also Chapter 7, section 1, for gardens)
G. Alessio, *Oplontis* in *Studi Etruschi*, 1965, pp. 699ff.
A. Barbet, *La peinture murale romaine*, 1985
F. Coarelli (ed.), *Guida archeologica di Pompei*, 1976, pp. 346ff.
J. Engemann, 'Architekturdarstellungen des frühen zweiten Stils' in *Römische Mitteilungen*, Suppl. 12, 1967
F. Fedele and G. Guadagno, *Campania archeologica*, 1984
A. De Franciscis, 'La villa romana di Oplontis' in *Parola del Passato* 153, 1973, pp. 453–66, in B. Andreae and H. Kyrieleis (eds.), *Neue Forschungen in Pompeii*, 1975 *Gli ori di Oplontis* (exhibition), 1987
W. Jashemski, *Ancient Roman Gardens*, 1981
W. Jashemski, *The Gardens of Pompeii, Herculaneum and the Villas Destroyed by Vesuvius*, 1979
C. Malandrino, *Oplontis*, 2nd ed., 1980 (1977)
H. Mielsch, *Die römische Villa: Architektur und Lebensform*, 1987
K. Schefold, *La peinture pompéienne*, 1972
'Splendors of a Newly Discovered Villa' in *Horizon*, 16, 4, 1974, pp. 22–5
The Villa of Oplontis, 1988 (1980)
J. B. Ward-Perkins and A. Claridge, *Pompeii* AD *79* (exhibition, London), 1976, p. 338

CHAPTER 6: THE AUGUSTAN EMPIRE

1 Nicopolis: Monument for Actium
J. M. Carter, *The Battle of Actium*, 1970
D. Earl, *The Age of Augustus*, 1968
J. Gage, 'Actiaca' in *Mélanges d'archéologie et d'histoire de l'École Française de Rome*, 53, 1936, pp. 37ff.
M. Grant, *A Guide to the Ancient World*, 1986
N. G. L. Hammond, *Epirus*, 1967
W. Murray and P. Petsas, 'The Spoils of Actium' in *Archaeology*, 41, 5, 1988, pp. 28–55
M. Reinhold, *The Golden Age of Augustus*, 1978
A. Weis, 'Nikopolis' in R. Stillwell (ed.), *Princeton Encyclopaedia of Classical Sites*, 1976, pp. 625f.

2 Primis (Qasr Ibrim): Egyptian Frontier
W. Y. Adams, *Nubia: Corridor to Africa*, 1977
W. Y. Adams, J. A. Alexander and R. Allen, 'Qasr Ibrim 1980 and 1982' in *Journal of Egyptian Archaeology*, 69, 1983, pp. 43–60
J. A. Alexander and B. Driskell, *Qasr Ibrim*, 1984
D. J. Breeze (ed.), *The Frontiers of the Roman Empire*, 1986
L. P. Kirwan, 'Rome Beyond the Southern Egyptian Frontier' in *Proceedings of the British Academy*, 63, 1977, pp. 13–31

3 Caesarea Maritima: Herod's Port

(see also Chapter 8, section 6, on air photography.)

D. C. Braund, *Rome and the Friendly King*, 1984

R. J. Bull, 'Caesarea Maritima, the Search for Herod's City' in *Biblical Archaeology Review*, VIII, 1982, pp. 24–40

M. Grant, *Herod the Great*, 1971

R. L. Hohlfelder, 'Caesarea Beneath the Sea' in *Biblical Archaeology Review*, VIII, 1982, op. cit. pp. 42–7

K. G. Holum and R. L. Hohlfelder (eds.), *King Herod's Dream: Caesarea on the Sea*, 1988

L. I. Levine, *Roman Caesarea: An Archaeological-Topographical Study*, 1975

I. Malkin and R. L. Hohlfelder (eds.), *Mediterranean Cities: Historical Perspective*, 1989

A. Negev, *Caesarea*, 1967

J. P. Oleson (ed.), *The Harbours of Caesarea Maritima*, Vol.I, A. Raban, *The Site and the Excavations*, 1981

A. Raban (ed.), *Archaeology of Coastal Changes* (Proceedings of the First International Symposium 'Cities of the Sea', *Past and Present*, 1986), 1988

A. Raban (ed.), *Harbour Archaeology* (Proceedings of the First International Workshop on Ancient Mediterranean Harbours: Caesarea Maritima), 1983

A. Schalit, *König Herodes: Der Mann und sein Werk*, 1969

E. M. Smallwood, *The Jews under Roman Rule*, 1976

L. E. Toombs, 'The Stratigraphy of Caesarea Maritima' in P. R. S. Moorey and P. Parr (eds.), *Archaeology in the Levant: Essays for Kathleen Kenyon*, 1978

4 Rome: The Imperial Sundial

E. J. Bickerman, *Chronology of the Ancient World*, rev. ed., 1980

E. Buchner, *Die Sonnenuhr des Augustus*, 1982

A. E. Samuel, 'Calendars and Time-Telling' in M. Grant and R. Kitzinger (eds.), *Civilization of the Ancient Mediterranean*, I, 1988, pp. 389ff.

A. M. Snodgrass, *An Archaeology of Greece*, 1987

CHAPTER 7: THE POST-AUGUSTANS

1 Noviomagus Regnensium (Fishbourne): Prince in a Province

(see also Chapter 5, section 5 (villas).)

D. C. Braund, *Rome and the Friendly King*, 1984

B. W. Cunliffe, *Fishbourne: A Roman Palace and its Garden*, 1971

B. W. Cunliffe, *Fishbourne: Site Guide*, 1983

B. W. Cunliffe, P. Connor and K. Pearson, *Fishbourne: The Roman Palace and its History*, rev. ed., 1969

G. W. Dimbleby, *Plants and Archaeology*, 1967

A. Down, *Roman Chichester*, 1988

S. Frere, *Britannia*, 3rd ed., 1987

P. Grimal, *Les jardins romains*, 2nd ed., 1968

W. Jashemski, *Ancient Roman Gardens*, 1981

W. Johannowsky (etc.), *Le ville romane di età imperiale*, 1986

D. E. Johnston, *Roman Villas*, 1983 (1979)
E. B. MacDougall (ed.), *Ancient Roman Villa Gardens* (Dumbarton Oaks Colloquium), 1987
A. G. McKay, *Houses, Villas and Palaces in the Roman World*, 1975
J. Percival, *Recent Work on Roman Villas in Britain: Caesarodunum*, 17, 1982, pp. 305–20
C. Taylor, *The Archaeology of Gardens*, 1983

2 Aphrodisias: School of Sculpture

E. Akurgal, *Ancient Civilizations and Ruins of Turkey*, 5th ed., 1983
G. E. Bean, *Turkey Beyond the Maeander*, 1989 (1971) K. T. Erim, 'Aphrodisias: Awakened City of Ancient Art', *National Geographic Magazine*, 141, 6, June 1972, pp. 766ff.
K. T. Erim, *Aphrodisias: City of Venus Aphrodite*, 1986
J. de la Genière and K. Erim (eds.), *Aphrodisias de Carie* (Colloque du Centre des Recherches Archéologiques de l'Université de Lille, III, Paris, 1985), 1987
S. Lloyd, *Ancient Turkey: A Traveller's History of Anatolia*, 1989
A. D. Macro, 'The Cities of Asia Minor under the Roman Imperium' in H. Temporini (ed.), *Aufstieg und Niedergang der römischen Welt*, II, 7, 2, 1980, pp. 658ff.
D. Magie, *Roman Rule in Asia Minor*, 1950
J. M. Reynolds, *Aphrodisias and Rome*, 1982
C. Rouéche and J. M. Reynolds, *Aphrodisias in Late Antiquity*, 1989
M. Squarciapino, *La scuola di Afrodisia*, 1943
M. Squarciapino, *La scuola di Afrodisia: quarant'anni dopo*, 1983

3 Masada: Siege-Warfare

S. J. D. Cohen, 'Masada: Literary Tradition, Archaeological Remains and the Credibility of Josephus' in G. Vermes and J. Neusner (eds.), *Essays in Honour of Y. Yadin*, 1983
C. Dobinson and R. Gilchrist (eds.), *Archaeology, Politics and the Public*, 1986
I. A. Richmond, 'The Roman Siege-Works at Masada, Israel' in *Journal of Roman Studies*, 52, 1962, pp. 142–55
Y. Yadin, *Masada*, 1966

4 Herculaneum: Skeletons

S. C. Bisel, 'Human Bones at Herculaneum' in *Rivista di studi pompeiani*, 1 1987, pp. 123f.
A. Boddington, A. N. Garland, R. C. Janaway (eds.), *Death, Decay and Reconstruction*, 1987
R. Branigan, *Archaeology Explained*, 1988 ed., pp. 71ff. (palaeopathology)
D. R. Brothwell and A. D. Sandison (eds.), *Diseases in Antiquity*, 1967
J. J. Deiss, *Herculaneum: Italy's Buried Treasure*, 2nd ed., 1985
H. Duday and C. Masset, *Anthropologie physique et archéologie* (Toulouse Conference, 1982), 1987
R. Gore, 'The Dead do Tell Tales at Vesuvius' in *National Geographic Magazine*, 165, 5, May 1984, pp. 557–73

M. Grmek (etc.), *Diseases in the Ancient Greek World*, 1989
R. Jackson, *Doctors and Diseases in the Roman Empire*, 1989
R. G. Klein and K. Cruz-Uribe, *The Analysis of Animal Bones from Archaeological Sites*, 1984
K. Manchester, 'Skeletal Evidence for Health and Disease' in A. Boddington (etc., eds.), *Death, Decay and Reconstruction: Approaches to Archaeology and Forensic Science*, 1987
K. Manchester, *The Archaeology of Disease*, 1983
D. B. Ubelaker, *Human Skeletal Remains*, rev. ed., 1988
S. Zivanovic, *Ancient Diseases: The Elements of Palaeopathology*, 1982

CHAPTER 8: THE MIDDLE EMPIRE

1 *Augusta Trevirorum (Trier): Tree-Rings and Bridge*

S. Champion, *Dictionary of Terms and Techniques in Archaeology*, 1980 (pp. 34f., 104)
Conservation du bois (UNESCO ICOMOS), 1983
H. Cüppers, *Die Römer in Rheinland-Pfalz*, 1989
H. Cüppers, *Die Trierer Römerbrucken*, 1969
H. Cüppers in W. Sölter (ed.), *Das römische Germanien aus der Luft*, 1981, pp. 153–76
J. F. Drinkwater, *Roman Gaul*, 1983
P. Gazzola, *Ponti romani*, 1963
E. Hollstein, 'Jahrringchronologien aus vorrömischer und römischer Zeit' in *Germania*, 45, 1967, pp. 70ff.
E. Hollstein, 'Mitteleuropäische Eichenchronologie' in *Trierer Grabungen und Forschungen*, 11, 1980, pp. 133–53
J. McIntosh, *The Archaeologist's Handbook*, 1986 (dendrochronology)
R. Meiggs, *Trees and Timber in the Ancient Mediterranean World*, 1982
D. Miles in K. Branigan (ed.), *Atlas of Archaeology*, 1982, pp. 16ff. (dendrochronology)
M. Neyses, 'Holz macht Geschichte' in *Holz aktuell*, 5, 1985, pp. 67f
B. Ottoway (ed.), *Archaeology, Dendrochronology and the Radiocarbon Calibration Curve*, 1982
Past Worlds: The Times Atlas of Archaeology, 1988, p. 25 (dendrochronology)
W. Reusch, *Augusta Treverorum: Rundgang durch das römische Trier*, 1985 ed.
Trier: Augustusstadt der Treverer, 1984
R. G. W. Ward, *Applications of Tree-Ring Studies*, 1987
E. M. Wightman, *Gallia Belgica*, 1985
E. M. Wightman, *Roman Trier and the Treveri*, 1970
D. R. Wilson, *Science and Archaeology*, 1978 (1975) (dendrochronology)

2 *Vindolanda (Chesterholm): Writings on Wood*

J. N. Adams, 'The Latin of the Vindolanda Writing Tablets' in *Bulletin of the Institute of Classical Studies* (London), 27, 1975
P. T. Bidwell, *The Roman Fort at Vindolanda*, 1985
R. Birley, *Vindolanda: a Roman Frontier-Post on Hadrian's Wall*, 1977

A. K. Bowman and J. D. Thomas, *Vindolanda: The Latin Writing Tablets*, 1983
A. K. Bowman and J. D. Thomas, 'Vindolanda 1985: The New Writing Tablets' in *Journal of Roman Studies*, 76, 1986, pp. 120ff.
D. J. Breeze, *Roman Forts in Britain*, 1983
S. Frere, *Britannia*, 3rd ed., 1987
A. E. Gordon, *Illustrated Introduction to Latin Epigraphy*, 1983
M. Hassall, 'The Internal Planning of Roman Auxiliary Forts' in B. R. Hartley and J. Wacher (eds.), *Rome and her Northern Provinces* (papers presented to S. Frere), 1983
P. Holder, *The Roman Army in Britain*, 1982
B. W. Jones and R. D. Milns, *The Use of Documentary Evidence in the Study of Roman Imperial History*, 1985
M. W. Todd (ed.), *Research on Roman Britain 1960–1989*, 1989

3 *The North and Wadi Fawakhir: A Soldier's Diet*

D. R. Brothwell, 'Foodstuffs, Cooking and Drugs' in M. Grant and R. Kitzinger (eds.), *Civilizations of the Ancient Mediterranean*, I, 1988, pp. 247–61
D. R. and P. Brothwell, *Food in Antiquity*, 1969
D. R. Brothwell, J. Clutton-Brock and K. D. Thomas (eds.), *Research Problems in Zooarchaeology*, 1978
R. E. Chaplin, *The Study of Animal Bones from Archaeological Sites*, 1971
R. W. Davies, 'The Roman Military Diet' in *Britannia*, II, 1971, pp. 122ff
R. W. Davies, 'The Roman Military Medical Service' in *Saalburg Jahrbuch*, 27, 1970, pp. 84–104
S. J. W. Davies, *The Archaeology of Animals*, 1987
B. A. Knights (etc.), 'Evidence Concerning the Roman Military Diet at Bearsden, Scotland, in the 2nd century AD' in *Journal of Archaeological Science*, x, 1983, pp. 139–52
R. M. Luff, *A Zooarchaeological Study of the Roman Northwestern Provinces*, 1982
K. McLeish, *Food and Drink* (Greek and Roman Topics), 1978
M. Maltby, 'Iron Age, Romano-British and Anglo-Saxon Animal Husbandry' in M. Jones and G. Dimbleby (eds.), *The Environment of Man*, 1981
G. Webster, 'On Diet at Waddon Hill', *Proceedings of the Dorset National History and Archaeology Society*, 86, 1965, pp. 143ff.

4 *Novae: Danubian Legionary River Port*

B. Böttger, B. Döhle and K. Wachtel, *Bulgarien: eine Reise zu antiken Kulturstätten*, 2nd ed., 1977
D. J. Breeze (ed.), *The Frontiers of the Roman Empire*, 1986
D. P. Davison, *The Barracks of the Roman Army from the First to the Third Centuries AD*, 1989
R. F. Hoddinott, *Bulgaria in Antiquity: An Archaeological Introduction*, 1975
A. Mocsy, *Zur Entstehung und Eigenart der Nordgrenzen Roms*, 1978
A. G. Poulter, *Town and Country in Moesia Inferior* (Papers Presented to an International Symposium on the Ancient History and Archaeology of Bulgaria, Nottingham), 1983
L. Press, W. Szubert, T. Sarnowski, 'Novae in 1979 – West Sector' in *Klio* 64,

1982, pp. 471–83, and 'Novae in 1981 – West Sector' in *Klio 66*, 1984, pp. 281–90

L. Rossi, *Trajan's Column and the Dacian Wars*, 1971

S. Settis (etc.), *La Colonna Traiana*, 1988

C. G. Starr, *The Roman Imperial Navy*, 1960 (1941)

V. Velkov, *Roman Cities in Bulgaria*, 1980

V. Velkov, 'Thrace and Lower Moesia during the Roman and Late Roman Epoch' in *Klio* 63, 1981, pp. 473–83

5 Egypt: Novel on Papyrus

(see also Appendix II(ii) on the Herculaneum papyri.)

G. Anderson, *Ancient Fiction: The Novel in the Greco-Roman World*, 1984

R. Bagnall, 'Archaeology and Papyrology' in *Journal of Roman Archaeology*, 1, December 1988

R. Beaton (ed.), *The Greek Novel* AD1 – *1985*, 1989

I. Gallo, *Greek and Latin Papyrology*, 1987 (1986)

T. Hägg, *The Novel in Antiquity*, 1983

N. Lewis (ed.), *Papyrology*, 1985

T. S. Pattie and E. G. Turner, *The Written Word on Papyrus*, 1974

S. A. Stephens, 'Book Production' in M. Grant and R. Kitzinger (eds.), *Civilization of the Ancient Mediterranean*, 1, 1988, pp. 421ff

E. G. Turner, *Greek Manuscripts of the Ancient World*, 2nd ed. (P. J. Parsons), 1987

E. G. Turner, *Greek Papyri: An Introduction*, 1980 (1968)

6 The Samara (Somme) Valley: Air Photography

R. Agache, 'Détection aérienne de vestiges protohistoriques, gallo-romains et médiévaux' in *Bulletin de la Société Prehistorique du Nord*, 7, 1970

R. Agache, 'La Somme pré-romaine et romaine' in *Mémoires de la Société des Antiquaires de Picardie*, 24, 1978

R. Agache, 'La villa gallo-romaine dans les grandes plaines du nord de la France' in *Archéologia*, 55, February 1973, pp. 37–52

R. Agache and B. Bréart, *Atlas d'archéologie aérienne de Picardie*, 1975

M. Cosci, *Fotointerpretazione archeologica*, 1988

J. F. Drinkwater, *Roman Gaul*, 1983

Étude de la photogrammetrie appliquée aux monuments historiques, 1969

J. Hampton (ed.), *The Mapping of Archaeological Evidence from Air Photographs*, 1985

K. Hudson, *Industrial History from the Air*, 1984

G. S. Maxwell (ed.), *The Impact of Aerial Reconnaissance on Archaeology*, 1983

D. N. Riley, *Air Photography and Archaeology*, 1987

D. N. Riley, *Early Landscape from the Air*, 1980

T. G. Schmidt, *Atlante di aerofotogrammetria degli insediamenti*, 1970

J. T. Smith, 'Villa Plans and Social Structure in Britain and Gaul' in *Caesarodunum*, 17, 1982, pp. 321–36

D. L. Way, *Terrain Analysis: Guide to Site Selection Using Aerial Photographic Interpretation*, 1973

E. M. Wightman, *Gallia Belgica*, 1985

D. R. Wilson, *Air Photo Interpretation for Archaeologists*, 1982

D. R. Wilson (ed.), *Aerial Reconnaissance for Archaeology*, 1975

7 *Cruciniacum* (*Bad Kreuznach*): *Water Supply*

L. Baruchello, 'Antiche techniche di ingegneria idraulica' in *Archeologia Viva*, 3, 11, 1984, pp. 60ff.

H. Bullinger, 'New Understanding of Water-Supply and Drainage as seen in the Roman villa in Cruciniacum' in *Acta of the XIth International Congress of Classical Archaeology* (London, 1978), 1979, p. 291

Die römische Peristylvilla (Kreuznach), n.d.

G. Garbrecht (etc.), *Die Wasserversorgung antiker Städte*, II, 1987, III, 1988

O. Guthmann, *Kreuznach und Umgebung in römischer Zeit*, 1969

D. Hill, *A History of Engineering in Classical and Medieval Times*, 1984

J. G. Landels, *Engineering in the Ancient World*, 1978

J. G. Landels, 'Water Engineering' in M. Grant and R. Kitzinger (eds.), *Civilizations of the Ancient Mediterranean*, I, 1988, pp. 338ff

J. P. Oleson, *Greek and Roman Mechanical Water-Lifting Devices*, 1984

G. Rupprecht, 'Die Kreuznacher Palastvilla: Kurzbericht über den Stand der Erforschung im Herbst 1979' in *Mainer Zeitschrift* 75, 1980, pp. 219–26

G. Rupprecht, 'Quellenkunde zur Forschungsgeschichte der römischen Palastvilla in Bad Kreuznach' in *Landeskundliches Vierteljahresblatt* (Trier), 24, 1978, pp. 59–72, 136–53

CHAPTER 9: THE LATER EMPIRE

1 *Byblus: Buildings on coins*

K. Butcher, *Roman Provincial Coins: An Introduction to the Greek Imperials*, 1988

T. L. Donaldson, *Architectura Numismatica*, 1859, reprinted 1966

M. Dunand, *Byblos: son histoire, ses ruines, ses légendes*, 3rd ed., 1973

M. Dunand, *Fouilles de Byblos*, I (1926–1932), 1939; II (1933–1938), 1958

J. Ferguson, *Among the Gods: An Archaeological Exploration of Ancient Greek Religion*, 1989

M. Grant, *Roman History from Coins*, 1968 (1958)

K. W. Hart, *Civic Coins and Civic Politics in the Roman East,* AD *180–275*, 1987

M. Henig and A. King (eds.), *Pagan Gods and Shrines in the Roman Empire*, 1986

A. H. M. Jones, *Cities of the Eastern Roman Provinces*, 2nd ed., 1971

M. Lyttelton, 'Temples and Sanctuaries' in S. Macready and F. H. Thompson, *Roman Architecture in the Greek World*, 1987

M. J. Price and B. L. Trell, *Coins and Their Cities*, 1977

J.-P. Rey-Coquais, 'Byblos' in R. Stillwell (ed.), *Princeton Encyclopaedia of Classical Sites*, 1976

B. L. Trell, 'Architectura Numismatica Orientalis' in *Numismatic Chronicle*, 7th series, X, 1970, pp. 29ff

2 *Betthorus* (*Lejjun*): *Late Rome's Eastern Frontier*

G. W. Bowersock, 'Limes Arabicus' in *Harvard Studies in Classical Philology*, 80, 1976, pp. 219–29

G. W. Bowersock, *Roman Arabia*, 1983
S. Johnson, *Late Roman Fortifications*, 1982
D. L. Kennedy, 'The Eastern Frontier' in D. L. Breeze (ed.), *The Frontiers of the Roman Empire*, 1986
J. Lander and S. T. Parker, 'Legio IV Martia and the Legionary Camp at El-Lejjun', in *Byzantinische Forschungen*, 8, 1982, pp. 185–210
D. L. Kennedy and D. Riley, *Rome's Desert Frontier from the Air*, 1990
H. I. MacAdam, *Studies in the History of the Roman Province of Arabia: The Northern Sector*, 1986
S. T. Parker, 'Exploring the Roman Frontier in Jordan' in *Archaeology*, 37, 5, September/October 1984
S. T. Parker, 'Preliminary Report on 1989 Lejjun Campaign' in *Annual of the Department of Antiquities of Jordan*, 1990
S. T. Parker, *Romans and Saracens: A Study of the Arabian Frontier*, 1986
S. T. Parker, 'Towards a History of the Limes Arabicus' in W. S. Hanson and L. J. F. Keppie (eds.), *Roman Frontier Studies* (1979), 1980
S. T. Parker (ed.), *The Roman Frontier in Central Jordan: Interim Report on the Limes Arabicus Project (1980–1985)*, 1987
M. P. Speidel, 'The Roman Army in Arabia' in H. Temporini (ed.), *Aufstieg und Niedergang der römischen Welt*, II *Principat*, 10, 2, 1982, pp. 850–60

3 Mediolanum (Milan): The Last Western Emperor

M. Grant, *The Fall of the Roman Empire*, 1976
M. Grant, *The Roman Emperors*, 1985
J. P. C. Kent, 'Julius Nepos and the Fall of the Roman Empire' in *Corolla Memoriae E. Swoboda Dedicata*, 1966
J. P. C. Kent, *Roman Coins*, rev. ed., 1978
J. P. C. Kent and K. C. Painter (eds.), *The Wealth of the Roman World* AD *300–700*, 1977

APPENDIX I: ARCHAEOLOGY AND THE CLASSICS

See above (at beginning of Bibliography, II Modern Works)

APPENDIX II: A FEW TASKS FOR THE FUTURE

(i) Lavinium: Archaeology and Myth

Archeologia Laziale, 9, 1988
F. Castagnoli, 'La leggenda di Enea nel Lazio' in *Atti del Congresso Mondiale degli studi su Virgilio*, II, 1984, pp. 283–303
F. Castagnoli, *Lavinium*, I, 1972; (with P. Sommella), II, 1975
F. Castagnoli, 'Lavinium' in *Enciclopedia Virgiliana*, III, 1987, pp. 149–53
F. Coarelli, *I santuari del Lazio in età repubblicana*, 1987
F. Coarelli, *Lazio*, 2nd ed., 1985
T. J. Cornell, 'Aeneas's Arrival in Italy' in *Liverpool Classical Monthly*, 2, 1977, pp. 77–83
G. D'Anna, 'Virgilio e le recenti scoperte archeologiche a Lavinium' in *Sandalion* 6–7, 1983/4, pp. 93–101

A. Dubourdier, *Le sanctuaire de Vénus à Lavinium* in *Revue des études latines*, 59, 1981, pp. 83ff.
G. Dury-Moyaers, *Énée et Lavinium*, 1981
G.K. Galinsky, 'The "Tomb of Aeneas" at Lavinium' in *Vergilius*, 20, 1974, pp. 2–11
Greci e Latini nel Lazio antico (Atti SISAC Convegno 1981), 1982
N. Horsfall, 'Enea: La leggenda di Enea' in *Enciclopedia Virgiliana*, II, 1985, pp. 221–9
J. Poucet, 'Un culte d'Énée dans la région lavinate au IVe siècle avant J. C?' in *Hommages a R. Schilling*, 1983, pp. 197–201
P. Sommella and C. F. Giuliani, 'Lavinium: compendio' in *Parola del Passato*, 32, 1977, pp. 365–72
M. Torelli, *Lavinio e Roma*, 1984
R. Turcan, 'Énée, Lavinium et les treizes autels' in *Revue de l'histoire des réligions*, 200, 1983, pp. 41–66

(*ii*) *Herculaneum: Villa of the Papyri*

(For other discoveries at Herculaneum, see Chapter 7, section 4. For papyri and papyrology, see also Chapter 8, section 5.)

M. Capasso, *Storia fotografica dell'Officina dei Papiri Ercolanesi*, 1984
S. Castelnuovo and V. Litta, *The Papyri of Herculaneum*, n.d.
B. Conticello, 'Dopo 221 anni si rientra nella Villa dei Papiri' in *Cronache Ercolanesi*, 17, 1987, pp. 9–13
A. Fackelmann, 'The Restoration of the Herculaneum Papyri and Other Recent Finds' in *Bulletin of the Institute of Classical Studies* (London), 17, 1970, pp. 144–7
La Villa dei Papiri (II suppl.), *Cronache Ercolanesi*, 13, 1983
M. Gigante (ed.), *Contributi alla storia dell'Officina dei Papiri Ercolanesi*, 1980
M. Grant, *Cities of Vesuvius*, 1971
G. Gullini, 'Il progetto di esplorazione della Villa dei Papiri' in *Bollettino del Centro Internazionale per lo studio dei papiri ercolanesi*, 14, 1984, pp. 7f.
C. Knight and A. Jorio, 'L'ubicazione della Villa ercolanese dei Papiri' in *Rendiconti dell'Accademia di Archeologia, Lettere e Belle Arti di Napoli*, 55, 1980
M. Manfredi, *Quaderni della ricerca scientifica*, 100, 1978
D. Mustilli (etc.), *La Villa dei Papiri*, 1983
F. Sbordone (ed.), *Ricerche sui papiri ercolanesi*, 4th ed., 1983
A. de Simone, 'La Villa dei Papiri, rapporto preliminare 1986–7' in *Cronache Ercolanesi*, 17, 1987
M. R. Wojcik, *La Villa dei Papiri ad Ercolano*, 1986

(*iii*) *Puteoli: Movements of Earth and Shore*

M. and L. Carapezza, 'Energia eruttiva ed energia geotermica nei Campi Flegrei' in P. Amalfitano (ed.), *Il destino della Sibilla: mito scienza e storia dei Campi Flegrei, Atti del II Convegno Internazionale della Fondazione Bibliopolis* (1985), 1986, pp. 195ff.
J. D. D'Arms, *Romans in the Bay of Naples*, 1970
N. C. Flemming, 'Classical Harbours and Relative Changes of Sea-level' in *Acta*

of the XIth International Congress of Classical Archaeology (London, 1978), 1979, p. 291

G. Gialanello and V. Sanpaolo, 'Pozzuoli' in *I Campi Flegrei*, 1987

P. A. Gianfrotta, *Un porto sotto il mare*, *ibid.*

R. Gore, 'A Prayer for Pozzuoli' in *National Geographic Magazine*, 165, 5, May 1984, pp. 615ff.

C. A. Livadie (ed.), *Tremblements de terre, éruptions volcaniques, et vie des hommes dans la Campanie antique*, 1986

A. G. McKay, *Cumae and the Phlegraean Fields*, 1987

A. Maiuri, *The Phlegraean Fields*, 3rd ed., 1958

Puteoli: Studi di storia antica, 1–8, 1977–84

(*iv*) *Rome*

Archeologia del centro, 1985

Bullettino della Commissione Archeologica del Comune di Roma, 91, 1986, pp. 313–778 (various Roman excavations)

A. Carandini, 'Lo scavo delle pendici settentrionali del Palatino' in *Archeologia*, November 1987, pp. 14f., May 1988, p. 1

F. Coarelli, *Il Foro Romano*, I, 1986, II, 1989

F. Ghedine, 'Il Foro' in *Archeo* 38, 1988, pp. 102ff.

D. Manacorda (etc.), 'Roma: il futuro del passato' in *Archeo*, 48, 1989, pp. 3–103

S. Moscati, 'Le Mura di Romolo?' in *Archeo* 41, 1988, p. 3

INDEX

INDEX